FOOLS' GOLD

The Voyage of a Ship of Fools Seeking Gold

A Mock-Heroic Poem on Brexit and English Exceptionalism

JOHN HUNT PUBLISHING

First published by O-Books, 2022
O-Books is an imprint of John Hunt Publishing Ltd., No. 3 East St., Alresford, Hampshire SO24 9EE, UK
office@jhpbooks.com
www.johnhuntpublishing.com

For distributor details and how to order please visit the 'Ordering' section on our website.

ISBN: 978 1 78904 587 1
978 1 78904 588 8 (ebook)
Library of Congress Control Number: 2021941982

A CIP catalogue record for this book is available from the British Library.

Design: Stuart Davies

UK: Printed and bound by CPI Group (UK) Ltd, Croydon, CR0 4YY
US: Printed and bound by Thomson-Shore, 7300 West Joy Road, Dexter, MI 48130

FOOLS' GOLD

The Voyage of a Ship of Fools Seeking Gold

A Mock-Heroic Poem on Brexit and English Exceptionalism

Nicholas Hagger

BOOKS

Winchester, UK
Washington, USA

Also by Nicholas Hagger

The Fire and the Stones
Selected Poems
The Universe and the Light
A White Radiance
A Mystic Way
Awakening to the Light
A Spade Fresh with Mud
The Warlords
Overlord
A Smell of Leaves and Summer
The Tragedy of Prince Tudor
The One and the Many
Wheeling Bats and a Harvest Moon
The Warm Glow of the Monastery Courtyard
The Syndicate
The Secret History of the West
The Light of Civilization
Classical Odes
Overlord, one-volume edition
Collected Poems 1958–2005
Collected Verse Plays
Collected Stories
The Secret Founding of America
The Last Tourist in Iran
The Rise and Fall of Civilizations
The New Philosophy of Universalism
The Libyan Revolution
Armageddon
The World Government
The Secret American Dream
A New Philosophy of Literature
A View of Epping Forest
My Double Life 1: This Dark Wood

My Double Life 2: A Rainbow over the Hills
Selected Stories: Follies and Vices of the Modern Elizabethan Age
Selected Poems: Quest for the One
The Dream of Europa
The First Dazzling Chill of Winter
Life Cycle and Other New Poems 2006–2016
The Secret American Destiny
Peace for our Time
World State
World Constitution
King Charles the Wise
Visions of England
Fools' Paradise
Selected Letters
The Coronation of King Charles
Collected Prefaces
A Baroque Vision
The Essentials of Universalism
The Promised Land

"The man of letters as such, is not concerned with the political or economic map of Europe; but he should be very much concerned with its cultural map.... The man of letters... should be able to take a longer view than either the politician or the local patriot.... The cultural health of Europe, including the cultural health of its component parts, is incompatible with extreme forms of both nationalism and internationalism.... The responsibility of the man of letters at the present time... should be vigilantly watching the conduct of politicians and economists, for the purpose of criticizing and warning, when the decisions and actions of the politicians and economists are likely to have cultural consequences. Of these consequences the man of letters should qualify himself to judge. Of the possible cultural consequences of their activities, politicians and economists are usually oblivious; the man of letters is better qualified to foresee them, and to perceive their seriousness."

T.S. Eliot, 'The Man of Letters and the Future of Europe', 1944

"Since, broadly speaking, the distant consequences of actions are more certain than the immediate consequences, it is seldom justifiable to embark on any policy on the ground that, though harmful in the present, it will be beneficial in the long run."

Bertrand Russell, 'Philosophy and Politics', 1946

"We make out of the quarrel with others, rhetoric, but of the quarrel with ourselves, poetry."

W.B. Yeats, 'Anima Hominis' in *Per Amica Silentia Lunae*, 1918

"Poetry and politics.... Poetry is art, which involves seeing all sides of a question in depth. Politics is about getting things done and generally involves a point of view, which in poetry can appear to be propaganda unless it's treated in a rounded way and not in black-white, right-wrong terms."

Nicholas Hagger, letter to Sir John Weston, 1 February 2010

"Wer sich für ein Narren macht
Der ist bald zů eym wisen gemacht."
"He who recognises himself as a fool will soon become wise."

Sebastian Brant, introduction to
Das Narrenschiff (*The Ship of Fools*), 1494

*

"Fool's gold, iron pyrites."

Concise Oxford Dictionary

"The Prime Minister promised that this Queen's Speech would dazzle us – on close inspection it turns out to be nothing more than fool's gold."

Jeremy Corbyn, Leader of the UK Opposition,
on the Queen's Speech, 14 October 2019

"A new Golden Age for the UK is now within reach."

Boris Johnson, Prime Minister,
on the Queen's Speech, 19 December 2019

"Johnson circles with a rapacious shark's eyes.
O Hermes, please can we vote to ostracise
A public menace to remotest Syria?"

Nicholas Hagger, *Fools' Paradise,* canto XVI, lines 303–305, 2020

"Yet let me flap this bug with gilded wings,
This painted child of dirt, that stinks and stings."

Alexander Pope, 'Epistle to Dr Arbuthnot', lines 309–310

"All that glisters is not gold...."

Prince of Morocco in Shakespeare's *The Merchant of Venice,* 2.7.69

"Lord, what fools these mortals be!"

Puck in Shakespeare's *A Midsummer Night's Dream,* 3.2.115

"Come to London, to plaguey London, a place full of danger and vanity and vice."

John Donne, 1607

"No man is an island, entire of itself; every man is a piece of the continent, a part of the main; if a clod be washed away by the sea, Europe is the less, as well as if a promontory were, as well as if a manor of thy friend's or of thine own were; any man's death diminishes me, because I am involved in mankind."

John Donne, *Devotions upon Emergent Occasions*, XVII, 1624

The front cover shows the Ship of Fools in the 1499 Basel edition of Sebastian Brant's 1494 German poem *Das Narrenschiff, The Ship of Fools*. The Ship of Fools is heading for Narragonia, the fools' paradise, to find gold, which in *Fools' Gold* turns out to be glittering fool's gold, iron pyrites, a lump of which is shown behind the ship.

⌜Symbol

A corner-mark (⌜) at the beginning of the line denotes that there is a break or gap before that line which has been obscured because it falls at the bottom of a page.

CONTENTS

Preface

The Man of Letters and the Cultural Consequences of Politicians, Reconciling Eliot and Tennyson

A sequel to Fools' Paradise

Fools' Gold follows on from *Fools' Paradise* (2020) in telling the story of Brexit, Britain's exit from the European Union.

Fools' Paradise focused on Theresa May's premiership and her inability to get her Withdrawal Agreement through Parliament, which resulted in a paralysis widely derided in Europe. The poem describes the UK's attempt to leave the EU in terms of the voyage of a Ship of Fools to Narragonia, the Fools' Paradise, in Sebastian Brant's German poem, *Das Narrenschiff* (*The Ship of Fools*), first published in Basel, Switzerland in 1494.

The Brexiteers had been promised a paradise funded by savings from annual budget payments to the EU, which would provide an extra £350 million a week for the NHS, and new trade deals would replace the European single market that took 43 per cent of UK exports. Zeus was exasperated by Brexit as his plan to create a United States of Europe as a staging post to a World State that will solve all the world's problems has received a setback.

Fools' Gold

Fools' Gold continues the story by focusing on Boris Johnson's premiership. Johnson won support at the hustings to select May's successor by announcing there would be no deal with the EU. He succeeded May and announced that the UK would be leaving the EU on 31 October 2019. However he was unable to get the Withdrawal Agreement through Parliament, which was the most unpleasant Parliament in living memory, completely deadlocked and full of personal abuse. After winning a general election with a stunning majority of 80, during which many promises were made of coming 'gold', Johnson tweaked May's Withdrawal Agreement – of the 599 pages less than 5 per cent of the divorce deal was changed – and got it through Parliament. The UK exited the EU on 31 January 2020. There was then a transitional period in which a trade deal was supposed to be agreed.

There was now alarm that the Withdrawal Agreement with the EU had created a border down the Irish Sea, and that Northern Ireland had in effect been lost to the United Kingdom. With Scotland and Wales having voted Remain and wanting independence in varying degrees, there were fears that the United Kingdom would break up and would pass into a Federation of the British Isles.

The costs of leaving the EU were estimated by Bloomberg Economics at £203 billion by the end of 2020: £39 billion for the divorce settlement; £125 billion in loss of growth amounting to 6 per cent of gross domestic product (GDP) worth £2.2 trillion over two years; and a proportion of £160 billion to repay loans. These costs were soon swamped by further costs as a result of the Covid-19 pandemic that spread from China, and lockdown: borrowing estimated at £391 billion by the end of 2020; at least £174.6 billion in loss of growth amounting to 9 per cent (possibly 14 per cent) of GDP; and unemployment rising to 2.5 (possibly 4) million.

All the promises of 'gold' turned out to be worthless fools' gold, and ahead was the worst recession for 100 years (since the outbreak of Spanish flu from 1918 to 1920), and possibly for 300 years (since the bursting of the South Sea Bubble in 1720). And with the world order breaking down and the breakdown now compounded by Covid-19, the simultaneous rise of China (where Covid-19 originated) and the paralysis of the Western economies, there were fears that the West would be in decline for a long while and that power was shifting from the West to the East.

At a time when there was such economic devastation in the West and little prospect of the promised trade deals as other trading nations had their own problems relating to Covid-19, it was questioned whether this was the right time to be leaving a single market that took 43 per cent of British exports and precipitate a 'double whammy' to the British economy: paying for four months' of lockdown and lack of economic activity *and* for the departure from the EU.

The Foul Parliament

UK parliaments are often known by nicknames: The Mad Parliament (1258–1264), The Addled Parliament (1614–1621), The Happy Parliament (1624–1625), The Useless Parliament (1625–1626), The Short Parliament (April – November 1640), and Barebone's Parliament (1653–1654).

The 54th UK Parliament (2005–2010) was known as "The Rotten Parliament" because of the expenses scandal: so many MPs were found to have overclaimed their expenses and to be "rotten". The 57th Parliament from the general election in June 2017 to December 2019 was a fetid swamp in which both parties were stuck. May's three Meaningful Votes were lost, and though Johnson won a vote on his tweaked version of May's deal it was felt to be worse. Johnson made the keynote speech at Northern Ireland's DUP's 2018 conference and promised there would be no economic border down the Irish Sea, and then broke his promise and cancelled May's red line on having no economic border down the Irish Sea.

This Parliament was one of broken promises, intemperate language and shouted abuse. In 1381–1382 Chaucer entitled a satirical 700-line poem 'Parlement of Foules' (in the sense of 'birds'), and, writing in his tradition, I echo Chaucer in calling this Parliament 'The Foul Parliament': a Parliament of foul deeds and behaviour.

Covid-19

The coronavirus Covid-19 (SARS-CoV-2) had been worked on in a laboratory in the Institute of Virology, Wuhan in China.

There had been a US-funded program to work on a benign bat coronavirus for five years from 2014 with a view to discovering the aetiology of diseases, and US and Chinese research scientists had worked together without a problem, funded by the US NIH (National Institutes of Health, $3.4m for the program). This was renewed for a further six years in 2019 (funded by the US NIH and NIAID, the National Institute of Allergy and Infectious Diseases, another $3.4m for the program). This time the experiments modified a benign bat coronavirus with gain-of-function add-ons to make benign bat coronaviruses more airborne, attach themselves to the ACE-

2 receptors in lungs and enter human cells, and with an envelope protein from HIV (GP141) impair immune systems. Whether it was wise to be creating a pathogen, an organism that causes a disease and is therefore a quasi-bio-weapon, to research into diseases is a moot point. But out of the first program seems to have come Remdesivir, which was sponsored by NIAID, an antiviral drug used against Ebola and later promoted as a treatment for Covid-19.

Covid-19 is thought to have escaped from Wuhan City's Biosafety Level (BSL) 4 laboratory between 6 and 11 October 2019, presumably by accident but at the time of writing deliberate intent cannot be ruled out. There were Wuhan phone records mentioning roadblocks and satellite images of full hospital car parks from 14 to 19 October. This second joint US-Chinese research programme was terminated on 24 April 2020.

The Americans knew of the escape in November 2019, and alerted Israel that same month. Covid-19 seems to have reached the UK by early December 2019 as Professor Stefansson, who was then in charge of Iceland's track-and-trace, has said that Covid-19 arrived in Iceland that month via skiers returning from the Alps and travellers from the UK. It was probably active in the UK during the general election of 12 December 2019. Yet Prime Minister Johnson did not attend five consecutive Cobra meetings on the coronavirus on 24 and 29 January and 5, 12 and 18 February 2020 when arrangements for a pandemic could have been put in place. Hancock, chairing the meetings in his place, described the risk from the virus as "low". Johnson spent two of these weeks in Chequers with his pregnant fiancée formalising his divorce, and did not attend a Cobra meeting on the virus until 28 February 2020.

There was talk of a second 'spike' or outbreak, but in fact the virus was permanently present as was the plague of 1347–1351, the Black Death which killed half England's – and Europe's – population via rat-fleas. The 1347 plague had forty 'spikes' during the next 318 years, the last one being the Great Plague of London of 1665, when blind Milton left for Chalfont St Giles with his family and dictated *Paradise Lost* to his daughter while isolating or 'shielding' with the plague outside. It was not impossible that there would be further outbreaks of Covid-19 for years to come if no vaccine could be developed that worked.

The plague turned all necks, armpits and inner thighs black, and death followed within 12 hours. Covid-19 was dangerous for the elderly and those with underlying health conditions, but it was not as severe. Nevertheless, the UK suffered the highest death rate in Europe and also the highest number of excess deaths, despite Prime Minister Johnson describing the Government's arrangements to contain the virus as "world-beating", a claim so at variance with the facts that it turned many against his Government.

Poetry as quarrelling with oneself: the cultural health of Europe

The poet Yeats wrote: "We make out of the quarrel with others, rhetoric, but of the quarrel with ourselves, poetry" (*'Anima Hominis'* in *Per Amica Silentia Lunae*, 1918). The critic, and world authority on Tennyson and Eliot, Christopher Ricks quoted this during his walk round Oxford with me on 21 June 1993, when he advised me to use blank verse in my epic poem *Overlord*. He said that great poetry comes from a poet quarrelling with himself. So Keats wrote in the 'Ode on Indolence':

> O, for an age so shelter'd from annoy,
> That I may never know how change the moons,
> Or hear the voice of busy common-sense!

He was arguing that he should live in "honey'd indolence" with negative capability, just receiving impressions and working on them with his imagination, not understanding them scientifically. It can be argued that a poet *should* know how the moons change, but the point is, Keats wanted a life of ease he had not got, he was arguing with himself. Ricks said to me, "Yeats was right. Great poetry is produced from a quarrel with oneself. I hate Yeats, but he said something that is true. You must quarrel with yourself."

A poet should not present a political point of view in his work as it then becomes one-dimensional propaganda and probably invective, certainly rhetoric: "the art of effective or persuasive speaking or writing; language designed to persuade or impress (often with an implication of insincerity or exaggeration)", *Concise Oxford Dictionary*. A poet should present both sides in a balanced way, reconciling opposites, in accordance with the wisdom of the East which the Japanese poet Junzaburo Nishiwaki wrote out for me in Japan on 5 October 1965: +A + –A = 0. Just as all opposites – day and night, life and death, time and eternity – can be reconciled within "great zero", so all political opposites can similarly be reconciled within an underlying harmony.

Christopher Ricks sent me a 1944 first edition of *Horizon* containing T.S. Eliot's essay 'The Man of Letters and the Future of Europe' in July 2004, when I was putting the finishing touches to my *Classical Odes*. Many of my odes were on the culture of Europe, and a handwritten message from Ricks tucked inside the magazine said: "Apt to your thinking, no?" In this essay Eliot wrote:

> The man of letters as such, is not concerned with the political or economic map of Europe; but he should be very much concerned with its cultural map.... The man of letters... should be able to take a longer view than either the politician or the local patriot.... The cultural health of Europe, including the cultural health of its component parts, is incompatible with extreme forms of both nationalism and internationalism.... The responsibility of the man of letters at the present time... should be vigilantly watching the conduct of politicians and economists, for the purpose of criticizing and warning, when the decisions and actions of the politicians and economists are likely to have cultural consequences. Of these consequences the man of letters should qualify himself to judge. Of the possible cultural consequences of their activities, politicians and economists are usually oblivious; the man of letters is better qualified to foresee them, and to perceive their seriousness.

In this important extract (the first epigraph in both *Fools' Paradise* and *Fools' Gold*) Eliot is saying that the man of letters has to be very concerned with the cultural health of Europe as it is incompatible with extreme forms of nationalism and internationalism. (Writing in 1944, he was thinking of Fascism and Communism.) He argues that the man of letters should vigilantly watch the conduct of politicians and economists as their decisions and actions are likely to have cultural consequences – of which the politicians and economists are usually oblivious. He argues that the man of letters is better qualified to foresee these consequences and to perceive their seriousness than the politicians and economists.

The Europeanness of the British

In both *Fools' Paradise* and *Fools' Gold* I have foreseen the cultural consequences of Brexit, and have quarrelled with myself on the Europeanness of the British while at the same time putting forward the case for a global Britain that is scarcely credible in view of the UK's woeful lack of resources.

In *Fools' Gold* the Europeanness of the British is a historic fact. Practically all the UK's population has arrived from Europe – the Celts, Romans, Anglo-Saxons, Vikings, Normans and many other such ethnic groups – and it seems that my own ancestor Carolus Haggar arrived from Bruges in 1366. The UK has always been a part of the European civilisation, especially since the Dark Ages, and has shared Christianity, the Church and the Pope with the rest of Europe. The UK's history has been intricately connected with European history from the time when England ruled part of northern France through to fighting two world wars in Europe, and helping the Eastern-European nations break free from the Soviet Empire and join the European Union.

Nationalism versus regionalism

I have also quarrelled with myself over nationalism and regionalism (the European Union). The UK is a Union of four nations in current danger of breaking up, and it acts as one nation-state and is represented at the UN as such. Having been a British intelligence agent for four years and risked my life many times for my nation-state, I am arguing with myself regarding the merits and demerits of nationalism as opposed to regionalism (the European Union), and I have foreseen a coming World State not in my lifetime but perhaps in my grandchildren's lifetimes. For this to happen the US, a coming United States of Europe including Russia (an integrationist EU with fiscal union) and a Pacific Union including China need to form a united federation of the world that will preserve internal independence but combine externally to abolish war and nuclear weapons, solve the world's problems relating to poverty, famine and disease, and have a united policy towards climate change and on viruses to prevent future pandemics. The Eastern wisdom of seeing that all opposites – *yang* and *yin* – are reconciled in the *Tao*, +A + –A = 0, applies to nationalism + regionalism (Europe), which are reconciled in the political Universalism of a World State: +nationalism + –nationalism (regionalism) = the Universalism of a World State.

As a quarreller-with-myself in *Fools' Paradise* and *Fools' Gold* I am seeking to preserve the cultural health of the European civilisation, to which the UK has always belonged and always will belong, by arguing with myself about both the Europeanness of the British and the nationalism of nation-states which always leads to wars and trade wars, as the experience of the two 20th-century world wars and colonial competition, and Trump's 'America First', fully bear out. Brexit is a move away from Europeanness to a new nationalism, and, I would argue, from a Union to a new Federation of the British Isles. This move has profound cultural consequences the politicians and economists may not have foreseen, but which are apparent to a discerning man of letters.

Mock-heroic verse

In *Fools' Paradise* I wrote in the mock-heroic tradition – heroic couplets with an epic tone – of Dryden's political perspective in 'Absalom and Achitophel' (1681) and of Pope's social satire in 'The Rape of the Lock'(1712–1714) and *The Dunciad* (1728–1729, 1742, published as a whole in 1743). Like these works by Dryden and Pope, my *Fools' Paradise* is in rhymed heroic couplets, which I used in my 'Zeus's Ass' and 'Zeus's Emperor', poems about Blair.

It is appropriate for the man of letters to hold politicians to account for the need to maintain the standards of the cultural health of Europe, as Eliot urged, and one way of doing this is via the heroic couplet, which affirms standards while ridiculing and satirising follies and vices. A prose model for such an approach would have to be the incomparable Swift. In *Fools' Paradise* I continued the tradition of the rhymed heroic couplet, which is admirably suited to mock-heroic and ridicule.

Heroic verse

In *Fools' Gold* I have, on reflection, gone back to heroic verse, blank verse, which I used in my two epic poems *Overlord* and *Armageddon,* to hold politicians to account and uphold the standards required to maintain the cultural health of Europe as advocated by T.S. Eliot in 'The Man of Letters and the Future of Europe' (1944). The catastrophic turn of events that saw Brexit overtaken by Covid-19 has shifted the public tone, and the nature of responding to politicians, beyond mock-heroic into the territory of epic, my two poetic epics and my three masques (*The Dream of Europa, King Charles the Wise* and *The Coronation of King Charles*), all of which have serious implications and are also in heroic verse.

In this I am reminded of Milton's preface to *Paradise Lost* in which, under a heading *The Verse,* he champions "English heroic verse without rimes as that of Homer in Greek and of Virgil in Latin" and laments "the troublesome and modern bondage of riming" which is "the invention of a barbarous age, to set off wretched matter and lame metre".

Quite simply, in *Fools' Gold* the coronavirus pandemic compounds Brexit in bringing disaster to lives and livelihoods, and to the UK's economy. At the time of writing there have been 141 million cases of Covid-19 worldwide and 3.01 million deaths, and Covid has killed more than 567,000 Americans and more than 127,000 British citizens. For comparison, more than 291,000 Americans were killed in combat in the Second World War, and 43,000 British citizens were killed in the Blitz – and between 1940 and 1945 61,000 British citizens were killed by air attacks.

To put it another way, the tone of *Fools' Paradise* is of the follies and vices of the politicians which have led to a colossal mistake, the biggest mistake in British history since the Second World War (and perhaps since the loss of America). The tone of *Fools' Gold* is of the consequences of this mistake, which are compounded by Covid-19, and the heroic verse of my epic poems and masques is more suitable and appropriate to the rawness and mortality of these consequences.

Fools' Gold, then, is in heroic verse. What the heroic line loses in rhyme it gains in music. Dr Johnson wrote in his 'Life of Milton' in *Lives of the Poets*: "The music of the English heroic line strikes the ear so faintly that it is easily lost, unless all the syllables of every line co-operate together." In my heroic line I use the iambic pentameter, which has been central to English verse over 600 years from Chaucer to Tennyson, and I have sought to avoid "lame metre" (Milton) by varying my iambic feet with trochees (– ᴗ), anapaests (ᴗ ᴗ –) and dactyls (– ᴗ ᴗ) that add a lively skip. I recall a rhyme that conveys what these metres do:

> The iamb saunters through my book,
> Trochees rush and tumble;
> While the anapaest runs like a hurrying brook,
> Dactyls are stately and classical.

I also use other less-well-known feet such as tribrachs (ᴗ ᴗ ᴗ), bacchiuses (ᴗ – –), cretics (– ᴗ –) and amphibrachs (ᴗ – ᴗ), that allow individual words and syllables to be stressed within the musicality of the regular metre.

In this I am conscious of being the son of two musicians: my mother was a violinist who gave recitals in the 1930s and my father was a singer, a tenor with a very rich voice, and they performed together at many musical evenings in the 1950s. Such musicality as can be found in my verse can be attributed to the classical music that was constantly played and performed in the family home when I was a child.

When I was nearing the end of *Fools' Gold*, on 10 November 2020 (the morning after a new Pfizer vaccine against Covid had been announced) I was woken early from sleep by a series of seemingly pre-prepared revelations from the beyond that reminded me of how I encountered the heroic line and its varying skips at school. I was shown chunks of verse I had learned while reading the heroic couplets of Chaucer's *Prologue* and the heroic verse of Shakespeare's *Macbeth* for 'O' level English Literature at the age of 14, and the skips in Chaucer's "As wel in cristendom as in hethenesse" and in Shakespeare's "Tomorrow, and tomorrow, and tomorrow" and "To the last syllable of recorded time". I was shown chunks of verse I had learned during 'O' level Greek and Latin from Euripides' *Alcestis* and the dactylic hexameters of Homer, Virgil and Ovid, and dwelt on a particular skipping line from book 12 of Homer's *Odyssey*:

> ἀλλ᾽ ὅτε δὴ τὴν νῆσον ἐλείπομεν, οὐδέ τις ἄλλη
> φαίνετο γαιάων, ἀλλ᾽ οὐρανὸς ἠδὲ θάλασσα....

I was shown myself sitting reading Milton's *Paradise Lost* by the Seine in Paris in April 1959 when I was 19 and a skipping line from the opening passage: "And chiefly Thou, O Spirit, that dost prefer ..." I was also shown that my use of cantos in 'Zeus's Ass', 'Zeus's Emperor', *Fools' Paradise* and *Fools' Gold* came from my reading of Dante in the summer of 1957, just after I turned 18, and from my visit to Ezra Pound in Rapallo. And I was shown that my use of Zeus in my poems and masques came out of my Greek studies at school.

In short, I was alert to varying the heroic iambic pentameter at school while I was getting 89 per cent for 'O' level English Literature and three As for my 'A' level Latin, Greek and Ancient History (which won me an Essex County Major Scholarship and enabled me to go to Oxford, hence my lifelong loyalty to Essex). In giving me a good grounding in traditional syllabic verse, which is beneath the stress-based system of modern European poetry, my early education worked. There are many instances of varying skips in my heroic lines – my epic poem *Overlord* has over 41,000 heroic lines and my epic poem *Armageddon* 25,000 – and there are many instances in *Fools' Gold*, for example in the last two lines of canto XXIV: "And where is British pragmatic common sense,/ The realistic eye that detects fools' gold?"

This extraordinary pouring-in of revelations ended in a sequence of at least a dozen expanding circles of Light each radiating outwards into my mind one after the other like rapid ripples from a stone thrown into a pool but with the force of the expanding shock wave of an exploding nuclear bomb, as if the Muses and angelic orders were priming my earthbound consciousness for my coming work on

Fools' Gold, indicating that they were working with my heroic verse to chart the end of the pandemic in *Fools' Gold*.

The good thing about English Literature is that it is a tradition and one can link oneself to previous models within the tradition – in the case of *Fools' Gold*, Milton and Tennyson – while avoiding slavish imitation, varying what the masters of the past did to achieve effects more appropriate to our time when today's readers follow "24-hour news" and the phrases of news reports form part of their everyday language. I have used the heroic line to hold politicians to account and uphold the standards required to maintain the cultural health of Europe in a more serious way, as the cultural future of the UK and wider Europe during the rest of the 21st century will be affected by the blunders associated with Brexit and Covid-19.

Poet of decline and world unity

I became a poet in Japan in 1965–1966. My Modernist poem 'The Silence', written during 18 months while I was a Professor there, reflects Western decline and Eastern wisdom, and in 1966 I visited China, and then Russia twice (on my way back on leave from, and again during my return to, Japan). In those days I was thinking deeply about Western decline – the Japanese asked me to teach a year's course to my postgraduate students called 'The Decline of the West' from 1966 to 1967 – and while on leave in England in the summer of 1966 I wrote in 'Archangel', my poem on Communism:

> How but by containing both sides, can we heal
> This split down the mind of Europe and the world?

In Moscow I had visited the Cathedral of the Archangel within the Kremlin compound on 9 June 1966, and staring at the icon of the Archangel Michael I glimpsed a united Europe and a united world, and I wrote of a "World-Lord" who presided over a World State, and its leaders:

> Decades of contemplation
> Show in their white-haired peace

As, trusting to perfect feelings,
They value each equal they greet;
Until, whispering on silence,
They glide to the Leaders' Hall,
Their hearts, with a World-Lord's wholeness,
At the centre of life, of all,
Their hearts where all past and future meet.

On 22 April 2019 I told an audience in Moscow that I had first glimpsed a united world inside the Kremlin, and was roundly applauded. The audience included a number of Russian servicemen in military uniform.

In 'Old Man in a Circle', which I also wrote on leave in 1966, I saw the West in deep decline. I wrote of the strength of the UK's military at the time of the First World War, and its weakness in 1966:

And all down Piccadilly, the indomitable Grand Fleet steamed,
71 battleships and battlecruisers, 118 cruisers,
147 destroyers and 76 submarines;
And on the dreadnoughts our guardian angels sang
"Rule Britannia, Britannia rules the seas."...

Aegospotami and Midway. Ah the maritime:
One blink and a whole armada is knocked to bits
Or sold abroad, or stored, as "obsolete",
And shipless Admirals' voices float from aerials
To 4 aircraft carriers, 2 commando ships,
2 cruisers and a few destroyers and frigates –
O Senior Service.
As I left Downing Street during the Seamen's Strike,
Big Ben peered over the trees and pulled a face
And Nelson raised an arm.

Today's ship count would show an even steeper decline.

I have seen the European civilisation rising into a United States of Europe and the UK declining towards the break-up of its Union and the establishing of a Federation, further on towards decline, similar to Russia's decline from the Soviet Union to the Russian Federation. In a sense, *Fools' Paradise* and *Fools' Gold* are within the tradition of my 'Old Man in a Circle' and similarly hold a mirror up to Nature to reflect the UK's decline. I have written what I have seen, the dwindling and diminishing of my nation-state from ruling a quarter of the world when I was born before the Second World War to Little England, at odds with Scotland, Wales and Northern Ireland, and the European Union.

In the Victorian time the British Poets Laureate were expected to reflect national events in their works. Hence Tennyson's 'Ode on the Death of the Duke of Wellington' (1852) and 'The Charge of the Light Brigade' (1854). Their works were expected to lift the morale of the serving forces throughout the British Empire. The last thing a Poet Laureate should be doing is dwelling on national decline. I am grateful to have been left free to be a court poet (in the sense that my subject matter is drawn from the court) who reflects what I have seen even though it dismays me, and has dismayed me for 54 years.

The poet is a truth-teller who holds his mirror up to Nature, the universe, the Age, and the court. Like Hans Holbein the Younger he reflects the main royal and political figures of his day. Holbein truthfully painted Sir Thomas More, Henry VIII, Jane Seymour, Anne of Cleves, Thomas Cromwell, Erasmus and (on the day they heard that England was finally leaving the Catholic Church of Rome) The Ambassadors. I have truthfully painted Eisenhower, Churchill, Montgomery, George W. Bush, Hitler, bin Laden, Tony Blair, Van Rompuy, Theresa May, Boris Johnson and Prince Charles. In the course of painting the universe the poet will truthfully paint what is going on in the court. The poet should aim to put his easel up in the seat of government and power and paint the court from an independent point of view.

The true poet reflects the Truth and is not a propagandist for his administration or regime. Queen Elizabeth I in 'The Rainbow Portrait' is shown clutching a rainbow – a symbol of the State's control of the dramatists' inspiration in the 16th century – and there may still be an expectation that a State appointee today will be a flattering propagandist and not be truthful.

As I wrote in the Preface to *Fools' Paradise*, the true poet stands apart from society and reflects the true state of his civilisation's cultural health. The true poet has to be a truth-bearer in a mendacious Age to reflect the central idea of his civilisation and culture, in my case the European civilisation and culture. I believe I caught its positive vision in *The Dream of Europa*, the first of my three masques. This has to be read alongside my second masque, *King Charles the Wise*, in which the case for Brexit is put to Prince Charles by Britannia. All my works have to be read in conjunction with another of my works as there is a dialectic, +A + –A = 0, at work between pairs of my works, behind the scenes.

All my works are aspects of winning through to world unity: my vision of a coming World State, as forecast in my third masque, *The Coronation of King Charles*. And a vision of a united world lies behind both *Fools' Paradise* and *Fools' Gold*. My quarrelling with myself enables me to tell the truth to imperfect politicians without being locked up in the Tower of London like the first Metaphysical poet, Sir Walter Raleigh, but in such a way that the positive side of the politicians' message is also shown, and there is a tension between the two. For in +A + –A = 0, the +A and the –A are tethered together and are inseparable, even though they are reconciled within a larger underlying vision.

A Universalist poet: reconciling Eliot and Tennyson

Fundamentally I am a Universalist poet. *In Fools' Paradise* and *Fools' Gold* I endeavour to show all conflicting points of view and opposites within an underlying unity. Universalism affirms the fundamental unity of the universe and of all humankind, and the Universalist poet shows where the misjudgments and self-interested decisions and actions of nationalist and internationalist (regionalist, European) politicians make things worse for their civilisation and culture with cultural consequences, as T.S. Eliot urged men of letters (including himself) to do in 1944 when the British Empire was at its height.

Fools' Paradise and *Fools' Gold*, two national poems by a man of letters, attempt to foresee, take a longer view, criticise and warn of the cultural consequences and seriousness of the decisions and actions of the UK's nationalist and the EU's internationalist politicians, of which the politicians and economists – and SAGE scientists – may be oblivious and which they need to understand. As Sebastian Brant wrote in the introduction to *Das Narrenschiff* (*The Ship of Fools*) in 1494:

Wer sich für ein Narren macht
Der ist bald zů eym wisen gemacht.

This can be translated:
"He who recognises himself as a fool will soon become wise."

In following Eliot's concern for European civilisation and culture and in warning of the cultural consequences of politicians, and in following Tennyson's focus on national events and a "Federation of the world" in 'Locksley Hall' in Tennysonian narrative rather than in the abbreviated, concentrated narrative of the Modernist sequence of images, both within the Classical heroic couplet of Dryden and Pope and the Classical heroic line of blank verse of Milton and Tennyson, I believe I have brought about a Universalist reconciliation of the approaches of Eliot and Tennyson in *Fools' Paradise* and *Fools' Gold* – and, indeed, in all my poetic works that use the heroic couplet ('Zeus's Ass' and 'Zeus's Emperor' as well as *Fools' Paradise*), the heroic line of blank verse (my two epic poems *Overlord* and *Armageddon* and my five verse plays as well as *Fools' Gold*) and rhymed stanzas (my *Classical Odes* and the majority of my poems in *Collected Poems* and my more recent poems).

8–10, 18, 21, 25 August; 10–11 November 2020; 5 March; 20 April 2021

Das Narren Schyff.

Gen Narragonien.

Hi ſunt qui deſcendunt mare in nauibus
faciẽtes opationem in aquis multis.
Aſcendũt vſq; ad celos/ & deſcẽdunt vſq;
ad abyſſos: aĩa eorũ in malis tabeſcebat
Turbati ſunt & moti ſunt ſicut ebrius: &
omnis ſapientia eorũ deuorata eſt.
Pſalmo .Cvi.

The Ship of Fools in the 1499 Basel edition of Sebastian Brant's 1494 *Das Narrenschiff, The Ship of Fools,* with a caption in Old German: *Gen Narragonien,* 'travellers going to Narragonia'.

Fools sailing to Narragonia (the destination on the ribbon banner), captained by Dr Griff (see flag), from the 1499 Basel edition of Sebastian Brant's 1494 *Das Narrenschiff, The Ship of Fools*. The music (top right) relates to a Gregorian chant for all saints:

"Gaudeamus omnes in Domino diem festum celebrantes sub honore Sanctorum omnium de quorum solemnitate gaudent Angeli et exsultant Archangeli et collaudant in caelis Filium Dei. Exsultate justi in Domino: rectos decet collauditio."

("Let us all rejoice in the Lord, celebrating the feast in honour of all the saints, in which solemnity the angels rejoice, while the Archangels rejoice and in the heavens praise the Son of God. Rejoice in the Lord, O you just; for praise is fitting for the upright.")

Canto I
Proroguing Parliament

Sing, Muse, of humankind and harmony,
Of politics and international laws
Rooted within the rhythms of wildlife,
Of Nature that nurtures human affairs,
Sing in images of Nature's variety,
Of sun on sea, hills, plains and sheep on dales,
Of every animal, bird and insect. Sing
Of a vision of a World State's unity
And battered hopes for international peace.
And sing of wilfulness and of self-harm
As a nation-state damaged its global role
By charting a lone course apart from Europe
Under a blustering Prime Minister,
A good campaigner but a bad leader.
Sing of his attempts to get Brexit done.
And sing of prorogation of Parliament
Which branded his Government undemocratic,
And of how Parliament took back control,
Of lack of scrutiny and colossal debts
And sing of viruses and contagion,
Of Government dithering and of lockdown,
And the biggest crisis in three hundred years,
Of an economic crash and decline of the West,
Sing of a disastrous exit from Europe
And implosion of a three-hundred-year-old Union.
Sing of Europe's integration and progress
And how the UK became its satellite
Without a seat at the decision-making table.
Sing of dismay and rising discontent
As golden promises ended in disappointment.
And sing of Zeus's exasperation
As his plan was threatened by foolhardiness,

Sing of follies and vices and delusions
Of grandeur as global Britain went alone.
    A gasp rang round the heights of Olympus,
Of consternation, "*Hwaet*?" (or in modern
Transcription, "What?"), like the squawk of a parakeet
Challenged and shocked, as Zeus, stunned, learned Johnson
Was Prime Minister, having said in a Beowulfian
Flourish there will be 'no deal' in talks with the EU
To get the UK to leave and honour
The referendum of three years before.
Johnson was vague on facts, your poet saw
Him at the last of the hustings at the Excel
Centre (later a Nightingale), wave a kipper
Like those once posted by kipper-smokers,
Now to be posted in a plastic ice pillow
Because of EU regulations, he said –
But in fact UK regulations made the change.
If it had been known there would be a virus
The Tories would have preferred his rival, Hunt,
Who had been Secretary of State for Health.
Johnson was known to be reckless and semi-detached
From the truth, from facts and from evidence –
Facts, policies, people were dumped if they got in the way –
And to be unreliable, as Zeus well knew.
    At the G7 Trump manspreads like an ape
That has ownership of the room, declining
To attend a session on climate change as "a waste
Of time" as climate change is "a Chinese lie".
Johnson's foot manspreads onto Macron's table.
The West seems to be run by simian narcissists,
Manspreaders who care about their own image
More than the world out there, or the evidence.
    Johnson has no mandate from the public,
Only from his Party, yet there is talk
Of his proroguing Parliament for five weeks
Like Charles the First or Cromwell, so MPs

Can't meet to make plans to rule out 'no deal'.
The Opposition parties still meet and agree
That they will seize control of Parliament
Business and vote down and ban a 'no deal'.
    Now breaking news, a bombshell, Johnson will
Shut Parliament for four-and-a-half weeks,
Giving only six days when MPs return
In which to discuss the biggest decision
The UK's had to make since the Second World War.
There's immediate uproar, many statements
That "taking back control" could never mean
Shutting Parliament to deny MPs a voice.
Johnson has barricaded Parliament
Just as a king parakeet perched squawking
On a nut feeder pecks at approaching birds
And bars them access to where they want to be.
There'll be a Queen's Speech on October the fourteenth,
Proroguing's been timetabled, Johnson really has
Followed the path of King Charles and Cromwell,
Both of whom lost their heads (one when exhumed),
And of Gaddafi, who closed Parliament.
It's been plotted for months, only Cummings,
Cox, Gove, da Costa, Rees-Mogg and Johnson
And a few others knew, it was 'top secret'.
As a bluebottle lays eggs in a carcass,
So Johnson's buzzed and settled in Parliament
But the maggoty plan was leaked and Rees-Mogg was observed,
Like a croaking frog squatting on a lily leaf,
Flying to Aberdeen with the Leader of the Lords
And the Chief Whip, bound for Balmoral
To receive the Queen's consent to prorogue
In what's been regarded as a *de facto coup*.
An aide of Javid's sacked for leaking the news
And been frogmarched by police out of Downing Street.
Cummings is accused of a reign of terror
For ordering this public humiliation,

He's like a ferret catching rats for a sack.
Johnson's adored and hated in the country,
Where passions are now running very high.
    Now politics has become frenetic.
Like a farmer opening a drawer of cockroaches
Corbyn calls on Momentum to shut down streets,
Occupy bridges and barricade roads.
Courts in England, Scotland and Northern Ireland
Study the legality of proroguing.
Like a brazen squirrel recklessly scattering nuts,
Johnson launches the biggest advertising
Drive since the war to prepare for 'no deal' –
And starts twice-a-week talks with the EU.
He pledges fifteen billion more for schools.
An election campaign's already begun.
Bercow's been ringing Letwin from Turkey
To plan a blocking of coming 'no deal'.
Major has joined the legal squeeze from court,
An ex-PM's pursuing the incumbent.
The Defence Secretary blurts that the proroguing
Was because Johnson has 'no majority'.
    Like a woodpecker persistently tapping at bark
For hidden insects, morsels to devour,
Cummings is running the Government, he's
A Messiah guiding all to the promised land,
According to Johnson's supporters, by game
Theory, the study of decision-making,
Understanding opponents' objectives
And wrong-footing them to gain advantage.
Will the EU blink at economic chaos
Or be tough in the eyes of the twenty-seven?
Now the EU is wrong-footing Cummings
By seeking to extend Article 50
To avoid a 'no deal' that must otherwise
Take place on October the thirty-first.
Barnier says the backstop won't be removed.

It's the "maximum flexibility"
Brussels can offer and any solution
Must "be compatible with the Withdrawal
Agreement", which defies Johnson's optimism.
Johnson's told Cabinet there's a good chance
There will be 'no deal', a shift from his saying
'No deal' is only a million-to-one chance.
An opinion poll shows the Tories would have
An eighty-four-seat majority in
A general election if the Brexit Party
Stands aside. Now in the three legal actions
In England, Scotland and Northern Ireland
There's a debate on the legality of the advice
Given to the Queen when she gave her consent
To the unusual proroguing of Parliament.
Johnson says all rebels will be sacked
Like wasps smoked out of a nest in a loft.
And it transpires that Dover waiting times
For lorries will be two days, not two minutes.
Now Johnson stands outside 10 Downing Street,
With eyes darting like a venomous snake,
And speaks of how he wants to get things done
And calls for MPs to support his cause
If the agenda's seized in Parliament
The next day and there's legislation
To block 'no deal', otherwise he will seek
A general election immediately.
There's uproar. Does Johnson believe losing
Scottish and South-West seats will be balanced
By gains in Labour 'Leave seats' in the Midlands
And North, or is this a punt, a chancer's gamble
That could return one more hung Parliament?
Like a cunning fox with an ulterior motive
He wants Parliament to block him so he can be
Seen to fight for the people against Parliament.
It's said the negotiations with the EU

Are a sham that is running down the clock
To 'no deal'. Johnson's blaming the EU
And Parliament, and's setting up an election
Before the consequences of 'no deal'
Become apparent. He has no mandate
And no national support for a 'no deal'.
    Now twenty-one rebels who vote against
The Government are expelled from the Party
Like mice locked out of an attic's rolled carpets
And cannot stand for it at the election.
Johnson, like a cuckoo, has pushed young birds from the nest
He has occupied and fatly opens his beak.
Hammond, Gauke, Stewart and Churchill's grandson
Have been drummed out of the Party.
It's a purge of the moderates that Stalin might have carried out,
A Berian purge in a democratic party.
A strategic mistake's been made, the move
To suspend Parliament was an error,
The ending of careers has inflamed all.
Like a housewife boiling a kettle to pour
Scalding water on a hatching of flying ants
To protect her children out in the garden,
Cummings is ruthless, he has purged the Party,
Some say he should be frogmarched out of Downing Street.
It was ill-judged to sack Churchill's grandson.
Twenty were ex-ministers, it's bad tactics.
Cummings sees it as ferreting out more rats.
    The executive's thwarting of Parliament
Has delegitimised the Government
In the eyes of the EU, its referee
Has blown the whistle on a succession of fouls:
Shutting Parliament for the longest time
In ninety years, sacking an aide, police
Marching her publicly down Downing Street,
Threatening rebel MPs with deselection –
Whistle, whistle, whistle, foul, foul, foul, foul!

⌜The Government's lost its working majority.
And now in Parliament the MPs vote
To ban 'no deal' and Johnson rubs his hands
And like a sparrowhawk seeing blue tits round nuts
He calls an election for October
The fourteenth, planning to extend the date
So the UK crashes out of the EU
During the election campaign, one more foul.
To echo Chaucer, whose "foules" meant 'fowls', birds,
This Parliament is a 'Parliament of Fouls'.
    The rebels have succeeded, and progress
To getting Letwin's Bill to block 'no deal'
Amended and quickly back from the Lords.
Like magpies flying at a retreating fox
And pursuing it away from their nest,
They have seized control of Parliament's business
And can ban 'no deal' so it's illegal.
If the Government call an election the Bill
May be dropped before a 'no deal' is banned.
Labour don't want to vote for an election
Till they know the Government can't go to 'no deal'.
If Johnson says he has no confidence
In himself, then just a majority
Of MPs, not two-thirds, can vote it through.
Tactics can prevent a strategy winning.
    Like hooded crows sitting along a fence,
And one cawing importantly, in charge,
The tellers stand before the mace, one speaks.
Letwin's motion has passed by twenty-seven,
The MPs have seized control of business
And can now turn the vote into a law.
Flushed and waving his arms as if Hitler,
Johnson requests a vote for an election
Which the Opposition parties decline,
Wanting to ensure there's not 'no deal', suspicious
He'll advance the date so there's 'no deal' before the result.

Like a raven in the Tower clad in black,
Rees-Mogg, in a peck at Letwin, says those
Supporting the emergency motion
Are "an Illuminati who are taking
The powers to themselves" – knowing that Letwin
Was employed by Rothschilds who both founded
And funded the Illuminati in
1776 and own or control
All central banks except for North Korea,
Cuba and Libya as a dynastic
Élite of world bankers, who'll bank the world.
The third reading has passed, the Bill has gone
To the Lords. The MPs have blocked Johnson's plan
To leave the EU on October the thirty-first
And have demanded a new extension.
Johnson again calls for a general
Election, but Labour, not trusting him,
Suspecting he might advance the vote beyond
October the thirty-first and crash out
During an election campaign, are waiting
Till the Bill passes through the filibustering
Lords to Royal Assent before they agree.
Like a flock of parakeets round a nut feeder,
The MPs have taken power from the Government
But have rejected a general election.
The twenty-one can appeal to the Chairman
Of the 1922 Committee, Charles Walker,
With whom your poet sips red wine on a terrace
Overlooking a slope to distant woods
And says: "Like literature, Conservatism
Is an oak tree with branches for each decade
And many contributed to its tradition
And did well in their time and still have a place.
Some may be out of date and should stand down,
But the present should not lop off past efforts
Which were made in good faith during past issues.

Today's problems require new solutions.
I say it's wrong to purge like Beria,
Or prorogue or dismiss and victimise,
March staff off with police on either side.
The courteous who rebelled from sincere motives
Should be treated courteously and not be banned
Like lopping a leafy branch from a two-centuries-
Old oak tree laden with acorns that shouldn't be pruned."
The twenty-one rebels agreed in advance
A plan for an extension with the EU.
    Johnson says he won't ask for an extension
But would rather be found "dead in a ditch"
And would rather defy the law – go to prison
For contempt of court, but a civil servant
Could sign the document in his place. In his first
Three days he lost his majority, sacked
The twenty-one and his own brother resigned.
He flails and national division mounts.
There's talk of sacking Cummings, Vote Leave's guru
Who follows Sun Tzu's advice to make feints
To disorientate your opponents
Like a self-interested fox that conceals cunning.
You rule out an election and then call one.
Cummings is like a cunning prowling fox
That trots past a pecking hen to reassure,
Then turns when it's off guard and attacks and kills.
It's the Tory Party that's disorientated.
    Sun Tzu's *The Art of War* requires Johnson
To use war language – "Collaborators",
"Surrender" – and now he needs a Plan B.
Labour says it will refuse an election
Till after October the thirty-first
And having wrested control from a Government
Bent on wrecking the UK with 'no deal',
They plan to keep him a powerless prisoner
In Downing Street so he breaks his promise

To leave by the thirty-first of October
And appears a useless, tetchy windbag.
Now Rudd has resigned saying she has not seen
Any real work to secure a good deal.
Like a rampaging bull that crashes round a field
Johnson has split his Party and broken
The political system and constitution.
He says he'll break the law that requires him
To ask for an extension, and is heading
For a showdown before the Supreme Court
And perhaps a deposing of himself.
There is division that Johnson has said
He'd "rather be dead in a ditch" than ask
For an extension, and there's talk that he
Will veto a Commission appointment
To wreck the EU's plans. Like a new Macbeth
He's wading in blood and cannot turn back,
But like Samson he's pushing the pillars
Of Parliament and bringing it crashing down.

The last day before prorogation, now
Like a cockerel crowing in a new dawn,
The Speaker has announced he is leaving
On October the thirty-first or if
An election's earlier, then on the last day
Parliament sits before an election.
A debate called by Grieve to hand over
Prorogation documents and the Yellowhammer
Report on 'no deal' is won by the rebels.
    Now a debate to force the absent PM
To obey the law. There's a call for impeachment.
The demand is nodded through. And at last a vote
On the Government's call for a general election.
He's failed to get two-thirds of all MPs.
There's no election and Parliament's prorogued.
    Now Johnson's prorogation has been found

Unlawful by the Scottish Court, a foul.
It now seems that the Queen has been misled
Like a rabbit following a hungry fox.
The judges suggest Johnson lied to her
To avoid Parliamentary scrutiny.
They don't believe his reasons for proroguing.
There's a call to reopen Parliament.
The Supreme Court, the highest court in the land,
Will reach a decision in London next Tuesday.
    Operation Yellowhammer (named after
The yellowhammer's song, 'a little bit
Of bread and no cheese' as under 'no deal')
Is released, a five-page summary
That makes it clear there will be no access
To pure water, medicines, fresh food or fruit
For many months, and flu will spread, there'll be
A rise in electricity prices,
Fuel supply will be affected, lorries
Will queue in Kent for two days, there'll be
An increase in inflation, food prices
Will rise and there'll be a risk of rioting.
A responsible Government would not proceed
Along this course. No one voted for this.
This was not what was promised three years back.
A political fraud has taken place.
It's said the politicians who led the UK here
Should not be in office for they are not
Patriotic. It was right to block 'no deal'.
There has been a ferocious reaction,
The PM's played fast and loose with the truth
And should resign to free all from Cummings.
    Like sheep flocking round a gate at feeding time,
Now there's pressure from MPs to return
To Parliament. After two months in office
Johnson has hurtled into a massive
Constitutional crisis. Independent

Judges can halt the executive in its tracks.
Carrie was right in the row when wine was spilt:
Johnson does not care about the hardships he'll cause,
He only cares about his self-interest.
In six weeks he has demeaned the office.
He's lost six votes and lost his majority,
And gone from one to minus forty-three
By expelling the twenty-one, and he's lied to the Queen,
And is about to lose in the Supreme Court.
He's been a disaster as Prime Minister.
    Johnson's asked if he has lied to the Queen
About his reasons for proroguing
Which were, it's said, to escape scrutiny.
Like a parrot croaking pre-learned words by rote
He says, "Absolutely not," and also says
Negotiations with the EU are progressing.
The EU say there are no major changes:
"We have no reason to be optimistic.
We've had no legally-operational proposals."
Cameron says Johnson was appalling
In saying on a bus that the NHS
Would receive three hundred and fifty million pounds
A week more when the UK's left the EU.
Like a farmer cackled at by indignant geese
Johnson is heckled in the North and told
To open the prorogued Parliament now.
Remainers are planning to revoke
Article 50 when Parliament returns.
Parliament has made 'no deal' illegal,
But if one of the twenty-seven says No
There will be 'no deal' despite Parliament.
There may be a deal if Northern Ireland
Is allowed to stay close to the EU's rules
To become part of a united Ireland,
Which May red-lined, and Johnson has also.
The EU has received no proposal.

Johnson's in Luxembourg to meet Juncker.
Like two wary stags ready to lock horns
They have a drink in a room with bouldered walls
That looks like a prison. There are handshakes
For the press, is Juncker's handshake Masonic?
There is a lunch of snails, salmon and cheese.
Though Merkel asked for a UK proposal
Within thirty days, no new proposal's been
Received. There's a press conference in the open air,
With loud heckling: like geese honking, cackling,
Outdoing each other, booing, whistling, shouting
"Shame on you, stop the *coup*". Johnson heads for his car.
Like a fox scenting hounds he's bolted for cover
And squats sullenly at bay in a thicket.
The Incredible Hulk has become the Incredible Sulk.
There's an unattended UK podium,
The PM for Luxembourg, Bethel, speaks unopposed,
Channelling the irritation in Europe.
He points to the space, the optics are not good.
He says only the Withdrawal Agreement
Is on the table, and that it protects
The Single Market and Good-Friday Agreement.
People need certainty, one man should not
Hold a country and the EU hostage.
It's a blow to Johnson's strategy and pride.
Bethel's told Johnson not to blame Europe
And not to hold the future hostage for
Party political gains. The protesters' noise
Was so cacophonous Johnson drove off
And did not answer questions on the deal
He says he can see the shape of. There were
Only fifty protesters, he flunked it
Like a farmer avoiding hens at feeding time.
Luxembourg's been laughing in Johnson's face.
Johnson has abandoned a news conference,
It has ended in jeers, he's been ambushed.

His visit to Juncker's ended in chaos.
The PM of a country with a population
No more than Bristol's has mocked the showman.
The Ineffable Sulk's bombast has gone,
Like a peacock that's flown off over a hedge
He's flustered and becomes the Invisible Man.

The new mutineers have now seized the ship
And have turned it round to head for the true
Narragonia. The captain knows the way
And has told all of the gold they will find there
And bring back so there are riches for all.
He's said, "We're heading for true paradise.
Only I know how to steer the correct course."
All crew and passengers are overjoyed
At the prospect of finding and bringing back gold.
Their greed's personal as well as national.
The captain talks of how things will change for them,
How two birds in the bush are worth more than one in the hand.

Canto II
The Supreme Court and the Foul Parliament

Sing, Muse, of justice and the people's right
To be represented in their Parliament,
Sing how the Supreme Court took the people's side
And walloped the PM for his abuse
Of the people's right to debate their future.
Sing of judges and scheming politicos
Who involved the Queen in their duplicity.
Sing of populists who deny the people.
And sing of rebellion on the back benches,
Sing of support for an Opposition Bill
That would make 'no deal' impossible, which the PM's
Called "the Surrender Act" as it would not
Challenge the EU by threatening 'no deal',
Sing of the rancour on all sides of the Commons,
Sing of the inglorious Foul Parliament.
The Supreme Court with clever justices
Staring like unblinking owls, fazed by nothing,
And an appeal against the judgment of the High Court
And the Inner House of the Court of Session
That the courts have no jurisdiction over
A political prorogation of Parliament.
Like a wagtail dipping its tail and earnestly
Making point after point, virtuous wags,
One counsel speaks of an abuse of power.
Counsels speak for and against, John Major
Is a witness. Was the Queen misadvised?
It's said no PM in the last fifty years
Has abused his powers as much as has Johnson.
Where does the balance of power lie between
The executive and the legislature?
Do the courts have the right to stop the PM
Proroguing Parliament, and can it be proved

That he misled the Queen and will the PM
Abide by the ruling? Will he prorogue again?
Like a killdeer luring predators from its nest
Johnson has not signed a witness statement
Suggesting that he has something to hide.
Proroguing may have been legal and yet
He could have misled the Queen, and trust has gone,
PMs should not ride roughshod over institutions.
Parliamentary democracy's been pushed aside
And the Scottish judges' neutrality's questioned.
  Now the Supreme Court's President has asked
Downing Street to write down what Johnson will do
If he loses, not an encouraging omen.
Like a hawk perched on a branch and stonily still
Lord Garnier, your poet's libel lawyer,
Major's counsel, reads out a statement by
Major that Johnson acted like a dodgy,
Dishonest estate agent, who had had
Ulterior motives when he prorogued.
Devolution brings Parliament and people
Together, prorogation drives them apart.
  The summing-up, and the arguments seem clear.
There's no witness statement by the PM.
Five weeks' closing of Parliament when there
Are only seven-and-a-half weeks until
The end of October seems unreasonable.
It's for Parliament to decide a recess,
And the executive's decision has
Taken that decision away from Parliament.
A number of important Bills are lost.
The motive was fear, to avoid scrutiny.
There is an appeal for the Supreme Court
To grant a declaration that Johnson's advice –
And therefore the Order in Council – was unlawful
And the prorogation should be null and void.
Parliament would then determine the way forward,

It would reopen as soon as possible,
The Speaker should decide how to proceed.
Could Johnson then prorogue Parliament again?
    Now Johnson's gone to the UN and said,
Like a fox allowing chickens to feed on a lawn,
That the UK'd agree that regulatory checks
On agricultural products and some goods
Passing from Britain to Northern Ireland
Could take place in ports along the Irish Sea,
And the EU'd agree to check that the right
Custom duties are paid on goods travelling
Between Northern Ireland and the Republic
Without physical checks at the border.
Juncker says that a deal can now be done.
He says he doesn't like the idea of 'no deal'
Which would have catastrophic consequences.
If all the objectives are met, the backstop can go.
He thinks that Brexit will happen, he wants
An agreement and thinks one's possible.
Many in Brussels say he may want a deal.
    A leaked EU document shows 'no deal' is near:
"Proposals for a deal fall short of what
Would be a legally-operable solution."
Officials call the proposals a "backward step"
And "totally insane", which is deflating.
Both sides want to seem helpful and to blame
Each other if a deal cannot be struck.
Like a fox lying low from hounds in red dogwood,
Johnson has boxed himself in with red lines
And has said 'no deal''s better than a bad deal
And has been boxed in by the bloc to 'no deal'.
Johnson's at the UN General Assembly,
Meeting Macron, Merkel, Varadkar, Trump.
    The judgment of the Supreme Court is read
By Lady Helen, the Chairperson, who wears
A black dress with a glittering spider,

Suggesting she's in the centre of a web
(And that Johnson's a trapped buzzing bluebottle).
She says the case is Justiciable.
Since a 1611 Act the sovereign
Can only do things that can be reviewed in court,
And the Government has been scrutinised by MPs.
There was no good reason for proroguing.
The decision was unlawful as it frustrated
The ability of Parliament to carry out
Its constitutional function, and brought
Parliament to a halt for five weeks, not six days.
Like an unblinking owl, censorious,
She says the Court's concluded the proroguing
Was unlawful as it frustrated Parliament,
And the Privy Council's Order in Council
Was unlawful and of no effect, Parliament
Has not been prorogued. It is for the Speaker
And Lord Speaker to take steps for each House
To meet, and the PM is not involved.
She blinks like a tawny owl sitting in a tree,
Peering down at a scurrying squirrel, its prey.
The Speaker says Parliament was adjourned,
Not prorogued, and so the State Opening
Of Parliament has been cancelled, and the laws
That were lost are back on the agenda.
The verdict was unanimous, eleven–nil.
    It could not have been worse for the Government.
She's calmly excoriated everything
The PM's said about prorogation.
He advised the Queen to act unlawfully.
The Court spoke with unanimous clarity.
Like hounds baying for blood and an impending kill,
On all sides there are calls for "Johnson, out",
And his resignation. He's misled the Queen,
Lost every vote in Parliament and now his biggest
Decision's been overturned by the Supreme Court.

Like a wolf that howls to all other wolves
Johnson assumed he was above the law
Of the land and that he could override
Parliamentary sovereignty, and the four nations
Of the UK, and it's rebounded on him.
    Like an angry cat hissing with an arched back
The Queen is livid, Johnson has leaked she asked
Why anyone would want to be PM
At this time of national uncertainty.
He expressed his regret rather than said sorry.
She was angry with Cameron, who leaked
"The Queen purred", and again that he asked her
To help in the Scottish referendum and she
Asked all to consider the future carefully.
Like a dog that chases a cat out of bounds,
Now Johnson has pursued the monarchy
Into a row involving Parliament.
Neither he nor Cameron, nor Blair (who also
Leaked) will receive the Order of the Garter
While she's alive. It's said Johnson's not fit to be PM.
The Cabinet was not shown the legal advice
For prorogation, just given assurances.
And should the Queen retire as she was duped
And at ninety-three may not be as sharp
As she once was – just as Prince Philip's retired
From driving after crashing his Land Rover?
    Growling like a Rottweiler and ready to bark
Johnson speaks from New York, says that he
Disagrees with the judgment and will carry on.
The judges expressed an opinion, not the law.
He's the standard, not the legal system.
Like a grey squirrel chased from a nut bag
He bristles and returns to munch more nuts.
There's been foul play involving Parliament,
And it's now revealed by Johnson – *cui bono* –
The Attorney General advised prorogation.

Johnson's only been PM for sixty-two days
But everything's gone wrong, and he has lost
His majority, twenty-three Tory MPs
And even his brother, from his Government;
He's lost his battle with the Supreme Court,
He's hoodwinked the Queen into wrongly ordering
The closure of Parliament for five weeks;
He's lost his prorogation and may well lose
His Party conference as Parliament's reconvened;
He's been accused by Scottish Supreme Court
Judges of misleading the Queen; two ex-PMs
Have said he's "dishonest", he's lost six votes
Out of six in Parliament, he's been accused
Of misusing public funds when London Mayor
To support a "close friend", a blonde ex-model,
In her new role as a US tech entrepreneur.
His political strategy is in smithereens.
Like a Rottweiler baring its teeth and ready to bark
Johnson is livid in America.
    Now like a Red Admiral on a blackberry bramble
That shyly takes wing when it hears footsteps
Johnson refuses to answer questions
If he had an affair with the American
Ex-model when he was Mayor of London
And she received large sums of public money
For her failing company. She had a pole
In the sitting-room where Johnson visited,
And sat in his chair in City Hall and stood
Outside 10 Downing Street, posted online.
He's being investigated by the police watchdog
To see if he's committed a criminal offence.
    A day ago Johnson was saying proroguing
Had nothing to do with Brexit, and he's now said
The Supreme Court's decision was to foil Brexit,
Admitting that Brexit was behind proroguing.
Like a jackdaw flying from crusts, then returning,

A day ago Johnson was saying the judiciary
Is the best in the world and he'd always respect it,
But now he's saying it's interfering
In the process of Brexit. He's briefing against
Judges, calling them "enemies of the people",
Like a jackdaw flying this way and then that.
It's very damaging to the system.
    It's said it's time for a written constitution
As a wave of right-wing populism
And authoritarianism's scorned convention
And wrecked the unwritten constitution.
And your poet agrees, for that is why
He wrote a constitution for the world.
When people cease to behave like gentlemen
Convention must yield to codifying.
Yet an unwritten constitution's flexible
And no new PM will prorogue again.
Precedent is a powerful force for good
But there's no substitute for hard and fast rules:
Voting by button saves time wasted in lobbies.
    Johnson has to get a deal from the EU.
He can't be seen to be breaking the law
After this judgment, he can't be seen to be
On the wrong side of the law a second time.
The EU has no incentive to reach a deal,
He's no authority over the Commons now
And can't get a majority for a deal.
He lacks the confidence of the Commons,
They won't allow him to have an election,
And are forcing him to act against his will.
He can't extend – no ifs, no buts, he must
Do or die, come what may, die in a ditch –
But he can't not extend at the same time
Because the law requires him to extend
And he can't infringe it. Unless he gets a deal.
    It's scissors-paper-stone. The Government

Is the scissors that are cutting Parliament,
But the stone is the Court blunting scissors. Johnson
Has pushed aside Parliamentary sovereignty,
The monarch and the Cabinet, three fouls.
Like a referee the Supreme Court has ruled
His prorogation a foul and confounded
His strategy and what he planned to do.
    Like an octopus changing colour for camouflage,
In New York Johnson's forced to phone the Queen,
Now an errant schoolboy excusing breaking the law,
And discuss the unanimous ruling
That his advice to prorogue Parliament
Was illegal. Did he apologise
For advising her to break the law she's enforced?
In a Cabinet conference call languid
Rees-Mogg has accused the judges of mounting
A "constitutional *coup*". The Attorney
General Cox says the Supreme Court's overturned
Decades of precedent, "a revolutionary
Decision", a new principle of law
Which has passed into Common Law. Soames says,
"Be ye ever so high you are not above the law."
Sitting manspread next to Trump Johnson's asked
If he'll resign. Trump says he's going nowhere.
Johnson glares like a falcon whose leg is chained.
Verhofstadt says the rule of law prevailed,
That Parliaments should never be silenced
In a real democracy, and he never wants
To hear Johnson or other Brexiteers
Say the EU is undemocratic.

Parliament has reopened, and now Cox
At the dispatch-box says he lost a case,
That a lower court had agreed with the Government.
He gave his legal opinion to the PM.
Like an octopus changing colour for defence,

He says he's not permitted to disclose
The legal advice he gave the PM.
Clarke asks if it's confirmed there will be no more
Proroguings in the future and Cox agrees.
It's the most damning judicial indictment
Of a recent Government. The rule of law
Must be upheld. Labour says Cox has been found
To lack credibility. Cox replies
In his rich baritone that flows through the House,
Puffing new colour into his tentacles:
Should the Lord Chief Justice, who has upheld
The Attorney General's advice, be asked to resign?
    Johnson has flown back from America
And now, at 6.30, the chamber fills
For his statement on the Supreme Court's ruling.
He comes in to cheers from his back benches,
Dishevelled hair, flustered, blustering, tired,
Like a hawk that's survived a farmer's gun,
And talks of this paralysed Parliament,
And says he is discussing opening
The Withdrawal Agreement, replacing
The backstop and arriving at a new deal.
He says the Opposition have Communist
Fantasies and delusions, and the Court was wrong
As it ruled on a political question.
He claims to speak for the people against Parliament.
He asks if Corbyn will dodge a no-confidence vote.
Corbyn says it's been ten minutes of bluster
From a PM who feels he's above the law,
And his statement was like his illegal
Proroguing – "Null and void, and of no effect";
This is a precarious moment in the UK's
History. The highest court in the land has found
The PM broke the law when he shut down
Parliament, and he should have resigned by now.
    Everyone is furious, there is rancour,

Like the screeching of a cawing flock of crows.
Johnson wants an election, Corbyn won't give one.
The anger is mounting and the PM's
Bellicose language – "treachery", "betrayed",
"Surrender Act" – recalls the death of Jo Cox.
Johnson says, "I've never heard such humbug."
('Humbug' means 'false talk' and 'speaking falsely'.)
He says "The way to remember her is to take
Britain into Brexit" – when she was murdered
While campaigning *against* Brexit by a supporter
Of Britain First. He means that the Benn Act –
The Surrender Act – will make it less likely
To get a deal as the EU will see he
Can't get it through Parliament, but it comes across
As Johnson again saying he'll 'do or die':
'Do Brexit, or you may die like Jo Cox.'
It's raucous, rancorous and at boiling-point.
Johnson peers like a sparrowhawk sensing prey.
Corbyn continues his onslaught, says the PM
Has been eager to avoid scrutiny
Of the Yellowhammer document, which the PM
Claimed was "out of date", trying to hide the truth
From the people about a 'no deal'. It would hit
Food and medical supplies and affect the poor.
No effort's been put into negotiating,
And there's no reason for optimism.
He calls for the PM to be investigated
For his funding of the American model
(His ex-mistress who sent him an arty photo
That caused him to quote Chandler's *Farewell, My Lovely*,
"A blonde to make a bishop kick a hole
In a stained glass window" – on high scaffolding?):
"For the good of this country he should go."
Johnson replies Corbyn's being held hostage
By members of his Shadow Cabinet,
And has been censored for calling an election now.

As a flock of geese honks approval in unison,
Johnson's leadership is greeted with applause
And waving of order papers for two minutes.
    The Leader of the SNP, Blackford,
Says the PM is not fit for government.
The PM who's fought the law is responsible
For the law, and he must resign. He has been
Chaotic and ignored the rule of law
To concentrate power in his own hands.
He says the Attorney General and he are "at one
In respecting the Supreme Court and in thinking them wrong".
The political, legal and judicial
Establishment have quietly blocked Brexit.
Now Johnson is asked, "If you don't get a deal
Will you ask for an extension as the Act requires?"
Johnson answers "No" and leaves the chamber,
A scowling sparrowhawk wanting to swoop.
    Next day there's fury at Johnson's language.
Howls of outrage reverberate far and wide.
It is not the language of a PM
Who is representing *all* UK citizens.
The exchanges have been bitter and acrimonious,
Squawks and screeches, cackles and shrieks and yells.
Johnson's said MPs are standing in the way
Of Brexit and Parliament needs to be pushed aside
As they're "traitors", "treacherous" and "betrayers",
They've "surrendered" and "capitulated".
There are many criticisms in Parliament
Of his inappropriate tone and language.
A man has been arrested for menacing
A Labour MP, Jess Phillips, who spoke up
For Jo Cox and spoke out against Johnson.
Her office phones have been suspended as
People have rung, shouting "Traitor, betrayal".
    Johnson's sister Rachel has called his language –
"Surrender", "capitulation" – "very tasteless",

He has honoured Jo Cox's memory
By saying "The best way to honour her
Is to get Brexit done" when she campaigned
Against Brexit and was murdered by a right-
Wing activist who proclaimed "Britain First".
It's like honouring Waterloo dead with '*Vive la France*'.
Rachel says Johnson should not be a bully,
The dispatch-box can be a "bully pulpit".
She wonders if her brother is being advised
By people who have invested billions
To short the pound, as they expect 'no deal'.
Johnson is using a jingoistic
War metaphor and using abrasive
Language as an election strategy.
It suggests the UK's at war with the EU,
It insults the intelligence of the electorate
Who see through the phoney war imagery
As if it's the barking of a snarling dog.
If he were really trying to get a deal
He'd be using more conciliatory language.
    Brexit was to strengthen Parliament and courts
And both have humiliated the PM.
Now Johnson's lost another vote – he's lost
Eight out of eight – and the foul Parliament
Cannot be recessed for his conference.
Parliament has simply refused to adjourn.
    Johnson has refused to apologise
Like a heron that's dropped a *koi* carp by a pond.
Major says no previous Government
In the UK's long history would have considered
Such reckless and divisive behaviour.
There are entrenched positions, Cummings says.
Brexiteers are enjoying the present position.
Cummings says there are loopholes in the law
That requires the Government to extend.
Major says Johnson can use the Privy

Council to bypass the Benn Act. It could pass
An Order *of* Council (which as distinct
From an Order *in* Council does not require
The consent of Her Majesty the Queen)
To bypass Statute Law and suspend the Act
Until after the thirty-first of October
And this could be done without the Queen's consent.
    If he takes this course he will disrespect
Parliament and the Supreme Court, it will be an act
Of political chicanery that
Would crash the UK out of the EU,
As deceptive as a cuckoo laying an egg
In a reed warbler's nest so its chick
Can push the other eggs and chicks out of the nest.
Labour's planning a new law to block this.
Juncker is ready to blame the UK
For lack of a deal if that is happening.
There is a Cabinet revolt as Cummings' plan
Has failed and there may be riots on the streets
If Brexit is not delivered (a Minister's warned).
Johnson has raised expectations of leaving
And there'll be anguish if he fails to deliver.

The EU are in despair at Johnson's cuckoo-like
Approach to Parliament, which has dashed hopes
That Labour will support a last-minute deal.
Cross-party support for a deal is now over.
The UK's papers are a "stalling tactic"
And are ill-thought-through. Barnier's said
The UK's alternative to the backstop
Is unworkable, and as the PM
Does not have the numbers to get a deal
Through Parliament, it's 'no deal' or extension –
And the rest is bluster. That's the EU's view.
    There's a revolution happening in the UK
But few world leaders understand its scope,

Its yearning for change, or see the globalist
Establishment as an *ancien régime*.
The British insurgency is seen as
Impertinent – as the British State blaming
Its deficiencies on external forces
When it's inward-looking and isolationist,
And out of Trump's stable – by globalists
Who seek global governance. Johnson sees
The UK coming together under Brexit
Round the idea of a "global Britain",
"A Brexit for Remainers", with unity.
There's a clash between global Britons and globalists,
There's turmoil in the UK that could last for years.
Now Johnson's been referred by the Monitoring
Officer of the Greater London Authority
To the Independent Office for Police
Conduct – as Mayor he was in charge of the police –
And an independent civil servant
Has begun a London Assembly inquiry.
He's been referred to the police watchdog
For possible criminal activity over Arcuri,
The American model and business woman
He visited hours before standing between
Princess Anne and his wife at the Paralympics opening,
Who received taxpayers' money shamelessly:
A hundred and twenty-six thousand pounds.
His conduct when he was in charge of London crime
Is now being looked at, he has to respond
Within two weeks. There'll be more stonewalling.
It's now clear that Johnson's backed by hedge funds
That have bet eight billion pounds on a 'no-deal'
Crash-out by Johnson's Leave, he has billionaire
Backers who will make billions from 'no deal'
(Including hedge-fund Odey who made two
Hundred and twenty million on referendum night).
No less than 4.6 billion pounds of aggregate

Short positions on 'no deal' have been taken out
By hedge funds that bankrolled Johnson's leadership
Campaign and another 3.7 billion
Pounds by firms that donated to the Leave campaign
But did not donate to the leadership campaign.
It smells foul, there is something not quite right
When proroguing is mixed up with hedge-fund bets
And a man who acts like a squirrel with cheeks full
Of sweetcorn yet greedily gnawing for more.
It's fanciful but one can't help wondering
Are Rothschilds at the bottom of it all,
To converge the pound, euro and dollar?
It smacks of Soros who made one billion
Dollars by forcing the UK to pull out
Of the ERM in 1992.
It's been denied by Full Fact, who had said
It's a misunderstanding of the data,
No spike in the number of short positions occurred.
The *FT* have said that 'no-deal' Brexit
Is not a secret hedge-fund conspiracy
Of currency speculators (or spivs)
But there are names in the *Byline Times'* report
And Labour has taken it up to investigate.
    Johnson has to deliver 'no deal' despite
The Benn law, which he must get round by talk
Of the 'Surrender Act' and so capture
The Brexit Party's vote and Labour's Leave
Voters to win a general election.
He's like a fox that's sidling past hens
While plotting when to turn and devour them.
There will be support, even a reward,
Out of the billions he hopes his backers will land.
With such an incentive, the stakes are high.
No wonder he's under strain from the Supreme Court
And Arcuri, and has become a blusterer
Who deflects questions and changes the subject

And speaks aggressively to ward off the truth.
It suited him to seek to leave Europe
And tie in with America (where he might meet
Arcuri), and receive a large windfall
From his pleased backers from their eight-billion bet,
And pose as a One-Nation, unifying PM.
It seems Brexit is at bottom about greed.
    But hold on a moment, the country's alarmed.
Communist Momentum fanatics shocked
With an extreme motion at the Labour
Conference that called for UK private schools'
Endowments, investments, properties and fields
To be seized by the State, in a latter-day
Dissolution of the monasteries, a Bolshevik
Confiscation's entirely illegal.
Like a sparrowhawk eyeing a blue tit,
Now Corbyn, the Bolshevik Bourbon, wants
To call for a no-confidence vote against
Johnson when he's in Manchester speaking
To the Conservative conference and cannot vote,
As Johnson can't be trusted to comply
With the Benn Act and Article 50.
Corbyn is reaching out to the Lib Dems,
Will there be an ambush in Parliament
While Johnson's MPs are in Manchester?
    Now a fight back at the Conservative conference
With a slogan "Get Brexit done." But it won't
Be done on October the thirty-first,
The UK'll be talking about a trade deal
With the EU for at least a decade.
Now preening like a parrot squawking slogans,
Now snarling like a Rottweiler with bared fangs,
Johnson says that Supreme Court judges should
Be accountable, and he'll move to the US system
In which judges are political appointees.
Judges should be appointed by politicians.

He's attacking institutions that oppose him,
First Parliament and now the Supreme Court.
The UK's institutions are not safe,
It's the end of the stable old England.
He says he will build forty hospitals.
Number Ten is probing Remain MPs'
Foreign collusion, as a link between foreign
Governments and MPs is behind legislation
That could force the PM to delay Brexit.
This will give meaning to his war language,
To the language of "betrayal" and "traitors".
Some MPs – Grieve, Letwin and Benn – have asked
Brussels what the extension period could be?
    Starmer says Johnson is whipping up fears
Of riots to avoid an extension
By invoking the Civil Contingencies Act.
The Opposition parties have discussed
Bringing impeachment proceedings against Johnson
To censure him for his unlawful suspension.
There's a plot to force Johnson into an extension,
The plotters will take control of Commons business,
They wonder if Johnson saying he will be out
Of the EU on October the thirty-first
Is bluster, or whether he's found a loophole.
There will be extra handcuffs but not a vote
Of no confidence. Johnson can't leave without a deal,
But he's goading the people and blaming the law.
    He's facing new claims about his past conduct,
Thigh-squeezing a journalist twenty years ago.
Two journalists have said that at a *Spectator*
Dinner, sitting between them, he put a hand on
Their upper thighs, a crime in MeToo times.
Cummings' wife says she was not one of the two.
Arcuri had made a mysterious loan
Of seven hundred thousand pounds to her company,
Hacker House, before it received a grant

Of a hundred thousand pounds from the UK
Taxpayer to fund her failing business.
Who put this money into her bank account?
The Sunday Times report that she told friends
She was in a sexual relationship with Johnson.
The issue's his allocation of public funds
To her and his conduct in public office.
The Opposition's dithered, and is split.
They can't decide who'd lead a caretaker
Government to oust Johnson, so he survives.
He needs to speak the language of harmony.
Like a gazelle that's survived a cheetah's attack
And is suspicious of its further moves,
The Queen is wary of cheating Johnson.
There's huge disquiet in the Queen's household at
Johnson's proroguing and there are now fears
That he will use the Queen's Speech as a device
To trigger a general election. There's
A breakdown of trust between Buckingham
Palace and Downing Street, now Johnson is
As distrusted as Cameron, who revealed
The Queen's conversations – neither will receive
The Order of the Garter while she is alive –
Whereas Major is trusted, he would not have joined
The legal action without tacit approval
From the Queen's advisers who were content to see
The PM's decision to suspend Parliament tested.
Major is very, very close to the Queen.
Courtiers have discussed whether Prince Charles should go
Alone to the State Opening and read the Queen's Speech,
But the Queen is determined to read the speech herself.
The problem is that the UK has been
A Parliamentary democracy
For centuries, and now the referendum
Has created a conflict between direct
And representational democracy

And no one knows how to reconcile the two.
Plebiscites are a folly that go back to the time
Of Harold Wilson, repeated by Cameron.
And so there's a broken, and paralysed
Parliament that's stuck through MPs' foul play
Like a rusty harvester that starts, then stops.
The fifty-fourth UK Parliament was
'The Rotten Parliament' of unlawful expenses,
And the fifty-fifth that has stuck for many months
Is 'the Foul Parliament' that bent the rules.
It's offensive, abusive and loathsome,
Unfair and ever ready to undermine
Institutions and circumvent the law
On all sides: Speaker, Opposition and PM.
First the Rotten, then the Foul Parliament.

The captain's now showing the passengers
The ship's store of prospecting equipment
That has been kept locked away in the hold
From previous voyages to look for gold:
Gold pans, rock hammers, pickaxes and spades.
He says the ship has got a good record
Of taking passengers where there's a gold hoard.
The last captain got the direction wrong
And landed in the wrong land, but now he
Will bring them all to great prosperity:
"Onward, all, to Narragonia, where
You can fill the ship and your pockets with gold."
A corrupt judge, a drunkard, an untrained
Physician, lustful and slothful men beam
Along with builders who do not complete
Their buildings, scholars who write unreadable books
And procrastinators who endlessly prolong.
All nod in anticipation of new wealth.
It's a long haul across a dipping sea
But the wind's in the sails, the ship's tossing.

The hundred fools are happy as a band,
Armed with gold pans, rock hammers and pickaxes.
Among them can be found all kinds of fools:
A parent who keeps his children out of schools,
A follower of fashion consumed with pride,
An obese man who gorges to excess,
A student who's neglecting his studies,
A litigant who wastes time on legal cases,
A man who carries the world on his shoulders
Like Atlas and staggers beneath its weight,
A gullible man duped by politicians.
On this ship are all follies and vices,
And all stare at the horizon beyond the waves
For a glimpse of Narragonia, land of gold.

Canto III
The EU Rejects Johnson's Plan

Sing, Muse, of how the PM had a plan
To ignore the border in Northern Ireland
With the EU and disregard a backstop
And sing of how it was bluntly rejected,
Sing of a trading threat to the Union
And of how a populist did not read details.
Sing how a promise collided with a treaty.
    Johnson is about to reveal his Brexit plan
Of customs centres away from the border,
Like an ill-prepared student reading out
A hastily-cobbled-together essay,
And will ask the EU to rule out an extension
To Article 50 as part of a new Brexit deal
Contrary to the Benn Act, to confront
MPs in Parliament with a binary choice
Of agreeing the revised deal or ensuring
That the UK leaves the EU with no agreement.
Like a blue jay imitating a hawk,
Presenting a false appearance for its own ends,
Johnson has to get his plan through Parliament
To avoid a 'no deal' on October the thirty-first.
Now Johnson says his Brexit plan's a change
Of policy, and says in interviews there will be
No physical border checks, but further back
There will be clearance centres with technology.
Ireland says there must be no checks in the Irish island.
It's the moment of truth for Dublin, Brussels and Berlin.
    Night, and Downing Street has told journalists
Johnson will be making in his conference speech
His final offer on the Irish border
To the EU, on a take-it or leave-it basis.
Brussels and Dublin have said: no checks in Ireland.

There may be 'no deal' by mid-October.
    But now he's speaking to the packed conference hall,
And as one might expect from a dissembler
His ultimatum does not get mentioned.
His speech is a fudge on the backstop. Northern Ireland
Would remain in the EU's single market
Until 2025 but leave the customs union
On the thirty-first of October, so there is
A time-limited backstop; by the end
Of 2025 Northern Ireland
Would decide whether to remain in the EU's
Single-market rules or join the UK.
    It's a mundane speech with little on the EU.
He's peeping out of a hole like a timid mouse.
It meanders with many jokes and Trumpian call-outs.
There's a lack of substance beneath the surface charm.
There's an emollient tone, saying technology
Will get Brexit over the line. The EU
Has declined to be impressed, his plan for
A border in Ireland breaches all undertakings
Made by the May Government, and so Johnson
Has deleted the ultimatum, it's a non-event.
There's no certainty the Government will leave
The EU on October the thirty-first.
There's been a two-minute audience reaction,
Not as long as usual, it has fallen flat.
It was a bit like watching a horse grazing.
    Johnson has written to Juncker – his letter's headed
"A fair and reasonable compromise: UK
Proposals for a new Protocol on
Ireland/Northern Ireland" – to replace the backstop.
The Government wants the future relationship
To be based on a Free Trade Agreement,
And as the backstop was a bridge to a future
Relationship with the EU, it's a bridge to nowhere.
Northern Ireland will leave the EU customs union

Alongside the UK but remain aligned
On all single-market rules for agriculture
And industrial goods for four years
And the two borders between them will have a kind
Of no-man's land between them, with no fencing.
Juncker replies in a phone call to Johnson.
There's a customs border within the Irish island,
And Northern Ireland has four years to decide
Whether to be with Great Britain or the EU,
And if it chooses Great Britain there'll be
A regulatory border down the Irish Sea.
Like a venomous snake, poised and ready to strike,
Corbyn says it's worse than the Withdrawal
Agreement, and it looks as if Johnson
Wants 'no deal' – and wants to blame the EU.
Like an eagle looking down and surveying the scene,
Barnier says a lot has still to be done
To fulfil the three objectives of the backstop:
No border, Northern Ireland's economy
And protecting the citizens inside the single market.
Now Parliament is proroguing on Tuesday
For a Queen's Speech on October the fourteenth.
There's dismay in Brussels as it does not match the backstop.
The EU will ask how it addresses the issues:
Can there be a customs union and checks?
How will it stop smuggling and loss of tax
Revenues for the EU? A deal seems unlikely.
The European Council President, Tusk,
Like a tutor unimpressed by an essay
But tactfully distancing rather than being blunt,
Has said they're open but still unconvinced,
And the Irish PM's said the plans "fall short".
The British have suddenly made themselves scarce
Like a flock of jackdaws bolting when a crow lands.
As roses relish soil mixed with horse dung
And bloom in appreciative bright colours,

But will wilt if grown in unnourished ground, so a deal
That's in rock-hard ground will wilt and look ragged.
The EU has doubts over Johnson's plan
For the Irish border, and Johnson in the Commons
Has talked of the two borders, and they have given
Johnson '*nul points*'. He's said, "It's a genuine
Attempt to bridge a chasm" but seems half-hearted,
His plan is dispiriting, yet it has united
The Conservative Party and may get through the Commons.
But the EU is against it and because of the Benn Act
There's no pressure on the EU to compromise.
An EU source says they can grant the UK
An extension without Johnson's applying
Under EU law, which is superior to UK law.
    Europe may force the PM to abandon
Northern Ireland and accept its proposal
For a province-only backstop. Johnson has
Made a big-money offer to Ireland
To compensate businesses for lost revenue,
Caused by a cross-border customs system,
But Varadkar has flatly turned it down.
Like a jackdaw loitering in the hope of crusts,
Johnson has offered to negotiate
With the EU throughout the coming weekend
But the EU Commission's snubbed his offer,
Saying his plans don't provide a basis
For concluding an agreement. Johnson's
Plan is now as good as dead in a ditch
And now Johnson's like a bull, hoofing sand back
With two dart-like *banderillas* stuck in its back
While the EU matador struts and readies his sword.

As terns dive-bomb beach walkers near their young
The EU's released a statement saying they've asked
Many questions of the UK, and its proposals
Do not provide a basis for an agreement.

To some they're not genuine proposals,
Johnson knows the EU will knock them back
And that he won't get them through Parliament,
But if he keeps them going a bit longer
He will soon secure a 'no-deal' Brexit
That'll be welcomed by his hedge-fund backers.
Like a squid releasing ink to ease its escape,
He's standing alone in a Churchillian manner,
Defending the people against the monstrous EU
And the Supreme Court, in a political ploy.
    The EU want there to be no customs,
The backstop has to remain till there's something else,
There are ambiguities in the document
And Brussels' reaction will be negative.
It's not a good way to treat the Troubles,
To give Northern Ireland a choice between
The Republic and the UK every four years.
    Now like a cuttlefish changing colour
To be male one side and female the other,
Johnson is being deceptive to escape
And there is talk of sending the EU
Two letters, one agreeing an extension,
And a second letter saying in effect
'We didn't really mean it' – a bit underhand.
Cummings appears confident and has said
If Brussels does not back down, it's 'no deal'.
But Brussels has refused to work over
The weekend, as there's no basis for a deal.
Cummings says the letter to the EU will be
A letter from Parliament, not the PM.
There's a stand-off like two skirmishing stags.
    The UK's narrative's the people being blocked
By Parliament and the Supreme Court, and Johnson
Standing up to an EU tyranny.
And like an octopus squirting a cloud of ink,
At the German Embassy Gove has compared

Brexit to the fall of the Berlin Wall,
Suggesting there's a parallel between
East Germany's fight for freedom and Brexit.
    The EU's called for fundamental changes
And the Government has said it could clarify
Its proposals. Johnson insists the EU
Should negotiate as the UK will leave
On the thirty-first of October. It's said
The UK will disrupt and sabotage
The EU if 'no deal' is forthcoming
By vetoing the budget and sending
A new UK Commissioner to Brussels
To disrupt – it's said it could be Farage.
Barnier's saying the British Government
Will be to blame if there is now 'no deal'.
    The EU's on the verge of saying No.
Silver-haired Barnier's said he won't allow
Passion or emotion into his approach,
Only facts and figures, what is legal
And operable, and the UK cannot change
The EU's support for the single market.
He will not go "into the tunnel", meaning
The process of line-by-line negotiating,
As that would signal a possible breakthrough.
He and Johnson lock horns like autumn stags.
    The EU, in the person of Barnier,
Says the UK'll bear full responsibility
For a 'no-deal' outcome, and it's a mystery
How Johnson can leave on the thirty-first of October
And observe the law. The reality seems to be
He's no idea himself, and's looking for loopholes,
And all the rest is electioneering,
Including a short proroguing so that the Queen
Can read the Queen's Speech as his manifesto
And a party political broadcast on his behalf.
    The reality is, devious as an ink-squirting

Sea hare, Johnson's put forward unworkable
And unacceptable proposals, expecting them
To be rejected so he can blame the EU
In the election campaign he so craves.
And if MPs try to unseat him for
A caretaker government led by the Speaker
Or an ex-minister, he will not resign
As the Fixed-term Parliaments Act does not mention
A need to resign. He'll squat on in Downing Street
And dare the Queen to sack him, the first time
A PM would be dismissed by a monarch
Since Lord Melbourne was sacked in 1834.
The Queen would dissolve Parliament and let
The people decide in an election.
Meanwhile the Opposition will try to force
Him to publish the entire legal text
Of his Brexit plan as it may confirm it
Brings infrastructure into Northern Ireland
And contradicts the assurances he gave the House,
And how he plans to replace protections
For workers' rights, MPs do not trust him.
    His moral leadership is now dismissed.
It's come to light Johnson recommended
The American model Arcuri to head
A government quango with a salary
Of a hundred thousand pounds a year, although
She was woefully underqualified for the post
Of chief executive of Tech City, and failed
To declare the conflict of interest.
The London Assembly have summoned him to provide
All his private text messages and emails,
Both private and public, and to appear
With these before their committee under Section
Sixty-one of the Greater London Authority Act
Of 1999, which can compel
An ex-Mayor to attend their proceedings

And supply documents when they require.
On TV Arcuri declines to deny
She had an affair with Johnson when he was married.
    It's been the longest Parliament for hundreds of years,
This Foul Parliament with its stench of abuse,
Its squawking, cackling and feather-pecking,
And now is the last day before it's prorogued.
It's been hard to undo the enmeshing
Of forty years, and ahead is the prospect
Of the UK being a small- to medium-sized
Country among many such on the world scene,
All competing for trade deals, which can take
Four to ten years to negotiate from the start.

Johnson may have to rework his proposals as
He's been told by Macron the EU'll decide
By the end of the week if a deal is possible,
Johnson's in a last-ditch bid to save his plan
Or else it – not he – will be dead in a ditch.
He and Macron are like two stags that have locked
Horns in a bout of fierce mortal combat.
    Now Parliament's voted to make Johnson
Publish his Brexit plan in full: forty-
Four pages when only a memorandum
And a letter – a summary, a précis
And an interpretation – by Johnson have been revealed.
It's said he's not honest, and Ireland's said
He's contradicted what the legal text says:
There'll be checks within the island of Ireland
Contrary to the guarantee he's given,
And there's a difficulty over workers' rights.
Dudderidge says the legal text will be
Published only when it helps the negotiations.
But MPs need to see the text they're being
Asked to support and not take it on trust.
    Now Johnson's ministers are threatening

The Republic of Ireland with what will happen
If there's 'no deal', leverage that includes
Shortage of medicines, most of which come from
The UK, and disruption of equine transport,
Not to mention loss of fishing rights
Off the coast of north Ireland and lengthy delays.
    It's now clear how stark the divide is between
Britain and Northern Ireland over Johnson's plan.
It's as wide as the Irish Sea, with the EU between.
In his plan all goods would be checked between
Britain and Northern Ireland to ensure
They comply with EU standards and then
Would be checked again to ensure they comply
With customs rules between Northern Ireland
And Ireland, a double border: Britain and Ireland.
So Britain would be outside the EU's
Single market and customs union, and there would be
A regulatory border for goods and food
Between Great Britain and Northern Ireland –
Which the DUP once opposed but has now agreed
In return for huge sums of money to Northern Ireland.
    But the EU objects to the untried technology
And the checks at locations away from the border,
And the plan is a non-starter with the EU.
There's a pretence of talks, which will limp on
Until the EU formally declares
Them unacceptable, and blames the UK.
    It's said Johnson rang Merkel at 8am
And had a frank and clarifying talk,
And locked horns in a fury that drew blood.
There will be 'no deal' unless Northern Ireland
Remains in the customs union.
The UK has repudiated much of May's deal.
No deal with Europe will be possible *ever*.
Johnson's angry and has had a massive row
With Merkel and the goodwill has ended.

Johnson says a deal's essentially impossible
After his clarifying call with Merkel,
Which was a game-changing, outspoken call.
The UK will have to borrow a hundred billion pounds
To meet spending commitments after a 'no deal'.
A video has gone viral showing Johnson
As a younger man saying no Government
Would be foolish enough to leave the EU,
And as an unprincipled man who now
Scorns his old beliefs out of self-interest.
Now Johnson's meeting the Head of the EU
Parliament, and Tusk has said the future
Of Europe and the UK is at stake.
"You don't want a deal or an extension,
Or to revoke, *quo vadis*?" (Where are you going?)
The talks are teetering. There are massive gaps
In the proposals, there have to be customs checks
Which were omitted. The Government wanted
The proposals to fail, to get to 'no deal'.
And now Parliament has been prorogued for
A Queen's Speech (an electoral broadcast).
Like an angry chameleon changing its colour
To red with a black stripe, reptilian
Johnson's trying to create a narrative
Of EU intransigence leading to breakdown.
Now the talks have broken down, there is no deal
Unless Northern Ireland stays in the customs union
And remains aligned with the EU,
And the hedge funds stand to get a return
On their eight-billion-pound investment bet.
Johnson's proposals have not changed hearts and minds.
He would like to take the UK out of the EU
By the end of October, and he's blocked by Parliament
And blocked by the EU, and it's unknown
What will happen next. The Government's campaign team
Is making Johnson a Brexit martyr,

His deal appearing to be foiled by Europe.
    Proroguing's happened. Two dozen in the Lords,
Five Commissioners, and a statement from the Queen
Read in neutral terms by Baroness Evans,
Of all her ministers have done in this Parliament,
Watched by two dozen MPs from the Commons
Standing at the bar. This Parliament is dead,
And so is the UK's hope for a deal.
    Ahead is a bleak time, a lower standard
Of living, an economy no longer booming.
It will be sixty billion pounds smaller
Than if the UK'd wanted to remain.
Johnson's been told his public-spending splurge
Could raise public debt to a fifty-year high.
Businesses will be hit with a fifteen-billion-pound
Customs bill if there's a 'no deal' Brexit.
    The EU have criticised the UK's plan,
And Parliament's prepared for a weekend sitting.
Cummings has said that the UK will cut
Security ties with EU countries who back
A Brexit delay, and Johnson has slapped him down.
    It has now been revealed that the EU
And Merkel say that if Northern Ireland
Were outside the customs union there would be
Checks on goods on both sides of the border.
This would disrupt the all-Ireland economy
And break with the UK's commitment under
The Good-Friday Agreement, which is fragile.
Also, the plan to get Irish consent
Would give a veto to the DUP,
And a vote every four years would further
Destabilise the peace process as every
Northern-Ireland party opposes this
Except for the DUP. Also, if the UK
Reduced its VAT there could be smuggling,
And deferring an alternative to the backstop

To the transition period was rejected.
And the UK would have an advantage
Over the EU as environmental rules
Can add to companies' costs, and electricity
Could be supplied more cheaply from Ulster.
  Like a stag twisting and tugging its locked horns
The EU's insisted Northern Ireland
Stays in the customs union, which could break up
The UK. The UK can only leave
The EU by breaking up the UK.
  Barnier says the EU is not at a point
Where a deal can be done. He's relentlessly
Downbeat about a deal. It all looks grim.
Merkel's "*nein*" – outright rejection of Johnson's
Deal – risks sudden catastrophe for all
In a chaotic, ill-thought-out 'no deal'.
Verhofstadt has called Johnson a traitor
Who risks steering his country to disaster.
The stags have unlocked horns and paused combat.
But Johnson and Varadkar are meeting
Even though there is 'no deal', so they can
Be seen to be trying to find a deal
With Northern Ireland in the customs union.

The ship prowls on through not-too-stormy seas.
When the captain appears all clatter their gold pans
In approval, all are behind his search for gold.
He says he's been to Narragonia
And gold can be found in rocks and a river.
They hang on his every word and discuss what he says.
All are convinced that their fortunes will change,
All have dreams of what their new gold will buy.
Under his direction there'll be prosperity.

Canto IV
Pathway to a Deal Blocked

Sing, Muse, of Ireland's European border
And how the Taoiseach met with the PM,
Walked in a garden and found a pathway
To a deal, sing of blurring and compromise,
Of no trade checks and trade checks happening
At the same time, with Great Britain and Northern
Ireland understanding opposite things from
The same wording, and of 'checks' meaning 'no checks'.
Sing, Muse, of warfare on the back benches,
Of a blocked deal and a Withdrawal Amendment
Bill in limbo as a stalemate prevails,
Sing of frustration and negativity
And of paralysis and self-division.
Sing of a nation-state that's in depression.
    Johnson's meeting Varadkar for three hours
At the mid-nineteenth-century Thornton Manor
In Cheshire's Wirral, a wedding venue.
Like two deer from the wild in a garden
They walk down a long path between mown lawns.
He's "seen a pathway to a deal", and compromised
On customs as the DUP had feared.
Seven defeats in the Commons and a defeat
In the Supreme Court's moved Johnson away
From 'no deal' and now towards Green, leader
Of the large One-Nation group of eighty
Tory MPs, who's said he can't support
A manifesto campaigning for 'no deal'.
There's a rift in Number Ten between Cummings,
Who's declared negotiations dead after Merkel's
Rowing, and Lister, who favours a deal.
Johnson's ruled out any 'no-deal' pledge in
The manifesto for the next election.

He's moving away from 'no deal' even though
Parliament is to meet on Saturday the nineteenth
Of October and vote on a deal or 'no deal'.
The papers are full of options: deal, don't send
A letter, send two letters (the second
Undermining the first), resign, vote on
'No deal' and, last, a no-confidence vote.
But Europe's got a plan and is waiting
For Johnson's promises during the referendum
To be shown to be hollow and a sham.
They're waiting for the electorate to find him out –
Then the British will wake up from the nightmare
They were plunged into by the intemperate vote.
Both leaders want to keep the talks going
So they're not blamed for their final collapse.
    Now, like chickens at feeding time, heads down,
All sides appear to be negotiating
And to strike an upbeat note. There are pictures
Of Johnson and Varadkar walking on a pathway
Having seen the pathway to a deal, a plan
For Ireland, a Northern-Ireland-only
Customs arrangement. The UK and Northern
Ireland would leave the EU's customs union
But all goods coming into Northern Ireland
Would be subject to tariffs. Northern Ireland
Would still be within the EU customs zone.
Its businesses would receive Government rebates.
A customs 'partnership'. Johnson has U-turned.
There's a sound of silence as talking takes place.
    Now details of the draft deal have emerged.
A product arriving in Northern Ireland
Would be subject to EU tariffs and import
Taxes, which would be paid by the exporter,
And there would be a check at the mainland port
To see it complies with single-market standards.
If it stays in Ulster, the importer

Would get a rebate from the UK Government
If the tariff is lower than the EU's.
The UK Government would collect the tariff and send
It to Brussels, and repay any difference.
If it goes on to the Republic of Ireland
No rebate, no single-market or customs
Checks will be needed as the tariff has
Already been settled. A new border
Has been created down the Irish Sea.
Johnson's agreed to a customs border in
The Irish Sea, abandoning Northern
Ireland, and therefore splitting the UK.
He's betrayed Ulster as a wolf betrays its partner.
  Last year Johnson said the idea's crazy
As the UK would collect tariffs for the EU
And the EU also rejected the idea –
Yet now Johnson is weirdly proposing it.
There's been a concession, and both sides can claim
The other side's backed down, it's a compromise.
It's the biggest U-turn since Disraeli split
The Party over Corn Laws in the 1840s
And sided with farmers against the poor –
Supported taxes on imported wheat,
Raising the price of bread – and when he became
PM, angered the farmers by refusing
To reinstate the Corn Laws as they wished.
  It's now come out that, like a cow stamping
On the pathway with pointed horns, Merkel rebuffed
Johnson's plan to take Northern Ireland out
Of the customs union with unproved technology.
She said he must work with Brussels and Ireland,
And Northern Ireland should remain in full alignment
With EU rules "for ever". She made it clear
The EU has a veto over the UK's
Leaving the customs union, and that a deal
Is overwhelmingly unlikely. Cummings then sent

The Spectator a seven-hundred-word text message
Detailing the UK's plans to disrupt the EU
Business if the UK is forced to extend.
Johnson's pulled away from Cummings' 'no deal'.
He wore a suit to Cheshire, forced to submit
To new sartorial rules, put in his place –
No sign of his unironed shirt, jeans and fleece.
Sedwill's now in charge of getting a deal.
Johnson will sign off on most of May's deal,
Which he voted against twice, and there's no discount
On the thirty-nine-billion-pound divorce settlement.
It's May's deal with a few tiny things changed:
Customs checks don't have to be done on the border.
He's moved from the ERG and has revived
May's Withdrawal Agreement with a tweak
To push it through Parliament at the last minute.
    The meeting with Varadkar under Sedwill's
Influence changed everything. Johnson gave ground
On the Irish border, he now accepted
A border down the Irish Sea, Northern
Ireland would continue to obey single-market
Rules and regulations for agricultural
Products and industrial goods, and would remain
In both the EU and UK customs zones,
And he also agreed new consent rules.
He was turned from 'no deal' by security
Reports that hundreds of terrorists would target
The customs infrastructure, and would blockade roads.
Johnson dismissed a similar idea
Put forward for a "customs partnership",
Which Rees-Mogg called "cretinous" – they support it now.
    Sixteen hours of technical talks in Brussels
Surrounded by silence, all is intense.
No spoken progress, only two days to go.
Both sides are talking but all have agreed,
A significant amount of work is still to be done.

Now a cacophony of shrieks and squawks.
It's been reported the EU is "baffled"
By Johnson's proposals, and Brexiteers
And the DUP are attacking the deal.
Brexiteers are furious as the EU's made
More demands for concessions by the UK.
The EU say Johnson should give more ground.
The problem of fraud has not been addressed.
There's anxiety as an election could lead
To a hung Parliament. 'No deal' looms again,
Brexit hangs in the balance. Johnson promised
To leave by October the thirty-first.
Time's running out on a deal, there's too much to do.
The State Opening of Parliament. The first
Day of the new Parliamentary session.
The Queen's Speech after two and a quarter years
Of the Foul Parliament, can things be any better?
As the Government has a majority of minus
Forty-five it will be a party political
Broadcast amid splendour from the steps of the throne.
With such a minority Johnson is telling all
Of the twenty-six bills he plans to pass
If he wins a general election.
The coach and six white horses pulls away
From the Buckingham-Palace doorway, and in rain
Heads up the Mall before the waiting crowds,
A golden coach, with gold wheels and gold roof.
The Queen enters the Palace of Westminster.
In the Commons the mace is on the table,
The MPs stand. In the Lords the peers are all
In ceremonial red robes and ermine.
The Queen has robed and sits on the gold throne
Assisted by Prince Charles. The Queen's handed
Her speech by the bewigged Lord Chancellor.
She's made sure she's had the text a week, so Johnson
Could not put something in at the last minute

That would embarrass her, she's on her guard.
Like a graceful but wary fallow deer
She reads the twenty-six bills in a thin voice,
Including seven bills on leaving Europe.
A legislative programme ends with an election.
There's going to be an election within days,
There will have to be another Queen's Speech next month.
The Queen says the programme offers a new age
Of opportunity for the whole country.
    As persistent as a rat-hunting ferret,
Corbyn says the Government's majority
Is minus forty-five and they are setting
Out a legislative agenda that can't be delivered
In this Parliament. He says, "The Prime Minister
Promised that this Queen's Speech would dazzle us.
On close inspection it turns out to be
Nothing more than fool's gold." It glints but is dross.
It's come across as an election programme,
As electioneering from a golden throne.
    The Commons looks towards next Saturday,
The first time there'll be a weekend sitting
Since the Falklands war. An election can be called,
Or talking about a deal may be tunnelling
Under the EU summit and emerging
In time for the thirty-first of October.
    Now Barnier, a regal eagle who sits supreme
Above the fray, says there must be a legal text
By midnight tonight, or else there will be no deal.
He suggests it's difficult but doable,
He's discouraging and encouraging at the same time.
The EU've asked Johnson for more concessions.
May said no British PM could sign up
To a border down the Irish Sea. Johnson's desperate
And has conceded more than the DUP want.
He's got to bring the two wings in Parliament
Together into a compromise, like May.

Tusk says the sticking-point's on the British side,
It's the consent mechanism, how communities
In Northern Ireland come out of the arrangement
And are not trapped in something they want to leave.
Also the alignment of VAT.
Johnson's held an eight-minute Cabinet meeting,
He has reported progress has been made
But there won't be a deal tonight. Barnier's meeting
The twenty-seven Ambassadors, and will meet
Them again tomorrow. But it's May's deal with tweaks
On the backstop, consent and future relationship.
Good progress because of a British change of heart.
The customs VAT's been sorted, now
It's the Political Declaration.
But it hasn't been put into a legal text.
Negotiations will go on past the EU's deadline.
There is to be a vote on Saturday
For a Brexit deal (or extension or second
Referendum, or even a general election).
Johnson is short of a majority.
The deal's on divergence, guarantees will be dropped,
So Labour will not vote. Now it sinks in,
Despite his bigging-up and blustering
Like a puff adder making itself look larger,
Johnson has surrendered. All the ERG
Are going back on what they said. There's no protection
For workers. Johnson will not want to give the text
Out to MPs before the vote as so much will be
Found unacceptable. He's not going to die in a ditch,
He's not doing or dying, he's taken out
Bits on closeness to Europe. He's given away
Northern Ireland – a border down the Irish Sea.

Now, arms spread, hunched and slouching like an ape,
Johnson says reaching the deal's like the prisoner
In *The Shawshank Redemption*, crawling through a mile-

Long tunnel to freedom and Red saying
Hope's a dangerous thing, and can drive a man insane –
While he's given away Northern Ireland.
He's a snollygoster, guided by personal gain
Rather than by virtuous principles,
As soon as something difficult comes his way
He bats it off with a flippant reference
And disarming quips, he's shallow, not profound,
He's not regarded as authoritative.
It's May's deal with changes, the backstop's replaced
By a border down the Irish Sea, changes
To VAT and consent – cross-community
Consent is required by the Good-Friday Agreement.
Labour and the DUP won't back the deal,
So it won't get through Parliament, it's going to be
A rerun of May's three defeats in the Foul Parliament.
It seems Johnson, who voted against May's deal,
Will be getting a taste of his own medicine.
    The EU countries are a bit like the states
Living under the Roman Empire, like Britannia.
The Roman Empire was good, it built new roads.
EU leaders will need Johnson to prove
He can get this deal through Parliament
Before they sign it off at a summit.
    Johnson has said that as there is now a deal
There's no need for an extension, and MPs
Now face a choice between this deal and 'no deal'.
The EU are trying to pressure MPs
Into voting for a deal. MPs have voted
That the Government should sit on a Saturday
To get the deal passed and then ratified.
    Now it emerges it's a bad deal for
The Union, and is not as it was sold.
The Declaration does not provide a close
Relationship with Europe, it's distant.
The ERG say Johnson's only had

Eighty-five days and the Withdrawal Agreement's been opened,
The backstop's been removed, and a deal's agreed,
It's a remarkable achievement for Johnson,
But it splits the UK and risks losing
Northern Ireland and Scotland, and ending
The prosperity that's interlocked with Europe.
It's not a good outcome for the UK.
It's worse than May's deal, the Tory Party
Is a right-wing rump now the twenty-one
Are out of the Party. If any MPs
Vote against on Saturday, they'll lose the whip.
It's emerged that at 6.30 on deal morning,
Johnson agreed to go ahead with or without
The DUP, just as Varadkar had asked for.
The DUP say Johnson lost his nerve
During the negotiations with the EU.
Northern Ireland stays in the EU, the UK leaves
Like a bull that's locked horns turning and slipping away.
There will be barriers to the trade between
Northern Ireland and Great Britain. New trade
With the US, Australia and New Zealand
Will not complement the lost trade with the EU.
Verhofstadt's officials referred to the UK
In the May text as a colony. Like Greece.
The Roman Empire built the roads, and Greece,
Which gave birth to the Athenian Empire,
Became its colony and received its aid.
Now Northern Ireland stays in the EU's
Single market, the UK's become Great Britain,
Which is now outside the EU Empire
And won't have European roads, clean air,
Water and other environment protections.
If the deal goes through Parliament Great Britain
Will be on its own and have to stand alone.
Johnson needs votes for his deal, he's seeking to persuade,
He sidles towards MPs in the tearoom and fawns.

It's now clear Letwin favours backing the deal
To avoid 'no deal' but having an extension
As insurance to prevent a crashing-out
With 'no deal' by accident if something goes wrong.
Letwin has an amendment to compel Johnson
To comply with the Benn Act and delay Brexit.
He's been helped to write it by Lord Pannick,
Who won the cancelling of the proroguing
Before the Supreme Court and has told him he must not change
A word of his carefully-worded amendment.
Letwin, who once worked for Rothschilds, wants this deal,
But with an extension, and if there's a deal,
The Benn Act will automatically fall away.
    The Letwin amendment will encourage MPs
Not to vote for Johnson's Bill. Macron has said
He would not support an extension and might block
Letwin's amendment. EU leaders feel
They are being gamed by UK politicians.
Now the DUP are accusing Johnson
Of an "awful betrayal" of the Loyalists
By agreeing to a border down the Irish Sea.
The only way Brexit would ever work
Was to have a border down the Irish Sea,
To tie Northern Ireland into the EU
But with no voice in the EU Parliament.
    The EU's October summit, and on the last day
Johnson's greeted warmly by all EU
Leaders, he salutes Macron and he beams
And shakes hands as all smile and crowd round him
As Red Admirals cavort round blackberries,
And meadow browns flutter near clover flowers
And azure blues dance sunwards in the sun.
He's the centre of attention for he has
Agreed – perhaps without fully realising it –
To a customs border down the Irish Sea,
May's red line from the outset of the talks.

All are happy to resolve the stuck Brexit
So they can get on with their own project,
An integrated Europe, a superpower
With its own army, which the UK would not back.
The smiles say, 'Good to see you're leaving, we
Can get on now without being held up by you.'
So Johnson has a deal he can take back.
    Like a peacock fanning its tail with many eyes
That struts and parades its agreement with all,
Johnson is shown on TV surrounded
By friendly, smiling, relieved EU leaders.
Why such warmth? Is something going on behind the scenes?
There may be years and years of arguments
With the EU, and the UK'll be opened up
To a deal with the US and falling standards.
The detail shows it's Brexit in name only,
That's why Macron and Juncker have been beaming.
The fishing rights have been betrayed, and France
Can fish in UK waters. The deal's what they want.
    Parliament is sitting on a Saturday
For the first time since the Falklands conflict.
It's Johnson's Day of Reckoning at last:
There's to be a Meaningful Vote on the new deal,
But also Letwin's amendment to compel
Johnson to comply with the Benn Act and request
A delay to Brussels. A good omen:
A flock of forty large birds fly in formation
And make a large V for Victory. Will it be
Victory for Letwin and his extension?
    A shock, the MPs won't vote on the new deal
But on Letwin's amendment. Johnson speaks
To a packed House. He says that if Letwin's
Amendment goes through he will pull the vote on the deal,
Let loose a bull to stand on the pathway.
A copy of Parliament's letter will go to Tusk,
But he will continue to say to the EU leaders,

'Get Brexit done on October the thirty-first
With the new deal and no delays.'
And there won't be a vote on the deal, a vote
For Letwin's amendment would render
The entire day meaningless and sum up
This broken Parliament. Hundreds of thousands,
Perhaps a million, squash down Whitehall towards
Parliament Square, all calling to stay in the EU.
The Letwin amendment says there cannot be
A Meaningful Vote until there has been a WAB,
A Withdrawal Agreement Bill, and the text
Has not been seen, it's a hundred pages long.
It's been signed off by the European Council
But not the European Parliament
Or Council of Ministers. Johnson offers
The DUP money to support him,
It's a bung, cash for votes. The vote takes place.
It's three hundred and twenty-two to three
Hundred and six, Johnson's lost. And now there won't
Be a vote on his deal. He is stunned.
Sulking like a squirrel that's barred from nuts,
Swishing its tail on a branch in annoyance,
He says, "I will not negotiate a delay
With the EU, and neither does the law compel me."
Corbyn says he must now send the letter
Requesting an extension to the EU.
And now there won't be a vote on his deal,
But an attempt at another vote on Monday
If the Speaker allows it, and does not rule
It out of order when the Benn Law states
He has to send a letter if there's 'no deal'
By October the nineteenth. That's today.
Johnson states he will not send the letter.
Will Parliament send it, or the Speaker,
If a court decrees that he should do so?
Or will he send the letter and another

Saying 'Please do not comply, I didn't mean it'?
Super Saturday has become Setback Saturday,
Scrabbling for Plan-B Saturday. It's dire.
    Are Rothschilds now clawing the UK back
Into the EU? They were behind the Treaty of Rome
And want a united Europe to go forward.
Have they blocked Brexit through their ex-employee
(Till he was made Shadow Chancellor) Letwin?
If the vote is passed on Monday, the PM could
Withdraw his letter and return to the deal,
But Johnson sees victory slipping away.
    Now it's announced an unsigned, typed letter
Has been sent in hard copy and email to Tusk,
With a covering letter by his envoy to Brussels,
Barrow, which makes clear it was from Parliament,
Not the Government, and a further letter signed by
Johnson, stating Government policy
And that asking for an extension is a mistake
And he doesn't want an extension, and how
Deeply corrosive an extension would be.
It's been written by Government lawyers.
In his calls to EU leaders Johnson's said,
"This is Parliament's letter, it's not my letter."
By not signing the letter, he may be
In contempt of Parliament and of the Court.
    The MPs are now clear there must not be
A Meaningful Vote on the Withdrawal Agreement Bill
To achieve the ratification the EU needs
Until it's clear that it's not a trapdoor
To a 'no deal'. Tusk's said he will take several days
To talk to the member states. They may grant
A technical extension, depending on what for.
A short extension would help the EU's
New Commission come in and get settled.
There is now no pass to get out of the EU
And the UK's heading for an election.

The Withdrawal Agreement Bill must become law
By October the thirty-first. It solves nothing,
There's still the trade agreement to come,
And that can take several years of more wrangling.
    Johnson said he would not send the letter,
Do or die, he'd rather be dead in a ditch.
The letter was accompanied by other letters
But it counts as a letter which he said he would not do.
Like a fox luring a chicken to a safe place
And then devouring it with gobbling bites,
He made a promise in his keynote speech
At the DUP's conference, then betrayed the DUP.
It's the most duplicitous Parliament in history.
Its MPs have promised to exit the EU
And again and again have broken their promises.
It votes against everything put before it,
It's a Foul Parliament, it's badly-behaved
With obfuscation, prevarication and obstruction.
It appears to be nothing but a House of Fools.
    The Speaker's now saying there can be no
Vote on the Withdrawal Agreement Bill until
The legislation against 'no deal''s complete,
In the spirit of Letwin's amendment.
    There has to be a specific reason for the EU
To grant an extension, such as an election.
As the consequences of the deal become clear –
The pushing of Northern Ireland and the Republic
Together, which could lead to the break-up
Of the Union – there will be a falling-away
Of support for the deal, which does not offer terms
As favourable as remaining within the EU.
The unlawful prorogation of Parliament
And Johnson's incendiary language have alienated
The Labour MPs he needed to persuade
To join his own Europhobe supporters
For whom Brexit's become a kind of religion

Of economic closure, the splitting-off
Of Northern Ireland and Scotland, and now
The domination of a once-great country.
At best, it's an act of egregious self-harm,
And at worst, an act of self-immolation.

Monday. There is news the EU will grant
Johnson a three-month flexible extension
If he can't get his deal through the Commons.
And there's a rumour that Speaker Bercow'll block
The postponed Meaningful Vote by a ruse.
But in Parliament, there's no sign of Johnson
As the Speaker rises for his 3.30 statement.
Like a magpie fluttering near a hawk in an oak
To protect its nest and drive it from its young,
He says he's had thirty points of order
From twenty-four colleagues expressing consternation
That they should be debating the deal again
After Saturday's proceedings; and in substance
The Withdrawal Agreement Bill motion
Is the same as the one debated on Saturday,
Circumstances haven't changed; and so in accordance
With Erskine May, the rule book of Parliament,
Page 397, a 1604 rule,
The same motion cannot be brought twice in the same
Session. The Government can now proceed
To legislate, and bring the Withdrawal
Agreement Bill for first reading that night.
It's a hundred and ten pages long, with forty
Clauses, and few have seen all the wording of the bits
That have been changed so there'll be no Meaningful Vote;
And the 1972 European
Community's Act can't be repealed today.
    The Bill can be amended after the second reading,
And with each amendment it ceases to be
The text the EU's agreed; and there can be

No EU ratification until the EU
Have seen the final text when it has gone
Through the Commons and the Lords into law.
The rush to leave before the EU's deadline
Of the thirty-first of October means there will be
Too little scrutiny of the text, it's better
For there to be an extension to study the Bill.
Benn says goods leaving Northern Ireland for
The UK will need customs declarations
To be submitted even though they will
Be leaving the customs territory of the EU,
Which makes it clear there is a customs border
Down the Irish Sea. Such points need studying.
  Meanwhile the Government has triggered its
Contingency plans for a 'no deal' caused
By the legal default position. The M20
Is closed for lorry-parking rehearsals.
The EU is intrigued and bewildered,
They don't want the UK to leave but want
To get on and carry integration forward.
Juncker says spending so much time on Brexit
Is a waste of time and the Withdrawal
Agreement Bill won't be ratified this week,
Verhofstadt says the UK Government
Is not ready, there's chaos in Parliament.
Johnson has threatened to axe the deal in view
Of the Letwin amendment. Rees-Mogg has announced
That the Withdrawal Agreement Bill's second reading
Will be ended a week before the deadline
For leaving the EU. It took twenty-two days
For the committee stage for the Treaty of Rome,
Twenty-three days for the Maastricht Treaty,
And only one-and-a-half days for this Bill,
Less than thirty-six hours to scrutinise it all.
  Now it's the battle of the timetable to get
The legislation for the Withdrawal

Agreement Bill done in less than thirty-six hours
When it's a hundred and ten pages and, as the most
Important legislation since the war,
Needs line-by-line scrutiny taking months
And the October deadline is looming.
The Government wants to ram the Bill
Unamended through the Commons and Lords
Even though there will now be customs checks
Between Northern Ireland and Great Britain.
More details emerge: the EU will continue
To have supremacy over British law
Until the end of the transition period.
The deal bears no relation to what was
Proposed before the referendum vote.
O Clio, Muse of History, don't despair.
The UK'll come through this nightmare again.
Please save us from shouting and foul abuse,
And finger-jabbing in our Parliament.
    Like a carrion crow bent on an impending kill,
Johnson rises to present the crucial Bill,
He takes many interventions and stresses
That many points dissolve in four years' time.
(This dissolving is not in the Bill's text,
And may in fact be a confusion between
The single market and customs union.)
The timetable should be fast-tracked to leave little time
For line-by-line scrutiny by MPs.
It's said the Bill's a trap to a 'no deal'.
Johnson himself is in *The Telegraph*
As threatening to axe the deal if it's not voted through.
There's a precedent for pulling a Bill
In the Lords' Reform of 2011.
He now says the Bill will be pulled if it's voted down,
And he will call for a general election.
    Corbyn says that the Bill is a charter
For deregulation, that Northern Ireland

Is within the EU's customs union
And there will be tariffs. The more divergence,
The harder the border and more danger
To the precious Good-Friday Peace Agreement.
Corbyn says the so-called sovereign Parliament
Is being treated as an inconvenience.
It's facing the severest impact on
The economy in peacetime history.
And not one promise made by the Leave campaign
Is in the text of the Withdrawal Agreement Bill.
    The summing up by the Justice Secretary.
Now they're voting on the Withdrawal Agreement Bill,
The UK's declaration of independence.
The result, 329 to 299.
A cheer for a majority of thirty,
The second reading of the Bill has passed.
Now the vote on the breakneck timetable,
And the DUP are sitting in their seats.
    There's a long delay. The tellers take their place
Like four house martins on a telephone wire.
The Government's lost 322 to 308.
Corbyn offers: "Work with us." Johnson crows
That his deal is in the national interest
And expresses his disappointment at
The delay and further uncertainty.
He says he will pause the legislation
And the UK will leave by October the thirty-first.
The SNP leader says the PM
Must now ask for an extension. Johnson
Storms off in a churlish sulk. He has blundered,
He could have offered several days' scrutiny.
Clarke asks the absent PM to cancel the pause.
The Speaker says the second reading has passed
But the MPs can't pass to the committee stage.
    Now there's turmoil in Parliament. Rees-Mogg
Says that because of the loss of the programme motion

He must make a business statement revising
What happens: for two days there will be a debate
On the Queen's Speech. He ignores Labour's offer
To work with the Government and there will be votes.
The Speaker says the Bill is in limbo.
Rees-Mogg says Pope Benedict the sixteenth
Abolished limbo, but it can be said
It's in Purgatory and suffering pains there.
Rees-Mogg says that the Bill has been withdrawn
And cannot be in limbo as it's dead.
The Speaker says that he is wallowing in
Metaphysical abstraction. Beckett
Says only pure souls get to limbo
And so not many Tories will be there.
Rees-Mogg says limbo is occupied by
Those who died young and those who have just died.
An MP says some souls ended in Dante's
First circle of Hell. Rees-Mogg says Dante
Is not reliable on the Catholic Church.
    It's now impossible to get this deal
Through the House before October the thirty-first,
The EU's deadline, so it's in fact dead.
It was blocked by Letwin's amendment, then passed,
But was blocked again by the hasty-timetable vote
And blocked yet again by Johnson's sulky pause,
And is now "in limbo". Why have the PM
And Leader of the House decided not to progress
The Bill? In blocking the Bill for the third time,
They are the architects of their own misfortune.
They've over-rushed it through and are paying the price.
A snorting bull is standing in their path,
From their own farm, they can't blame the EU.

The captain's brought the ship to a strip of land.
"It's Narragonia," he declares, "all out
In relays to shore to dig for the gold

We'll take back with us for our prosperity."
Narragonia, the Promised Land, it's here.
The crew and passengers can't wait to land,
They arm themselves with picks and, believing
They've reached their destination, head for the boat.
The boat is lowered and rowed to the beach.
The first party clamber out, and then walk
Through a meadow full of clover, tiny
Stitchworts like stars and yellow buttercups
And cavorting meadow browns and tortoiseshells
To a cliff, and the captain cries out, "Gold."
All rush forward, trampling flowers, and there in the cliff,
Sure enough, gleams the glistening promised gold.
"We don't have to journey inland, it's right here,"
The captain calls. All set to and hack out
Lumps of the precious ore and make a pile
That will be lugged and loaded onto the boat
And rowed back to the ship and stored in the hold,
A cargo of precious glittering gold.
The next boat comes to shore and more climb out.
"Over there," the captain points, "that river bed."
He's organised his supporters into groups.
Some wade into the river's shallow side
And stoop and scoop up gravel and shake the pan,
Tip out the gravel and mud and peer for gold
That, as a dense mineral, will be at the bottom
Of the pan when it's been circularly shaken.
Some search the river beds for gold nuggets,
Scoop with their fingers, grope for a rough 'stone'.
Others dip their pan into the river sand
And make circular movements under water
To shift the light rock particles so they float
Back into the water, leaving the heavy gold.
Then they walk through the meadow to the cliff
And with cries of delight hack out more ore.

Canto V
Limbo, End of the Foul Parliament

Sing, Muse, of the breaking of a deadlock
And how a general election's at last agreed,
Sing of the end of the paralysis
And of the Foul Parliament no one will mourn.
Sing of a divided country that's perplexed.
    Now Tusk has tweeted he will recommend
An extension to prevent a 'no deal'
Following Johnson's decision to pause the Bill,
And the twenty-seven have yet to agree.
Johnson is telephoning EU leaders
Saying he will not accept a three-month extension,
Downing Street would rather push for an election.
He paused the Bill so there'd be no amendments.
His strategy's been to bury Brexit amid
Glittering policies – huge sums of money for
Police and hospitals – and tell the public
What it wants to hear, that the money will come from Brexit.
Huge sums released, seventy-six million Turks
Flooding in, no border down the Irish Sea –
If he were running a commercial venture
He'd be taken to court for deception.
    Now Johnson says he will attempt to call
An election on the twelfth of December,
And he will bring back the Bill and offer
Two more weeks for MPs to scrutinise it.
It will be the first December election since
1923. He has given up on his
Thirty-first-of-October deadline. Johnson says
MPs can have longer to scrutinise,
But there *must* be a December election.
Corbyn says he can have an election
If he takes 'no deal' off the table. Corbyn

May trap Johnson in Downing Street, as Johnson
Wants a 'Parliament-versus-people' election,
And Corbyn won't want to give it to him.
The Queen's Speech is approved with a majority
Of sixteen (310 to 294).
But Johnson's in limbo, he cannot get
His deal through and can't get an election.
In a letter to Corbyn Johnson concedes
That he can't leave by October the thirty-first.
As a camel walks sedately with one hump
That stores enough water and energy
For it to trudge a hundred desert miles,
A dromedary that sways and plods and trots
With the irregular rhythm of Donne's Muse,
So Johnson faces a long desert plod.
Johnson is a prisoner of Parliament
And he can't get his Brexit done or an election.
He is in limbo. Now he has threatened
To suspend all Parliamentary business.
He'll park his Bill and not proceed with it,
But he is trying to get his deal through.
Johnson has postponed the November budget
And Labour won't grant an extension until
He has taken 'no deal' off the table.
A winter election as in 1974,
School nativity plays cancelled so school halls
Can be polling-booths, in a bid to end
This Foul Parliament that's dysfunctional.
A winter election has short days that are cold.
There's to be a vote on an election.
Johnson is bartering inspection of his deal
For an election, but the deal's a new treaty
And it should be inspected anyway.
The EU Ambassadors agree an extension
But will wait until after the vote before saying how long.
There is one problem with taking 'no deal'

Off the table, it can be 'no deal' on
October the thirty-first, or after an extension
On January the thirty-first, or on
December the thirty-first at transition's end,
And the only way to guarantee 'no deal' on these
Three dates is to revoke Article 50.
    France has vetoed the deal until after the vote.
Tusk's replacement Michel is an ally
Of Macron and will support his view. The two
Will press ahead towards integration.
Germany can do nothing, the UK has to wait.
The UK's just five days from a 'no deal'.
All Barnier's red lines are in the Political
Declaration, so the UK is heading
Into a three-year-long EU-controlled nightmare.
A leaked document says the Government
Is set to diverge from the EU after Brexit.
The UK's drifting aimlessly and seems
To have a declinist mentality.
Cummings says it's the worst Parliament for
Four hundred years, it's a Foul Parliament.
    To Churchill and Macmillan after the War
The UK was the linchpin in three circles:
Empire and Commonwealth; America;
And Europe. It has looked back with fond dreams
Of imperial nostalgia and battleships,
And leadership of the Commonwealth; and fond dreams
Of the special relationship, but has not embraced
The aims of the Treaty of Rome, and would not support
"Ever-closer union", join the euro
And be in the triumvirate that would counterbalance
The erratic US and expansionist Russia
And China. All this together means the UK'd be
A middle-sized nation trading on its own,
A low-tax Singapore in a no man's land,
In decline after its erstwhile world role.

But now the UK's role has been resolved,
It's to be global Britain with free trade,
And the Carolingian Age will see UK support
For a World State that will be reciprocated,
And the UK'll have a place in world affection.
Johnson has lost his bounce, nothing's gone right,
He's like a fretting bull lashing its tail.
And he's manoeuvred and done untrustworthy things:
He had to send a letter he said he would not;
He pulled the Bill before the committee stage
So it wouldn't be amended out of recognition.
He's been blocked and now his lies are focused on:
Leave voters could have it all; a more sovereign
UK; a booming economy; newly
Funded public services; fewer immigrants;
Avoiding Turkey's seventy-six million
From coming to the EU; promising
An easy deal with the EU; blaming
Parliament instead of the lies he told
For the mess the UK now finds itself in;
Promising no border down the Irish Sea;
Blaming Benn and Letwin for colluding
With the EU; and blaming Hammond for
Leaking Operation Yellowhammer documents;
Proroguing Parliament for a Queen's Speech
And shutting it down for five long weeks;
Saying he'd deliver Brexit "do or die"
By October the thirty-first; pledging
To maintain all workers' rights, consumer
Protections and environmental standards
When a leaked document shows he won't;
Promising three times to appear before
The Liaison Committee and cancelling three times;
Saying his Government would go on strike
And withhold legislation if MPs did not back
His call for a general election, and not striking;

Threatening to table an election motion
Every day until MPs accede, even though
Parliamentary conventions would not allow this;
Making announcements in short media clips
So Parliament can't grill him on his inconsistencies.
    Like a wolf prowling near a flock of sheep,
He's not trusted and trust in the UK's
Democratic norms and constitutional
Principles has gone. Johnson's behaviour
And tactics have dragged political office down.
All are appalled at the decay in the UK's
Standards of public life, which once led the world,
And by its decline to be like an African state
Whose ruler is semi-detached from truth.

The EU leaders have agreed a "flextension"
Until the thirty-first of January
Unless Parliament ratifies the deal sooner.
Johnson has agreed to the flextension,
Which means he accepts that he cannot leave
"Do or die" by October the thirty-first.
Not dead in a ditch, he now rises and asks
For a two-thirds majority to have an election
In return for accelerated approval of his Bill.
Corbyn reads out a list of the PM's
Broken promises and says he can't trust him
Not to crash out on January the thirty-first
Or after then. The Labour benches are
Half empty as they've told their MPs to abstain,
Which will deny Johnson an election
On the twelfth of December. Redwood says
Parliament's full of abuse and must be better
Or have a general election to elect
A better Parliament. This one is foul.
    The SNP leader says there should be
An election on December the ninth so students

Are not disenfranchised, and EU citizens should vote
Along with sixteen- and seventeen-year-olds.
Lib Dems' Swinson rises and says she wants
A second referendum but as there's not
A majority for that she will support
An election. She says she cannot trust the PM,
He might change his date of December the twelfth
And crash out of the EU before then.
She wants to revoke and will go to the people
In an election to ask for this. Johnson
Glowers, in office but not in power.
    Like a gaggle of geese honking at an intruder,
The Opposition are arranging what will take place
And, like a daddy-long-legs trapped behind glass
And dancing up and down a window-pane,
He is now powerless except to consent.
It's a rancorous, divisive politics,
His third attempt to get an early election,
In which all sides are foul to each other.
And in the season of goodwill there may not be
A nativity play in the schools used as polling-booths.
A Christmas of bad cheer looms far and wide.
    The vote's been held, the tellers take their stand
As still as herons standing near a pond.
It's two hundred and ninety-nine to seventy,
But it's not reached 434, the two-thirds
Majority. Johnson says Corbyn's run away,
And announces a one-line Bill the next day
For an election so voters can pronounce
On the deal that passed its second reading.
Blackford says the Opposition does not trust
The PM and needs a cast-iron agreement
That the PM will not crash out before an election.
Clarke appeals for a return to the Bill
To take it through committee (and amendment)
And on to a third reading. Corbyn says it must

Be clear that 'no deal' is off the table
As the PM has form in breaking his word.
    Johnson has abandoned the Queen's Speech,
He's abandoned the second reading of his own Bill,
He should be discussing the border in the Irish Sea,
The Bill needs to be scrutinised line by line.
He's sleepwalking into dangerous territory,
He's like a bull lashing its tail at flies.
Thousands of students will be disenfranchised
As they were at the time of the referendum,
As they will have left their universities
To go home and many can't travel back.
It's not a wise choice to go to the country
In winter when some voters can't get around.
As a buzzard circles high in the air
And peers for movement in the fields below
So it can swoop on prey, or tack if it suits,
Now Johnson's agreed not to bring back his deal
To get an election in December.
    Next day, and Labour now wants an election.
The one-line Bill has been amended so
Non-Government amendments to the Bill
May be made. Johnson speaks and says he wants
To bring in a free-trade programme – more glitter.
Like a fierce jackal menacing at dusk,
Corbyn says he wants to rid the country
Of this reckless Government, and now 'no deal'
Is off the table. He says that Johnson
Has failed in his "do-or-die" bid to leave
The EU on October the thirty-first,
And that this may be the last day of this Parliament
And may mark the end of Johnson's tenure.
The Bill has been introduced, its first reading
Is completed and it can now be published.
    Now the MPs vote on the Bill's second stage.
There's no division, just a shout of "Ayes".

The Ayes have it, that stage is passed. Now they go
To the committee stage, and amendments.
The mace is now below the table top.
There is a debate on the election date,
On December the ninth versus the twelfth.
Northern Ireland's civil service requires
Legislation which can't be got through by December the ninth.
Now there's a vote on the election date:
A majority of twenty for the twelfth.
　Now the mace is on the table, the Crown's in the chamber.
Laing's in the chair and gives way to Bercow,
Who calls a vote for the third reading. It's passed.
Only twenty dissent, there's a majority
Of 418 for a general election.
The Bill goes to the Lords. It'll receive
Royal Assent the same day, and has gone
From start to law within only one day.
　The UK's direction in relation to Europe
And the Union is at stake, it's a gamble
By Johnson, a reckless breaking-out from
Being in office but not in power.
He's as content as a ruminating bull.
It's the last PMQs. Johnson commends
The Speaker, who's retiring, and then rants
At Corbyn (who's said he and Bercow follow Arsenal).
There are heated personal attacks on both sides.
There's election in the air as claims are made,
Records are recited, there's hatred on both sides.
　So this Foul Parliament has dissolved itself,
Extinguished itself after months of self-harm,
Blockage and delay. In the Bill's committee stage
Cash said Parliaments are called by names, he meant
They're given adjectives: there's The Addled Parliament
And The Mad Parliament. He said this Parliament
Should be called The Purgatory Parliament. Quoting
Cromwell, he said its MPs should be told:

"In the name of God, go." In fact, it was so foul
And treacherous on all sides, with such foul play,
It should be called – updating Chaucer's *Parlement*
Of Foules (meaning 'fowls') – The Foul Parliament.
So The Foul Parliament has at last been put out
Of its misery. Will the souls who've been
In the wretched limbo of Purgatory
Go backward to Hell or on to Paradise?

Like a jackdaw eying twigs for its chimney nest
Johnson plans to steal seats from the Labour left
And the Brexit Party's right to win the election,
And as his words will be both left and right
Like a strutting cockerel's cock-a-doodle-do
That's also a yellowhammer's bread and no cheese,
He will need to speak in slogans to appeal
To both sides without either side realising
They're being played so voters defect.
Johnson is in his element, blustering
And being evasive, not answering questions,
Which he knows better than anyone how to do.
It's Hallowe'en, when the UK should be leaving.
Johnson's visited Addenbrooke's Hospital
And is booed on leaving. Corbyn is cheered.
Johnson is repeating robotic messages –
"Get Brexit done", which, alas, is meaningless:
It will never be done, to replace
The seven hundred trade deals the UK
Already enjoys through the EU would take over
Thirteen years at one a week and fifty-eight
Years at one a month. Brexit is never-ending.
 Like an unblinking and scrutinising owl
Ridge asks him why anyone should believe
What he says now he can't leave on Hallowe'en.
She asks if he'd apologise to his Party
To those who voted for him over Hunt.

Like a sullen dog that's sulking from a telling
He says he was deeply disappointed
To have to write the unsigned letter to Tusk
Asking for a three-month delay in leaving.
He blusters, stutters and defends his deal.
He's looking to get his deal through, Farage
Is asking him to stop his deal for 'no deal'.
His rejection of Farage has split the Brexit vote.
He's split his own Party, the moderates have left.
Parris has announced he'll vote Lib Dem
(Like Clarke and other centrists who've been banned)
To defeat Tory zealotry over Europe,
Believing it's folly for the UK to leave the EU,
Unable to support a leader who lacks
Honesty and principle and is populist
From ambition, and has shifted away
From traditional centrist Toryism
And has crossed a Rubicon to the Far Right
While dangling glittering tax cuts as promises.
    Like a song thrush throstling in the evening air
Clarke says, sitting next to Duncan Smith, who looks
Sheepish and shifts uncomfortably, eyes down,
That Johnson and Barclay did not understand
They'd signed a deal that in the Withdrawal
Agreement had a real customs border
Down the Irish Sea (which is why the EU
Leaders greeted Johnson so warmly after he signed)
And this would have been found out at the committee stage,
Which is why they allowed such a short time for scrutiny;
And so he pulled the deal and is holding
An election to cover their mistake. So Johnson,
Having promised at the DUP conference there'd be
No economic border down the Irish Sea,
Allowed one by not understanding the Withdrawal
Agreement. Out of his depth, Johnson does not attend
To detail, and his ad-libbing's found him out.

For more than two centuries the Conservatives
Kept power through pragmatism, 'a broad church',
All contributing like branches, twigs and leaves
To the Tree of Tradition, their Party.
But now Johnson's effected a Tory split,
And the exodus of the moderates like Ken Clarke,
Soames (Churchill's grandson) and many others, to leave
A Leave party, is like several branches lopped.
Like a cockerel cock-a-doodle-doing hens
Johnson hopes to win power for a decade
But needs Leave voters in Northern working-class
Labour seats, and's appealing to nation-state
Nationalism in a Universalist time.
On TV he's blaming his stupid promise
To leave the EU by the end of October
On Parliament, whereas if he had paid
Attention he'd have seen it opposed 'no deal'.
He could have given his Bill more time, increased
Its timeline for scrutiny, but he pulled the Bill.
He uses flamboyant words, he's described Corbyn
As a 'coelacanth', a fish a hundred
Million years older than the dinosaurs
From the Marina Trench, a 'look-at-me'
Narcissism in an Age of Narcissism.
He's full of evasions and equivocations,
His jokes and punchiness – he punches the air
As he says "Get Brexit done" – show a great lack
Of earnestness and awareness of Truth.
Like squawking parakeets pecking each other
To secure sole perch on their own nut feeder
The Brexiteers have split and fallen out.
Farage – by contesting every seat – is right
That Johnson's deal is a very bad deal,
He's capitulated to the EU's red lines.
Johnson has said the UK will become
The largest and most prosperous economy

In the hemisphere – offering voters
Glittering gold. He's extrapolated
From an OECD forecast's time frame,
And *The Telegraph* (which paid him two hundred and seventy
Five thousand pounds a year as a journalist)
Has been forced to issue a corrective to its story.
Johnson has made false claims on the UK's
Economic growth, the third time this year
That *The Telegraph* has been forced to correct
Johnson's material. Juncker's been interviewed by
Der Spiegel and's expressed regret he did not
Counter the lies Johnson told in the referendum.
 As foxes drag the carcass of a deer
New Speaker Hoyle is dragged unwillingly
To the chair, and will shake off the tarnished
Reputation of Parliament under Bercow –
Who has stood up for MPs and Parliament against
Illegal manoeuvrings by Johnson and Cummings.
 Cummings wants to smash the Establishment,
Has no Party loyalty, he speaks for his
Vote Leave, not the Tories, is confrontational
Like a wild boar crashing out of undergrowth.
It's he who broke the proroguing law, sacked
The twenty-one, thus splitting the Party,
Driving out the moderates, and he caused
Collateral damage. To him disruption is good.
He hates the British State, wants to smash it up
Just as he punched a hole in the ceiling
Standing on a table, making a victory speech
After Vote Leave won the referendum.
 The Lib Dems believe that the economy
Would be 1.9 per cent bigger if
The UK stays in the EU, and that
Would also save some fifty billion pounds.
Glittering Johnson says the NHS
Will receive thirty-four billion pounds. The real

Figure's 20.5 billion
Over five years, less than the annual increase since
The NHS was founded. Johnson has lied
Again, or just not realised the truth.
The Labour leader says that the PM
Is hijacking Brexit to sell off the NHS
For a trade deal with the US. Now Corbyn says
That the NHS would have to pay twenty-
Seven billion pounds a year more for all drugs –
That is five hundred million pounds a week –
That came from the US if there's a trade deal,
And if not, the UK won't get access
To things it wants from the American market.
But under ten per cent of the UK drugs
Come from the US, so twenty per cent
Will not go up and the annual cost of drugs
May increase by fifty million pounds, not five hundred.
Labour has made a false claim
That's not accurate, says an authority
On NHS purchases from America.
    Seven days of near-silence from the Tories.
Now Parliament's closed and the MPs have gone.
Johnson goes to the Queen to start the election.
In *The Telegraph* he's compared Corbyn to Stalin
For targeting owners of corporations
Just as Stalin targeted *kulaks*, but they
Were affluent farmers, Stalin deported
Two million and shot hundreds of thousands,
And five million starved to death, and Corbyn's done
None of these things. The comparison is inapt.
It is odd to celebrate profit when
The election will be on Brexit, and Labour
Will criticise the Tory love of profit.
It's a mistake that can be blamed on Cummings.
Rees-Mogg on the radio is understood to say
The Grenfell-fire victims should have had

The common sense to ignore the fire brigade's
Advice and leave the tower block, suggesting
A casual callousness towards those trapped
In the high-rise tower. He's accused of saying
The victims were stupid, and's caricatured
As an uncaring toff, which is damaging.
And a Tory video has mocked Starmer
For not explaining a policy he did explain.
And the Welsh Secretary has resigned.
It's been a bad opening of the campaign for the Tories.

Now makeshift tents adorn the meadowy plain
At the prospect of Narragonian gold.
O Diodorus Siculus and Pliny
The Elder, who described how gold-mining
Took place under the Roman Empire, help me
Describe how the ship's fools toiled in their search for gold.
Prospectors dig with pickaxes and spades,
And crouch by a stream and pan by a river bed.
Surely they will find nuggets of great worth,
Surely there will be prosperity for all?
They scoop gravel and sift the dirt for gold,
They have a dream of plenty in their lives.
And surely this mineral they've found in rock
Is gold that will transform their poverty?
Quick, pick it out of the cliff with the axe,
If it glitters and glistens, it must be gold.

Canto VI
Election Campaign

Sing, Muse, of electioneering, of promises
Held out to voters like lumps of pure gold,
Sing of glittering policies and dreams,
Of slogans that will entice Northern voters,
Sing of trust, truthfulness and sincerity,
Sing of a Communist who'd seize each private school
And of whether it's foolish to believe a fool.
    Johnson has visited the Queen, and speaks
In Downing Street. He promises to end
Parliament's paralysis. A poll shows
The Tories are in the lead by eleven points.
Now Johnson launches the Conservative campaign
To five hundred activists in Birmingham.
Like a preening peacock displaying its fanned tail
He says he did not want an election
But had no choice as Parliament was blocking him.
(He was desperate for an election.)
Young men grin and hold up placards as he
Speaks while pointing and waving his arms. He says
He has an "oven-ready deal" to be put
In the microwave at "gas mark 1". (Microwaves
Aren't gas, they're electric, he's muddled his facts.
It's a mixed metaphor, a sign of a clichéd mind.)
Like a red kite circling and peering for prey
He attacks Corbyn, and it's now reported
That his deputy Watson's to retire.
So all the moderates are walking out on this
Foul Parliament, over sixty so far.
Johnson gives a Churchillian V-sign.
Elsewhere, Bercow says "Leaving the EU
Is the biggest foreign-policy mistake
In the post-war period", since the Second World War.

And the UK is a representational,
Not a plebiscite, democracy. Much gold
Is promised by both parties, by Labour
Fifty billion a year, by the Tories twenty-five.
There'll be more investments and more borrowings.
    Like Henry the Eighth holding a summit
With Francis of France and seeking to impress
By bringing tents with hangings of rich cloth
And gold beaten and worked into long strips
Set out on the Field of the Cloth of Gold,
Our new Henry, Johnson (who's overweight,
Has had six 'wives', has lived Merrie England
And 'broken with Rome', in his case the Treaty of Rome),
Has paraded promises like strips of gold
To dazzle English voters, whose votes he needs.
    More than ten thousand EU nationals have left
The NHS since the referendum.
Johnson promises six thousand new doctors
Over five years. (Five thousand GPs were promised
Four years ago, and never delivered.)
And fifty thousand more nurses (who'll include
Eighteen thousand five hundred existing nurses
Who are being persuaded to remain in their posts).
Johnson's said new money will be pumped in.
(It's in fact already in the NHS's reserves.)
    Now Johnson's spoken in Northern Ireland.
Like a herring gull aloof from its snatched fish
Standing still and peaceful with pink webbed feet
He says there will be no checks on goods leaving
Northern Ireland for the UK, but Barclay
Says there will be checks, customs declarations
On goods as the Withdrawal Agreement states.
Johnson's said these forms should be binned, and those
Asked to pay should ring 10 Downing Street.
It's a whopping lie that's upside-downed the truth.
As a nuthatch perches on a nut feeder

Downwards and pecks with its head below its tail,
An upside-down feeding posture unlike
That of all other birds, so Johnson pecks
His plan upside down with an untruthful approach.
He still seems not to understand the treaty
Which he has signed on behalf of the UK.
The Royal British Legion Festival
Of Remembrance, and Johnson's seated next
To Prince Andrew, well away from the Queen,
And applauds with slow handclaps, fingers not meeting.
Next day the leaders stand at the Cenotaph.
The Prince of Wales lays a poppy wreath for
The Queen, then one for himself, and eventually
Johnson ambles up with his wreath, and stoops
And lays it upside down, and backs away
And nods perfunctorily, then ambles
Back to his place. Corbyn, looking well-groomed,
Advances and lays his wreath and bows, eyes closed,
And says a long prayer, then returns to his place.
Next day a clip is shown of smart Johnson
With different hair laying a wreath – but look,
It's three years ago, he's in a different suit.
The BBC say it's an accident, not an attempt
To smarten scruffy Johnson up. Oh yes?
Farage announces the Brexit Party will not
Field candidates in three hundred and seventeen
Seats won by the Tories in 2017
Because Johnson's deal has gone further than May's deal,
And the UK won't align with the EU rules
But go for a Canada-style trade deal.
Now Johnson sees flooded streets in Yorkshire –
At last – and is tackled by residents whose homes
Are filled with water. He offers sympathy,
But does not seem to have much empathy. One says,
"No, thank you." Another, "I'm not happy talking to you."
He has received the wrath of the flooded.

It's his first contact with the electorate,
It's not a staged event with activists.
He's finding Northerners are not quite so
Adoring as he'd thought down in London.
The issues up North are living standards,
Health, education, floods and getting help,
Not 'getting Brexit done' but 'get me back
In my house and get my business moving again'.
  Tusk's farewell speech in Bruges as President
Of the European Council. He speaks –
Like a nightingale singing by a woodland lake –
Of unity, says Brexiteers want
To leave the EU to make the UK
Global again as they believe that only
By being alone can it be truly great,
They long to get their Empire back again.
But the reality is the opposite:
Only as part of a united Europe
Can the UK have a global role and confront
The world's greatest powers – China, the USA
And the EU. If the UK leaves it will
Become an outsider, a second-rank player.
It will be shown when the UK breaks up
That Brexit's the end of the British Empire.
Leaving the EU's a catastrophic mistake
Which will split the UK into fragments so
Scotland, Wales and Northern Ireland shear off
And Little England will be left alone,
And the world will know that the end has come
For the global role of the British Empire,
Which will have declined from grandeur before
The First World War to fragmented poverty.
Now Johnson refuses to nominate
An EU Commissioner, pleading convention
During an election. The EU have taken
The UK to court as it is now in breach

Of its treaty obligations, and the UK may be fined.
    There's a winter of crisis for England's NHS:
The worst A & E waiting times ever.
Labour says the Government is out of touch.
Treatment for cancer's delayed many times,
A quarter of those with cancer wait two months.
Patients languish on trolleys. The NHS
Tops the list of the public's voting concerns.
Now Labour says it will part-nationalise
British Telecom to give free Broadband
To all the British people, a stunning idea.
BT say it should be a priority
To step up the roll-out of fibre Broadband
And 5G across the country to build
The digital economy of the future.
They say Labour's undercosted the scheme.
Johnson says it's a crackpot scheme that will
Cost the taxpayer billions in nationalisation.
    What are election pledges but fantasy?
Look down the totals of promised billions:
The Tories two hundred and ten, Labour
Four hundred and seventy-three, Lib Dems
A hundred and ninety-three, and the Greens
A whopping nine hundred and fifty-nine.
Such huge sums cannot come from taxation.
The UK will shrink when it leaves the EU.
If it leaves the EU's customs union
And single market its economy
Will be 3.5 per cent smaller than if it had stayed,
With a 4.9 per cent loss of GDP.
UK-EU goods trade will be forty
Per cent and service trade sixty per cent down.
Now raffish Johnson quotes Ibn Khaldun,
A Tunisian sage in the fourteenth century:
Cut taxes of the olive harvest and then
People grow more olives and taxes go up.

But no Tory tax cuts can replace the loss
Of income from exiting the EU.
And there are disquieting developments:
It transpires eight Brexit-Party candidates
Have been offered jobs or peerages to stand down
And give the Tories a free run at their seats,
And the police are checking more Tory foul play.
    At last the debate, Johnson versus Corbyn.
Both make their opening statements, Corbyn gives
An outline of how Labour will share wealth.
Hoping the voters will have a strong instinct
Like sheep to follow the sheep in front of them
When they've been led onto grassless, furrowed earth,
Johnson talks of Brexit and getting it done
And says the transition will end in a year
(Which is why Brexit-Party candidates have stood down).
Corbyn says Johnson will try for a trade deal
With the US which would take seven years,
He reads out evidence that the Government
Have been in secret talks with the US
Which have endangered the NHS. Both men
Are asked if the Union's more important
Than Brexit. Johnson denies there will be
A customs border down the Irish Sea
Like a heron denying it speared that lifeless carp.
    Both are asked how the nation can trust the two leaders
To have personal integrity after their lies
(Such as the 1.2-trillion-pound costing
Of Labour's as yet unpublished programme)
And abuse of each other. Johnson is asked
If the truth matters. He says he thinks it does,
The audience laughs. It's pointed out Johnson
Promised forty times the UK would leave
The EU on October the thirty-first,
And it did not happen, so why should he be believed?
Both are asked about their borrowing, have they both

Found magic money-trees? Now the summing-up.
Corbyn is factual and is cheered, Johnson
Waffles and blusters, a poor debater.
  There's reaction in the BBC's Spin Room.
The poll is fifty-two to forty-eight
For Johnson – no knock-out gaffes or switching.
Both tried to define what the election is about,
Both have been playing to their own audiences.
The poll benefits Corbyn, the underdog.
Some of Johnson's answers have raised eyebrows
(Forty hospitals, not twenty being built)
And he disintegrated in the second half.
  Next day Johnson visits helmeted workers.
One asks, "Are your tax cuts to benefit you, or us?"
Johnson leaks the manifesto in his answer:
"Tax cuts will be up to nine thousand five hundred
And will save five hundred a year." But the true figure
Is eighty-five, it's five hundred when it reaches
Twelve thousand, an ambition, not yet.
Once again Johnson has told an untruth.
Now it's transpired the Conservative Party
Has rebranded a Twitter account Factcheck,
A fake 'fact-checking service' to endorse
Johnson during last night's leaders' debate,
And it's declared Johnson "a clear winner".
Verhofstadt says it's disinformation
Of the kind seen in authoritarian states,
To dupe voters into voting for Johnson.
  Jennifer Arcuri is in London,
Parading round television studios
Like a lost swan seeking its lifelong mate.
She says she's heartbroken as Johnson won't
Answer her phone calls, but when she's asked if
She had an affair with Johnson she declines
To comment. Some say it's romantic revenge
For an affair that lasted four years and ended

In Johnson "ghosting" her. She says she has kept
His secrets, she has diaries to disclose.
Johnson's just sold, for 3.7 million,
The house in Islington he shared with his wife
Marina, until she began divorce
Proceedings because of his affair with Carrie.
It's all disreputable for a PM.

It's said Brexit will make the UK poorer
Yet the Labour manifesto screens huge sums
For a vast economic transformation
That will make the UK poorer as
Much will have to be loaned – as for Tory policies.
Two borrowers are vying for the UK's
Votes, it's Terrible versus Terrible,
Making promises they cannot deliver.
Some say it is an act of deception
To claim this scale of expenditure can be funded
By heaping taxes on higher earners without
Increasing taxes across the whole population.
Such an expansion of the size of the State
Can only be funded by taxing everybody.
Labour have overreached themselves and have put
People off. They say they can unite the country –
Johnson says *he* can unite the country
By leaving the EU – but no one can
Heal the festering wounds caused by Brexit.
    Johnson has refused to attend a hustings
In his Uxbridge seat, and it has been cancelled.
Now the four leaders of the biggest parties
Answer questions on a *Question-Time* Special,
One after the other, for half an hour each,
Being scrutinised on their own record.
Some of the questions are quite ferocious,
With open hostility to each leader.
Corbyn is received warmly, but would stay

Neutral in a second referendum.
Sturgeon (whose Scotland has the worst deficit
In the EU) is asked if she prioritised
Scottish independence over Brexit.
Like an albatross chick flapping its unused wings
In its cliff-top colony, ready for its first flight,
Swinson is unconvincing on revoking
Article 50. Johnson's jeered on trust
And the dreadful conditions in the NHS
(Patients dying on trolleys in corridors).
There are untruths: Johnson says the Tories
Are building forty hospitals, Corbyn says
Only the top five per cent will pay increased tax.
Reaction in the Spin Room is that all four
Are flawed individuals and weak leaders
With bad track records who can't be trusted
And there is no one who should be voted for.
Trust in leaders is at its lowest ever.
The election will be won by the leader
Who is distrusted the least, the shepherd
Who voters follow like sheep. The aftermath
Of the election may be that the new PM
Cannot repair the disillusion felt.
    An untrusting ex-Head of MI6
Has said Corbyn's a security danger
Who looks back to East Germany and Czechoslovakia,
Cold-War countries that no longer exist,
And says he's a sleeper agent who wants
The UK to give the Chagos Islands
To pro-Chinese Mauritius, including
Diego Garcia, where the US
Has a large naval base aimed at China.
    Now like a preening parrot mimicking words
Johnson presents the Tory manifesto
On a Sunday (the day of rest for trading)
In a large room in Telford in Shropshire.

He'll spend three billion on raising the National
Insurance threshold and says he will hire
Fifty thousand more nurses – actually
Thirty-two thousand as eighteen thousand
Are still in the NHS and haven't left –
And he will make sure that there will soon be
Fifty million more GP appointments a year.
No pledge on social care or anything else.
Labour is spending ninety-five billion,
Twenty-eight times as much in current spending.
The Tory manifesto's a bit of a mouse,
A continuity manifesto
With no promise to cut taxes, focusing
On the bottom end of society, signalling
The Tories will play it safe and leave the EU.
Perhaps they've been told how much this will cost,
And what damage this will cause to the UK's trade,
Hence only three billion's been pledged in spends.
Even so, the fiscal rules have been broken
And austerity's ended, but not as
Radically as under big-spending Labour.
The manifesto's about not doing things.
The lack of policy action's remarkable,
It's the most cautious manifesto in living memory.
There's no vision of England, and seems drab.
The policies in the Tory manifesto
Glint like a lump of rough-hewn stone with bits
Of gold gleaming here and there, the sparkling
Promises calculated to take in fools.
The slogan is 'Get Brexit done and unleash
Britain's potential'. His MPs stand and applaud.
    Like a horse galloping furlongs in a race
Johnson's ahead in the polls, if things stay this way
And if he holds on to his Leave voters
He will have a majority. But the manifesto
Is pared down, and there are deep anxieties

About his approach to Brexit, and fears
That in a year's time there'll be no trade deal.
Johnson does not seem to understand Brexit,
He thinks that if it's done the Government
Can go back to running Little England – now,
Somehow 'global Britain'. He doesn't care
About Brexit, it was his path to power.
He's not interested in trade deals, and doesn't seem
To understand the border down the Irish Sea,
And that Brexit will not be 'done' for years.
    The next day a Brexit-Party spokesman
Points out that the Tory manifesto states
In writing that the UK will now leave
The transition at the end of next year
And there won't be political alignment
With the EU – so the Brexit Party achieved
Its critical red lines by standing down
Three hundred and seventeen candidates.
Johnson has scooped up the Brexit policies
To win as the sole pro-Brexit Party.

The leaders' debate, seven leaders stand
Like magpies in a line at feeding time.
The Green says Johnson's "oven-ready" meal
Will be chlorinated chicken and make all sick.
Scotland, Wales and Northern Ireland all want
To remain in the EU, and 'no deal'
Still seems to be a possibility.
People get news from social media,
A third regard the PM as racist,
More think Tory austerity killed thousands.
    It's now dawning, to take the UK out
Of the EU will cost seventy billion
To the UK's economy, trade and jobs,
Which is missing from the Tory manifesto,
Which is therefore a risky, dangerous manifesto.

It will make the UK poorer, there will be less
For the NHS, police officers, teachers
And the standard of living will be worse.
The UK was told in 2016
All could have their cake and eat it, there'd be no
Difficulty in getting a trade deal.
And the voters are flocking to him like sheep.
The first of December, and there's a new guard
In the EU Commission who are suspected to be
Puppets of Merkel and Macron, handling
An EU divided over migration.
Another leaders' debate, stand-ins for Johnson
And Corbyn. They all argue with each other
Like chickens pecking when their feed is thrown.
Farage says the National Debt when the Tories took power
Was six hundred and seventy billion pounds and it's now
1.7 trillion, it's the day-to-day
Deficit they've tackled, not the National Debt.
People are going to vote for parties they've
Never voted for because of Brexit.
Johnson, interviewed by Marr, shouts over him,
Rudely continues on an old question
When Marr asks a new one. Ill-tempered, Marr
Mutters, "You just keep going on and on,
You're chuntering." The interview establishes nothing.
Trump is in London for NATO's summit.
He says he won't interfere in the UK's
Election campaign, that the NHS
Won't be in a trade agreement with the US.
He's greeted by the Queen and other Royals.
But the NATO meeting's marred by discord.
Trump's picked a fight with a US ally,
He says Macron's "nasty" and "disrespectful"
For calling NATO "brain dead", although Trump said
Two years ago that NATO's "obsolete".
He's disagreed over the number of foreign fighters

Who've escaped from Syria and whether IS have lost.
He's quarrelled over tariffs with Germany,
He's misrepresented the way NATO's funded
And disagreed with the Turks on Baltic defence
And Syria. It's all unsettling.
Johnson's not on TV or the red carpet,
He's holding his meetings off camera.
No one believes Trump on the NHS.
We are living in a post-truth age, and it's
All right to change your mind just days later.
NATO's leaders, at the Grove in Hertfordshire,
Have pledged that they will take stronger action
Against terrorism. Macron has threatened
To boot the US out of NATO unless
More is spent on their collective defence –
Two per cent of GDP for NATO.
Twenty-nine leaders have cited Russia
And China as threats, space is now a war zone.
A video taken in Buckingham Palace
Is shown on TV with subtitles. Johnson
Asks Macron, "Why were you late?" Trudeau, sipping,
Says jokily, "He was late because he takes
A forty-minute press conference off the top" –
A reference to Trump's impromptu press conference
At the start of his meeting with NATO's
Secretary-General. Rutte says, "Fake news,"
And as they laugh Macron tells an anecdote.
Trudeau replies, "Oh yeah, yeah. You just watched
His team's jaws drop to the floor," and he motions
A jaw dropping. Later Johnson and Raab
Are laughing behind Trump's back. Trump's being mocked
And ridiculed in gossip. Now he's seen
The video and's sulking, a narcissist
Who feeds on praise. He says Trudeau's "two-faced",
He cancels his press conference and heads
For the airport. There has been acrimony,

But despite the mockery, the alliance held
And took the decision to stand up to Russia.
And in the video Johnson comes across
As one of the Europeans – one of his great-
Grandparents was Turkish, two were German
(Both UK enemies during the First World War) –
And his Brexit looks a sham, a political way
Of seeing off the Brexit Party and then
Staying in – could that be what's happening?
Another leaders' debate, Johnson v. Corbyn.
Like a wood pigeon cooing its same song
Johnson misrepresents the Withdrawal
Agreement deal, he says there'll be no changes.
Corbyn holds a document that proves he's wrong
And that he hasn't understood his own deal.
Corbyn says Johnson will spend seven years
Negotiating with the US, and as
There won't be a good deal with the EU,
The UK'll be worse off than if it had stayed.
It's been a flat debate, Corbyn did not
Weigh in and Johnson hammered his main themes.
They've clashed over security and crime,
Over the economy and Brexit,
And made their case on public services.
They have set out separate agendas
And were appealing to their own core vote
With Johnson blustering to bring everything
Back to Brexit, denying there will be
Exit checks on goods going to and from Ulster,
Urging "get Brexit done" when it won't be done for years
And saying things are "fantastic" like Trump.
Corbyn says Johnson was in the Government
That voted for austerity and food banks.
An instant YouGov poll says Johnson won
Fifty-two to forty-eight – the same ratio
As the referendum – but one showed empty

Robotic bluster, the other clarity.
The leaders reinforced their images:
Johnson came across as the more likeable,
Corbyn as more in touch with ordinary folk.
    Johnson's interviewed. Leaked Treasury documents
Show there will be checks on goods going between
Britain and Northern Ireland under his deal.
Like a wood pigeon repetitively cooing
Johnson says they are wrong – is he lying?
Or just seriously confused? His hair
Looks as if he has just climbed out of bed.
    A photo that can swing the election:
A four-year-old boy asleep on a hospital floor
On red coats for four hours as he has not been
Admitted, he has got pneumonia.
Johnson in high-viz jacket in a warehouse
Is shown the shameful picture on a phone
By a journalist. He takes the mobile and puts
It in his pocket without looking at the boy.
Does he not care? Why hasn't he had a look?
It feels like the moment a dead three-year-old
On a beach in Greek Lesbos was picked up and held
Limp and lifeless, and turned Europe's loathing
Of migrants into horror and empathy.
Corbyn says Labour will end austerity
And reverse NHS cuts that have led
To what this little boy's had to endure.
    Another shock. Johnson's been asked to be
On *Good Morning Britain,* interviewed by
Morgan. He's declined – the narrative is now
That he's avoided scrutiny from Neil and Morgan –
And has shut himself in a large freezer container
At twenty degrees to escape being questioned.
The narrative is that he's evasive.
Barnier says it will take two years at least
To negotiate a trade deal, not one year.

It's been the most shallow and mendacious
Election in Brits' living memory.
   At last it's polling day, long queues in rain
For an hour to vote, including many young,
Students wanting to scrap tuition fees.
A gloomy overcast and rainy day
Everywhere, and in Loughton's shopping street
The rain pelts round the cars and wide streams gush
In the gutters. It's not a day to queue.
   The exit poll at 10pm predicts
A Tory win 368 to 191,
An eighty-six majority for Johnson.
It's a stunning development if it's true.
Labour's worst result since 1934,
The Tories' best since 1987.
Many Labour voters in the Midlands
And North have switched their vote, and if it's true
The UK will leave the EU next month.
It's not just about Brexit, for Corbyn
Will have to resign. The bumbling buffoon's appealed,
The voters did not want Corbyn and followed
The shepherd and the sheep in front of them
And have not arrived at the slaughter-house so far.
The EU wanted a Johnson landslide
So he could dump the ERG and move
To the centre and deal with them. The deal
Will now go through, ninety-five per cent May's.
The EU see a clear way forward.
Johnson can ignore his Party's extremists
And have a closer relationship with the EU.
   Next morning, the Conservatives have made gains
And are projected to have a majority
Of eighty seats. The Lib Dem leader has lost
Her seat. All day on TV there is talk
Of how Labour voters turned from Corbyn
And voted for Johnson, persuaded (some

Would say 'conned') by his promises to end
Brexit in January when it will go on
For years and seven hundred laws have to be rewritten.
As sheep follow the sheep in front they flocked
To the shepherd whose promises they trusted most.
The SNP have fifty-five seats and call
For a referendum on Scottish independence.
Sinn Fein has gained, the DUP are down,
And there's pressure from Northern Ireland to leave
The UK now there is a border down
The Irish Sea. The UK's breaking up.
There's also talk of Welsh independence.
"Get Brexit done" now means "end the UK".
    Johnson's won his landslide by occupying
The Labour and Brexit Party's programmes:
Moving to the Left on the economy –
Ending austerity, spending on services,
Investing in the regions – and to the Right
On cultural issues, controlling immigration,
Cutting crime and claiming to "get Brexit done",
Reassuring Labour and Brexit voters
In the Midlands and the North he'll deliver
Their economic interests and Brexit.
As a zebra parades its black and white stripes
In the bush to disorientate predators,
So Johnson's paraded Labour and Brexit stripes
To disorientate voters and win their votes.
He's poached from Labour and the Brexit Party,
Stolen their programmes, not stood for his beliefs.
    In Brant's 1494 poem a ship of fools
Heads for Narragonia, a Paradise.
Have the fools now found the Paradise they sought?
Or have they split the UK with a border
Down the Irish Sea and another against Scotland?
Are all seeing the break-up of the UK,
The further decline of the British Great Power?

Is their Narragonia delusory?
Is it Paradise, have they found true gold?
Time will soon tell as the UK's self-harm
Begins to be apparent, and its delusions
Crash the economy and leave the UK worse off.
It looks like gold but glittered to deceive.
Brexit will not be done, will take many years,
And will not benefit the economy.
Do the Tories have policies to do things for
The blue-collar workers who've voted for them?
The fools on the ship are talking a deal
But ahead is a drastic worsening
Of the UK's economy and less to spend
On the UK's institutions than under the EU.
    Like a peacock fanning out its hundred eyes
Johnson stands outside 10 Downing Street
Feeling pleased, everything has gone so well.
What could possibly go wrong? Hubris, pride –
Excessive pride in defiance of the gods –
Swells into atë – an act of folly,
Delusion, ruin – and flushed with success,
He thinks he's utterly unassailable.
It never occurs to him that nemesis –
Retributive justice in a downfall –
Might be lurking ahead to bring him down.
Bad news seems impossible, and right now
He can't be touched by fate, can't be brought low.

Some have found their way inland to a group of tents
Where wizened Narragonians in strange caps
Sell from trestle-tables what they have found
As Bedouin sell red-sandstone desert rose.
All buy, picking up ores that glint in the sun.
All currencies are welcome in Narragonia.
Soon the trestle-tables are cleared, the gold has gone.
Passengers have arms full of lumps to show

To jewellers who will surely verify
What they've bought and pay much more than they paid
At these primitive open-air market stalls.
It dawns on no fools that they have been conned,
They believe they have gold, not worthless rock,
And surely now they'll have the prosperity
They've long longed for and always believed in.
Their leader's assured them all the gold is real.
It's unthinkable that they will be worse off than if
They had not had high hopes from such imperfect gold.
Just as a party's manifesto policies
Glitter and glister like gold promises
And the voters take them at face value,
So the passengers took the captain at his word.

Canto VII
Withdrawal Agreement Treaty Passed

Sing, Muse, of promises like glistening gold
And of a stunning victory, how young and old
Believed in the spending of a reckless man
Who's never run a business, balanced books,
Or paid by the due date or made ends meet,
Because his opponent's spending was widely deemed
Unbelievable – and he's the least-worst choice.
Sing how the Withdrawal Agreement was passed
And of how he agreed a border down the Irish Sea
Without realising what he had signed.
He'll understand the plight of the common man
Even though he's from Eton and can't read a treaty.
It's the first time in ten years there's stability.
Now as contented as a well-fed lion
Johnson's speaking outside 10 Downing Street.
He says he's forming a new Government
And will take the UK out of the EU by
January the thirty-first, he says he'll unite
And level up the UK, including
Northern Ireland and Scotland. He has won
A huge mandate to transform the country,
Having gambled on a December election.
Given the PM's lack of compassion
For the child sleeping on the hospital floor,
That he sacked twenty-one so ruthlessly,
That he wrote pro-Remain and pro-Leave articles,
That he's not a One-Nation-Tory
And is a racist (seeing Muslim women
Wearing "letter-boxes", writing of "piccaninnies"),
And was sacked from two past jobs for lying,
How could Labour not have defeated Johnson?
It was Corbyn who lost the election while Johnson

Pretended he was opposed to austerity
And the nine years of Government he was involved in,
And now he has a 1980s-style
Majority after the instability
Of Cameron and May – even though he's not trusted.
He's going to bring prosperity to the UK,
He's going to find valuable minerals.
"Let the healing begin," Johnson proclaims,
Standing in Downing Street, when *he* made the wounds.
Now like a humpback whale blowing a rainbow
He basks near his huge landslide, when in fact
The Tories advanced their share of the vote
By one per cent, and Labour crashed by eight.
The public on doorsteps wanted Brexit
Done and Corbyn kept out of Downing Street,
And English nationalism now seems strong.
They did what they had to do for now, but know
They've put a rascal in charge, a charming cheat,
They've held their noses because Corbyn's ghastly,
They're weary of Brexit and are hostile
To his challenge, they know he has no vision,
Mastery or personal virtue, but's a chancer.
He's told them foreign investment will avalanche –
There will be new trade deals with the US
And Australia, and of course with the EU,
There'll be forty new hospitals, twenty
Thousand more police officers and fifty
Thousand more nurses, more local-government
Spending in the Midlands and the North where
The new ex-Labour voters live, even though
There'll be no increases in income tax, VAT
Or National Insurance. He has told them
He's Unionist, that Scotland and Northern Ireland
Will stay in the UK, not allowed to leave
Even though the UK's leaving the EU.
He'll not have the money to fund his promises.

He's like a hawker selling "gold nuggets".
    Will the UK now move from deficit
To prosperity and improved lifestyles?
The aircraft-carriers *Queen Elizabeth*
And *Prince of Wales* are symbols of English
Self-importance, they're unaffordable
Pretensions to world greatness, swanky warships
That reflect the UK's unwillingness to cut
Its cloth to match its purse, gaudy symbols
Of national delusions that an imperial past
Has been revived and is present again.
Johnson's Government will be like these warships.
The UK'll stand alone and rule the waves
As Britannia used to do, and trade with all
And be the most prosperous nation on earth,
Brexiteers assert, but in truth it will be
An offshore island off the United States
Of Europe, like Cuba off the US,
With little impact on how the world is run
Save for the vision of a few thinkers
Who see a United States of Europe
Heading towards a democratic World State.
    Like a displaying peacock with eyes like smiles
Johnson stands with the Tory winner in Sedgefield,
Blair's constituency, and a group of supporters.
He reads out the constituencies that have turned Tory,
And each one is cheered. Now he has to find
Money for the NHS and public services,
But also bring courtesy and politeness
Back, so the people can be reunited.
He tells the EU he wants no regulatory
Alignment in exchange for a tariff-free,
Quota-free trade deal, which will make the deal he wants
Harder to negotiate in eleven months.
He's preparing to axe a third of his Cabinet
To give him support for a hard Brexit,

He signals that like a budding Cromwell
He'll be a ruthless leader and get his way
Like a shepherd penning his flock for their well-being.
    What kind of man is Johnson, who now wields
Power that is unrestrained by Parliament?
He's really an ordinary Tory right-winger,
But his narrative's that Britain is Great again,
An island nation with global interests,
Unique and apart from all power blocs,
But allied to Anglophone America.
When a man is climbing he conceals his thoughts,
But when he obtains power he reveals himself.
A camouflage is no longer necessary
And what he reveals often disappoints.
Johnson's narrative is that he's opened a door
In a brick wall and revealed a rural landscape
On which the sun shines, and a road paved with gold.
But the gold is the reflection of the sun,
The gold is not as the narrative describes.
On the trestle-table, the gold has all gone.
Out there's a people who have bought fool's gold
And they can only soon be disappointed.
    Johnson's going to pass a law that the NHS
Has to have thirty-four billion pounds more
Over the next five years, roughly the amount
On the side of the bus for two years, now spread
Over five years. The trouble is he's promised
No increase in income tax, National Insurance
Or VAT, and this will have to be paid for
By economic growth – but the economy
Will shrink because of Brexit, or borrowing.
A new tax may have to fund the NHS.

The EU has said as the price of a trade deal
The UK, which will become a competitor,
Must align itself with European rules

On competition, the environment
And workplace rights in return for tariff-free
Access to the EU's single market.
If there's no move on alignment there will be
No zero-tariff, zero-quota deal –
Certainly not one agreed quickly. The EU
Will not open its single market to a competitor
Who undercuts European economies
On regulations, the EU won't cut its own throat.
Now it is announced that the Withdrawal
Agreement Bill that passed two pre-election
Readings will be tweaked and have three clauses removed,
Including the old clause 30, which allowed
The transition period to be extended
If MPs voted for it. There will be
A new clause making it illegal for
Parliament to delay the transition, so
Any delay to Brexit will be blocked by law.
Like a mouse that's trespassed into a large loft
And curiously sniffed cheese on a spike
And snap! now lies dead in a steel-sprung trap
Clause 30 of the Bill's been taken out.
A new law will prohibit Parliament
To extend the date beyond the thirty-first
Of December 2020, and if by then
There's no deal, the UK'll end the transition
Period with no deal. The EU has said
This is not a realistic timetable
And the negotiations may end in 'no deal'
At the end of December. So Johnson
Is to enforce a 2020 Brexit
In law and if there's not a deal there will be
'No deal', and the hedge fund which backed his campaign,
Bet on Vote Leave and won eight billion pounds,
May now stand to gain another windfall –
Thanks to the role of Cummings of Vote Leave.

The sheep are being told what's good for them.
    Like a bear that's broken free and roams the wild
Johnson will abandon all EU rules
When the UK leaves, there'll be no alignment
As it resembles applying to rejoin.
The new President of the European Council
Says there must be a level playing-field
If the UK is to have a trade deal, which means
Not undercutting the EU or lowering
Financial, product and health-and-safety
Standards as Johnson seems to want to do.
Johnson says that extending the trade deal
Beyond December would be like Prometheus
Chained to the Tartarean crag, having
His liver pecked out by an eagle, and when
It grows back having it pecked out again,
Endlessly. And he says Leave and Remain
Are now as pointless as the disputes of Swift's
Big-enders and Little-enders, or the feud
Between the Montagues and Capulets
At the end of *Romeo and Juliet.*
    Now the EU's set to block the City
Of London's access to European markets
And erect barriers to data flows vital
To all British commerce ("equivalence")
Of financial services and "adequacy"
Of personal data. A top European
Bureaucrat has threatened to delay trade talks
And extend the UK's transition period
Before it leaves the EU, as leverage,
Unless it aligns with EU regulations.
In June an EU summit will decide
If a free-trade deal with the UK's possible
By the end of the year, and by then there must be
A draft agreement on fishing, or talks will stall.
    The Queen's Speech has now taken place, the Queen

And Prince Charles were both less formally dressed.
It sets in law that Parliament cannot block
The Withdrawal Bill, which the next day is passed
By a hundred and twenty-four, with four clauses
Removed, and now Johnson's Tories don't need
To make concessions to Labour to get it through.
His talk of One-Nation Conservatism
Now seems baseless rhetoric, he's rejecting
Alignment with EU regulations
For an economically calamitous
Brexit that risks destabilising the Ulster
Peace process, awakening violence.
Parts of the UK want independence,
Their nationalism wants more devolution,
And the UK, which before the Second World War
Ruled a quarter of humankind that was shown red
On maps, may now dwindle like melting snow
To Little England, on its own and poor.
    Now like a market trader selling sunshine
Johnson hails a Golden Age for the UK.
A painting of the Golden Age based on
Michaelina Wautier's *Bacchanal*
(Before 1659) shows Bacchus
Lying back naked and being fed grapes.
Now a cartoon shows a naked Johnson, drunk,
Wine glass on its side and some red wine spilt,
Being fed grapes by Javid, his Chancellor.
Other ministers blow trumpets or ring bells.
Johnson says a Golden Age for the UK
Is not far off, a crock of gold at the end
Of the rainbow. "Get Brexit done" was the cry
To the voters but now seems like a cook
In a Christmas kitchen, the turkey still alive,
And, with 'no deal' ahead and Scotland going
And the prospect of Ireland reuniting,
Brexit looks uncooked, like a strutting turkey.

No one knows the kind of country Britannia,
Blindfolded, will find herself in, just that she has
To negotiate with twenty-seven EU countries
That will regard her as a rival and give less help
For defence and defeating terrorism than before.
It may be a hard Brexit – a trade deal on goods,
Not services – and defeats will be sold as victories
In the years to come, the crock of gold as gold.
Christmas Day, and Johnson is in Downing Street
With Carrie, his girlfriend, and his father hosts
His wife Marina and his grandchildren
(And plans to become a French citizen).
Johnson, hater of the EU, having scorned it
To win an election by eighty seats
As a populist – his Christmas broadcast began
"Hi, folks" without any trace of a cringe –
Now jets off with Carrie to warm Mustique,
The island of the rich (where Princess Margaret
And the Cambridges stayed), as guests of Count
Leopold von Bismarck, direct descendant
Of the Prussian and first German Chancellor
Otto von Bismarck, who unified Germany
And formed the German Empire – whose dominance
Johnson wants to replicate in the UK while
Sending a message to the twenty-seven
EU member states that he's friends with the Bismarcks
And that his "Golden Age" will be like Otto's
(And of course the Emperor Augustus's
Regeneration of the Roman State).
He says to Leopold, "Life is perfect."
Be careful, Johnson, too much hubris and the gods
May send a plague to bring you down to earth,
A nemesis that will preserve order.
But he's latched on to something Bismarck once said:
"With a gentleman I'm always a gentleman
And a half, and when I have to deal with a pirate

I try to be a pirate and a half."
(He will say this to his chief negotiator Frost,
Who will repeat it. Be careful, Johnson.)
So Johnson the populist, anti-EU leader
Is cosying up to rich German friends,
Perhaps there'll be a soft Brexit after all.
    Johnson struts and swaggers his stonking win,
He's lord of all he surveys, your poet can see
He's puffed up with hubris like a fat toad,
And is already swollen with atë,
As he seeks someone to pay for his winter break
With Carrie in Mustique, as he's entitled.
O Johnson, the gods punish arrogance,
Be careful lest they send a nemesis
Like a dreadful plague to cut you down to size.
    Wanting acolytes who will think outside the box
And wage war on the Establishment he hates,
Basing his criteria for excellence on himself,
Like a furry mole burrowing under a lawn
And throwing up a mound like an anthill
Cummings now calls for "weirdos" and "misfits"
To apply for jobs in Downing Street to shake
Up the civil service. The UK's to be governed
By weirdos and misfits, it is so sad
The once-mighty UK has descended to this.
(Uri Geller and Jennifer Arcuri
Are two of thirty-five thousand who've applied.)
    Now Trump's assassinated Soleimani,
The Iranian menace linked to militias
In Iraq, Syria, Afghanistan and Yemen,
And has left the Middle East in uproar.
There's now a threat to Western interests
And security will now be an issue.
Terrorism has woken from its slumber,
Iran is back to creating a nuclear bomb.
US troops will have to leave the Middle East.

Johnson has to choose whether to go with Trump
And support a war with Iran, or whether
To go with Europe and de-escalate:
Johnson was not warned of the drone attack
In advance, and's been cold-shouldered by the US –
And now by Europe as the UK can't be trusted
With EU secrets, its voice is no longer sought.
    Now like a grizzly bear meeting a gazelle
Johnson's meeting with the EU's new President
In Downing Street, Ursula von der Leyen.
He's said he wants a trade deal by December,
Otherwise he'll walk away with 'no deal'
(As the hedge fund that backed Vote Leave would like).
Workers' rights, food standards and the environment
Will all be worse. He's got to decide if he
Wants trade tariffs or alignment with the EU.
She's said time's short, and warned him not to erode
The protections for EU citizens living
In the UK after Brexit. It's stalemate.
    Johnson appears in Parliament for PMQs
And at last speaks of the American drone attack
That killed Soleimani, the Iranian mastermind
Of proxy militias' attacks throughout the Middle East.
Killing him will cause the US to be
Turfed out of Iraq, and Iran will strive to have
Nuclear weapons so it will never again
Have a major-general drone-attacked
By the US from five thousand miles away.
Johnson has to agree with America in
Order to secure the trade deal offered by Trump,
And agree with the EU who want to de-escalate
To secure a trade deal with the EU.
It is a fraught time, and so he's silent.
What is global Britain? There's a global
Crisis on Iran, and no one has heard
From the UK's PM for five long days.

Where is the leadership of global Britain?

Like a shepherd Johnson ushers MPs like sheep
Into his Aye lobby to continue
The passage after two pre-election readings
Of the Withdrawal Agreement Bill. It's passed
Its Third Reading by ninety-nine votes, it's now
With the Lords, and the long-awaited moment
The UK faces being global Britain
With a tiny army and no military power
Has crept nearer. Nation-states like Russia
With a smaller GDP than the UK
Pack a larger punch. Von der Leyen says the UK
And the EU will be the best of friends
But a trade deal in eleven months is impossible.
    After the Second World War the US replaced
The British Empire as the regional power,
But now the US dominance is fading.
It's now clear the US, UK and EU
Have separate approaches, are diverging
And their electorates won't vote to intervene.
A united front is difficult to maintain.
To speak of "the West" as one entity
Makes little sense, the West's ceased to exist.
It's a disorderly world unless humankind
Can unite in a federal World State
As Zeus would like, and does his best to intrigue.
    In an interview where he looks bleary-eyed
With drooping bags under his puffy eyes,
His hair dishevelled as if he'd just got up,
His socks hurriedly at half-mast, showing legs,
Like a toad croaking beside a muddy pond
Johnson has called for crowdfunding to fund
Big Ben to bong in Brexit at 11pm
On the thirty-first of January,
But many will be grieving, many in tears,

And the EU will take down the UK's flag
And quietly place it within the Museum
Of European History – so perhaps
A tolling bell for the severing of a link
That is centuries old and won two world wars,
And for the loss of a hundred and thirty
Billion pounds in lost European trade
By the end of the coming year, is more
Accurate and far more appropriate
Than celebrating illusory fools' gold?
The dangers of voting for Brexit were
That the UK might break up; that it would need
European support to block Russian expansion;
And that it would endanger forty-three
Per cent of the UK's exports to Europe.
Now Ireland is heading for a Union
Which would take Northern Ireland out of the UK;
The ruler of Iran's said the UK
Is America's lackey (along with the EU);
And the EU wants the UK to follow
Its rules on tax, state aid and the environment
In return for a "zero-tariff" free trade agreement,
And Javid has warned that some UK businesses
May do less well after Brexit – all risks
Your poet identified before the vote to leave.
And yet there's to be a laser-light show –
A clock projected on the black-brick walls
Of Downing Street, all Whitehall buildings lit
And flags on every pole in Parliament Square –
That seems triumphalist nationalism
And looks like gloating and divisiveness.
Johnson's called a charlatan, "a person who
Falsely claims knowledge or a skill" – he doesn't care
And is reckless, and so by definition
Lacks the skill that's required to be PM.
Brexit's not been done well, with an eye to jobs,

And it's now slipping into trade, which does not enthuse,
And an endless tussle between the UK
Saying the trade agreement will be agreed
By December, and the EU saying it will need
Five months' extension, and there will be no deal
By the end of the year. And yet the IMF
Have said the UK'll grow faster than the eurozone
This year and only the US and Canada
Will grow faster during the next two years.
The trouble is, in an age of rising
Protectionism the UK's chosen
To walk out of the biggest free-trade area
In the world where nearly half its trade goes,
And its economic and trade prospects now
Depend on making new and better deals
With a range of countries including the EU
Where trade will be smaller than what it's been.

Now there's a pile of gold heaped high to be
Transported back to the ship, and in each tent
Are individual piles of gold. And now
The captain's making promises to all
As he calls for all the ores to be loaded
Into bundles to be carried back to the ship.
All have become prosperous, all are smiling.
'*Gaudeamus omnes*' ('We all rejoice')
As the Gregorian chant for all saints intones.
Reluctantly all pack away the tents
And trek back to the ship with large bundles.

Canto VIII
The UK Leaves the EU

Sing, Muse, of rupture, and of a bond ripped,
Of forty-seven years of entanglement,
And sing of leaving and of great sorrow,
Of triumphal jeering and great anguish.
Sing of the rearranging of a world
As boastful nation-states enter conflict,
Sing of how a Union is teetering
On the edge of fragmenting into separate bits.
In a time of unity sing of fracturing
And the sombre solitude of sad divorce.
Sing of rejoicing and of quiet despair.
Sing, Muse, of recklessness and sad dismay.
   Now there's a constitutional crisis
As all three devolved administrations –
The Welsh and Northern-Irish Assemblies
And the Scottish Parliament – rejected
The EU's Withdrawal Bill. Could the UK
Collapse into four nations, three of which
May find their way back into the EU?
And the House of Lords has voted against
Three of the Bill's measures, including granting
Settled status digitally, without
Written evidence of citizenship.
Peers have voted for EU citizens
To have written proof of their right to stay.
The Government's rejected what they've said.
   Now the Lords has bowed to the will of the Commons.
The Queen's signed off the EU Withdrawal Bill.
There's now Royal Assent. And Johnson's claimed
That the Brexit finishing line has been crossed.
The UK's devolved nations are still opposed.
   Like two lions roaring at a wildebeest

The US and EU are both hostile.
Trump's threatening retaliatory trade
Tariffs on the UK's cars if it taxes
US tech giants such as Google and Facebook.
The EU's preparing to offer the UK
A trade deal that's tougher than those
Given to Canada and Japan and a host
Of others as it would be a mistake
To allow some UK industry bodies
To certify that goods conform to EU
Standards. Now new migrants will be allowed in
Without having to have thirty thousand pounds –
And Johnson appeals for Africans to migrate.
Africans are to replace Europeans.
    On the thirty-first of January there will be –
Along with a light show and countdown clock
On Downing Street and the White Cliffs of Dover –
A new 50p coin that says on the back
"Peace, prosperity and friendship with all nations".
The lack of an Oxford comma before 'and'
Groups prosperity and friendship with all nations
Together, when the UK's de-friended
The twenty-seven and shown the opposite,
Making the legend on the coin vacuous
And somewhat hypocritical. Many
UK Remainers have said they'll refuse
To accept this 50p coin as the words
On the back are the opposite of actuality
And should say "War, poverty and conflict
With all nations". They say the coin's designed
To rub Remainers' noses in their defeat.
Few have seen that the legend's inspired by
Jefferson's first inaugural address:
"Peace, commerce and friendship with all nations."
Why does the UK have to borrow from the US
In what is said on the back of its new coin?

It seems to align itself with the US
To get a new trade deal for chlorine-washed
Chicken and hormone-treated beef – while in dispute
With the US over digital tax,
Huawei on 5G, and extradition.
Perhaps these are bargaining counters so
The UK can become the fifty-first state
Just as late Greece aligned itself with Rome?
    Nothing has been settled with the EU,
It's not even the end of the beginning.
Brexit's barely half-done, there's a trade agreement
To negotiate with the EU, and how close
The future relationship is to be.
Half the UK's trade is with the EU.
This must continue to come in, somehow,
Or there'll be low growth and catastrophe.
Johnson says he wants a 'Canada plus' –
Ninety-eight per cent of tariffs eliminated,
Plus financial services included –
With control of laws, money, borders and not
Being rule-takers. But if he does not want
Tariffs on EU goods and services
And if the UK's lost trade with Europe
Can't be made up so the economy suffers,
He'll have to stay aligned with EU rules
And so stay within the single market
And wriggle out of his past promises
Just as he wriggled out of his promise
To the DUP and Northern Ireland. Then
UK-EU relations will stabilise,
And will then improve and the UK will once more
Snuggle up to Europe with growing calls
To share in rule-making again, and dump
Not-being rule-takers, which will by then
Be seen to be bad for the UK's trade.
Alignment or divergence? Diverging

Moves away from EU rules and frictionless trade
Which business likes, so divergence can only be
In areas business welcomes. The debate is now
To what extent the UK takes back control
Over its own rules, and how much it moves away
From EU rules, and what impact that will have
On the closeness of the trading relationship
With the EU and so on UK businesses
That depend on that close relationship.
It seems the Cabinet is split on this
And trade groups fear that ideology
Will trump practical considerations
In the coming talks. There is confusion
And contradiction in the Government.
Like a bumbling and ungainly wild boar
Johnson doesn't seem to know what to do next.
Iran, Huawei, HS2 and the Budget
Are all subject to internal divisions
As is alignment versus divergence,
Trade with the US or trade with the EU.
There's no plan ahead as there's no clear vision,
Just a muddle that does not bode too well
For the UK's prospects in the coming year,
And Johnson's determination to bolt
From the EU, like a muntjac buck with tusks
Running squatly down a field to a hole in the hedge.
The UK has a leader who could see
To the end of the election but does not know
What is to happen next and what path to take.
O how many long for the certainties
Of the EU and its frictionless trade rules!
Now Johnson's agreed that Huawei hardware
Should be used in thirty-five per cent of the UK's
5G network, on the fringe rather than the core,
As banning Huawei, which is already
In the system – Huawei already runs a third

Of the UK's infrastructure – would have set
5G back three years and would have cost
A hundred and twenty billion pounds in
Lost productivity. There's an outcry
In Washington, a Trump official says
There's no distinction between fringe and core
And as the US and UK exchange
Intelligence what's in the UK system
Would swiftly get into the US system.
The Dragon's now guarding the UK hen-house.
It's as if the KGB were installing
A national telephone service in the UK
During the Cold War for eavesdropping.
Forty-two US Congressmen have urged
The Commons Defence Select Committee
To reconsider as the Government
And private industry in China work
Together to expand the influence
Of the ruling Communist Party. Short-term
Financial savings using Huawei will
Evaporate due to the long-term cost
Of monitoring, and the cost will be
Catastrophic if Johnson goes ahead.
And intelligence-sharing between the US
And the UK will be frustrated.
    Now there's an outcry from ex-military
MPs on Johnson's back benches, and a call
To reconsider such a reckless move.
But Johnson promised to upgrade Broadband
During the election campaign, and he thinks
He's chosen the best option, to take a hit
From the Americans rather than voters
And have an underperforming economy.
For him it's the least worst option to take,
To put the economy before security.
The UK has freed itself from Brussels

Only to cede sovereignty to Beijing.
China spies on its own citizens, Huawei
Receives billions from the State and has eighty
Thousand staff, more than the UK army.
    America's furious with its ally,
The special relationship has been ignored.
Varadkar, the Irish prime minister,
Says the UK has to come to terms with the fact
It's now a small country and lacks the clout
To impose its will upon the world: the EU
Has four hundred and fifty million people,
The UK only sixty-eight million, so
The EU is the stronger team and will win.
Now the UK seems "a small country" to Poland:
Seventy-five years after the liberation
Of Auschwitz, and not one British Minister
Is present at the memorial. The UK
No longer counts, it's just an offshore island.
    More differences with the United States:
The Environment Secretary has said
The UK will not import US hormone-
Treated beef or chlorinated chicken,
And the US Ambassador to the UK
Has called for British farmers to accept
Chicken washed in chlorine – or there won't be
A big, speedy trade deal with the US.
Collision with the US or China,
Divergence and distance from EU,
The UK's nation-state's at loggerheads
And a pandemic virus shutting down trade –
Things don't bode well for the isolated UK.

News that the EU Parliament has approved
The Withdrawal Agreement by six hundred and twenty-one
To forty-nine, so the UK will leave
On Friday evening. An anti-EU rant

By Farage (who'll live off his EU pension,
Seventy per cent of his monthly salary
Of seven thousand six hundred pounds) in praise
Of populism, and then MEPs
All join hands and sing 'Auld Lang Syne', drowned out
By cheers from Brexit Party MEPs,
And many eyes are filled with tears. Some UK
MEPs wave goodbye as they leave the chamber,
Hoping it's *au revoir* and not *adieu*.
Johnson says he will accept border checks
To free the UK from the EU's rules –
And so there will be a lorry park in Kent
And long queues waiting for passports to be checked
And there'll be an end to frictionless trade.
TV screens show all round the bleak UK
Sadness, foreboding and rueful dismay.
    January the thirty-first and it's overcast
With light rain. The Brussels Mayor has put on
A pro-British light show with a red telephone
Box in the Grand Place to stress the friendship
Between Belgium – and Europe – and the UK.
There is a sad feeling in the chilly air.
The Union Jack is lowered in Brussels
In a quiet low-key, courteous hauling-down.
Johnson's Cabinet has met in Sunderland
To show it's on the side of Northerners.
Now a crowd gathers in Parliament Square
Where brash Farage celebrates independence.
As swanky as if his two thumbs tugged at
His braces and spread fingers screamed 'Look at me',
Johnson's holding a reception in Downing Street,
Serves sparkling English wine to eighty guests,
Shropshire blue cheese, fillet of lamb on toast,
Mushroom tarts, crab cake and beef in mini-
Yorkshire puddings topped with horseradish sauce.
Cummings, the leader of the Leave campaign,

Believes he's won – but many feel Brexit
Will undermine the British economy
And no one knows the future relationship.
Many say Johnson has no plan. He's said
Eighty per cent of British trade
Will be covered by free-trade deals in three years.
There are already signs things won't go well.
Barnier's said there's no chance of a zero-
Quota and -tariff trade deal on Canadian lines
Unless the UK promises to stick
To EU standards when transition ends.
Johnson's said no chance, there's a collision ahead,
And the prospect of 'no deal' (as the hedge funds want).
Australia's Government's turned down a trade deal
Sought by the UK that included visa-
Free work and travel between the two countries
To prevent a brain drain to the UK.
The UK's science will lose 1.52
Billion pounds of European Research Income,
Which will do great damage to UK science.
The UK economy grew at nought per cent
In the last three months of 2019.
The Treasury's said the UK economy
Will bring in five per cent less than when it
Was in the EU, and the man in the street –
In the North and cheering in Parliament Square –
Will be hit by job losses and price hikes.
An Austrian stamp shows a blue Europe
On a white background with Great Britain missing –
And 30.10.19 crossed through and replaced
By 31.1.20 – the UK's vanished
And is an insignificant hole in the map.
Farage's measure of success is freedom
From the yoke of the EU's colonialism,
But that is a self-serving fantasy,
And success must be measured by economic gain

And there is going to be economic loss.
Ahead's a rocky, rocky, rocky time.
    The thirty-first of January, and there's anguish
As dusk falls on a fruitful period
Of contemporary British history.
Rain's falling on Parliament Square, a crowd
Wrapped in shiny macs waits for their demagogue
Who's in the boastful tradition of Greek Cleon
More than two thousand four hundred years ago.
Johnson earnestly addresses a camera
In a video – he's jerky and is reading
What he's saying and appears insincere.
He's punchy and stays inside 10 Downing Street.
He says it's a beginning, not an end.
The BBC ignores this video
As self-promotion, and not shot by them.
Farage is asked, "Was it that bad? In the EU?"
He waffles on what he calls Independence Day.
He hails a great "national liberation",
But it's hard to see who's being liberated –
Not Scotland, Northern Ireland, or the Welsh
Assembly or London, who all want to remain,
So it must be England without London,
And there is no English Parliament, just
A Parliament representing four nations,
Three of which want to stay. It looks a mess,
As the muntjac reaches the gap between hawthorn trees,
Certainly an act of monumental folly
That was received with an exhausted shrug
And listless torpor by most who believed
Johnson when he said Brexit would now be done.
    On the walls of Downing Street the time says
48.40 on a ticking down,
And there's also a clock on the White Cliffs
Of Dover. But, hush please, in Brighton sits
A silent vigil, with candles, in grief.

Scotland, Wales and Northern Ireland all see
Independence ahead and the UK
Crumbling into fragments, from a Union
To a Federation of the British Isles.
And your poet, the poet of decline,
Who charted the loss of the British Empire
More than fifty years ago, may live to see
The mighty UK reduced from Union
To federation and decay, to be
Little England. The UK's on its own
With many decisions to make, and years
Of hard work start now. Johnson's said, "It will
Be easy, there will be trade-offs." But that's
Not the case, and he will be in for a shock
As things will get much tougher from now on.
His promises will be tested and found out.
Juncker told him that he used lies during
The referendum campaign, and these will
Come back to haunt him and show who he is.
Verhofstadt said, "Sad to see a nation
Leaving, a great nation that has given
Us so much economically, culturally,
Politically, even its own blood in two world wars."

Eleven o'clock and in virtual reality
Big Ben on the walls of Downing Street bongs eleven.
Bong. Welcome to new vassalage, will it be
To the EU or US and its trade deal?
Bong. Share your fisheries with the EU
Or guard your fishing waters with armed vessels
And lose access for your financial services?
Bong. US trade commissioners or ECJ?
Bong. Chlorine-washed chicken or straight bananas?
Bong. British taxes on Google or US
Tariffs on your Jaguar Land Rover?
Bong. More East-European pickers or

Fewer cabbage fields or raspberry plots?
Bong. Fewer nurses in the NHS
Or more immigrants from the Commonwealth?
Bong. No European health insurance
Cards, or more health tourists in the UK?
Bong. More alignment to the EU's rules
Or more divergence and bare-bones trade deal?
Bong. Keep half of all our trade with the EU
Or have much less from Africa and Asia?
Bong. Remain with a prosperous economy
Or lose five per cent of our annual take?
Accept a drop in British influence
Or side with undemocratic dictators?
    00.00 hours on the digital clock.
We're out, and the UK's left the EU.
    Like a timid muntjac heading for a thicket
Johnson does not come out and address the throng
But inside gongs a Chinese gong to cheers,
An ornamental gong, with a mallet,
Eleven bongs to shadow virtual Big Ben,
Cheered on by his eighty wine-bibbing guests.
There's rowdy cheering in Parliament Square
And staunch singing of patriotic songs.
Farage sings 'God Save the Queen' fervently.
    O sad, the UK has left the EU
And will now have less influence in the world.
Just as beech trees in Loughton Camp recall
The Roman time of Caesar's sloping walls
Of mounded earth that kept his soldiers safe,
So Britain, a member of the European
Civilisation since Julius Caesar's
And Emperor Claudius's Roman conquests,
And since Augustine's mission into Kent
And sharing the Catholic Church and rule by
Norman kings who then ruled northern France,
And sharing the Reformation, is rooted in

The European civilisation
And cannot leave its two-thousand-year-old
European identity even if
It no longer funds the political
Union that's preserved peace for seventy years.
As a skylark rises twittering towards the sun
And then drops like a stone as rain is nigh
So those with continental ancestors
Plunged from a sunny height into deep despair.
O sad that the UK's a small country
With less clout than it had with the EU's strength.
Now Johnson can't blame the EU any more
As he squashes through the thorns of the hawthorn hedge,
From now on he will be held to account:
Economic growth or lack of it, cuts in
Immigrants and nurses in the NHS
Are now down to the achievement or mistakes
Of Johnson and his Government, no one else.

The UK's left the European Union
And its Permanent Representative
To the EU has been swiftly replaced
By the British Ambassador's Mission,
And Johnson wants no alignment, no concessions
And no court involvement by the EU.

With a sudden lurch, as if the earth tilted
On its axis, history has turned and now
The UK's Union is tilting downwards
And heads towards a splitting within itself
With Scotland, Northern Ireland and Wales all
Wanting to rejoin the EU, perhaps
An outcome the EU has quietly sought
So it has the four nations separately.
And how stark now is the contrast between
The foot of the rainbow's gleaming crock of gold
And the fool's gold, iron pyrites, it's been found to be.

Now the ship's been loaded, bundles are piled
In the hold and stacked on deck after many journeys.
Just as on England's Jurassic coast where
Ammonites washed from cliffs lie between stones
On a beach stained dark-brown from ancient iron,
And a sole trader covertly hammers out
Lumps streaked with dull gold, puts them in a bag
And returns to his car and drives away,
So these hundred 'fossil'-hunters dislodged gold
Into cloth bundles they lugged back to their ship.
The ship's weighed down with precious ore hewn from
Cliffs and dredged up from mud in the river bed,
And all the pans, picks and hammers are back
In the storeroom down in the hold. Job done.
The captain led them to Narragonian land
And all will now benefit from the gold,
And there's a communal pile that will sell well.
Everything's excellent, no one has any doubt.

Canto IX
Covid Ruins the Economy

Sing, Muse, of a new virus and of the end
Of the old world of intermingling
In crowds and on transport with all strangers,
Sing of how Covid-19 paralysed
Society and ruined the economy
As mixing increased infection and led to death,
Sing of the silent advent of a plague,
Of isolation at home besides from Europe.
Sing of the nightmare of social distancing.
    The next day's sunny and a bit windy,
Johnson says there's a new dawn and era
But nothing practical has changed, only
A symbolic leaving to a light show
By a post-imperial power with a feeling
Of exceptionalism – being exceptional –
And in a tired economy with low
Productivity and a sense of entitlement
To health and welfare benefits afforded by
Ever and ever higher taxation.
Half the country was pained by the delay,
Now there's relief that the democratic vote
On the referendum has been honoured.
But ahead, to be negotiated, is what
Is to happen next, a new EU trade deal
That in eleven months can only be
A WTO bare-bones, off-the-shelf deal
At best, or 'no deal' and long lorry queues.
'Global Britain' must always stay aligned
With the single market and customs union
Or show downward economic decline
With no new trade deals and slow closing-down
Of car manufacturers, fast-rising

Unemployment and looming recession,
And Northern Ireland and Scotland detached
And the end of the UK and Great Britain
And, as Wales follows, of Britain, leaving
Only England with half its exports gone
And now a target of revolutionaries,
Of neo-Bolsheviks and Trotskyites.
Britain's been European since Roman times,
And this fine morning has not left European
Civilisation, just a political bloc
Of (now) twenty-seven European nation-states
With which it's fallen out of love and preferred
To separate and now go it alone,
Following nationalism (which results in war)
And patriotism (country before all else).
The UK's Europeanness still remains.
    As a cunning fox differs from a grazing sheep
Johnson and Barnier have different visions
For trading with the EU. Barnier's stressed
A level playing-field in state subsidies,
Environmental standards and workers' rights.
He's said the question is, will the UK
Still adhere to Europe's societal
And regulatory model or will it seek
To diverge? The UK's answer will be
Fundamental to the level of ambition
For its future relationship with the EU.
    But Johnson, speaking in the Painted Hall
At the Old Royal Naval College, Greenwich
(With nymphs and cherubs round Baroque symbols
Of British mercantile power), where Nelson
Lay in state, on the UK's first working day
Outside the EU since 1972
Has charted a course that will collide with
The EU's red lines on trade. He has said
There is no need for the UK to abide

By the EU rules, and the UK will
Prosper regardless of its relationship
As a sovereign equal taking back control.
    He meant Britain won't accept the EU's rules
As the price of a favourable trade deal.
He's said the UK wants a comprehensive
Free-trade agreement that's like Canada's
But if the UK does not get it trade will
Have to be based on the Withdrawal Agreement.
But he's got a divorce deal, not a trade deal.
He's said he'll walk away from a trade deal
If it means the UK must follow Brussels' rules.
He's said there won't be 'no deal', the question is,
Will it be like Canada's or Australia's,
Which is like WTO rules, and in either case
He has no doubt the UK will prosper.
Time will tell. Government economists say
Johnson's Brexit deal will knock six per cent
Off the UK's GDP in the next fifteen years
Compared with if the UK had stayed in.
The UK'll lose much of the forty-three per cent
Of its exports that go to the EU and may be unable
To make them up by trading far away.
Before the election he said there's no chance
That the UK would leave without a deal,
But now he speaks of the UK's heading towards
Australia's nothing deal, and 'no deal' looms.
Barnier and Johnson seem many miles apart,
And look set for a future collision.
The Withdrawal Agreement aside, little is known
About the future relationship, and 'no deal'
Is still very possible in December.
    And now how much Johnson understands is called
In question by a former minister.
Claiming to be an internationalist globalist
And not a nationalist nation-stater

Johnson has sacked ex-Minister Claire O'Neill
From President of the UN Climate Change
Conference, COP26 (Conference
Of the Parties, the 26th session)
To be held in Glasgow, and Cameron and Hague
Have declined to succeed her. O'Neill has said,
"He told me he doesn't understand climate change,
He doesn't get it," and "My advice to anyone
To whom Boris is making promises –
Whether it is voters, world leaders, ministers,
Employees or family members – is to get it
In writing, get a lawyer to look at it,
And make sure the money is in the bank."
Nothing lasts for ever, and nation-stater
Trump's being impeached and will eventually give way
To an internationalist who has a world view.
And nation-stater Johnson will, too, make way
For a leader with vision who will reconnect
Isolated Britain to Europe and the world.
Just as a beast of burden, a donkey,
Is laden with daily loads and worn out,
And is gloomy and stoical and tired,
Now the last three months catch up with Johnson,
A nightmare he did not see coming as
He blustered under the Greenwich ceiling,
Sending coded messages to the EU.
In November US spies alerted base
About an out-of-control disease in China
From intercepts and satellite images.
The US notified Israel and NATO
Early, in the second week of November.
In January, during Johnson's holiday
On the private Caribbean island Mustique,
Paid for (Johnson declared in the register
Of MPs' interests) by a Carphone-Warehouse
Businessman, "value fifteen thousand pounds"

(Which the businessman, Ross, has denied paying),
A US drone's killed the Iranian Soleimani.
There's talk of war, and Johnson's by the sea.
But far more seriously, there's been an outbreak
Of a new coronavirus, Covid-19,
In Wuhan in China. It is believed
To have originated in a food market
Selling wildlife, probably bats for soup.
There's talk of bats being illicitly
Sold to the market by a researcher
At the Institute of Virology,
Where scientists work on wildlife viruses.
China reported the outbreak in December
But played down its gravity and the need to act.
Johnson, holidaying after his election
Exertion, is not instructing laboratories
To prepare for mass testing like Germany,
Which has activated a hundred and fifty labs.
All through January the situation in Wuhan
Deteriorates. Two Chinese nationals test
Positive after staying at a York hotel,
And Britons are brought back from Wuhan on
An evacuation plane and are quarantined
At a specialist hospital in the Wirral.
But tests in Iceland have found that the virus
Was established early on in the UK,
And travellers brought it to Iceland in December.
The first UK transmission of the virus
Is confirmed in February. Unlike China
And Italy, which impose restrictions on
Liberty and movement, the UK goes
For social distancing, and if there are symptoms,
Self-isolation and quarantine, the thinking
Being that herd immunity can be reached.
Five Cobra meetings, one a week, take place
Without Johnson's chairmanship or presence –

Like a donkey put out to grass he's not working,
He's gone to the grace-and-favour Chevening House
While Chequers is being renovated,
For a "working holiday" for a fortnight,
And agrees his divorce and battles with his children,
And announces Carrie's pregnancy and their engagement.
He likes his country breaks, doesn't work weekends
Or chair meetings or do urgent planning,
He's like a mallard always near its drake
And grins at the world with a beak and green sheen.
There's been no leadership in the lost five weeks
When snowdrops startled on the frozen ground.
No PPE (gowns, masks), tests, ventilators
Have been ordered, the NHS is unprepared.
There's no plan to deal with a pandemic,
Johnson has said it's just another flu
And wants Whitty to inject him with Covid
On TV to show that it's no worse than flu.
Johnson changes his mind ten times a day,
Administrative lions are being led by donkeys.
There's a lack of action and a sense of drift,
As snails gather under a street light at night
And cling to blades of grass and leave a trail
Of slime as they inch their way towards their goal
Ministers mutter Johnson's giving no lead.
Corbyn's called him "a part-time Prime Minister".
    On the fifth of March the first virus death
Takes place in the UK. On the eleventh of March
The World Health Organization declares
A global pandemic, and says five days
Later, "Test, test, test." On March the fifteenth
A harassed Hancock, the Health Secretary,
Announces that over-seventies will be asked
To self-isolate by not leaving their homes
Within weeks, and the next day Johnson warns
Against non-essential travel and going to pubs,

Clubs and theatres. All should work at home if they can.
Johnson announces twenty-five thousand tests a day
On the eighteenth of March, but there's no timetable.
    Competing reports to the Government
Have had different outcomes and therefore outlooks.
A study by Oxford University
Suggests the virus spread a month before
The first recorded death in the UK
And that most UK citizens have been infected
And so have acquired herd immunity.
A relaxed approach. But on the second of March
At last Johnson chaired a Cobra meeting
Which saw a new model put forward by SAGE
(The Scientific Advisory Group for Emergencies):
The Imperial College's Neil Ferguson
Has forecast two hundred and fifty thousand deaths –
Perhaps even half a million – in the UK
And hospital beds having to increase eightfold
Unless there is lockdown. And now in panic
The Government changes its strategy
And after dithering between the two for three weeks
Abandons herd immunity for lockdown
And the assembling of Nightingale hospitals.
    Like a sparrowhawk whose presence sends birds to their nests,
Johnson orders all pubs, cafés, restaurants,
Bars and gyms to close, and employees to be furloughed.
The Chancellor announces at the daily news
Conference the taxpayer'll fund eighty per cent
Of the wages of employees temporarily sent home.
On the twenty-third of March there's total lockdown.
Key workers can work, everyone else must stay in,
Go out once a day to exercise or buy food,
And the vulnerable over-seventies must stay in
For twelve weeks. The virus is virulent,
It attacks breathing, the country's paralysed.
    The streets and skies are empty, there are few cars.

The economy's ground to a halt, everything's shut.
Strict social distancing and isolation.
The PM's gone for lockdown to prevent
The worst-case scenario, but, the old apart,
The worst may soon be over, and restrictions
Could be eased within weeks, not months or years.
The Institute for Fiscal Studies states
Lockdown will create a UK deficit
Of two hundred billion pounds, a quarter more
Than the banking crisis caused in 2008,
And 10.8 per cent of GDP.
It took the UK fifty-seven years to repay
The US and Canadian war loans.
    All TV interviews are conducted from home.
There's talk of a three-hundred-and-fifty-billion cost,
Twice as much as in the banking crisis.
It's unprecedented since the Second World War.
All cower at home from an invisible virus
That's in the air and settles like a frost
That kills some plants by expanding the water
Inside plant cells and blocking nutrient sap,
And watch the daily news briefings at five
With graphs showing rising deaths and cases
And less and less travel in the cities.
Promises have been made without timetables:
There are 3.5 million antibody tests,
But there's no timetable. Johnson declares
There will be two hundred and fifty thousand tests
A day – a glittering promise – but there's
No timetable, and the labs have not been found.
There are no tests, and there's no protection
For doctors and nurses on the front line.
It's shocking incompetence, Johnson's promises
Of more and more tests are again fools' gold.
    Prince Charles has tested positive and has gone
To Birk Hall and is self-isolating

In two rooms there in the Scottish Highlands
With an armed policeman at the wooded gate.
And simultaneously his son Harry
Has moved to LA's Hollywood with his wife.
    There are complaints at the daily conference
And on *Question Time* that there's a shortage
Of ventilators, masks and PPE,
That doctors and nurses on the front line
Are among patients with Covid-19
With substandard protection. There's a clap
For carers across the nation at 8pm
To cover up that the Government has left
Doctors and nurses exposed. Prince Charles claps
In his room, Johnson outside Number Ten.
He looks flushed and feverish, and seems unwell.
    Now it comes out the EU Commission
Asked all its twenty-seven member states
On March the sixteenth how many face masks,
Ventilators and personal protective equipment
Items they would need for a bulk order
In four bulk-buying procurement schemes to buy
Supplies with combined purchase powers and keep
Prices down, and twenty-five EU states
And their associate Norway all responded
While placing their own orders separately.
The first order going to twenty-five
Member states covers masks (types 2 and 3),
Gloves, goggles, face shields, surgical masks, scrubs
And overalls, all needed by the UK.
The European Procurement Initiative,
Of seven-hundred-and-fifty-billion euros
Funded by the European Central Bank,
Has secured on the world market offers
Of great scale at short notice, while the UK
Has ordered ventilators from Dyson,
Who makes vacuum cleaners, and his machines

Will have to pass regulatory tests
That will delay their delivery to the new
Nightingale Hospital in the Excel Centre,
Where your poet saw Johnson wave a kipper
In the last hustings of the leadership contest.
    Like a green woodpecker preferring bark crevices
To sharing a feeder with other birds,
Keeping itself to itself, independently,
Johnson has said the UK would place
Its own order as it's leaving the EU,
He has ducked out of the procurement scheme
And's branded ideological, as doctors
And nurses need protection of WHO
Standards, and Johnson's declined to participate.
Downing Street has offered no coherent
Explanation – it was Cummings who said No.
Johnson's said the UK did not receive
The EU's email, but there were meetings,
And all are clear that this is another lie.
    The Contain-Delay-Mitigate-Research
Strategy of the Government has failed
Because ministers did not follow the WHO's
Advice to "test, test, test" each suspected case,
And did not isolate and quarantine,
Did not expand testing capacity
In February, buy WHO-approved
PPE and set up training programmes
And guidelines to protect NHS staff.
And so there's panic among NHS staff
And patients, many die in intensive care.
Two hundred and sixty have died in one day
And the staff have no masks or equipment
And may be asymptomatic carriers
And may be infecting patients, there've been no tests
So no one knows. It's all a shocking mess,
And the virus has spread stealthily, unobserved.

Your poet thinks of the streets in the time of the plague
When under cover of darkness a body-collector
Wheeled a dead-cart on the cobbles between houses
Calling out, "Bring out your dead," and relatives
Dragged out and heaped a body on the cart.
It's quiet out there in the silent city streets,
Deserted shopping centres, chained-up playgrounds,
Almost empty skies, but a thousand have died.
There is a battle within hospitals
And care homes to save hundreds of gasping lives,
And the Government's not supplied ventilators,
Tests and protective equipment, plastic
Gloves are four years out of date, and stickers
Blot out expiry dates, and nurses are
Asking how the UK's so bad at testing
And supplying care beds and ventilators.
As the way things are going the UK
May soon have the worst death rate in Europe.

A new fine day and shocking news. Johnson
And Hancock, the Health Secretary, have both
Tested positively for Covid-19.
Johnson's had a temperature and a mild cough,
He has mild symptoms and will not leave
His flat above 11 Downing Street.
He is self-isolating for seven days,
An invalid who's surrounded by work,
And is that a death-watch beetle he can hear
Clicking behind old wood as it bores through
Timber tunnels and bumps its head while staff
Sit outside and hear sounds portending death?
He has been reckless and not carried out
His own advice, he has boasted that he's
Shaken hands with coronavirus patients
And has been too close on stairs with Hancock
And the Chief Medical Officer Whitty –

Who has also now tested positive.
The three key men are now isolating.
At PMQs Johnson and Hancock were
Not two metres apart, so did they get it
From negligence, from not following their own rules?
On Friday evening Johnson has rung Trump,
Who's asked, "How are you feeling?" Johnson's replied,
"We need ventilators." He's begged him to send
Ventilators he could have had from the EU.
Trump's said he must look after America first.
The Head of the NHS says six thousand
Are now in hospital with coronavirus,
And NHS staff will be tested this weekend
So they are not infecting their patients.
Death numbers are sometimes doubling each day
As all stay in their homes and, like horses
Peering over their stable doors, peep at the plague.
The UK economy's forecast to shrink,
A fourteen-per-cent fall in GDP,
The biggest slump in three hundred and ten years,
Since the Great Frost of 1708 to 9
(Europe's coldest winter in five hundred years),
And is heading for the deepest recession
Since the financial crisis, and a new hole
Left by lockdown and payments to workers
Totalling at least two hundred billion pounds.
The Bank of England's Ways and Means account
Has paid medical costs and businesses'
And furloughed workers' bridging cash, and soon
The Bank will create two hundred billion pounds
And lend it to its subsidiary company,
Its Asset Purchase Facility Fund, which will buy
New gilts from the Treasury's Debt Management Office
That will offset this balance that's due, so that
The Bank's in effect funded the virus.
But the Bank can't save the UK from recession

Or the jolt when it loses the EU's trade;
And all this has to be blamed on China.
Now the Government's blaming China's secrecy
For its own slowness in ordering tests
And declining to take part in the EU's
Bulk-purchase of ventilators and masks.
It's said art comes from quarrelling with oneself.
Your poet is constantly self-quarrelling,
And now he sees that to the extent that all
Are keeping clear of the virus and slowing
The peak of the curve, this self-isolation
Is a good thing; but to the extent that all
Are taking pressure off the NHS
Because there are too few ventilators when
Johnson declined to participate in a bulk-
Order via the EU and was rebuffed by Trump
And has now ordered thirty thousand from China
Where the virus originated and which has been
Less than transparent in sharing its true death rate
When the ventilators have yet to be made,
This self-isolating may involve several
Weeks' waiting for ventilators to arrive,
And then there is a lack of trained doctors
And nurses to use them as many have
Returned to Europe following Brexit,
And, it has to be said reluctantly,
Self-isolation is therefore a bad thing.
On Friday Cummings ran off down Downing Street
Like a lolloping hare bounding towards a gap,
And vanished, was not seen returning home.
It's now been announced he has the virus.
It's said he's rushed home to look after his wife
But developed symptoms and is very ill
With a high fever and spasms which made
The muscles lump and twitch in both his legs,
And he can only breathe in a shallow way.

The Prime Minister, Health Secretary and Chief
Medical Officer, who are in charge of keeping
The people from getting the virus, have all had it.
Three weeks till a hundred thousand tests a day
And they haven't found an antibody test
('Have I had the virus?') that works, only
An antigen blood test ('Have I got it?').
The testing's gone wrong and the UK's found
It has small bargaining power as an offshore island.
Another daily conference, and Vallance,
A grim harbinger of tidings of woe,
Like a crow bringing news of impending death,
Chief Scientific Adviser, says the UK
Is on the same trajectory as France,
And the curve must be kept below intensive-care
Capacity, and the numbers testing positive
(In a thousand tests for each day) will continue
For a couple of weeks and will then stabilise.
He's asked by Beth Rigby, were other countries
Faster in getting testing than the UK?
Germany tests seventy thousand a day
And the UK's aiming at twenty-five thousand,
And one in four doctors are now off work
Isolating without being tested
As there are no tests ready for the front line.
A cough or fever are the main symptoms
And social distancing's now being enforced.
The UK's becoming a police state,
Police are fining people for buying
The wrong thing (inessentials) when shopping,
Or resting on a bench to get their breath.
Wrong numbers of deaths have been broadcast
As there's a lag in verifying data
And last week's data may be given as this week's.
In the NHS there are half a million staff
And only ten thousand have been tested

And deaths are up by 563 in a day,
Like marigolds consumed by severe frost.
The UK did not take part in the EU
Order of equipment and ventilators
As it's leaving the EU and would make its own arrangements.
The Penlon machine, adapted from existing
Ventilator designs, more like a CPAP machine
Than a ventilator, has been approved by
The Medicines and Healthcare Products Regulatory
Agency, and is now on a production line.
Tens of thousands have been ordered, but only
Thirty will be delivered to the NHS next week.
An NHS supplier in Nantwich has said
It found twenty-five thousand ventilators
It could have supplied if there'd been a Government order.
The Defence Secretary's isolating with symptoms.
    Germany began testing in January.
The Government (especially the PM
Who vacillates) has dithered between herd
Immunity and lockdown, and testing is woeful.
Laboratory capacity's going unused.
How to end this lockdown nightmare without testing?
A quarter of the world is in lockdown,
Fifty thousand deaths globally till now,
Thirteen billion NHS debts written off.
    At a daily news conference, Hancock,
Bustling and pecking, busy as a starling,
Now back from isolation, says there'll be
A hundred thousand tests a day within
Four weeks, by the end of April, covering
Swab testing and blood tests, with a drive
From the diagnostic industry as the exit
From lockdown is mass testing, for the virus
Is in outbreaks in different parts of the country
And testing helps to identify where they are.
The Government has bought seventeen and a half

Million tests, but not all of them work well.
One identifies only one in four who have
The virus, three are free to infect patients.
Public Health England denies it bought these tests
Or any tests, it's embarrassing.
The Germans began testing earlier
As they had better diagnostics labs,
A hundred could produce tests in January.
The Government's sending tests to Germany
As they're processed and returned the same day.
The UK has to build labs like the pop-up
Nightingale hospitals gone up in a week
In London, Birmingham, Manchester and Glasgow.
The truth is, the UK wasted a month
Waiting for herd immunity on wrong advice
When Germany was testing and plotting
Where the virus was strongest so it could be suppressed.
  Fingers are now pointing at the PM
As he was missing from five Cobra meetings
Like a wizened fox lurking in its burrow.
It's said he doesn't know his limitations,
He's a generalist who doesn't do detail,
Drilling into science or resourcing,
And he's angry when his targets are not met,
Unrealistic, unfunded, can't-do goals.
He needs Hunt, Hague and Cameron in his Cabinet
For when the virus's second wave begins.
Health bureaucrats have collapsed the economy
By being slow to embrace testing, which some
See "as a side issue", the important thing
Being social distancing, economic shutdown.
The Government's tardy, incoherent
And constantly shifting, its wishful
Thinking hasn't thought through the economic consequences
Of indefinite lockdown, and how to resume.
It has a confused political direction,

There's managerial incompetence
And logistical inadequacy,
Hence tests have to be sent to Germany
As UK companies can't get quick results.
Arguably, lockdown has been reckless,
There's a manageable illness, and he has shut down the economy
At the wishes of health bureaucrats
Who are not considering the wider picture.
There's a case for lockdown to end after Easter
To get the economy going again, while there's
A mitigation strategy so those at risk
Continue their self-quarantining lives.
  Again the national clap. All round Britain
People come to their balconies and doors
And stop in supermarkets and offices,
In palaces and outside Downing Street
At 8pm and clap the NHS.
Johnson's risen from his sickbed looking dreadful,
Like a mangy dove that's feathers are sticking out
After surviving a sparrowhawk's attack,
And is standing by the door of 10 Downing Street,
Panic and struggling to cope in his bleary eyes,
Clapping with the Chancellor two metres apart.
He was raised to deny pain and discomfort
And personal inconvenience and his classical
Education taught him to be stoical.
Cummings has organised the national clap
For risking their lives while unprotected –
As a result of Government incompetence.
  Hancock again at the daily briefing.
Earlier he said Easter might be the peak
According to the model, now he rows back
In case large crowds go out this warm weekend
And increase transmission of the virus.
There are teams testing malaria and HIV
Drugs on patients with the virus to see if

A treatment can be found from an existing
Cure while a vaccine is sought for and found.
  Starmer's now Leader of the Opposition.
Carrie says she has been in bed for a week
With symptoms of the virus, when pregnant.
The UK has no diagnostics industry
And has to buy masks on the market, but
Fifty-four countries have placed export curbs
On stock, which means countries are competing.
The US takes masks ordered by Germany.
There's a form of piracy out there in the world.
  Another press conference, and journalists ask:
Can the PM, who's ill enough to be in
Hospital, be well enough to run the country?
And what's the plan to exit the lockdown?
Raab, Johnson's uncertain deputy, presides
And like an automaton says that Johnson's
In good spirits and is working "on full throttle".
He hasn't spoken to him since Saturday
When he was asked to deputise if need be.
It's a waste of time even listening.
He's sticking to a script, and no one knows.
  Neil Ferguson of Imperial College,
Whose report led Johnson to order lockdown,
Gobbling statistics like a strutting turkey
Agrees the curve will peak over Easter
With seven to twenty thousand deaths in all.
It looks as if there may be an escape
From lockdown at the end of May, a mix
Where the elderly and vulnerable stay indoors
But shops and offices reopen on amber
With green still months away – this would balance
Economic and medical concerns.
He agrees there's economic, social,
Financial and health harm in staying in,
And ways must be found to get back to normal

But millions of antibody tests bought
From China do not work as they only
Identified immunity in those
Who had been seriously ill in the past.
    The UK's lost a quarter of GDP,
It's two hundred billion pounds down, and it's
Said that lockdown is costing the UK
2.4 billion pounds a day.
Five and a half days' lockdown, thirteen billion
Pounds, the amount the UK Government
Paid to the EU budget every year –
Gone in one week, Monday to mid-Saturday.
The Henry Jackson Society, a foreign-policy
Think tank, concludes the G7 countries
Have a bill for 3.2 trillion pounds
Following Beijing's disinformation programme
Denying that the virus originated
In an animal 'wet market' in Wuhan,
And that Britain should sue the Chinese Government
For three hundred and fifty-one billion pounds
For covering up the accidental leak
Of bat viruses sold through a market
From Wuhan's Institute of Virology
That caused this new virus and pandemic.
The G7 could sue for 3.2 trillion pounds.
    There's division in the Government, there's blame.
It's failed to provide virus tests and personal
Protective equipment for NHS staff.
There's an absence of policy or plan.
Downing Street's irritated by Hancock's
Grandstanding and his failure to fulfil
Public promises on testing and equipment.
Cummings says he should have been sacked twenty times.
And Hancock's at odds with Gove, who's interfered
In the labour market and the Chief Executive
Of NHS England for non-supply,

He was too ready to believe his promises.
China, where the virus started, is now claiming
The credit for saving the rest of the world
By exporting testing kits – most don't work –
And face masks while denying it's to blame.
    After ten days of coughing and spluttering,
Johnson still looks dreadful and is still unwell
With Covid-19, it's about now when
Acute pneumonia begins and gasping for breath.
It's been said Johnson is the new Churchill,
But he doesn't look like it on his Twitter feeds.
He must know all his plans for a pro-Brexit
Golden Age appear fools' gold now the virus
Has taken three hundred and fifty billion pounds
From the nation's funds while the economy's stood still.
    Like a clucking contented hen who rules her roost
The Queen broadcasts to the nation from Windsor
In the run-up to Easter, only the fifth time
She's addressed the nation outside Christmas
In her sixty-eight-year reign, the previous times
Being on the death of Diana, the Gulf War,
The Queen Mother's death and her diamond jubilee.
She's the longest-serving Head of State in the world.
In a rallying call to the nation to be strong
She appeals to young and old: "I hope in the years
To come everyone will be able to take pride
In how they responded…. Those who come
After us will say that the Britons of this
Generation were as strong as any,
And that the attributes of self-discipline,
Of quiet good-humoured resolve and of fellow-
Feeling still characterise this country."
Morale needed lifting, harder times are to come.
    Barely has this been digested than we hear
Johnson has been taken to St Thomas'
Hospital while the Queen was speaking, struggling

With coronavirus ten days after
Testing positive on the twenty-seventh of March,
And will have tests on his high temperature.
It's not an emergency, he's been admitted
As a precaution as his symptoms are persistent.
But days ten to seventeen are the worst, when
The body's exhausted and its antibodies
Flood in and the immune system breaks down.
He's overweight, seventeen-and-a-half stone
When only five foot nine, with a BMI
(Body mass index) of thirty-six, and the obese
Suffer most from Covid's invasion of the lungs.
Johnson's on oxygen to help his breathing.
It's ironic that during a conference call
With over sixty manufacturers
On Monday the sixteenth of March, Johnson
Joked, trying to be jovial, that in making
Twenty thousand ventilators they would be part
Of an emergency project that would be known
As "Operation Last Gasp", a remark
That left them all extremely unimpressed.
That was three days after he declined to join
The EU Commission's bulk purchase for
Twenty-five EU member states and Norway
Of masks, gowns and ventilators at four
Meetings shown in EU minutes between
The thirty-first of January and the thirteenth of March.
And it was nine days before he contracted
Coronavirus, having been filmed on
A surprise visit to Kettering General Hospital
Just after midnight on February the twenty-eighth,
Shaking hands with coronavirus patients,
Believing he was unassailable
And invincible, and it may seem to some
That he brought it on himself with his recklessness.

And now shock news, at seven o'clock Johnson's
Condition has worsened, and he has been moved
To an intensive-care unit in case he should need
A ventilator to help his breathing.
He had breathing difficulties about seven,
And was given four litres of oxygen, a low dose,
But there's a national mortality rate for fifty-
To-sixty-year-olds who are intubated
Of forty-six per cent, which is worrying.
He was conscious, he'd have to be unconscious
To be connected to a ventilator.
A ventilator requires heavy sedation
As it takes over the breathing process.
The patient's given a paralysing agent
Like curare, which stops muscles working
So the machine can take over and do its work.
Patients lie flat and are turned onto their tummy
In cycles of sixteen hours. Meanwhile,
A needle in an artery allows
Blood levels to be monitored all the time.
His doctors are stabilising his breathing.
If he survives he will recover his strength
In a week to ten days. He is now in
A still position and in good spirits.
The man who put a false slogan on a bus –
"We send the EU three hundred and fifty million
Pounds a week, let's fund our NHS instead" –
Is being saved from death by the NHS.
He'll be monitored in depth and guarded
With twenty-four-hour specialist care against
Auto-immune disease, a cytokine storm
And against blood pressure failing and, when blood vessels
Constrict, the need for inotropic support.
Sedwill tells the Cabinet in a phone call:
It's very serious, he's critically ill.
Hearing the news on Mount Olympus, Hera

Looked accusingly at Zeus, and said softly,
"Dearest, have you decided to remove
Johnson from the UK's chaotic scene?"
Zeus stared into the distance and did not reply.
Hera continued, "I think that was a yes."
Staring ahead, Zeus said: "You know that plagues
Come and go regardless of what we do.
That was so in the time of Moses and Ramesses the Second.
This one seems to have been man-made in a lab
By the self-interested Syndicate to bring in
Their authoritarian New World Order
As a response to the blunder of Brexit.
But there's no doubt Europe would be a better place
If it could move from division to unity,
From nationalism to regional integration,
And the same applies to the world. We gods
Observe and try to plot a clear way through
The mess humankind creates, and this one man
Has created an enormous amount of mess."
O humankind, let this be a lesson.
The gods take note of all excessive pride.
He was puffed up with hubris from his win,
And swollen with atë, and now the gods –
With Zeus's permission – have brought him down,
With microbes that have put him in hospital
And have laid him low in intensive care,
Like a marigold impacted by hard frost,
Its watery cells frozen and its sap blocked,
A downfall that fills all with pity and terror.
Johnson rang Raab from his bed about seven
And asked him to deputise when necessary.
Raab's taken over the day-to-day running.
Johnson's now fighting for his life in intensive care
With assistance from a CPAP machine
And resembles a tranquillised donkey on a vet's table.
It may be ill-at-ease and nervous Raab,

Who came nowhere during last year's hustings,
Who is socially awkward and wooden
On TV and cold and even abrupt,
Like a startled goose that takes a few steps and honks,
Who reads his words and says nothing, is now
In charge of the day-to-day decisions.
At the press conference he either did not know,
Or was unwilling to be open about,
Johnson's condition, and may be hopeless.
The news has come as a tremendous shock.
The lack of openness has ended in disaster.
There's a national crisis deepening by the day
In health, politics and the economy,
Of wartime proportions and uncertainty,
And the UK may have to face it without the PM,
And with reduced authority, for Johnson
Had an eighty-seat majority and authority,
Whereas Raab is one of a now squabbling Cabinet,
And lacks their confidence among tensions.
And now it emerges Johnson has not got
Pneumonia, which is a relief at this stage.
Another news conference. Why has Germany
Done so much better than the UK – with a million
Tests while Public Health England has been slow,
And more plotting of where the infected are
And fewer deaths than the UK has seen?
Germany has a hundred and fifty labs
Working on testing of Covid-19
And contact tracing. The UK needs new labs,
Not just Public Health England's eight labs, but
NHS facilities, pharmaceutical
And commercial companies, and there's difficulty
In procuring chemicals. It's all a mess.
Trump says the UK's desperate for ventilators
And has asked for two hundred – he'll send them.
The Chief Medical Officer of the US

Has said the UK has a lot to learn
From Germany in testing for Covid-19
As deaths are at a much slower rate there.
    A new study by Seattle's Institute
For Health Metrics and Evaluation
Predicts that the UK's death toll will be
Sixty thousand due to the long delay
Caused by doing nothing and waiting for
Herd immunity until the twenty-third
Of March, when social distancing was imposed
After the study by Imperial
College in London showed that hospitals
Would be overwhelmed. There is anger in
The NHS that Government inaction
Has left medics exposed to the virus
Without personal protective equipment.
The UK's death toll will be the worst in Europe.
There's sympathy for the PM, who's
Still in intensive care but his response was wrong
And the death toll has to be laid at his door
As he turned his back on the EU's bulk purchase
And ignored German testing – and did nothing.
The UK's lack of preparedness is a case
Of incompetent manslaughter rather
Than deliberate premeditated murder.
    Now the Queen sends a message to Carrie
Saying she's in her thoughts (as she bears her child)
As she isolates from her husband-to-be
Stuck in intensive care with no visitors.
Johnson's the driving force behind Brexit,
And has called the lockdown that will kill it off
By highlighting Germany's preparedness.
    Questions at the daily conference, like finches'
Chattering when alerted to danger. Is it wise
To leave the EU during this crisis?
The Chancellor, whose plan's costing forty billion,

Is evasive, there will be a Cobra
Meeting with all the four devolved leaders,
The Mayor of London and scientific
Advisers the next day to discuss lockdown.
The question on the EU's reverberated,
And it now emerges that Johnson chose Raab
As his deputy because during the election
He was strong on Brexit and popular with Vote Leave –
Cummings, Johnson's chief adviser – and would take
Britain out of the EU if Johnson's incapacitated.
(But in a choice between Raab and Starmer,
Starmer would win and apply to rejoin.)
    The person who was supposed to defend
The UK population against the virus
And protect the life and liberty of all
Has been struck down having shaken the hands
Of coronavirus patients recklessly,
And he's applauded the NHS he hasn't
Defended by ordering tests and PPE,
His eyes rheumy, his face a sickly sheen
From his high temperature, looking confused
In a crisis he's completely unable
To handle. Now the Cabinet have agreed
To leave the decision to end lockdown
Until Johnson's health improves and he returns,
Which may be weeks away as he'll be off work.
His relentless energy and impatience
Is missed, and his rationale for what's being done.
It will be lockdown into May, at least.
    Global trade's heading for its worst year in
Decades, with falls of thirteen to thirty-two per cent,
And there'll be painful consequences for people
And companies worldwide, the WTO says.
The eurozone's thrashing out a four-hundred-
And-forty-billion-pound rescue package,
And the UK'S furlough scheme is set to cost

Forty billion pounds, says the Resolution Foundation.
Many think back to the wonderful decade
At the end of the last century and the beginning of this,
A summer of progress and prosperity
Ended by the financial crisis, just as
The Edwardian summer was ended by the Great War.
The noughties was our Edwardian decade
When it was very Heaven to be alive.
Now, beset by plague, your poet sits, like Milton
In Chalfont St Giles, who escaped the Great Plague
Of London to write there, with spring's green trees
Below this window and writes this anguished work
Of a Paradise lost with a virus outside
That is killing more than five hundred a day
Like spring flowers laid low by a severe frost,
Sitting in lockdown, society at a halt,
The economy frozen, all forbidden to leave
Their homes unless they're key workers.
He sits in harmony with the universe
And basks in spring sunshine under empty skies,
Near a quiet road, in air that makes the may
A vivid white in the hedgerows from his window,
And, eighty, is at ease with the world that has given
Him fifty-five books and much to be pleased
About despite the global pandemic
That ravages and decimates all nations.

The ship's heading back to England, dipping
And rising and rolling amid deep troughs,
Low in the water, overloaded with ore.
Waves swoosh across the deck and wet the fools.
Many feel ill, are they feeling seasick,
Are they landlubbers not used to a swell?
No, one or two have difficulty in breathing,
They're feverish and have a persistent cough.
The captain too is unwell, and suddenly

The passengers' health is of more concern than gold.
One of the fools, gasping for breath, has died.
The word's gone round, keep apart from each other.
Now there's misery on the deck as passengers
Clutch their bundles and, as the ship tosses
And rolls, dips and rises, try to stay well.

Canto X
Lockdown

Sing, Muse, of lockdown from the rampant virus,
And of how city- and town-centres fell quiet,
Sing of the eerie silence on the streets
As the economy crashed, sing of the deaths
In hospitals and care homes and at home,
Of how the PM was brought near to death.
And sing of how money not given to Europe
Was spent many times over in funding the costs
Of the virus and millions sitting at home.
Sing of universal misery and despair.
    Now Johnson's been moved out of intensive care
And back to a general ward at St Thomas'
Where he's receiving close monitoring
During his recovery. There's rejoicing
In the media that he's out of danger.
It was touch and go as to whether he'd survive,
He was more ill than the bulletins made out,
And he was saved by immigrant nurses
(Who he'll surcharge with six hundred and forty
Pounds for NHS treatment they may receive).
Even some who think him a liar and charlatan
Felt a wave of sympathy for the PM.
Good Friday, and he was very near death.
Easter Sunday, and he's risen again.
There's hope as there are now flattening curves
And slowing down of the rate of deaths,
Seven hundred and forty-five million pieces
Of PPE have been delivered to the front line
By the NHS, industry and armed forces
(Yet some places are still short of PPE
And nineteen doctors and nurses have died of the virus).
There's also an admission that he thinks

Lockdown's got out of hand. It wasn't the plan,
It was expected more schools would remain open
And more businesses, with some working at home.
Three million claimants for job retention
Were anticipated, not nine million.
Lockdown's costing 2.4 billion pounds
A day – fifty billion after three weeks.
There are fears lockdown may cost more lives than
The virus – one estimate says a hundred
And fifty thousand against twenty thousand –
And that a quarter of the British economy
Will have simply disappeared by the summer.
A third of the private-sector workforce
Will cost the taxpayer forty billion pounds
Each three months. There'll be a fall of fifteen
Per cent in the UK's economic output –
Without lost access to the single market.
It's 'lives versus money' and less than ten per cent
Of UK citizens will have caught the virus.
It's time to return to offices and shops
And minimise risks with social distancing.
    There's a decision to be taken as to when,
Like stable doors being opened and bridled horses
Being led out to resume their galloping,
Lockdown is lifted and under what terms.
The Government's paralysed as Johnson's
Power grab fused the Treasury, Cabinet Office
And Number Ten under the PM's control,
A triangle of power, and the PM has been
Removed from it in intensive care, while four
Of his inner circle of advisers –
Cummings (Thomas Cromwell to his Henry),
Lister (his loyal chief of staff), Gascoyne (his
Political secretary) and Cain
(His communications secretary) –
Have all been laid low by Covid-19.

There's a deficit of two hundred billion pounds
At least, if not three hundred and fifty,
And coping with it will affect the promises
Of more NHS staff and more police
And levelling up the North. The EU
Has its own difficulties, a five-hundred-
And-forty-billion-euro rescue deal
For all its member states and as much again
In a second wave, and focus on borders
And national survival and the UK's trade
With the EU is bound to be affected.
Ahead is a time when promises will be dumped,
And the glittering gold dandled before voters
Will be shown to be worthless iron pyrites,
Fool's gold, and competent Starmer is waiting
To point this out at the next election –
'You were offered gold and all you had was dross' –
And, when the lessons have been learned that togetherness
Is better than national isolation,
To take the UK back into the EU
As its trade needs the EU's customs union,
And also the single market, to head off
A new great depression and to prevent
The country sliding into irrelevance.
Easter Saturday and a news conference,
As yellow gorse burns in the Easter sun,
Bright furze that blazes as a prickly hedge,
And may, hawthorn blossom, is brilliant white
And blossoming cherry trees dazzle like snow,
There's a chorus of questions to Priti Patel
About the delay in getting PPE
To front-line staff and the poor testing results –
One thousand five hundred a day at the new centre
When it's to be a hundred thousand by April's end.
There's huge disquiet at the Government's slowness.
Like a screech owl screeching to portend death

But also blaming to hide its mistakes,
Hancock speaks of the "misuse" of PPE.
Doctors who have no PPE are furious.
Johnson's told colleagues that he owes his life
To the staff at St Thomas' Hospital –
Two nurses from Portugal and New Zealand
Watched over him and gave him oxygen
On a CPAP machine they monitored
At night and kept him breathing and alive.
He's had a profound experience of near-death
And may have changed his attitudes towards
Immigrants and public services. Time will tell.
He's been discharged and's recovering at Chequers.
(Seven in ten intensive-care patients experience
Memory and concentration problems for years
Afterwards, and have trouble with processing
Multiple stimuli such as group conversation.)
Now there's more 'news' – fake news? – of the virus.
It was allegedly identified
By Shi Zhengli on January the second
In gene-sequencing and related tests
As originating in caves in Yunnan
A thousand miles north of Wuhan and – misinformation? –
It was found on January the fourteenth
That the new virus could infect people.
News was suppressed, a whistle-blowing
Doctor, Li Wenliang, was forced to sign a retraction
Of "untruthful statements". Articles now ask:
Is coronavirus a biological
And economic warfare operation?
Did Russia or China release the virus
To finish off Western capitalism?
Kissinger hints at the Third World War, he says
Failure to safeguard the liberal world order's
Principles – mainly order, security,
Economic well-being and justice –

In the virus crisis "could set the world on fire".
Has the whole world been locked down to fend off
A military operation against the West?
It now comes out that Bill Gates' pandemic
Exercise on October the eighteenth
Predicted sixty-five million deaths from
A respiratory virus. There is now
A new global industry for selling
Tests, PPE, antivirals and vaccines.
There's talk of the virus having HIV
Insertions to destroy the immune system.
There's also talk of English exceptionalism,
Of feeling superior to other nationalities
And so pursuing a different strategy
Towards the virus from that of other nations;
And herd immunity, which led to late lockdown
And is on course, now the UK has passed
Ten thousand deaths, to bring to the UK
The highest number of deaths anywhere.
There's talk that in taking the UK out of the EU
Johnson has given the English a false sense
Of exceptionalism that has resulted in
His disastrous response to Covid-19.
There's talk of the Queen's broadcast to the nation
Identifying national characteristics –
Self-discipline, quiet resolve – as challenging
Liberal universalism which removes identity
From place, tradition, history and culture.
But universalism's for all humankind
And sees all nation-states as transient
As the city-states of the Renaissance time,
And all city- and nation-states and unions
As growing into a glorious World State.

Like a wolf baring its fangs and savaging,
Now the press has turned on the Government.

The UK did not take part in a 1.3-
Billion-pound order for masks, gowns and gloves
To protect staff against Covid-19
Despite shortages in the NHS.
It missed three opportunities: the EU's
Procurement of February the twenty-eighth
Did not attract suppliers. It was relaunched
On the fifteenth of March, and the UK took part
In a meeting on the nineteenth. It did not attend
A meeting on the twenty-fifth of March
When it was agreed requirements must be notified
By the next day. The UK is not involved
In the joint procurement of lab equipment.
Care homes are in uproar: more than twelve thousand
Outbreaks of the virus, seven thousand
Five hundred deaths not in the official figures,
The elderly airbrushed from overall numbers
As Covid patients were sent from hospitals
Into care homes to infect residents,
Care workers not tested and lacking kit,
Some on minimum wage being coughed over,
Staff isolating, care workers going into homes
Without protection, old people dying
Surrounded by unprotected staff, some
Left alone due to understaffing and separated
From their loved ones as they struggle to breathe.
    The Office of Budget Responsibility
Funded by the Treasury to make forecasts
Say a three-month lockdown will cause the economy
To shrink by thirty-five per cent this spring
And unemployment will rise to ten per cent.
Lockdown will cost forty-five billion pounds a month,
GDP will be down thirteen per cent for the year.
The amount that Government will have to borrow will rise
From fifty-five to three hundred billion pounds,
A sixfold increase, the biggest borrowing

And single-year deficit since World War Two,
The deepest slump since 1720
(The South Sea Bubble), two million unemployed;
An economic slump unparalleled
Since the Great Depression of the 1930s,
The deepest crash for nearly a century,
The biggest recession for three hundred years.
The anti-virus measures are going to cost
A vast sum – more than three hundred billion pounds
And more to follow for leaving the EU –
And cancel out the decade of austerity
That reduced the national debt, which will now grow
To more than the total value of the economy,
And all that effort has gone and the UK
Will be repaying this borrowing for years to come.
And doing all this is the man at the helm
Of an incompetent, blundering, ideological
Government that won't have any truck with the EU's
Bulk-purchase orders, and so thousands have died,
Who is still sick from the virus and is stuck
With glittering promises voters believed
And he now has to turn into Fort-Knox gold.
    Like a horse at last released from its stable
Johnson walks in the grounds of Chequers, and now
The sky is bluer, pollution haze has gone,
The air is cleaner, waters are clearer,
Streets and flight paths quieter, wildlife happier.
The planet is cleaner and healthier,
Pausing civilisation's improved the environment.
He's with pregnant Carrie and their dog, recovering
From his encounter with death which nearly snuffed out
The architect of Brexit, wondering
If he should express his thanks to the NHS
By appearing to give it three hundred and fifty
Million pounds a week as promised on the bus,
By settling its 13.4-billion-pound debt

(Owed by Government-owned NHS agencies
To the Government, a bookkeeping exercise).
Isolating from figures he doesn't want to hear,
Having let scientists shut down the economy
As the NHS was underprepared, he looks ahead.
His hopes for a global Britain that can lead the world
And finance many initiatives have faded,
The cost of this crisis will last a generation.
All economies will be at least five per cent
Smaller, and that will affect the amount they trade.
There can't be free-trade agreements on time
With the EU – both Barnier and Frost
Have the virus; the US or Japan,
Australia, New Zealand, Canada,
Singapore and Uruguay. There's now
A protectionist, nationalistic mood
And some blame globalisation for the virus.
There's no global body that's managing
And co-ordinating the virus's spread,
Not the G20 or the World Health Organization.
If there's no EU extension, there'll be 'no deal'
And trading on World Trade Organization rules.
With a four-hundred-billion-pound deficit
And calls for austerity for many years,
And the accusation – instinctive knowledge –
That Johnson, who's never run a business,
Crashed the economy as the NHS
Was unprepared for a new pandemic.
    For two days of his seven in hospital
His lungs had been overwhelmed by the virus,
His life had hung in the balance, he'd fought,
He'd coughed up congealed blood, Covid-19
Had attacked his digestive system, he
Was barely able to eat and lost a stone
And now was a frail shadow of his former self,
Unable to walk more than a few hundred yards

Without stopping to put his hands on his knees
Or lift anything heavier than a small parcel.
He was sleeping twelve hours a night and napping
An hour in the morning, an hour in the afternoon,
Yet at the end of each day he was still exhausted,
Washed out and completely lacking in energy.
He's still short of breath and is deeply fatigued.
It affected his nose and throat, his lungs, his heart
And blood vessels (made him prone to blood clots),
His liver and kidneys, and also his brain
(Made him prone to strokes, seizures and confusion).
He was told that he could develop a throat
Infection that may last a week as his
Immune system had been very weakened
And he could lose his voice. He should really
Take six weeks off, and not think about
The decision he had to make, when to lift
The lockdown – and if too soon risk a second
Wave of the virus, and if too late risk
A dire long-term economic impact –
A hard choice for someone in the best of health,
Let alone having to make it while suffering the virus,
Seeing the world through a sick-of-the-virus prism,
And having to bear in mind that to the healthy
The impact of lockdown could be much worse
Than the havoc spread by coronavirus.
It took four years for GDP to recover
From the Great Depression of the 1930s,
And this economic crash is more dramatic.
Ahead is a decade of misery and strife
Compounded by the damage from Brexit.
He was late in locking down and very slow
In organising equipment and testing,
He's technically responsible for many
Of the forty thousand deaths (counting care homes).
It's easier to talk to the dog than think of such things.

The country's national debt is now more
Than the value of the economy, the UK
Is technically bankrupt. He's leaving the EU
So the country can be on its own, and the virus
Has blown away prospects of new trade deals,
And the illusion of new national gold.
Four years of campaigning in the referendum,
On the hustings and in a general election
Have taken him to Downing Street, but what
He wanted to do's been removed, and he's unwell
With unknown consequences to his body from
His encounter with death, and the gold he saw
Four years back has turned out to be fools' gold.
The Black Death's fall-out lasted forty years,
And o for a world rule that would fund all our needs,
A World State that would act promptly and keep
Us all safe from new deadly viruses.

Morning in Chequers, and the papers scream
Lockdown has paralysed the economy.
Now the figures have congealed and are startling:
Seven trillion pounds lost to global GDP
In this year and the next, and the UK
Will borrow two hundred and seventy-three
Billion pounds this year, two hundred and eighteen
More than expected, even three hundred
Billion, twice what's spent each year on the NHS
(Against a hundred and sixty billion pounds
Borrowed in 2009), and forty-three
Billion was borrowed last year and eighty-eight
Billion more's expected this year (election promises).
It's half a billion a day to furlough staff,
Every day of lockdown costs 1.5
Billion pounds due to lower tax receipts
And higher spending, economic output
Falls two billion every day of lockdown.

The UK's output will fall 12.8 per cent
This year, the OBR say, against six per cent
In 2008 to 9. The national debt
Will increase by four hundred billion pounds
To 2.2 trillion pounds next year. Oil
Price will fall fifty-three per cent this year.
    Politicians, including Johnson, have let SAGE,
Scientists from the Scientific Advisory Group
For Emergencies (an acronym suggesting
Wisdom and intelligence), a group of a hundred
And twenty scientists, some unnamed, to make
All the big decisions, and they have overlooked
The economy. Only a hundred and twenty
Thousand have died worldwide from the virus
Against two to six hundred thousand from seasonal flu
And two hundred and eighty thousand from H1N1
In 2009, and the economy's suffered.
A Great Depression looms, there's hardship ahead,
An L-shaped, not a V-shaped, recession
Which stays down and does not bounce back and could be
As bad as the time of the bubonic plague.
There's permanent economic damage ahead.
    O Johnson, you turned your back on Europe,
Dreaming of gold, and what you now have is this,
Far worse than if you had stayed in Europe, and what
You hold is now seen by all to be fools' gold.
And now your promised gold has turned to dross,
All the promised gains were never there as
The UK turned its back on half its income
And dreamt of trade deals it would never find,
But now, even this glittering gold has gone,
Ravaged by coronavirus which has swept
Three hundred billion of new prosperity,
Hugely weakened the economy, and set
It back into a recession far worse
Than in the financial crash of 2008,

With services, the UK's strength, much worse
Than in 1996. If all had known
This pandemic would hugely disrupt trade
Would any wise person have planned new obstructions
To goods flowing between the UK and Europe?
Now the virus has disrupted the timetable
Of Brexit, with both Barnier and Johnson
Falling ill with the virus and having to isolate,
Which has set the discussions back and edged
Johnson towards 'no deal' as Disaster
Capitalism wants, so he'll leave transition on time
Before the UK has to pay towards
The post-viral reconstruction of Europe.
    Another daily briefing, and three more weeks
Of lockdown as (ministers quietly admit)
There is no strategy for ending lockdown,
And ministers are waiting for Johnson
To return to work and take charge of policy
Like a pride of lions bereft of its pride male
Who will return and protect all in the pride.
The scientists are effectively in charge.
No one will take a political risk,
The Cabinet's in a holding pattern,
Even though the peak was reached on April the eighth,
Waiting for Johnson to say what happens next
And there's evidence the cure's worse than the disease,
And Johnson has been told by his doctors
He risks killing himself if he returns too soon.
So it's lockdown, ramp up testing and hope
The epidemic's life is just eight months,
That it will shrink quickly and so avoid
Economic collapse, then reopen
While logging every case of infection.
It may take many months for a safe vaccine
To work and be got out on a mass scale
And bring about a herd immunity.

The policy is hoping for the best.
The man who led the UK out of Europe
Is sitting like a shell, unable to think,
And all are waiting upon his next word,
Like waiting for a fool to speak wisdom
And point a finger to a direction.
The Bank of England's Governor has said
The UK may be heading for its worst
Three months since records began, with a third
Of the economy lost as the OBR
Has said that there may not be a bounce-back.
Now there's news all medical staff must wash and re-use
Their PPE as there's not enough to go round,
And will it still be virus-contaminated?
Some have been told to use aprons instead of gowns.
It's left all doctors in consternation.
Some question the Government's motivation
In backing the national clap for the NHS.
Could it be to distract attention from,
And cover up, its blunder in missing out
On the European Commission's bulk-purchase
PPE order? Now forty thousand deaths
Are expected in the UK, the highest in Europe.
Now the Government's blaming China's secrecy
For its own slowness in ordering tests
And declining to take part in the EU's
Bulk-purchase of ventilators and masks.
There's no strategy to leave lockdown until
Johnson returns – Cabinet government's collapsed.
The PM is the first among equals,
The rest should be able to reach a decision without him.
But they don't want to take responsibility,
And leave that decision until he returns.
US scientists have found that sunlight, heat
And humidity act to disinfect the virus.
It struggles to survive in warm temperatures

And humid environments such as beaches.
Trump, at a news conference, recommends
Injections of disinfectant, and is mocked
For suggesting by implication that people
Should take swigs of bleach, which would be lethal.
But above all, self-isolating lockdown
Has paralysed the UK's economy.

The ship has reached calmer waters and yet
The passengers are suffering, some gasp for breath.
Two more have died, their bodies have been stripped
Of their clothes and flung overboard to the fish and gulls.
This is not how things were meant to turn out.
All try to isolate on the cramped deck
And snatch sleep when they can, when so many,
Short of breath, are labouring to gulp air.
Some are sweating from a high temperature,
From a fever, not the warmth of the sun
That sparkles on the waves so beautifully.
Word had gone round, the plague is on the ship.
Did they catch the plague in Narragonia?
The Ship of Fools, the Ship of State, is now
A plague ship, best left on the tossing waves.

Canto XI
Questionings

Sing, Muse, of bewilderment at the virus,
Of questioning why there's a high number of dead,
Of secret fears of going out, of shock
That a Western way of life has suddenly stopped.
Sing of shielding, isolating at home,
And sing of yearning to go back to as it was,
And recognition that will never be.
Sing of sorrow, resolve and endurance.
    Now there is questioning of the virus.
Humans, locked up like caged egg-laying hens,
Are pondering on the virus that has caused
Their close confinement within cage-like walls.
Is it a plague with a natural cause,
Coming from Nature like all diseases,
Or has it a laboratory origin?
It's said the virus was manufactured
At the Wuhan Institute of Virology's
Lab in a research project co-funded
By the US to find out if animal
Viruses could be altered to affect humans.
A Norwegian-British research team claims
That Covid-19 has been engineered
In a joint US-Chinese research project
And is in effect a weaponised pathogen
That escaped from a Biosafety Level-4 lab.
It began as a benign coronavirus
And has been modified to integrate
Spike proteins so it can enter human cells
By attacking ACE-2 receptors in lungs
And to integrate a protein from HIV,
GP141, which impairs the immune system,
And to involve nanotechnology

To allow it to remain airborne longer.
Jehovah's Witnesses see coronavirus
As the Great Plague that heralds in the end-days,
Armageddon, and they'll only be saved
If their belief in Jehovah's strong enough.
    And thinking back to 9/11, when,
It's since been established, the Twin Towers
And WTC7 were demolished
After Cheney stood down the air defence system
For a 'training day', giving the pilots
An unopposed flight path over New York,
Believing they'd evaded US defence,
So America and world public opinion
Would support an invasion of Afghanistan
Organised by the self-interested Syndicate,
Dynastic billionaires behind the New
World Order that was looting the earth's resources,
Your poet wonders if this virus has come
From the same stable. The CIA informed
Israel of the virus in November,
And the US and UK have had the most
Deaths until now (though Brazil's not far behind),
And the European countries most affected
Have had populist nationalism,
And China has dominated world trade –
Was the virus to target the US,
UK and European nationalism,
And create mistrust regarding Chinese trade?
And with every country now deeply in debt
After lockdowns, will Rothschilds, the world's bankers
Who own or control every central bank
Except for three, make billions from lending
To impoverished governments throughout the world?
"*Cui bono*," Cicero asked, "to whose advantage?"
    Just as farmers with animals on hills or fields
Resent self-interested break-aways,

The New World Order want to see the back
Of Trump and of Johnson and his Brexiteers
And of undercutting in trade by China,
And revive its financial grip on the world –
Did a New-World-Order agent working
At the US end of the co-funded project
Release the virus into the US
And the UK, where it surfaced early
And through travellers infected Icelanders
According to Iceland's test-trace-isolate?
Were the targets of Covid-19 the US,
European nationalists and Chinese trade?
Your poet shakes his head in disbelief
Just as he did at the time of 9/11
(Before he wrote of the hidden demolition
Of the Twin Towers and WTC7
In *Armageddon*, book 1, holding
A mirror up to events to reveal Truth).
There's no evidence but it all feels right,
It can't be ruled out they've done it again.
    How early did Iceland catch the virus?
An Icelandic professor, Stefansson,
Interviewed, says that Iceland's 'test and trace',
Which successfully reduced cases to one,
Has established the virus was brought to Iceland
In December or January across
The Alps by people skiing in Austria
And Italy, and then by travellers from Great Britain,
And so it seems the virus was widespread
In Great Britain at a very early stage
And the UK was one of the first countries
To be infected, which is why the death rate's so high.
As the UK was so early, did something covert happen?
    Did the self-interested New World Order behind
9/11, fed up with the rise of populist
Nationalism in many EU states,

See Johnson's election victory coming from polls
And nationalist Trump's re-election looming,
And release the virus in Wuhan, to blame China
And halt Brexit – as the UK economy
Would be ruined by the virus, and a 'no deal'
Following soon after would be catastrophic?
Has the UK been a Syndicate target?
Has the world been given a jolt to move away
From populist nationalism and return
To support for a world government of self-interested
Dynastic families (such as Rothschilds,
Who will make billions lending their trillions
To governments bankrupted by the virus)?
There's no evidence, your poet, who supports
A democratic World State that will control
Self-interested *élite*s, surveys the scene
As a possibility, and then looks away
From such an alternative view of history
And won't look back until there's some evidence.
    Like farmers protecting their livestock's health
EU trade negotiators have rejected
The UK's demand that UK-based testing labs
Should certify their exports to the EU,
Their cars, chemicals and pharmaceutical products.
These will have to be certified by EU-based
Authorities, which will add to UK businesses' costs.
The EU won't let a third country set
Conditions for access to the single market.
Barnier says the trade talks between the UK
And the EU are about to collapse
Into 'no deal', trade on WTO terms,
As the UK won't agree a level playing-field
With tax, labour rights, state aid and the environment,
And access to the UK's fishing waters,
All under the existing conditions.
The UK's moved teams of civil servants

Back from Covid-19 to plan for 'no deal'
Under the Government's XO (exit operations)
No-deal planning committee, chaired by Gove.
The Treasury sees a trade deal with the US,
With whom the UK does fifteen per cent of its trade,
As bringing in 3.4 billion pounds
While the loss of forty-three per cent of its trade
With the EU would lose a hundred and twelve billion.
  All want to restore world control of pandemics,
And so all want to combat populism in Europe,
And the virus has wiped out a hundred and sixty thousand
Older voters who let in the nationalists –
And Rothschilds, the world's banker which owns or
Controls a hundred and ninety central banks,
Can lend trillions to desperate countries.
Just as the Syndicate exposed the US
To 9/11, allowed al-Qaeda's planes
To strike by standing down its air defence
For a 'training exercise' which never happened,
And detonated controlled explosions
To bring three towers down so Western voters
Would support going into Afghanistan to defend
Oil pipelines and so increase its wealth,
So now has the same Syndicate latched on
To the US-Chinese corona project
In the Institute of Virology, Wuhan
Funded by the US National Institutes
Of Health for 3.7 million dollars,
A five-year project on bat coronaviruses,
And for another 3.7 million dollars,
Another project from 2019
Which did "gain-of-function" (modifying)
Research on a benign bat coronavirus
And made it more airborne and attach itself
To the ACE-2 receptors in human lungs
And with HIV GP141

Swamp immune systems and arrange for it
To escape from the Biosafety Level-4 lab
In Wuhan around the sixth of October
2019, so roadblocks were erected
From the fourteenth to the sixteenth round the Institute,
Filling the car parks of Tianyou Hospital,
To target populist nationalist Trump
And Johnson's Brexiteers and populists
In France, like Le Pen, Spain, Italy, Austria
And side-swipe Iran for fighting in Syria
And of course China for dominating trade,
To present China to the world as untrustworthy?
Was the US funding and involvement
Of the NIAID (the National
Institute of Allergy and Infectious Diseases)
Under Dr Fauci, advisor to every
US president since Reagan, and the British
New-York-based Daszak, to explore the cause of diseases
And animal-to-human transmissions,
And did this 'bio-weapon' somehow escape
By accident from its lab or by design,
Was it released to decimate voters
And create markets in which bankers could lend trillions,
Get the United States of Europe back on track,
And the US, the EU and China all
Supporting the Syndicate's New World Order?
They've spent fifty billion dollars on making
A town in Saudi Arabia automated
And they've got all Estonian citizens
Carrying one digital card, which fulfils
Many functions from passport to ID and banking.
They've invested too much to see it snatched away
And the virus has given them an opportunity
To raise unlimited funds for a world government
And implement a new AI programme,
Bring in their New World Order for a self-interested

World government with control of the world's resources.
There's been a cover-up, so who was doing it –
The Chinese, Americans or the New World Order
Who exposed the US defences on 9/11?
And why were Americans funding Wuhan lab research?
    China has been ahead of the US
With a more effective system of government,
Greater global popularity and a stronger
Economy, the US's economic
Primacy is at an end as it has put
Protectionism above free trade. It's ahead
In artificial intelligence, robotics,
Life sciences and space technology,
And its China-centred globalisation
Has made it invincible to the divided West
And the rules-based international order.
Now China's rejuvenation's been halted.
Deng crept up on the West without a challenge.
Xi reasserted the Communist Party's
Dominance and crushed all dissidents,
Jailed rivals and grabbed intellectual
Property, threatened cybersecurity.
There were demonstrations against this in Hong Kong,
And now he's suppressed the facts about the outbreak
Of the virus in Wuhan and it has spread
Round the planet and made the whole world ill –
And despite mass death Xi's saying he's saved
The world, and the US army is to blame.
It's rivalry between two superpowers.
And Trump's stopping funding the WHO
As its Head is pro-Chinese and part of this.
But withholding three hundred million dollars a year
Will not help the dying in Asia and Africa.
And the UK wants the Chinese government's State-
Owned Huawei to control the UK's 5G,
Trading investment for being at the mercy

Of a brutal and autocratic government
That will spy on Britain and steal all
Its military and commercial secrets.
The "Golden Era" of relations between
The UK and China has come to an abrupt end.
    The UK's moving away from the "Golden Era"
Of Sino-British relations under Cameron
And Osborne, moving away from Huawei
As the Telecom's Security Bill won't get through
Parliament, to friendly powers with know-how –
Japan, South Korea, Finland, Sweden
And the Five Eyes of the US, Canada,
Australia, New Zealand and Britain –
And away from an expansionist power that's repressing
Hong Kong with a new security law that will lock
Up protesters as subversives, as in China,
And use the cyber world to make more prevalent
Surveillance, spying and intellectual-property theft.
Raab used to be a Foreign-Office lawyer
And as Foreign Secretary he has continued
The previous line without thinking strategically
About the UK's role in a global world
But now China's virus has made him reassess.

The Government's still grappling with Europe.
The managing director of the IMF
Has appealed to the UK to extend
The transition period to avoid adding
To the global uncertainty caused by the virus.
But the UK's Frost has said that the UK
Will not extend the negotiating period
For a Brexit trade deal beyond December
The thirty-first, when it will finally leave
The single market and customs union.
He says a delay would keep the UK bound
By evolving EU laws when it needs to control

Its own affairs. Macron wants the EU
To proceed towards "ever-closer union"
And the UK is against such unity
And does not want to pay towards the fund
To help Italy and Spain to recover
From the economic blight caused by the virus.
It'll take five years for the UK to recover
From the economic crisis the virus leaves.
    Like a farmer protecting his flocks and shoals
Barnier says the UK is dithering,
Wasting time and saying that there will be
No extension to Brexit's transition
And blocking a deal on fishing waters
Without which the trade talks cannot begin,
And is refusing to implement its commitment
To preventing a hard Irish border by
Doing customs checks in the Irish Sea.
    But having told British voters that leaving
On the thirty-first of January to Big Ben's bongs
Was the only thing that mattered – the climax
Of the opportunistic project that shook up
The EU's political landscape, brought
A big election victory and confirmed
Johnson's ascendency – it is now clear
The UK's paying a great price for being
Distracted by Brexit in January
When he and his ministers did not pay
Enough attention to the migrating virus,
And ensure the UK's health and social
Services were prepared and equipped for
The looming emergency. And now, at this time
Of lockdown and economic shut-down,
It's unwise to risk further disruption
To vital trade, business and investment,
And have a second catastrophe approach,
A jump off the 'no-deal' cliff when it's vulnerable.

Like caring managers of an enormous farm
The EU leaders won't spend effort and resources
On a rushed negotiation to suit Johnson's
Artificial timetable, their priority
Is Europe's reconstruction and the UK,
Accused of dragging its feet by Barnier,
Has no coherent plan for a free-trade
Agreement, not even a bare-bones one.
The Brexiteers have been that irresponsible
And did not factor in an unforeseen
Crisis such as a war or pandemic
That could eliminate free-trade markets
And make the EU's single market more
Vital to its survival and well-being.
The UK has withdrawn from an alliance
That originated in geography
And is anachronistically seeing
Its future as a nation that's a walled city.
A transition extension has to be agreed
By June the thirtieth, the chasm is there.
It's not a policy, it's the failure
Of irresponsible political leaders
Who've failed to see Brexit was delusional
And dishonest, and now live in a fantasy
That's become a collective nightmare and risks
Additional damage to a country struggling
To survive the pandemic. The only rational course
Is to extend transition for a year or two
To make time for a proper trade agreement
Based on measures to rebuild a pan-European
Economy vital for UK prosperity.
Intransigence towards an extension
In those who want to 'take back control' means
Kicking away human, economic and social
Props as the national edifice trembles
And people suffer and die – which is not common sense.

'Get Brexit done' was the election mantra,
It's not done until a trade agreement's reached
And that means co-operating with the EU and extending.
    There's questioning of lockdown, it was too slow.
Starmer says the Government has been too slow
To enter the lockdown, too slow to increase
The number of people being tested, too slow to get
NHS staff the equipment they need to keep them safe.
The Government ignored warnings from scientists
And lost five weeks at the beginning of the outbreak.
The Prime Minister has been at the helm and has had
A three-hour meeting with Raab, and criticism
Of the handling of the crisis is aimed at him.
The Government's sleepwalked into pandemic catastrophe.
Resentful prisoners held behind closed doors
Like force-fed, factory-farmed cows, pigs, turkeys
And chickens raised for meat mutter at their lot.
Guidance on equipment's driven by shortages,
Not clinical evidence. There's a shortage of oxygen.
Hospitals can't pump oxygen around in the right quantities.
The hospitals weren't adequately prepared.
The health of the economy impacts on society,
And lockdown has created new problems.
    The scientists' support for lockdown has evolved.
At first they advised that the way forward
Was herd immunity, when sixty per cent
Of the country contract the disease and, when recovered,
Their antibodies protect themselves and the rest
Of the entire British population.
This was abandoned when Imperial
College showed that there would be two hundred
And fifty thousand deaths along the way
As the British crowded together as if at
Cheltenham races. The idea was then
Many would die – hence the pop-up Nightingale
Hospitals which now have many empty beds,

Doctors and nurses having gone back to Europe –
And not that they'd need tonnes of gowns, masks, ventilators.
Now social distancing will have to remain
Until there's a vaccine and the British
Can rise like Shelley's lions after slumber.
Now it's reported that Cummings – before
He ran off down Downing Street and vanished,
And was said to have the virus – has been
Taking part – listening in on – the scientific
Advisory meetings, arguing for lockdown
And the Government's *omerta* on even discussing
How it intends to lift the restrictions.
There are concerns that his political voice
Is polluting the scientific evidence
And contributing to the continuation of lockdown.
There are two ways out of lockdown: a vaccine,
Which will take many months, or testing to hunt down
The virus, but tests are in short supply.
Johnson has to decide: how much can lockdown
Be eased while keeping R (reproductive rate)
Under 1 (each victim infects less than one other)
And enough critical-care beds empty?
Questions to the Government on equipment.
Why have there been such chronic shortages
Of protective clothing for the doctors and nurses
When so much PPE has been sold abroad?
Why is the Government so adrift from its target
Of a hundred thousand tests every day?
And what's going on in care homes? There's a five-
Fold increase in deaths in a week to more
Than a thousand. The virus is spreading like wildfire.
America has sixty-thousand deaths,
More than it had in the Second World War.
The UK has twenty-six thousand deaths,
More than died in London during the Blitz,
And will have the worst death rate in Europe.

There are three million cases round the world.
There are questions about the failure to take part
In the EU's procurement scheme. Now
The head civil servant in the Foreign Office has said
Ministers were fully briefed on the scheme
And it was a political decision not to take part,
It wasn't the case of an email going astray.
There are questions over lockdown. The Government fears
A second wave which may undo the present work.
Every three months the UK remains in lockdown
Will cost the Exchequer forty-five billion pounds.
It's said Johnson is not making decisions
But he's re-engaged by ringing Trump about
A joint approach and a free-trade agreement,
And he will ring the Queen later this week.
    Like squabbling parakeets pecking at each other
To take possession of *their* nut feeder,
The Cabinet has split over lifting
Lockdown, scientific advice is that easing
Will increase the number of cases. Vital
Equipment was shipped to Italy, Germany, Spain,
Turkey and China instead of the NHS.
Time was wasted on ordering ventilators
Which can't be used on coronavirus victims,
Who have athlete-like shortage of oxygen.
Eighty per cent die after using ventilators.
Deaths peaked between the fourth and eighth of April,
So infection rose three weeks before then.
The actual peak was well before lockdown.
    Like an indignant jackdaw kaaarring at something wrong
A report in *The Sunday Times* condemns Johnson.
He missed five Cobra (Cabinet Office
Briefing Room A) meetings over five weeks.
He did not chair meetings or work weekends,
He didn't do urgent crisis planning
And did not take the pandemic seriously

Before it arrived in the UK, and so the country
Was woefully unprepared. He was fixated
On Brexit, distracted by his private life
At critical moments when the pandemic spread.
He ducked crucial decisions, went missing in action.
He went to sleep at the wheel and the country crashed
And thousands died as consequential loss.
The shortage of ventilators and PPE,
Predicted in 2016 if there were a pandemic,
Happened. Because the NHS was unprepared
The UK was doomed to lock down by austerity
And Johnson's hubris and incompetence.
    He's skipped five weeks of Cobra meetings
On the virus, ignored calls for protective gear
And was deaf to the scientists' warnings.
The military are aghast at the lack of planning
And the logistics in the delivering
Of masks, aprons, gloves assigned to hospitals
Without regard for need, some oversupplied
And some woefully short of everything.
He's taken a back seat in the planning.
The Sunday Times investigator asks,
Did his February failings cost thousands of lives?
And of a hundred NHS and care workers?
The Government's response was proportionate to the risk
Until it lost its nerve on Mother's Day
And gave in to clamour for a lockdown
Which damaged the UK more than the virus,
And has wrecked the economy for good.
And amid this negligence the key members
Of the Government caught Covid-19.
    Like a squirrel that's been blocked and thumps its tail
Johnson is furious, he is livid.
Gove, who said just before the referendum,
"Britain's had enough of experts", is asked
About the inexpert chaos he's caused

Along with Johnson and Cummings, in lack of tests,
Care deaths, PPE running out, the key
Workers in the Government including the PM
Missing in action, then ill with the virus,
And stutters, "The PM is inspirational,"
And repeats there's no plan to lift the lockdown.
He may have said there's no plan. It will be said
If the death rate falls it's proof lockdown's working,
If it rises then there'll be more lockdown.
Everything's a shambles, the English think
They're better than they really are, and need
Experts to place the orders and deliver.
  A hundred doctors and nurses and care staff
Have died of the virus, from lack of PPE,
Just as during the First World War young soldiers
Armed with single-shot-stop-and-reload rifles
Charged German machine-guns across a field.
The headlines are on betrayal, the Government
Has blood on its hands. Johnson is seething,
Downing Street's published a six-page rebuttal
Of the *Sunday-Times* investigation that shows
He missed five Cobra meetings and lacks leadership.
  A virtual PMQs, with fifty MPs
In the chamber and some of a hundred and twenty
Coming in on eight screens, and Starmer's being
Forensic: a capacity for forty thousand tests
But only eighteen thousand had and a hundred
Thousand the target within the next ten days.
The Government's policy in two documents
Of March the nineteenth and April the second
On discharging elderly coronavirus patients
From hospitals into care homes has been
Branded as reckless and is now being blamed
For the soaring death rates in residential homes –
It's said twenty-five thousand have been discharged –
And behind the policy, ultimately in control,

Is reckless Johnson who does not think things through.
    Banging pots and pans and Thursday clapping
Cannot conceal the rising number of deaths.
Twenty thousand have died in UK hospitals,
Forty including houses and care homes.
Johnson will be back at work on Monday
After a fortnight convalescing at Chequers,
But having nearly died he's reluctant
To ease the lockdown for the economy.
Some senior Tories are saying the cure
Is worse than the disease (Health and Safety
Carried to excess), and exaggerated fear
Of falling ill, hypochondria. But models
Are based on assumptions that are speculative
Rather than evidential, and are a bit 'crystal ball'.
True leadership requires honesty in choices,
Even a leader with a raffish private life
And a rascally public one must be honest
While (in Churchill's words) his "success consists
Of going from failure to failure without loss
Of enthusiasm" – going from being
Distracted by Brexit in January,
Thinking about Big Ben's bongs and not the virus,
Staying away from five Cobra meetings
And being too slow to go into lockdown
To believing the scientists' models.
    Like a dove cooing calm reassurances
Johnson says the UK's on a downward slope
With R (the rate of increase) less than one.
So a Covid case infects less than one other
And infection is on a downward curve.
The five tests Johnson's set have now all passed:
The NHS can cope, death rates are falling,
The R rate, disease's transmission rate,
The infection rate, has fallen from 3.7
To somewhere between 0.6 and 1,

Testing and PPE can meet demand
And the risk of a second peak has been contained
So the UK can now be given a plan
To exit lockdown and reopen schools
And businesses in phases. It's said lockdown
Was a mistake as only 0.1 or .2
Per cent of the population will get Covid
And isolation loses immunity
And increases deaths from other diseases,
For the old would anyway die of underlying
Conditions. The 'new normal' will now include
Risk aversion and hypochondria,
Social distancing, fear for the robustness
Of Western civilisation, living in a new way.
Now all nation-states are in recession
After a record slump, the fastest since
The South Sea Bubble of 1720
When the UK was loaned seven million pounds
To finance its war with France and in return
The Lords passed the South Sea Bill to bestow
On the South Sea Company a monopoly
In trade with South America, and no
Trading could happen, and the stock collapsed.
It will be seen if there is now a move
To globalisation to control viruses,
Or a nervous strengthening of borders.
The old world now in retrospect appears
A Golden Age that all foolishly took
For granted and, now that their search for gold
Has ended in failure, realise it was good.

Like an injured ape that's been nursed back to health
And cared for in a wildlife rescue home
And has been released back into the wild,
Johnson returns to Downing Street. He's been away
Only three weeks, but the country

He leads and the world have both changed beyond
Recognition, political consensus
Has begun to fray, he has big decisions to make –
With people out in cars and on the streets –
On whether to intensify or end lockdown.
There may be a hundred thousand deaths if the old
Stay in but the young come out, he will take charge
Of the Brexit talks for a deal or extension,
And he has to keep the Union together
When Scotland, Wales and Northern Ireland have all
Begun to announce exit strategies.
He's going to get the UK moving again.
He returns on Sunday quoting Cicero,
"Salus populi suprema lex esto"
("The people's health should be the supreme law"),
Meaning that lockdown is not over yet.
There's talk that he'll still be feeling fatigued
As the virus seems to linger on for months.
    Now like a slouching gorilla with a stoop
He stands at the lectern in Downing Street
At 9am and reads his address to the nation,
Looking pasty and drawn and struggling
To fill his lungs with air so he can declaim.
He, who was once reckless, is overcautious.
The gist is, the tide's turning, but it's too soon
To come out now and transmit the virus.
He talks urgently and enthusiastically,
He shouts and punches the air, does his Churchill impression,
But it's clear he has no plan to end lockdown.
He stammers and brays most vigorously,
Emphasises each line but says little.
The people's health comes before the economy.
    There's silence on the paltry PPE
And the trickle of tests that tell little.
There's a silence on when the lockdown will end:
The structured exit that the governments

Of Italy, France, Germany and Spain
Have given their peoples, for which the British yearn,
A boil that has festered and needs to be lanced.
Politicians and civil servants, scientists
Without experience of running a business,
Forget that the private sector pays the tax
That keeps the State and NHS afloat,
And now overcautious Johnson has stayed true
To ideology: Brexit and now science.
He's full of praise for the brilliant NHS,
Seeing the virus as an external enemy
That he hopes will reunite the British people,
But the death rate has been more severe in
The UK, which now has one tenth of all
Reported global fatalities, although
It has just 0.87 per cent
Of the world's population in its shores –
Because the UK was infected early on
And was slow to act and go to lockdown.
　Around him as he stands, to your poet's eye,
Is the sick aura of his past policies.
His words glitter as if he can still find
The prosperity he promised at Brexit,
And transform himself from a populist rabble-rouser
And clown (who joked the search for ventilators
Should be renamed Operation Last Gasp,
But has not made such jokes since his life was saved
By breathing with life-saving oxygen)
To a national statesman uniting all
With a compliant, obedient Cabinet,
Against a common enemy, the virus,
But all can now see the ruined economy
And the coming catastrophe of a reckless 'no-deal'
End to the transition with no trade agreement,
And all can now see as he falsifies
And punches the air with new opportunities

That the gold he promised all months before
The referendum, during the election, and now,
Is worthless iron pyrites: fool's gold.
And all can now see that all his policies
Were worthless bits of rubble he's sold as ore,
And that this Cicero-quoting charlatan
Is still selling nationalism to fools
In a world that cannot control viruses
Yet still can't see the need for a World State,
And is still hawking his glittering lumps as gold.

Now passengers are openly muttering,
Venting their discontent. The captain's to blame,
He should have kept the ship free from disease.
This gasping for breathing is now the main concern,
The stacked bundles of gold are forgotten.
Each passenger sits apart when they can,
Given the crowding on the wooden deck.
The ship's encountering rough seas again,
There's misery on deck, it's a plague ship
And all know they're not welcome in England
As they'll be bringing the plague to English shores.
There's questioning of why they're ill, and now
Of why they're all apart, will they really
Catch this plague they can't see from each other?

Canto XII
Coming out of Lockdown

Sing, Muse, of attempts to ease lockdown after
The disgrace of the scientist whose model
Shocked the Government into bringing it on,
And sing of the reluctance of the people
To go back to normal while keeping distance.
Sing of liberation from being locked up,
And of preferring a prison to risk.
Sing of conflicting life and livelihood,
Virus-free health and a booming economy.
    Next Wednesday your poet's switched on TV
To see the first Johnson v. Starmer duel.
But the PM is not at PMQs
As Carrie's given birth (out of wedlock)
To a baby boy who is well, despite
His parents having had Covid-19.
Johnson will take paternity leave later.
Now Starmer, clear-minded and forensic, says
Twenty-seven thousand have died from the virus
And the UK's on course for the worst death rate in Europe.
He asks if the aim to keep deaths below twenty
Thousand as announced on the seventeenth of March
By the Chief Scientific Adviser
Means – though Johnson said in front of 10 Downing Street
That the world is looking at the UK's success –
The figures are truly dreadful, not a success.
Raab, deputising, waffles, and is soon asked
For an exit strategy from the lockdown.
The SNP leader (on a virtual link)
Says the Government is gambling the UK's
Economic future on a 'no-deal' Brexit
In the middle of an emergency.
Why is the Government threatening to isolate

The UK's economy at the end of the year
In the biggest economic crisis of our time?
Raab says the Government plans to do a deal
By the end of the year. The SNP leader
Says the UK should be removing uncertainty
And protecting business, the OBR have said
The economy may be down thirty-five per cent
And at least two million face losing their jobs.
To refuse an extension's not a tough tactic
But a reckless gamble, the Government should extend
The Brexit transition so all citizens
Can tackle the health crisis together.
    Johnson's been interviewed on his brush with death.
He now says he was groggy while he worked in
Isolation in Downing Street. He did not want
To go into hospital but doctors insisted
As his readings were not what they should be.
There he was put on a nasal mask, then
A full-face mask, then moved to intensive care.
He went through litres and litres of oxygen
As his blood's oxygen levels kept going down
And the doctors were wondering if they should intubate,
Put a tube down his windpipe, put him into an induced
Coma and connect him to a ventilator.
He overheard doctors discussing how
To handle his death presentationally
And he had to come to terms for the first time
With his own mortality as the indicators
Were in the wrong direction, and he reflected
There's no medicine or cure for the virus.
A buoyancy within kept convincing him
That everything would be all right in the end.
The interviewer says it's clear his brush with death
Has left him a changed man, he no longer feels
A need to play to the crowd, within a month
He's come close to death and witnessed the birth of a son,

And the look in his eyes shows it's had a marked effect.
His baby's been named after his part-Turkish grandfather
And the two doctors named Nick who saved his life.
    The Imperial College team's predictions
Published by Neil Ferguson on the sixteenth of March
Claimed waiting for herd immunity would kill
A quarter of a million. 'Professor Lockdown'
Warned that without a lockdown hospital beds
Would have to increase eightfold. At the end of March
The Imperial team predicted five thousand
Seven hundred deaths if social distancing
Was in place – and now there are over twenty-
Eight thousand. Now the Imperial team claim
A hundred thousand will die if lockdown's lifted.
And despite their flawed guesses the Government
Believes them and is reluctant to lift lockdown.
Johnson's trapped in his putting of science first
Even though the scientists disagree.
    Now it's revealed Ferguson was visited
At home twice by his married lover in breach
Of his own advice – he acted in the belief
He was immune after testing positive
For the virus and isolating for two weeks.
He's broken the rules he advocated,
It's all right for others, but not for him,
It smacks of exceptionalist hypocrisy.
The UK has the highest deaths in Europe,
Having overtaken Italy – on the day
Raab's saying the UK statistics are
Better than other countries': exceptionalist.
    The first day of trade talks with the US
And Trump is reviewing whether spy planes
And intelligence officials should be withdrawn
From the UK now Johnson's agreed Huawei
Can help build its 5G network although
Huawei sends intelligence back to China

And hackers backed by China and Russia have tried
To steal vaccine secrets with cyber attacks.
    Now Ferguson's predictions are questioned.
His figures on Sweden (forty thousand deaths
Rising to ninety-six thousand) have proved wrong
For there have been less than three thousand deaths.
His record as a forecaster is dismal.
In 2002 he warned that 'mad cow disease'
Would cause a hundred and thirty-six thousand
Deaths in the UK – there were 178.
In 2005 he said two hundred million
Would die from bird flu, 292 died. He
In 2009 claimed that swine fever
Would cause sixty-five thousand deaths in the UK,
But only two hundred and fifty-seven died.
His shaky stats, and now his lover Staats –
Some wouldn't ask him to predict Christmas Day.
There's intellectual weakness over R,
The reproductive rate from a model
That misforecasts, so if the model is wrong
Why continue to use it to guide future
Policy and continue with lockdown,
Which is needlessly prolonged by the Government's
Reliance on an irrelevant infection rate,
An average that includes hospitals and care homes,
Pockets of high infection, and the under-fifties,
Who have hardly been affected but are cooped up
For the worst economic slump in three hundred years?
Professor Lockdown's scandal has brought lockdown
Close to collapse and it may be loosened soon.
    At last Johnson has to face clinical Starmer,
Like a wounded bull attempting to lock horns,
He can't postpone his interrogation any more,
He can't plead he's just become a father.
He walks from Downing Street to Buckingham Palace
At 7am, then back, in suit and tie,

Followed by two protection officers.
Starmer took Raab apart twice, Johnson can't
Bluster in his answers with his usual um and er.
Now in the deserted chamber he is asked
Why Britain abandoned its testing programme in March,
Only to resume it now. The true answer
Was it could not reach the capacity required.
Just as an ill-prepared teenager's challenged
And, eyes in corners, hunts for an excuse
And answers evasively, clutching at fibs,
Making his argument up as he goes along,
So he says verbatim with halting prolixity,
Waffle and intellectual confusion:
"A-a-as I think is readily apparent,
Mr Speaker, to everybody who
Has studied the, er, the situation
And I think scientists would, er, confirm
The difficulty in mid-March was that,
Er, the, er, tracing capacity that we've had –
It had been useful... in the containment phase
Of the epidemic, er, that capacity
Was no longer useful or relevant,
Since the, er, transmission from individuals
Within the UK, um, meant that it exceeded
Our capacity.... As we get the new cases down,
Er, we will have a team that will genuinely
Be able to track and, er, trace hundreds
Of thousands of people across the country,
And thereby to drive down the epidemic.
And so, er, I mean, to put it in a nutshell,
It is easier, er, to do now – now that we
Have built up the team on the, on the way out –
Than it was as, er, the epidemic took off."
He goes on to promise two hundred thousand
Tests a day by the end of the month of May.
He does not look well and is not leading,

Like a pig suffering from swine dysentery.
There are reports of confusion in Downing Street
And he does not appear to be up to the job.
He says it's like the Blitz and boasts how well
The UK is doing when its death rate is
The worst in Europe – it's a mass delusion,
Exceptionalism, that blind optimism
Is better than judicious leadership,
And where, o where is the leader's clarity
And sharp intellectual incisiveness?
It has not been in evidence at the dispatch-box.
The inquest in Downing Street will be sombre.
    On VE Day, in old black-and-white film,
See crowds throng streets, cheer Churchill's victory speech.
Just as Churchill led the British in the war,
And they longed for a change when it ended,
So after coronavirus and lockdown
The British may again yearn for a change.
Johnson reads a recently-discovered poem
By Blunden (who your poet once lunched with
In Japan), 'VE Day', which foresees the vision
That would sweep Churchill aside and will do for him.
The State and its institutions will strengthen,
Revolutionaries will redistribute wealth,
Johnson will be out, and Starmer will lead
The UK back into a reformed EU
And there'll be a move for global unity,
A united policy on climate change
And also (as it's now revealed Wuhan
Was in lockdown after a hazardous
Event in the Institute's National
Biosafety Laboratory between
The sixth and eleventh of October, which led
To roadblocks from the fourteenth to the nineteenth)
On the control of all virology.
Thirty thousand dead of the virus against

Sixty thousand civilians killed in the war
And four hundred thousand armed forces dead –
The war was worse than this virus: rationing,
Black-out, the Blitz, the wailing of sirens,
And it lasted six years, not three mere months.
    The Queen, seventy-five years after appearing
On the balcony with her father, the King,
And Churchill on VE Day, addresses
The nation movingly at 9pm,
The same time that her father, the King, spoke,
About the terrible war and now about
The love of people looking after each other.
She says the message of VE Day is
'Never give up, never despair'. She says
The streets are not empty but are filled with love.
She's lived through the war and now the virus
Has prevented national celebrations
And decimated the elderly in care homes
Which shelter the remnants of the generation
Who achieved the VE Day she's honouring.
The tragedy in the care homes may have been fuelled
By British exceptionalism, which believes
That the UK won the war with Germany,
Not the US or Russia, the "big two",
When out of seventy million killed in the war
The UK had less than half a million deaths –
And that Brits are above all viruses.
Now it's announced the Queen will withdraw from
Public life, and the virus, for several months.
The virus is impeding the Queen's role
Which requires her (she says) "to be seen to be believed".

Johnson's Sunday-evening speech on video:
After seven weeks in lockdown he presents his plan
For a cautious escape in slow changes
To thirty million viewers in lockdown

Hoping to escape seven weeks' imprisonment.
And like a sow that's convalesced in a sty
After a bout of coccidiosis
And feels down and has lost its appetite
And squeals with delight when it's at last let out
Into the farmyard, to run with other pigs,
He speaks animatedly reading from autocue.
The fifty-page document was assembled
And printed by a core task force – and not seen
By the rest of the Cabinet, which has been running
The country while Johnson's been in hospital.
They were shocked, just as May's Cabinet was shocked
When the Withdrawal Agreement was placed
Before them without any input from them.
He punches the air but it all sounds false,
And shows crude, oversimplified graphics.
It's empty rhetoric. He sets out five
Alert levels, the UK is being
Stood down from level 4 to level 3,
Construction and manufacturing workers
Can return to work but not on public transport.
Everyone can go out into the sun in parks.
It's an aspiration that some classes in
Schools will at last be back from June the first.
A slogan's changed – 'Stay alert' instead of 'Stay home' –
But not in Scotland, Wales or Northern Ireland.
The directions are vague, they smack of ineptitude.
    Like a teenager impressing with his maths,
Quoting a formula to win admiration,
Johnson tries to give objectivity
To a finely-balanced political judgment
Between the economy and lockdown by saying
That C (the Covid-alert level) = R
(The rate of infection) + N (the number
Of infections). But this is gobbledegook:
C, an alert level of 1 to 5,

Cannot equal R, which is below 1,
Plus the number of infections (more than two
Hundred and twenty-three thousand cases).
It's performance algebra and it's meaningless –
Just as R's phoney as it's the UK's average
For the high rate in hospitals and care homes
And the low rate among the under-fifties.
Yet R is central to Johnson's thinking.
    His instructions are like a flock of gulls
Flying in different directions with raucous cries.
His message is full of confusion: Go back to work
On Monday but it doesn't come into force
Until Wednesday; don't go by public transport
But if you've a child your employer must let
You stay at home as there is no child care;
Meet your parents, but actually only one
And in a park, not a house or garden;
Go to the seaside but don't stay the night
In your holiday home and if you cross
Into Wales or Scotland you'll be arrested.
There's quarantine for all travellers arriving,
But you can go to France without being checked
And travellers can enter freely via France.
It sounds like get outdoors but stay at home,
And fines have an R factor, they double up
For repeat offences till three thousand two hundred pounds.
Johnson admits there may never be a vaccine,
It's not guaranteed, there isn't one for SARS
After eighteen years, despite all the trying,
But there may be some therapeutic drug control.
Only fifteen per cent of the population's been tested.
    The end of lockdown and summer is here.
Cowslips no longer smile from a bank in the sun,
Now yellow bellis daisies beam in May
And goldfinches flit round the thistle-seeds
And fields of buttercups bask in sunshine.

As bees buzz in a smiling summer's flowers
And in slow flight hover and then nuzzle
In heather, lupins and now lavender,
Blessed with wide choice and a homing compass,
And a blackbird sings throatily in a tree,
And blue forget-me-nots turn orange eyes to the sun
And climbing jasmine fills the air with scent
And peacock butterflies and small fritillaries bask
In the sun on brambles amid blackberry flowers
Near fields of birds'-foot trefoil and clover,
The press says it's chaos, Britain's confused
And divided, there is no clarity.
Later Raab says that two parents can meet
Another parent in a park, but then
Contradicts himself, it's as it was before.
A hundred thousand deaths are forecast before
The end of the year by the London School
Of Tropical Hygiene. The UK's flown
Fifty thousand virus tests to America
As its labs have problems and cannot cope.
Twenty-five million goggles are substandard
And Johnson's shouted at Hancock and has blamed
His Department for not having a grip on the crisis.
Hancock's said petulantly, "That's not fair."
　Monday in Parliament. The PM's speech
And the released document contradict each other.
All have to return to work without transport,
Child care or PPE. There are no guidelines
For being safe at work until later that week.
Starmer protests that there's no clarity.
Does quarantine apply to all arrivals
Or just airlines? And there's now divergence.
Travel to outdoor spaces is permitted,
But in England only, not Scotland, Wales or Ulster.
The PM does not have answers, guidance
Still has to be given in all these areas,

And there'll be different rules for different nations.
It's said Johnson is PM for England
As Wales, Scotland and Northern Ireland are not
Changing the slogan from 'Stay home' to 'Stay alert'.
    At the evening briefing Johnson looks flustered.
His statements fly in conflicting directions like gulls.
There's confusion and division, and he says
All should use their common sense. Common sense is all
That's left when there's no PPE or testing,
When it's all presentation and colour schemes
Without much substance, and the UK must muddle through.
Like a centipede crawling across a field,
All legs moving to inch slowly forward,
Johnson's progress to freedom is laboured and slow.
    The fifty-page document contains common sense,
It's what the Europeans are doing: social distancing,
Hand washing. But why release this information
On a Sunday night, and then release the document
Eighteen hours later after briefing and rebriefing
And the guidelines aren't ready, and say on Sunday night
"It doesn't apply till Wednesday", it feels shambolic:
Work and hope you don't bring infection back
To your family. It's a question of clarity,
Johnson has provided no clear direction,
His incoherence may be driven by
Having to keep in his Cabinet the hawks
Who put the economy first, and the doves who
Put public-health lockdown first, but back-benchers
Are worried about Johnson's competence
And that of his team, their misleading use
Of statistics and of mixed messages.
Johnson is not a details man and he
Is winging it in a crisis, there's grumbling
Among voters who gave him an eighty-seat
Majority, and exasperation
In Cabinet for the lack of consultation,

And competent Starmer's coolly waiting.
The Government's using the 'Potemkin model'
In which all decisions are made before Cabinet meet.
It's said the Party – and Johnson – will pay
A heavy price for their handling of the pandemic
As a couple of million about to be unemployed
Will soon vent their fury on the PM.
    It's now revealed that the Cabinet Secretary
Sedwill had the virus the same time as the PM.
There's tension between him and Johnson, who asked,
"Who's in charge of implementing this delivery
Plan? Is it you?" And after a silence
Sedwill said, "No, I think it's you, Prime Minister."
The Cabinet are angry that the quad
(The inner circle of four ministers,
The hub and not the spokes) made the decision
To ease lockdown without consulting them.
And now a poll has shown the approval rating
Of the Government's gone from plus forty-two per cent
On the twenty-sixth of March to minus three
Per cent after the changing of the slogan
To 'Stay alert' and the going-back to school.

The truce is over, the people are irate
Like flocks of sea-birds screaming for more fish.
The PM's been saying the R rate's the most
Important factor in British policy,
And it's gone slightly up, yet Harries says
It's the number of cases that's most important –
The criteria have been changed, it's relaxation
At a time when Public Health England say
There are only twenty-four new cases a day
In London, of which a quarter involve
Diabetes – and at this rate the virus
Will be gone from London in a couple of weeks,
Suggesting the Israeli expert who said

The virus only has an eight-week life
Was right all along, and lockdown has been
An over-reaction and run up at least
A three-hundred-billion-pound borrowing and debt.
    A report from the Treasury to the Chancellor
Of the fifth of May sees a deficit
Of three hundred and thirty-seven billion pounds
On a base-case (most likely) scenario,
Or of five-hundred-and-twelve billion pounds if
There's an L-shaped decline, not a V-shaped
Bounce-back recession. The Bank of England
Have been doing quantitative easing,
Another two-hundred billion pounds it's given
To its Asset Purchase Facility Fund
To be drawn down as required, so it can buy
Treasury bonds from financial institutions
And from the Treasury's Debt Management Office,
And there will have to be more QE, creating
New digital money and releasing it
Into the money supply so it can buy
Government debt though new fifty-year gilts
Which will only be worth a tenth in fifty years' time
When they have to be renewed, and thus spare
The UK from a new round of austerity,
Tax increases and a public-sector pay freeze.
Now Johnson again rules out austerity.
    The UK's been through three catastrophes,
'Natural' disasters, within just three years:
The decision to walk away from Europe,
The advent of Trump's 'America First'
And now the virus that's shut down the West.
There are 1.6 million viruses,
Nearly half of which can infect people
And act like weapons of mass-destruction.
Many wonder in unspoken unease,
Has the West been targeted by a covert,

Invisible, deadly bio-weapon,
A viral warfare to beat nuclear powers,
So China can become number-one superpower
And seize Hong Kong, Kashmir and sundry islands?
    Like a naughty boy owning up at last to his lies
Now the Government's agreed that a Brexit deal
Does mean that goods will have to be checked in
Northern Ireland, contrary to denials.
There'll be checks on food and animal products
Coming into Northern-Irish ports from Great
Britain, with new paperwork for businesses.
The EU are unhappy as the ports
Could be a back door into the single market.
Businesses in Northern Ireland will face
Additional barriers to trade with Britain
Despite Johnson's promises to the contrary,
As Northern Ireland stays part of the EU's
Customs territory after Brexit to prevent
A hard border on the island of Ireland.
    Prime Minister's Questions. Starmer says the Chief
Executive of Care England has said
Patients were discharged from hospitals to care homes
Without being tested – twenty-five thousand
Of them may have been infected – and there's no testing.
Like a bull that's been charged by another bull and gored
Johnson says the UK's tested more than
Other countries in Europe. Starmer says
Tracing was abandoned on the twelfth of March.
There's been no tracing for ten weeks, and there
Have been thirty-four thousand deaths. Will there
Be test-track-and-trace by the first of June?
Johnson blusters that it will be world-beating
(When there's no tracking now). Starmer asks if it's right
That carers from abroad, who are clapped on Thursdays,
Should pay a surcharge of hundreds of pounds
To use the NHS themselves. Johnson blusters

That it's the right way forward. Starmer says
The fee for care workers to receive NHS
Treatment will soon be six hundred and twenty
Pounds and that will take seventy hours' work.
Behind his question is the sending-home
Of foreign care workers and charging those who stay.
    Now there is an outcry against lockdown
And the modelling which made it seem worthwhile,
Especially Imperial College's.
The gulls are swooping screaming above a shoal
Of miscalculations, contradictions and errors.
Imperial's programming under Ferguson
Could go down as the most devastating
Software mistake of all time, its finding
Of five hundred and ten thousand deaths unless
There was lockdown had fifteen thousand lines of code
When industry's best practice has five hundred
Separate files and uses models that factor
In randomness and give the same results,
Given the same initial parameters.
The model appears to be unreliable.
    Lockdown's been a nonsense. The NHS
Should protect the people, not the other way round.
Governments left it unprepared for a pandemic.
The NHS was unprepared, and so
The entire UK population was deprived
Of its liberty, pushing it into the worst
Recession in three hundred years, destroying
Millions of jobs and hundreds of thousands
Of businesses, crippling families with debt
And undermining schoolchildren's education.
It's for the people to say what risks they'll take
With their health, not for the Prime Minister
To say, "Walk in the park, but don't sunbathe,
Drive to Cornwall but not your second home,
Meet one person, not two, in your front, not back,

Garden, and be fined if you break the rules" –
Absurd rulings that discredit the law.
As horseshoe bats hang in loft eaves by day
And fly out at dusk and swoop on insects and spiders
And may carry SARS coronavirus,
So people emerge and go to essential shops
Wearing masks as anyone could have Covid.
The Government's terrified the people into submission
When the death rate for under-fifties is tiny,
And under one per cent infected actually die,
And of those eighty-seven per cent are over sixty-five,
And ninety per cent have multiple causes
Other than Covid-19. Johnson's broadcast
Was not Churchillian but that of a man
Imprisoned in his past mistakes, and afraid –
Terrified – of being blamed for thirty-five
Thousand deaths that somehow took place on his watch.
He's like a disgruntled pig that's finding it hard
To integrate with the rest of its drift (or drove)
After suffering a bout of porcine parvovirus.
Now Johnson, who when he went to hospital
Was five foot nine and seventeen-and-a-half stone
With a BMI of thirty-six, obese,
Is leading a fight against obesity
Which seems to attract Covid-19. Every
Morning he processes round St James's Park
With a disposable coffee-cup. Has he,
Who used to be a libertarian,
Believing 'What I want goes' – food, women,
Boasting of his own greed and idleness,
Now learned the way to live's not 'I, I, I'
But from the feelings of the deeper soul,
In the centre hidden away below
The rational, social ego of politics
(The centre all true poets have long known)?
Has he learned from his post-Brexit hubris,

His belief in British exceptionalism,
From his economic priorities
And habitual negligence, his ignored warnings
And delayed action on the pandemic,
His stunted awareness and intellectual collapse
Under Starmer's interrogations and a void
Beneath his glib blustering, the emotional
Void that accompanies incompetence?
Has he now learned to care for all humankind?
To put his arms round everyone in the world,
And learned sincerity from his near-death experience?
The answer from his broadcast is: he has not.
    Ahead may be the long-term damage from
The virus: lung scarring (or fibrosis)
That leads to chronic breathlessness and a cough
Such as he displayed at the Liaison Committee;
Kidney failure that may need dialysis
Or kidney transplants and acute fatigue;
Symptoms in brain, heart and blood vessels – migraines,
Heart palpitations, and phantom smells – for the virus
Destroys the small hairs in the nasal passage
That help to move mucus from the sinuses
And lungs. And loss of taste, stomach cramps, a rash,
A tingling sensation in hands and feet, lung
And breathing problems, breathlessness. It could
Take years for Covid-attacked lungs to recover.

Now the ship's off the English coast in quarantine.
So many of the passengers are ill.
Three more have died in breathlessness, gasping.
The captain has recovered, but is unwell.
The voyage began full of optimism
And is ending in despondency and rage.
Many want an expert to come aboard
And examine the gold they have brought back,
But quarantine rules will not permit this.

All sit with their bundles and stare solemnly.

Canto XIII
Johnson's Ratings Collapse

Sing, Muse, of populism and of polls,
Of how populists follow focus groups,
And sing of how advisers break the law
They've helped to put in place as it's not for them.
Sing of the justice of the gods, who will
That if advisers err, leaders' ratings must fall.
Sing of the turning-point that alienated
The public from the law they've rejected.
    It's come out that Cummings, Johnson's close adviser,
Made a two-hundred-and-sixty-four-mile trip
To his parents' farm in Durham at the end of March
When his wife was thought to have the virus. He took
His son and his wife in the cramped space of a car
And was infected by her, and had symptoms
Of Covid-19. On the fifth of April
Witnesses saw him in their Durham garden
With Abba's 'Dancing Queen' playing loudly,
And photographed him with his child. He's broken the law
That he helped form, like Ferguson. Those who make
The rules should lead by example so there's not
One rule for the *élite* and another
For the rest of the UK. It's revealed
He drove thirty miles to Barnard Castle.
Like chimpanzees jumping up and down pointing
The public's aghast, he's delivered the policy
Not to travel when under lockdown, he's a hypocrite
Who does the opposite of what he preaches,
Visiting grandparents when the Government
Had said they shouldn't, and on the same day
A Scottish minister resigned in Scotland
For quietly visiting her second home.
If both Cummings and his wife had Covid-19

How did they get to Durham without coming
Into contact with people at petrol stations?
    Johnson needs Cummings, he's woefully unclear
In explaining policies – the balance of risks
That a return to school will be better than staying at home –
As Pericles or Churchill would have explained them.
(They gave many details of their frightening wars
While saying the present risks could lead to hope.)
Johnson's ratings are falling and there's no sign
He's in charge, he's muddling through with U-turns:
The WHO declared a pandemic
On March the twelfth, and the UK decided to stop
Testing and tracing on the fifteenth, and only
When Imperial said there'd be five hundred thousand deaths
Was lockdown decided on the twenty-third,
And a SAGE scientist has said that because lockdown
Did not happen earlier thousands of lives were lost.
    At the day's briefing every question to Shapps
Is on Cummings, and where is the PM?
Like a crab scuttling to hide under a rock
And sink and bury its shell in the sand
Johnson has gone into hiding from the press.
Shapps doesn't know when Johnson knew of this,
Johnson needs to explain why his adviser
Is able to work when flouting policy.
The police say they found Cummings in Durham,
Spoke with his father and took no further action.
But the British people feel treated with contempt,
And so the public can break lockdown if they want:
People were asked to stay at home to save lives,
And did, and the rules have been broken by those
Who created them, there's a call for Cummings to go.
Now *The Sunday Times* Insight team has set out
Twenty-two days of dither and delay,
From March the second, when Johnson said the UK
Is very well prepared, to the twenty-third,

Lockdown dithering and delay that have led
To the UK's having the worst death toll in Europe.
The Insight team have found, having interviewed
Many scientists and civil servants,
That the preparations were for pandemic flu,
The modellers didn't model tracing, besides
Indecision there was working to the wrong plan.
Europe was going into lockdown in February and March
And Johnson was recommending washing hands
While he shook hands with coronavirus patients.
Thirty thousand lives could have been saved if he had
Not dithered for three weeks. That dithering
Has extended lockdown and crashed the economy,
And Johnson has disappeared and won't address the people.
R's an average, most are at R = zero.
It's a bank-holiday weekend, people are heading
For beaches, for if Cummings can, so can they.
  Number Ten has been a shambles, Cummings has tried
To get Sedwill and McNamara sacked,
And Johnson's got Case back from Prince William
As a firewall between them and Cummings.
He was an aide to Cameron and May
Before becoming William's secretary.
Now Cummings is under pressure, Durham police
Have investigated whether he broke lockdown rules
By driving north with a symptomatic wife.
His father rang the police regarding
Cummings' security – he had received death threats
Made to his London home – and was told he
Should not have travelled (transporting his wife's
Virus to Durham). Johnson has denied
The police were involved. What happened was,
Just after Johnson had symptoms and isolated
Cummings rushed home to look after his wife
And decided she and their child would be best cared-for
At his parents' Durham farm, but once there

He developed symptoms and was very ill
With a high fever and spasms which made
The muscles lump and twitch in both his legs,
And he could only breathe in a shallow way.
    Like a muntjac peering from behind hawthorns
Now Johnson takes the Sunday press briefing
And makes a statement supporting Cummings,
Who, with his wife suffering from the virus,
Acted reasonably and legally in
Taking their child to where he could be looked after
(Even though there was a relative in London).
Johnson blusters, as if it will go away.
He says Cummings followed his instincts like
Any father, but nowhere in the guidance
Does it say all can follow instincts rather than rules
Or that it's reasonable to transport the virus
From the South to the North (catching the virus
During the journey) to have your child cared
For by vulnerable over-seventies.
Nowhere does it say a child is vulnerable.
It's not said Cummings' maternal uncle
Lord Justice Laws died of the virus in
London while he was in Durham and grieving.
    The journalists are waiting till questions,
And unleash a storm of indignation.
It's said he broke three rules: he left his house,
He transported coronavirus and he
Stayed with elderly parents. Can all do this?
He followed his instincts as opposed to rules.
Can all do this? He got the virus from
The car journey. Johnson's asked, Were you told
He'd made the trip, did he visit Barnard Castle?
Did he stop on his way to Durham? No answers.
He's hiding in undergrowth like a shy deer.
Will the public understand? Have they read
The public mood right, or have they misread it?

Essential travel does not include second homes.
All can be fined for breaking lockdown, which is now
Virtually repealed. Cummings came up with slogans –
Such as 'Take back control' and 'Get Brexit done' –
And is part of the drive to get a 'no deal'
And win Disaster Capitalism's bet.
    The next morning's papers picture the two,
The *Mirror*'s serious: "A cheat and a coward."
Johnson was too cowardly to stand up to the cheat
(Who is his enforcer and behaves strongly,
And will help his supporters through to a 'no deal').
No apology, no inquiry, no sacking.
It's said Johnson's failed, Cummings felt he had
The authority to do whatever he likes.
The police say it's impossible to enforce lockdown.
Like a male elephant that's broken away
Johnson is shunned by the rest of the herd.
    Now the realisation's dawned, as Soubry says
The truth is Johnson simply can't operate
As PM without Cummings telling him
What to do, his Rasputin, a voice in his ear
Giving him detail as he's a big-picture man
And does not do detail. Now it comes out
That on the night the UK left the EU
Amid the champagne flutes in the Downing-Street
State Room, Johnson put his arm round Cummings' shoulder
And hailed him "a genius" – for getting Brexit done.
And so he's desperate to keep him, and all
Can now see the paucity of his leadership
And that he's not called the Great Charlatan for nothing.
Johnson's an imposter who's been told what
To promise and has promised gold, gold, gold
To win an eighty-seat majority,
And now he's been found out by his timidness.
He's a pretender who can't operate on his own.
Cummings and his wife went to a new region

As Covid carriers, and went round the region.
It's 'Do as I say', not 'Do as I do', and it's now
Tougher for front-line police to enforce lockdown,
Which only works through public sacrifice
To stop infection and dying by giving up work.
The people who made the rules can't break the rules.

Fresh news, Cummings is to make a statement
And take questions at a press conference.
The adviser has now become the news.
It's a high-risk strategy as he disdains the press.
Sturgeon says political interest has taken
Priority over public interest and trust.
(Some of the public say Sturgeon's daily
Briefings are clearer about what to do than Johnson's.)
The Downing-Street rose garden, and it's expected
Cummings will come out fighting, be defiant.
He's not an MP or Cabinet minister,
It's the first time a Special Adviser has held
A press conference for journalists while in the post.
He keeps all waiting half an hour in warm sun.
It's not the way to conduct government.
He's the driving force behind lockdown and quarantine,
Proroguing and expelling the twenty-one,
And the danger now is he's dragging Johnson down.
Like a timid, nervous and faltering goat
Cummings walks out alone in a shirt and sits
At a table, reads several sheets of A4.
He says he's speaking about his own actions.
He left because his home was a target,
He did not consult the PM, who was ill.
He gives an account of driving, feeling unwell,
And how his child was sick and taken to hospital.
He did what he did for child-care reasons
And was afraid he had Covid-19.
He was not tested but thought all three had it,

And had shouted conversations with his parents.
He was able to get home but was seen.
Questions, and his story begins to unravel.
He's asked if he regrets what he did
And whether he's considered resigning.
No, he hasn't. He says the rules require
Exercise of judgment. He drove to Barnard Castle
To test his eyesight to check he could drive home.
Should he have driven if he doubted his eyesight?
There's no apology as he was doing
His best for his family and his child.
He's unconvincing during question time.
   It's all defiant, it seems he didn't tell
The full story of what he said to Johnson.
His London house was a target, but there's
A central unit to improve security.
It's strange to drive with a child, with eyesight problems.
Can his account be trusted? There's hypocrisy
And all afternoon Johnson's been hiding.
There's no hint of a mistake, everything was right.
His decision lacked concern for the community.
   Now Ross has resigned as junior minister
In Scotland in protest at Cummings, who's
Divisive and has re-fractured the Party
After the split during the May years. Johnson
Is desperate to keep him because he can't govern
Without him, doesn't know what to say, dithers,
Even more now the virus has damaged *his* eyesight –
He wears spectacles for reading – and has seemingly
Impaired the clarity of his thinking.
   Cummings is an abrasive maverick
Who gets the job done and doesn't care what rules
He breaks – he gets Brexit done and brings on
The 'no deal' Disaster Capitalism want.
Around him in the court are the magnates
Who are jealous of his influence and would bring him down.

And in the middle's the monarch, Johnson,
Who only cares about maintaining his
Popularity with the common people.
There's a void at the heart of this Government.
The press conference hasn't ruled a line under
The Cummings affair, and a minister's resigned.
Cummings has damaged the Party and PM,
They appear truth-twisters amid calls for him to resign.
    A news briefing with Hancock, and more questions
On the loss of confidence in the Government.
The polls have dropped twenty points in four days.
Seventy-one per cent in a poll think Cummings
Broke lockdown. Hancock's asked if everyone can
Now use their discretion on whether to accept lockdown.
It's asked, Has Cummings a hold over Johnson?
    News that the polls have slumped, the Tories now
Have dropped nine points in a week during a Party
Revolt demanding Cummings' resignation.
Like a solitary bull elephant that's gone,
Johnson is being shunned by the national herd.
Many from the North say they won't vote Tory again.
Starmer's rating is now higher than Johnson's,
Yet so central is Cummings' drive for 'no deal'
To his premiership that Johnson's toughing it out.
    Johnson is before the Liaison Committee
Of the chairmen of key committees,
The first time a PM's appeared for a year.
Jenkin asks him to come to the committee again
Before the summer recess. Johnson declines.
Jenkin asks him why the Cabinet Secretary
Has not been asked to lead an inquiry.
Johnson blusters, ums and ers. He's asked
Why he's united the country in condemning
His handling of Cummings' breach of the rules.
Johnson says we should set aside the row,
Move on and concentrate on the virus.

Crabb says the UK's not acted as one nation.
Johnson denies that people will refuse
To follow lockdown after Cummings' drive.
Johnson's asked if he's seen the evidence and if
It should be published by the Cabinet Secretary.
Johnson ums and ers and repeats himself
And blusters and says the Cabinet Secretary
Has too much on his plate coping with Covid.
Yvette Cooper asks for clear advice on
What parents with Covid and a child should do.
Johnson says "Stay at home" and then blusters
And ums and ers. Cooper has rattled him.
She says, "You're ducking the question because you're trying
To protect Dominic Cummings." She says forty
Thousand are dead and there's been conflicting advice,
The advice should now be right, protecting Cummings
Should not replace the national interest. Johnson says
All must stick to the simple messages: 'Wash your hands,
Stay at home, keep social distancing.' He's told
People don't understand why Cummings is so
Pivotal and has become a distraction.
Johnson says people want to tackle the virus.
    Johnson says he doesn't read the scientific papers
But speaks to Whitty and Vallance from SAGE.
He's asked, can distancing be reduced from two
Metres to one, as the WHO recommends.
The science advisers say two metres is right
Even though it's the highest in the world.
He should get SAGE to review the two-metre rule.
He's asked, is staying at home compulsory
Or within people's judgment? He says people will be asked
To stay at home, and financial sanctions may follow.
A law? Fined by the police? Johnson ums and ers,
He blusters. No answer. When do tests happen?
When there are symptoms. If someone's been in touch
With someone who has coronavirus

That person has to stay at home and isolate
For fourteen days, and there will be a test.
Hunt says test, track, trace may be a game changer,
Why wasn't the hundred-thousand test target
In place until April when the first case was in
January? Johnson says the UK did not have the kit
And the trackers, it did not learn the lessons of SARS
And MERS and have a good testing system.
(He's blaming Hunt as past Secretary of State
For Health for not putting all this in place.)
   Hunt asks if lack of testing spread the virus
Into care homes. He says South Korea and Taiwan
Have the best records, and test results that are back
Within twenty-four hours when the UK's take twice as long.
A constituent of his waited a week.
When will Johnson announce that he has set
A twenty-four-hour target for testing?
As evasive as a badger near its burrow
Johnson says, "I've been forbidden to announce this now."
Who by? Who's the actual PM? Is it Cummings?
Johnson blames labs that are slow to process tests
For delays. It's always someone else's fault.
He's asked if the reopening of schools is safe,
And there are questions about women's roles.
He coughs and says, "Excuse me." Has he still got
Covid? He's still coughing. He says there will be
An economic recovery package.
   UK leaders did not lock down their country
During Spanish flu, which killed a hundred million,
Yet their plan in March 2020 to preserve
Hospital capacity turned into two months
Of near-universal house arrest and caused
Worker furloughs at two hundred and fifty-six
Hospitals, stoppage of international travel,
Forced closures of millions of businesses
And devastation of all economic sectors.

Errors in modelling mean lockdown was wrong
As the virus peaked a week before lockdown
Began in the UK, and deaths peaked two weeks
After lockdown began, so the victims
Caught the virus shortly before lockdown.
It will go down as a time of mass panic
And isolating from a plague at enormous cost.
The world's looked at the UK's incompetent
Handling of the Covid crisis with shock
And pity. The PM's leadership's more
Like Captain Mainwaring's than Churchill's, amid
The chaos there's been the Cummings affair,
And Cummings' reassurance in the rose garden
Has confounded, had the opposite effect.
The scientists say the affair has undermined
All they have worked to achieve, and the Government's
Strategy for handling Covid-19.
And now the real figure's sixty thousand dead.
Cummings' work continues: over one billion pounds
In State contracts to private companies
With no scrutiny, NHS duties privatised
And data sold off to US tech giants,
Trade checks between Northern Ireland and Great Britain
After all, and food and environment standards
After Brexit removed from the Agriculture Bill.
Sixty Tory MPs want Cummings to go,
And Johnson's approval ratings have nosedived.
Now no one will trust Cummings or Johnson.

As ready to hide as a rabbit seen in a field
Johnson takes the next day's briefing. All five
Tests have been met and so lockdown can be eased
To six people in a garden (both their grandparents)
While still maintaining social distancing,
So friends and family can reunite
As the R rate's dropped to 0.7 to .9.

The questions are all on Cummings, the PM
Forbids the two scientists from answering
A "political matter". The scientists are asked
To nod or shake their head if they're being blocked.
Both say they don't want to be dragged into politics.
Vallance is pessimistic about contact tracing
As two-thirds of all who've tested positive
For the virus had no symptoms, which will make
Contact tracing simply ineffective.

Now it is revealed that Cummings will quit
As Johnson's senior adviser in six months' time
After drawing a line under Brexit, cutting
The UK's last ties with Brussels and reforming
The Civil Service. Johnson will keep him so he
Can stick to the New-Year deadline to end transition
And see through a 'no deal' as his backers
Disaster Capitalism want, and his
Departure can be seen as resisting
Demands by his foes that he should be sacked
And Johnson could appear both loyal and strong
While Cummings' detractors would feel that they have won.
The Tories have squandered political capital –
Nine points in their opinion poll in one day
And twenty points in Johnson's in four days –
For an overrated adviser who's regarded
As having single-handedly won the referendum
And the general election, it's like a stain
That's indelible and now reflects the disgust
At the Government's handling of the pandemic:
Excess deaths in Britain are the highest
In the world, and the Government's not been in control,
But has been reactive towards the virus
And now has to cope with a nasty recession
And will be blamed for financial hardship
(Loss of jobs and pay cuts) and Labour is
Strong again under Starmer and can win.

Johnson's not husbanded the poll lead the Tories
Enjoyed during the election and under Corbyn.
A collapse in the Government's ratings is an event
In the next general election, for under
Starmer Labour's serious again and can win.
The drop in trust and support for the Government
Is unlikely to come back. The realistic
And ruthless Conservative Party has witnessed
An insecure PM and his flawed Rasputin
Drive the country into a wall and he can't
See where he is going (as near Barnard Castle).
Now a new take on anti-*élite* Cummings:
He drives a fifty-thousand-pound car, lives
In a 1.6-million-pound town house
With an extension that has a tapestry room,
A formal living-room and reading-room,
In Islington not far from the restaurants
And cocktail-bars of swanky Upper Street,
And stays in his in-laws' Chillingham Castle
In Northumberland whose grounds are home to a herd
Of Common-Agricultural-Policy-
Funded cattle. He felt the time had come
To end lockdown and return to normal life,
But millions were still terrified to leave their homes,
Go to work or send their children to school
And Johnson had grown nervous of loosening
Restrictions on the advice of the scientists.
And so Cummings decided to break lockdown
Himself and when he was exposed, he refused
Even to apologise, so when the British
People were indignant and appalled at
"One rule for him and another for us"
They'd refuse to accept lockdown and go out –
And so in a single inspired move he
Achieved precisely what he wanted and moved
The economy out of lockdown to a new normal.

It's the move of a genius and selfless
Man who's turned himself into a laughing-stock
And the butt of national jokes about eye tests,
Willingly chosen ridicule and sacrificed
His reputation to lead the British people
Out of their fears and insecurities
To where he (as *de facto* Prime Minister)
Felt they ought to be, back at work and school.
　But no, it's not credible, he transgressed
On March the twenty-seventh, just after lockdown,
And it was his own plan, it was too early
For him to set a route for getting out.
It's been heard Johnson gave him a final warning,
Behind it all is Johnson not knowing
How to get 'no deal' through without Cummings'
Direction till the end of the year, to please
Disaster Capitalism's investors
Who, having funded their referendum
And election campaigns, bet eight million on
'No deal', which Johnson's duty-bound to see through.
A similarly improbable story
That has a ring of truth and may be true.
　Now it's come out. Cummings was seen walking –
A bit like someone seeing a pheasant –
Outside shops and along a woodland trail
By the River Tees in Barnard Castle.
In his statement he said he'd "felt a bit sick"
And walked "ten to fifteen metres from the car
To the river bank nearby" while testing his eyes.
Cummings is an international laughing-stock
For claiming his outing to a beauty spot
Was nothing more than a glorified eye test,
And so is Britain and its incompetence.
He jointly owns the Durham farm where he stayed.
He's cheated on his blog as well, it says
He warned of an urgent need to plan for

A coronavirus pandemic on the fourth
Of March last year, but a digital library
That tracks changes to billions of web pages
Showed he added the reference to the virus
On April the fourteenth, the day he returned from Durham.
His backdating of his forecast's shown his vacuity.
The scandal of the Cummings affair has changed
How the country sees its Government and's worsened
Its opinion in a way that will endure.
    Now Johnson is seen as sending out ministers,
Like long-tailed tits who roost in family flocks
And huddle for warmth during cold winter nights,
To defend an adviser who holds them in contempt,
A demeaning posture for all to have to adopt.
Now he's seen to be dismantling restrictions –
Including those on the shielded, who can now go out –
To get his rule-breaking adviser out of the headlines,
Not because the virus's R rate has weakened,
And people ask if Cummings knows secrets
He would spill in revenge if Johnson sacked him.
It's come out that Johnson lost his temper
With Cummings that first Sunday, and gave him a final
Warning, told him to keep out of the news.
Johnson's halting performance before the Commons
Liaison Committee was that of an unwell man,
Irritable, tired, struggling with detail, coughing,
Fed up with his job, forgetful of facts
And unsighted on the impact of lockdown.
Cummings will stay to block an extension
But Johnson won't lead the Tories at the next
Election as he's made a mess of things.
The newspapers report the Tory lead
Has fallen from twenty-six points ahead
At lockdown to just a four-point lead now.
Like a lone elephant suffering from anthrax,
A bacteria that causes swellings and shiverings,

Johnson appears unwell and is shunned by the herd.
    The economic downturn is so bad –
A thirty-five-per-cent fall in the UK's
National income during the current quarter,
The economy shrinking thirteen per cent this year,
Three times the drop in the banking crisis –
That only rapid economic expansion
And growth will raise the UK from lockdown torpor.
Fighting the disease is doing more damage
Than the disease itself, as economic collapse
Also kills people by economically-driven
Deaths of despair. Across Europe, lockdowns
Are being lifted, businesses are reopening.
All children are back in school as in France.
It's said the young should be sent back to work, social
Distancing should be cut to one metre,
There should be full fibre broadband for all
And tax breaks and incentives to boost
Productivity and achieve massive growth.
The global economy's been detonated
To pursue a lockdown experiment that may not have worked.
    There are studies saying lockdown did not alter
The pandemic's course. In the UK infections
Peaked a week before lockdown, and daily deaths
Plateaued a fortnight after lockdown. A study
Suggests the virus has its own dynamic,
The models were flawed as they were exponential,
With the rate of growth related to the number
Of individuals present, who'll be infected,
As Levitt has explained. There have been no
Second waves save in Iran and Djibouti,
Where data's unreliable. It's said the healthy
Should carry on while the vulnerable isolate.
The Western strategy has been deeply flawed,
The West now needs to go for growth again.
    A daily briefing, Sunak announces

The end of furloughing in October,
A staggered end with employers gradually
Paying more each month from August, going for growth.
A question, will there be hardship ahead?
Sunak says yes, unemployment will go up,
Probably by another two million,
A quarter of the furloughed force may lose their jobs.
The alert level remains at 4, but easing,
Which should have begun at 3, is starting.
Sunak says the UK's meeting the five tests,
It's being done in a measured, progressive way.
The OBR says the cost of furloughing
And such schemes will exceed a hundred billion pounds.
Ahead's a time of central-bank money printing,
And financial repression. The workers,
Put to sleep to escape the virus, do not want
To wake up and return to having to work.
    Now the UK's economy is wrecked
And the opinion polls have narrowed again.
Questions are asked, can manifesto pledges
Be ditched as the world was different when they were made:
The triple tax lock (no income tax, VAT
Or National Insurance rises), increase in
Defence spending, HS2 – can the Government
Change course without being accused of political
Chicanery? *Omnia mutantur, nos*
Et mutantur in illis (all things change
And we change with them or: times are changed and we
Are changed with them) – a variation
Of Ovid in *Metamorphoses*, a saying
During the German Protestant Reformation.
    The UK has the highest excess deaths
Per million in the world: sixty-four thousand
And one of the worst epidemics in the world.
Johnson's approval rating's down twenty-nine
Points to minus seven per cent, while Starmer's

Has gone up four to plus twenty-seven per cent.
So Starmer's now thirty-four points ahead
Of Johnson in the polls and set to be
The next Prime Minister, as the public respond
To Johnson's handling of the corona crisis,
Care-home policy and then the upsurge.
Like a young elephant shunned by the herd,
Johnson feels unwanted by those he's helped.
Starmer's on course to win the next election
And perhaps lead the UK back into the EU.

Now the ship is still stuck, like a plague ship.
It cannot dock but has to ride the tides
And wait until it's safe for all to land.
And still no expert's boarded to see their spoil.
A passenger's shown an old hand a sample
Of gold he hewed from a cliff, and has been told:
"That's not gold, it's worthless iron pyrites."
He's tried to confront the captain, who won't see him.
He's told his friends among the passengers
And now there's a doubt spreading about the voyage
And the captain's being evasive, he won't comment
On the "erroneous" diagnosis of the gold.
He's promised gold and stands by what they've found
And brought back, he's delivered and won't be scorned.

Canto XIV
Moving away from China into Quarantine

Sing, Muse, of how Covid-19 began,
Of Chinese negligence or deliberateness,
Sing of superpowerdom and the rising East
When the West is reeling, its trade shattered,
And sing of the West's moving away from
Chinese influence and worldwide dominance.
And sing of quarantine, of public health
Being put above a prosperous economy.
Sing of grumblings as all try to stay safe.
    Now Downing Street has warned Brussels there'll be
No extension to the transition period
Because the UK will be snarled up in
A massive program of EU legislation
To shore up the single market after the virus,
And so the deadlocked trade talks must be made
To work. However, they've run out of time
And there are red lines on competition,
Regulations, fishing quotas, and the UK's
Access to Europol databases.
Global recovery will take years, when
Negotiating a free-trade-deal with the UK
Will not be foremost on countries' agendas,
And a 'no-deal' Brexit will not be stepping
Into the sunlit uplands of a global
Economy but into a wasteland
At a time when faith in British institutions –
The Government – having the skills to cope
Has diminished. It's been swagger, British
Exceptionalism – 'the UK's exceptional' –
And the 'no-deal' dream rests on all the failings
In PPE, testing, quarantining
And Government messaging, and now seems hubris.

The world has been shocked at the Government's
Handling of the coronavirus crisis, at
Its complacent, incompetent, negligent approach.
It lacks the commanding authority to secure
A lot of trade deals in a short space of time
And needs an extension for the maximum
Of two years as only one extension's allowed.
   Macron says the EU's a political project
And should now be looking towards integration;
The EU should not be inward-looking as each country
Suffers the virus, but should be outward-looking.
There is talk of the collapse of the EU
Under the financial strain of the virus,
And Brussels has asked to borrow seven hundred
And fifty billion euros to cope with the virus
But the fiscally conservative states –
Austria, the Netherlands, Sweden, Denmark
('The frugal four') – oppose EU-made grants
And want bail-outs to be in the form of loans.
   Britain's chief Brexit negotiator Frost
Says there's unlikely to be a fisheries
Agreement by the first of July, and a June
Summit will be the last chance for the UK
To request an extension of up to two years
Of the transition period that ends at the end of this year.
   Like a farmer protecting his herds, flocks and shoals
Barnier says Johnson should keep the promises
He made in the Political Declaration
Rather than row back on a level playing-field
For British and European businesses
On environmental, social and labour
Standards, security, governance
And access to British fishing waters –
If he wants to avoid a double whammy:
After the coronavirus, an EU hit.
He says the EU has much less to lose

From a 'no-deal' Brexit as it exports
Seven per cent of its total export trade
To the UK, which sends forty-seven per cent
To the EU, and WTO rules
Would put tariffs on most of its exports.
The world subject to the referendum
Doesn't exist any more, and now the UK's
Had coronavirus wrecking the economy.
It's funding lockdown, not thinking about Brexit,
So the UK needs a two-year extension.
A deal was promised in the Withdrawal Agreement,
But now that trade and travel have collapsed
Barnier's aim is to reach "a deal so hard
On the British they'd prefer to stay in the EU".
He's more concerned to teach the British a lesson
Than to get out of the worst slump the EU has known.
The EU regards the UK as if it were
Like a herd of cattle suffering from viral
Foot-and-mouth disease, slobbering from blistered tongues
Heads down above their blistered cloven hooves.
    Downing Street has now accused the EU
Of dragging out the negotiations
Till it's too late to do a Brexit deal,
And if the UK gets a breakthrough in
The fisheries agreement, there will be
Economic disruption, a blockade of Calais,
As the European countries will have lost
A significant part of their fishing catch.
    The pandemic's changed everything, and yet
Downing Street is still in the pre-Covid
Era in Brexit and is set to turn
The economic damage done by the pandemic
Into devastation by a 'no-deal' Brexit
That could have been avoided. The British public
Is not ideological, but was angry
With the British *élite* that supported Brussels,

And voted to upset the Establishment.
Johnson thought his premiership would be defined
By Brexit but he will now be judged on
His response to the pandemic, he has been
Overtaken by events and caught unprepared
And has not adjusted as the public have.
Like King Canute he sits upon a beach
And commands the rising virus tide to turn.

Now informed opinion is much troubled,
The intelligentsia are wondering:
What is this all-defining pandemic?
There have always been plagues, and Milton wrote
Paradise Lost while shielding from the plague.
They're always thought to have been natural events.
The truth is, all viruses are natural
And they're all transmitted from animals to humans.
Every virus has reached humans from animals.
Millennia ago tuberculosis came from goats,
Measles from sheep and goats, smallpox from camels,
Leprosy from water-buffalo, whooping
Cough from pigs, typhoid fever from chickens,
Bubonic plague, or the Black Death, from rats,
Malaria from mosquitoes, flu from chickens,
Spanish flu from birds, Russian flu from cows,
The common cold from cattle and horses,
'Mad cow disease' from cattle, Ebola
From fruit-bats and monkeys, SARS from civets
And bats, MERS from camels and bats, and Covid-
19 from bats and pangolins (ant-eaters).
Viruses always mutate, H5N1,
Hong Kong-based bird flu, from migrating ducks.
Forty variations of the virus were brought
Into the UK in February and March,
The genetic code of the virus is
Thirty thousand chemical letters long

With all the instructions to rampage round the world.
Decoding machines can track it and its mutations
In different parts of the world within a day.
Only a World State can control the food
That has mutating viruses and infects
Humans naturally by transmission.
    This is how the plagues and viruses start,
By accidental contamination,
And mutating out of control, sometimes
Helped by scientists searching diseases' genes –
Surely not by a human deliberately
Infecting other humans from self-interest?
That is what your poet wants to believe
Despite the Chinese Communist Party
Withdrawing its blaming of wet markets
And talk that the virus was made by scientists,
And despite having had personal experience
Of Chinese denials when he discovered the immense
Cultural Revolution fifty-four years ago
When visiting the University of Peking.
    The ex-Head of MI6, Dearlove,
Says he's seen a scientific report
In *Quarterly Review of Biophysics*
Discovery written by a Norwegian
Vaccinologist Sorensen and a Scottish
Immunologist Dalgleish proclaiming
The virus did not emerge naturally
But was made by scientists in a lab.
The report, *A Reconstructed Historical*
Aetiology of the SARS-CoV-2 Spike,
Suggests the virus is remarkably well
Adapted for human co-existence
And is the likely result of a Wuhan
Laboratory experiment to produce
Chimeric viruses of high potency.
Suspicious of the speed the Chinese rushed

Out publications blaming pangolins
And bats, Dearlove suggests that scientists
May have conducted secret gene-splicing
Experiments on bat coronaviruses
When Covid-19 escaped through a lapse
In biosecurity. It's presumption, not proof,
And he says it took place at the Wuhan
Institute of Virology or the Wuhan
Centre for Disease Control. If this can be proved
China may face the prospect of paying
Reparations for the deaths and economic
Catastrophe wreaked upon the rest of the world.
    He thinks the pandemic was started by accident,
But points to the way people were arrested
Or silenced to shut down any debate,
And the Chinese let a lethal SARS virus
Escape a Beijing lab in 2004,
And infect nine people during that April
Before the outbreak was at last contained.
And it contains genetic material
Of more than one virus, suggesting it's been
Modified in a lab as a bio-weapon.
The report says the virus is a chimera,
It contains material from more than one virus –
It can make use of co-receptors on
Human epithelial cells, noses and lungs –
And was perhaps created in a lab.
    Leitenberg, a biological weapons expert,
Has said in the *Bulletin of the Atomic Scientists*,
"The possibility of a laboratory
Escape of the pathogen was a plausible,
If unproved, theory." He says that in 2005
Wuhan Institute of Virology
"Initiated construction of novel" –
New – "chimeric coronaviruses"
That were "gain-of-function" experiments

To make a virus capable of infecting
A new kind of cell. He gave evidence
Of the inadequate security in two Wuhan labs,
Especially at the Centre for Disease Control
And Prevention. It's clear that China has
Scientifically well-founded questions to answer
About the virus's origin and nature
As Chinese concealment is hindering
The search for a vaccine throughout the world.
   The PM's spokesman says, "We have seen no
Evidence that the virus is man-made."
A Government official's said, "These are fanciful
Claims, world-leading scientists have clearly said
The virus was natural in its origin
And's likely to have moved into the human
Population through natural transfer from
Animals – not through a specific accident
Or man-made incident." And so it's all right
For the Chinese to continue investing
In the British economy and control G5.
The overwhelming consensus is that
Covid-19 originated in nature
And infected humans through trade in live
Animals – bats, pangolins – for the cooking-pot.
   It's slowly dawning on the Government
Something happened in Wuhan in October.
Satellite images show that more cars
Were parked outside Wuhan hospitals than
A year before, and Baidu, a Chinese
Search engine, shows far more searches for 'cough'
And 'diarrhoea' then than happened previously,
More evidence to add to the roadblocks
Found on mobile records in Wuhan then.
So if the outbreak was earlier than
November the seventeenth (when the Chinese
Announced it) why did the Chinese Government

Not alert the world sooner and prevent
A pandemic and the loss of half a million lives?
China is regarded as a herd of cattle
Where foot-and-mouth disease is rife, but no
Treatment with antibiotics and disinfectants
Is possible as its farm is out of reach.

Now China's passed a national security law
On Hong Kong to eliminate dissent.
It's Communist authoritarianism.
Johnson's announced the UK will offer
Three million Hong Kong residents visa-free
Access to the UK and perhaps British citizenship
As an alternative to Chinese repression.
Johnson's hoping bankers, computer operators,
Stock-market traders and consultants trained
By China will settle in the UK, strengthen
UK skills and will be grateful to Johnson
And vote Tory at the next election,
And replace Labour's Northern voters who lent
The Tories their vote once and won't do it again –
Just as Ugandan Asians voted for Heath
After being expelled by General Amin.
(Patel's parents fled Ugandan repression
In the 1970s, and Raab's Jewish relations
Fled Czechoslovakia in 1938
And lived in the UK during the war.)
It won't be long before Huawei's banned from 5G.

Like a fox that's found a garden where food's put out
And squats in a nearby burrow for daily feasts,
Now Johnson's forming a deeper relationship
With the UK's five eyes intelligence partners –
The US, Australia, Canada and New Zealand –
Which will end all reliance on China
With Cummings' policy of tech before trade,
Of making the UK a Silicon Valley,
And bring investment and research funding

To G5 and the nuclear-power stations.
But there's a split between Sunak, the Chancellor,
Who's warned against an economic wall
With the world's second-largest economy,
And will accept US chlorinated chicken.
So Johnson's sided with the US against
China in the contest of two superpowers
And China will withdraw its investment
In the UK's nuclear power and steel.
It will be Chexit along with Brexit,
The UK will be denied European
And Chinese goods as it tries to recover
From the crippling virus – and the Treasury
Wants more austerity. Sunak's waiting to succeed
Johnson if he goes on needing to nap in the day.
And the Chinese Ambassador to the UK's blurted
To British businessmen that China's produced
A vaccine ready to use against the virus.
He's said, "We always believed Covid-19
Has brought the world together, and we believe
In a shared future for mankind." It's on tape,
But his Embassy's saying he meant the Chinese
Have progressed a vaccine to its second phase
To be tested on humans. Yet if the virus
Was man-made in China, Chinese will know
The ingredients a vaccine needs, and are better placed
To produce a vaccine that can go round the world.
The UK's 'in quarantine' from China.
    China's behaviour has shocked all nations:
Its slowness in warning of coronavirus,
Its disregard for Hong Kong citizens' rights,
Its suppressal of the Uighurs' new births,
Its subjection of Tibet, its systematic
Thieving of intellectual property,
Its military ambitions in the South China Sea,
Its deal with corrupt third-world leaders to steal

Natural resources, its freezing-out of Taiwan,
Its expansionist exports and protectionist imports –
All ruthless empire-building by an aggressive,
Expanding power dreaming of world domination
(Like the Mongols, Romans, Spanish, Portuguese,
Ottomans, British, French and USSR till
Over-confidence, over-ambition, over-extension
And internal dissent brought on collapse,
And like the US which overreached itself
In Vietnam, Iraq and Afghanistan).

PMQs, and Starmer quotes Johnson as saying
He's now taking direct control of the virus,
He asks who has been in control so far. (Cummings?)
Johnson lists his achievements in protecting
The NHS and driving down the deaths
And asks for co-operation. Starmer says he
Wrote in private, asking if he could co-operate
To get children back to school – Johnson hasn't replied.
He says there's been a loss of trust in the Government.
And now it's announced that all visitors
To the UK and returning travellers
Must go into quarantine for fourteen days
Like cattle suspected of having foot-and-mouth.
Johnson's asking for support for quarantine.
    Quarantine three months too late's not the choice
Of an outward-looking nation that boasts
Of global Britain, but of Little Englanders
Pulling up the drawbridge, not caring about
The direction for tourism or the blow
To the UK's international reputation
As not wanting any foreign nationals,
Many from countries with fewer infections
And lower rates of transmission – all will
Have to quarantine for two weeks because
Cummings found the policy's popular

With focus groups and opinion polls: Brexiteers.
It suggests lack of trust in test-and-trace.
It will cost the airline industry twenty billion
And loss of billions that tourists and students bring
And the UK's reputation as an open
Trading nation. The UK now has more virus deaths
Than the twenty-seven EU nations combined
But Johnson's said there'll be a second peak
If arrivals don't quarantine. The UK
Has the worst infection and death rates in Europe,
And it makes no sense to exclude nationals
From countries that like Spain now have no deaths.
SAGE scientists have said it makes no sense.
    So why? The backers of the referendum
And the election, Disaster Capitalism,
Have bet on 'no deal' with the EU, which will
Lead to a shortage of medicines in a second spike,
And as 'no deal' is to be delivered to DC
It's vital there should be no second spike?
And so the UK's in lockdown from abroad
By quarantining all who are arriving?
    Quarantine's a shambles Cummings has pushed through.
And so all new arrivals must isolate for two weeks
Before they begin their holiday, it's three months
Too late, it should have been begun in March.
Holidays should not stop when the virus is dying out,
It's a disaster for domestic tourism
And signals foreign tourists are not welcome.
It's a blow to the UK's international reputation.
Cummings has found focus groups and polls show
Isolation in Little England is popular –
So what happened to outward-looking great Britain?
    The quarantine that Cummings is behind –
The three-hour delays at Heathrow as forms
Have to be filled in for arrivals and departures,
The group of ships moored off the British coast –

Is officially the UK's guarding against
A second wave of the virus, but in fact
(It's been said) is a pro-Brexit policy without
Scientific evidence, it's a tactic
Within the EU negotiations to prove
How powerful the British consumer's seen to be
By the European countries, whose economies
Are hurt when Spanish and Italian tourists
Are blocked from arriving in the UK.
Thirty thousand dead and the UK about to have
The highest death toll in Europe, above
The Italians, GDP thirty per cent
Down, one million jobs lost, and PPE
For doctors is thirty-seven per cent short.
The UK's a country been put to the test
By jingoism (the UK standing alone
Without feeling pain, as Brexiteers promised
In 2016) and has seen its leaders fail.
Johnson, a post-modern populist, has peddled
Cheerful myths with winks and smirks, calls for pluck.
The fatal failure to contain the virus
In February and early March when the UK
Was engulfed by the pandemic was caused by
Johnson's puffed-up nationalism, which saw Brits
As favoured by Providence, refusing
To be cowed like Europeans locking down,
The UK'd stand alone as in 1940
And cope with herd immunity as in the Blitz.
The Brexiteers, who invoked the wartime spirit,
Have never fought a war, and now the Brexit
Movement, impervious to reason or engaging
With complexity, has reached its terminus.
All the competent ministers with experience
Were fired for opposing a 'no-deal' Brexit
And sent to the back benches, and in their place
A dilettante PM, a Cabinet

Of nobodies and a civil service policed
By Vote-Leave propagandists who could fool
The country in a referendum but can't
Manage it in a crisis, a Government
Of sycophants, not of all the talents.
Their time has gone, they'll cling on in the slump,
Blame foreigners and turn to new saviours,
But the glib, deceitful spirit of 2016
With its promises that bills need never be paid
Is over. Having dismissed public-health warnings
As over the top – as it dismissed warnings
On Brexit as 'Project Fear' – the Brexit Right
Has been shown up in its final rally, and now,
Exhausted, even Johnson knows the UK
Will pay for being one of the last EU
Countries to go into lockdown by being among
The last to leave, and the counterfeit optimists
Who brought on Brexit are now frightened pessimists
Who can't forget the thirty thousand dead
And are now faced with GDP down eight per cent
From the virus and another five (some say ten)
Per cent from a 'no-deal' Brexit as the IMF
(Or NIESR) say – when the NHS has received
Only one per cent of GDP a year
Since austerity began in 2010.
Beside this, their hoped-for fifteen-billion-pound
Boost to the economy from US trade
Talks is minute, and the people have seen through
The charlatan Brexiteers' sale of fools' gold.

Still the ship rides at anchor off the land,
Biding its time, waiting for the plague to pass,
A plague ship in all but name with a load
Of sick passengers and crew, and of fake gold.
Word's passed among the fools: they've got fool's gold,
Iron pyrites. Many lies have been told,

They've been conned by the captain, whose policies
Glittered and glistened like sparkling gold.

Canto XV
Debt, Disorder – and Building

Sing, Muse, of colossal debt and deep recession
And of a PM who pretends everything's normal,
Sing of building within a new depression
And of disorder within society,
Sing of the hopelessness of the unemployed
As the downturn begins to hurt the poor.
And sing of the reckless policies that got all here.
    The figures tumble round the Chancellor's head.
The Treasury borrowed 62.1
Billion pounds in April, the biggest monthly
Figure in history, it's left a deficit
Far bigger than at the height of the financial
Crisis and without equal in peacetime,
More than was planned for the whole of the coming year.
And retail sales slumped 22.6 per cent
From the same month last year, wiping out fifteen
Years of growth in only one month, and there's
Been a knock-on effect for the Treasury.
The national debt has jumped 118.4
Billion pounds, seventeen per cent in a single year –
To 1.9 trillion pounds, the biggest
Yearly increase on record, and the Treasury
Are pushing for austerity and tax rises.
The Chancellor's under pressure to ignore
Johnson's growled pledge to do without austerity
(And leave the costs to a future generation).
    Now there's disorder in London, lockdown's
Forgotten as thousands demonstrate against
The killing of a black man in the US
(A drug taker who did five spells in prison,
An ex-convict who did five years for robbery),
In Bristol they've pulled down Colson's statue –

Premeditated, as they had the tools,
Wires strong enough to pull the statue down –
And rolled it to the dock's edge and pushed it over
So it's now sunk to the bottom of the harbour.
Statues remind all of their history,
Some are of good men, some of less than good.
Why should a mob decide if they should be shown
When there are learned men who can judge such things
And recommend a statue should be removed
To a museum if it's inappropriate?
    In London a mob have thrown a Boris bike
At a police horse, which bolted and crashed
A policewoman into a traffic-light
And put her in hospital. Crowds mill round King Charles Street
And fight with police, and set bins on fire,
Smash windows and throw bottles at the police.
And social distancing because of the virus
Has gone, along with accepting Government rules,
And there's a revolutionary feel to London,
Johnson's Government looks flimsy and fragile,
And where is Johnson? Not speaking in Downing Street,
Not exercising leadership while police scour.
The police have lost control of the streets, statues
Are being removed without democratic consent,
By a mob that's also daubed Churchill's
Pedestal "Was a racist", with no sense
Of the tradition of the past – that Churchill stood
Up to Hitler's racism and kept us free.
We are in an ill-informed and barbarous time
When there's criminal revolt against the strangling
Of the economy and throttling of liberty,
With little awareness there's a pandemic.
    Like screaming gulls swarming round a dead seal
A crowd has now gathered under Cecil Rhodes'
Statue outside Oriel College, Oxford.
On the road is painted "Post-Collonial

Attitudes matter" – a mob that doesn't know
How to spell 'colonial' is telling us what parts
Of our history should be thrown into a harbour.
There's a Cultural Revolution in the UK,
As Far Left seek to efface the national story
And replace it with one of racial oppression,
Editing and censoring past perspectives.
Nelson may be pulled down from his column,
Queen Victoria was a colonialist Empress,
Baden-Powell approved of Hitler and his statue
In Poole harbour is being guarded by scouts.
Wordsworth's cancelled, his brother sailed to China
And may have handled slaves before he drowned.
Ban Wordsworth from our libraries and schools.
Ted Hughes was descended from Nicholas Ferrar
Who funded Little Gidding where he was priest,
And's been found to be linked to the London
Virginia Company, to the slave trade,
So the British Library's dossier on links
To slavery and colonialism includes Hughes.
Your poet received cards and letters from him
And served as Heath's Unofficial Ambassador
To the African liberation movements,
And once owned Otley Hall, where Bartholomew
Gosnold organised his voyage to Virginia
And co-founded the Jamestown Settlement
That's associated with slavery. Does that mean
Your poet will end in a dossier on the slave trade?
    In Boston a statue of Columbus has lost its head.
It's a new bout of iconoclasm,
Like the Puritans cutting off all papal heads
And pulling down statues in Catholic churches.
Like packs of wild dogs iconoclasts sniff
The wind for statues and, snarling, savage them.
'We don't like Churchill, so pull his statue down.'
Now the Mayor has boarded Churchill up, the police

Are too weak to protect the man who saved
The UK and the whole of Europe from
A fascist and racist enslaving tyranny,
Britain's history seems to have been boarded up.
It's not just slave-traders, it's empire-builders.
Pro-colonial Hakluyt should be erased
(And of course his friend Bartholomew Gosnold who sailed
To America and founded the Jamestown Settlement).
British history matters, and should not be thinned down
By post-historical ideologies.
Will books be burned – Shakespeare's *Othello*?
What next to appease the mob of misspellers?
Police are grappled to the ground and filmed.
History's a conglomerate of ideas and beliefs,
Is complex and cannot be edited
To suit a sole narrative of black culture
And its roots in the slave-trade of the past.
    Like a chaffinch singing a repetitive song
Now in Parliament Starmer asks Johnson
If he's proud of the Government's record
As deaths from the virus have passed forty thousand.
The Office of National Statistics which records
Coronavirus on death certificates
Says deaths stand at fifty thousand and excess
Deaths stand at over sixty-three thousand,
The highest number in the world. Starmer says
There's no pride in these figures, and Johnson
Should take responsibility for his failings.
Johnson blusters that people must wait till
The end of the epidemic to draw
Comparisons. Starmer says there is no
National plan for early schools opening,
Commitment from parents and leadership,
And none of these is being shown. Johnson
Does not appear to understand the scale
And urgency of the challenge of reopening schools.

As sheep sit down on grass predicting rain
The markets slump down sensing bad forecasts.
Now the OECD has predicted the UK
Economy will be the hardest hit
By the pandemic among all developed
Countries in the West and will contract eleven
And a half per cent this year, or fourteen per cent
If there's a second wave towards winter.
Johnson's luck's run out, the scientists gave him
Wrong advice at the start – they did not realise
How many were infected by early March –
And the bureaucracy let the country down
By not ordering equipment and testing
And now he's making unforced errors –
The quarantine chaos and the failure
Of the test-and-tracing and the two-
Metre rule's dragging the crisis out much longer
Than in France, Italy, Spain or Germany
And now the UK's facing the sharpest recession
Of any rich country and will suffer worse
Economically than all its rivals.
The world has changed, and the UK has endured
Sixty-four thousand excess deaths caused by
The virus or lockdown, the worst in the West,
And the failure of the bureaucratic State
Has been clear for all to see – the incompetence
Of Public Health England, the lack of preparedness
And inability to order PPE,
The scientific advice, shifting, nothing
Learned from the SARS epidemic, and the blunder
That allowed the virus to rampage through care homes.
Another briefing and Johnson is asked:
Ferguson's told the Commons Science Committee
That had lockdown been a week earlier
The deaths would have been halved, twenty thousand
Who are dead would still be alive. But he

Did not say this in March – he's admitting
That his policy was completely wrong.
(He's said they missed ninety per cent of infections
Coming from abroad, from Italy and Spain,
And they assumed those in care homes would be shielded,
Which simply did not happen, so his estimate
Of twenty thousand dead under lockdown was wrong.)
Like a rattlesnake swaying at its full height
Johnson looks rattled and says now's not the time
To discuss deaths when data's still being collected.
He doesn't want to engage, he says it's too early
To judge, the epidemic is shrinking but not fast.
If he had attended the five Cobra meetings
In January and February, and had begun lockdown
Earlier at the same time as France and Italy
Twenty-five thousand people would still be alive.
His failure to chair five meetings meant he was slow
To implement what needed to be done
(As with PPE, masks, tests and everything else).
Now there's a looming economic storm,
High unemployment and high inflation –
Stagflation – or deflation, low prices,
As the bandages come off the economy.
The Government's been in intensive care
And now the sunlit uplands seem far away.
The Governor of the Bank of England's warning
Banks to ramp up their preparations for
A 'no-trade-deal' Brexit as time's running out
And no breakthrough's in sight. Johnson's reported
Ready to accept EU tariffs on
A small number of British goods to break
The deadlock in the trade talks with the EU.
The UK economy's shrunk 20.4 per cent
In April after dropping 5.8 per cent in March,
The biggest drop in GDP since records began.
The Bank of England's announced a further

Hundred billion pounds of QE, making
Three hundred billion in the present round.
The two-metre social distancing's slowing growth down.
Now it's announced the UK will not have
Full border checks on EU goods after Brexit
As companies can't cope with the fall-out
Of the pandemic *and* leaving the EU.
UK goods will still face full checks in Europe.
If there's no trade agreement by the end of July
The UK'll opt for 'no deal' and WTO terms
Even though it slows the UK's recovery
From coronavirus by adding high tariffs
To agricultural produce and cars
And strikes a blow on people's livelihoods,
Businesses and the NHS in what would be
A monumental act of national self-harm.
A plea from the first ministers of Scotland,
Wales and Northern Ireland for an extension
Of the post-Brexit transition period
While exiting the EU, but Gove declines
And the cohesion of the UK creaks again.
From January tariffs will be paid on all imports
But there will be a six-month delay for
Customs declarations and tariff payments.
So there's got to be a deal or else in December
It's 'no deal' and another economic hit
And businesses cannot cope with 'no deal'.
    Is Johnson still the PM? Tories are muttering
He's not fully recovered, has no direction,
Can't concentrate and his judgment is warped.
He may have to sleep three hours during each day,
And he's a poor shadow of the old Johnson
Who had always been an opportunist
With a minor talent for self-parody
To entertain and amuse the electorate.
He got into Downing Street through Brexit

But never believed in that foolish endeavour,
Yet as a charlatan, will not admit this.
(At Oxford Johnson spoke in the Union
On capital punishment and began by asking
"Can someone kindly remind me what the motion is?"
And when told said, "Crikey, Moses. I'm not
In favour of that," and walked to the other side
Of the table and began denouncing the motion,
Spoke against capital punishment, only half-serious,
And then stopped and said, "No, wait, I think I'm in favour
Of the motion after all," and crossed back and made
An impassioned case for capital punishment.
The audience roared with appreciative laughter.
He did the same with the EU, he wrote
Pro and con articles for *The Sunday Times*
Like a wild dog sniffing for the scent of meat,
And allowed the con to be published and took
The Leave side in the referendum, but could,
If it had been appeased with a juicy bone,
Just as easily have voted for Remain.)
And now the national coronavirus crisis
Has put the truth on show, and when voters
See Europe back to normal and more UK lockdown,
Soaring unemployment, widespread bankruptcies,
Empty Treasury coffers, no longer infatuated,
Unswayed by a calamitous 'no-deal' Brexit
With shortages of foods, medicines, and businesses
That survived the virus going under
Because of a man-made disastrous Brexit
They will turn on his Government ferociously.
He will fall and leave the stage, a charlatan
Who navigates by the opinion polls
And does whatever he thinks voters want –
Hence the quarantine shambles that may kill
The airline industry with a passenger drought.

The hottest week of the year, and sunlight kills
The virus (just as vitamin D's a shield) –
Half an hour of sunlight reduces its
Infectivity by ninety per cent,
Sunlight's ultraviolet radiation
Damages viruses' DNA – while it thrives
In humid and cold conditions. But one in three
Victims of the virus could be harmed for life.
Half patients treated in intensive-care
Units are left with a chronic fatigue
That requires naps to be taken during the day.
Many have long-term damage to their lungs,
Disturbances to memory, Alzheimer's.
Cognitive impairments befuddle thinking.
Breathlessness limits activity to ten minutes,
There may be anxiety, delirium
And signs of dementia, pressure on lungs
That lead to night shakes, seizure, nausea,
Tinnitus and a tightness in the chest.
    Now it's come out, the Threats, Hazards, Resilience
And Contingencies Subcommittee of the National
Security Council, chaired by Johnson,
Made up of intelligence chiefs and fifteen
Cabinet ministers, was wound up by Sedwill
To focus on Brexit exit strategy,
Cancelled by Johnson when it should have been
Ahead of pandemics and all such threats.
Minutes of SAGE meetings show the scientists
Called for caution, but after ignoring
The scientists by not attending five meetings,
Johnson was shocked when he saw the forecasts
Of Ferguson and his team – who'd overstated
The effects of mad cow disease (BSE),
Swine flu, bird flu and foot-and-mouth disease
(Which led to six million animals being killed) –
And, lacking his wife Marina's common sense,

Her intellectual input and home truths,
A new father with demanding Carrie,
And, as on a sure-footed donkey climbing a path
Up a mountain with sheer drops either side,
Reliant on Cummings, he and the Government panicked
And instead of isolating the elderly
And vulnerable while keeping society going
With masks and testing, rushed into lockdown,
One of the worst decisions in British history
As it wiped out eighteen years of economic growth
And crashed the UK's economy, education
System, performing arts, tourism and travel,
And blighted the life chances of a whole generation.
    Johnson's lost his ability to communicate,
He's indecisive under the virus,
His back-benchers hear nothing, he just looks
Exhausted and forlorn, sallow-faced, hollow-eyed,
Tired from sleepless nights with his baby boy
And a fiancée twenty-three years younger,
In a permanent dither and dysfunctional –
He and the Government are stuck in a quicksand
And can't emerge and break free from lockdown.
Like a dog that has rabies, with throat and jaw
Muscles paralysed and foaming at the mouth,
Johnson blunders on, blagging and bragging
On the pandemic, economic recovery
And on Brexit, trashing the country as he goes.
He has not taken back control, he's a PM
Who's lost control, looks fearful and panicky.
Now it's come out there's not been a Cobra
Meeting on the virus for more than a month
As last time Scotland and Wales would not change
The slogan from 'Stay home' to 'Stay alert'.
He's governed intuitively by his instincts
As a campaigner who sees what the public wants,
Without reading briefs, hoping the caravan

Of events will move on, as with Cummings,
Even while the dogs outside are still barking.
    Johnson wants a deal with the EU by August,
Europe by October to allow time
For ratification by the twenty-seven,
But will negotiate till the last day of December.
There's a lot of goodwill but no plan to make it happen.
Meanwhile the EU is preparing to back down
(So Barnier has hinted but not yet said)
On a Brexit fishing deal that gives EU fleets
An automatic right to fish in British waters.
The UK wants a free-trade deal with the US
By November, before Trump's out, which has blocked an EU
Deal, but Trump's top trade representative
Has said this is now "almost impossible",
And Trump could be out of office by the time
A deal with the US is ready to be agreed.
The UK faces no trade deal with the EU
Or the US by the end of the year
And a nightmare economic wasteland at home.
    The borrowing in April and May has pushed
Up the national debt by a hundred and seventy-three
Billion pounds, to 100.9 per cent
Of the entire economy's annual output,
The first time debt-to-GDP's risen
To more than a hundred per cent since 1963
When the UK was trying to pay down debts
Racked up in the Second World War which lifted
Public debt to two hundred and fifty per cent
Of GDP. In the EU, Belgium, France,
Spain, Portugal, Italy and (most of all) Greece
Now have higher debt-to-GDP ratios.
Unperturbed, Johnson's spending nearly a million pounds
Of taxpayers' money to paint a plane he'll use
Red, white, blue – again demonstrating
That he thinks in gimmicks, gestures and slogans.

Now the Bank of England's Governor's spoken
Of how panicking investors sold UK
Government bonds to realise cash and the UK
Had to auction gilts to fund crucial spending,
Which the Bank of England's funded with three hundred
Billion of QE, leaving the Treasury
To reduce the gigantic deficit this year.
He says he'll reverse the Bank's money printing,
Reduce its ballooning balance sheet of bonds,
Which has swollen to more than seven hundred billion
Built up through quantitative easing (QE),
Before raising interest rates from record lows.
He says the Bank must rebuild its war chest
Ahead of the next downturn, and without its QE
The Government would have struggled to fund itself.
The truth is, the Government would have gone bust
During the stock-market meltdown in March
If it hadn't been rescued by the Bank
Which averted a liquidity crisis.
With debt a hundred per cent of national income,
The highest it has been since World War Two,
During lockdown many have been living
In a fools' paradise, insulated from the prospect
Of widespread unemployment now ahead.
Now, like a shepherd removing a padlock
To let out sheep from the safety of their barn,
Exactly three months after it was imposed,
There is action to end lockdown and bring
The UK people out of hibernation
To stave off mass unemployment
And attempt a cautious optimism.
Johnson makes a statement in Parliament
On how measurements of the fall in the virus's
Prevalence (death rates, numbers on ventilators,
Downgrading the threat level from 4 to 3)
Means that in England only (not Scotland,

Wales or Northern Ireland) social distancing
Can be reduced from two metres to one
Plus mitigations – screens, face coverings,
Hand sanitisers and regular wiping down –
On July the fourth, but still, the fewer social
Contacts the safer. He lists twenty-five
Different kinds of business that can reopen –
Pubs, cafés, restaurants, hotels, cinemas,
Museums, hairdressers and places of worship –
But his guides in SAGE have advised caution.
Now Johnson hosts the briefing between his guides
Vallance and Whitty (the Chief Scientific Adviser
And Chief Medical Officer), and will they support
The easing of lockdown? He shows from graphs
That the five tests have been passed.
Whitty says a balance has to be struck
As there is co-existence with the virus:
Reducing contact between households to two
And operating in a safer – not completely
Safe – way as two metres is still preferable.
His approach is different from Johnson's, it's announced
There'll be no more briefings, just announcements
From time to time, so the scientists are stepping back.
This ninety-second press conference is the last,
With the scientists more cautious and worried and not
Whole-heartedly endorsing the changes,
And SAGE has not signed off this latest guidance.
But what happens if Whitty's right and the virus
Returns in the winter and the pandemic gets worse?
The Government's had an uncomfortable relationship
With its scientific advisers, it's evaded
Responsibility by passing the buck
To them for its own political decisions:
First came the essential medical services,
Then the unprepared last-minute decision
To lock down, using public-health legislation

Designed to control the movements of infected people –
Instead of cocooning the over-seventies
And people with underlying medical conditions:
A panic response to Ferguson's
Imperial-College statistical model.
When Sunak and Sharma explained the economic
Consequences, startled Johnson exclaimed, "Christ!"
Ahead was economic catastrophe:
Gross domestic product down a fifth and falling,
Three and a half million jobs set to be lost
In the hospitality industry, unemployment
Already two million, millions of businesses
To disappear, job openings for a generation
Of young people set to be extinguished.
Why was the PM surprised? What did he expect
To happen if he shut down the economy
For several months? The only plausible
Explanation is he hadn't thought about it.
Then the return to work was stymied by
The two-metre rule and by quarantine
Of incoming travellers, based on the belief
That the public would applaud it, according to polls.
The Cabinet is as devoid of talent
As was the Cabinet of the early nineteen-thirties.
The PM, like Cummings, was a good campaigner
But is poor at governing as everything
Has to be framed as part of a Brexit culture war.
He's incapable of studying a complex
Problem in depth, he thinks as he speaks – in slogans.
He can't think about more than one thing at a time,
Yet's destroying the British economy, cultural life
And children's education absent-mindedly.
Now the cricketer Botham is to be made a peer
For supporting Brexit. Are we to hear
His analysis of how much trade with the EU
Will be lost when the UK's under WTO

Rules, and is a third country? Is he deemed
More politically savvy than Bercow?
No, it's a Johnson joke, a dig against May
Who saw herself as having the staying power of Boycott,
And the cautious scientists, it signals the time
Of Boycottian caution is over and Botham's
Risk-taking's in. He's to have a seat in the Lords
As a walking metaphor for Johnson's PMship,
That will be full of risk-taking self-belief,
Not to speak on trade and the economy.
So populism has replaced statesmanship,
Wisdom and experience in high office
With support, cronyism and hero-worship
As qualifications for Parliament.
Your poet recalls standing outside Lord's
Last year (after a birthday outing to watch
A Test), waiting for a car, with Boycott behind
Him and Botham on the other side of the road,
Two knights looking at their phones, your poet between,
Equidistant from their opposites, reconciling
Their caution and risk, and did not think, 'I'm
Between May and Johnson, paradise and gold.'
    There are thirty-six new peers, including Botham
The legislator, and Johnson's brother Jo,
And May's silent husband's to be knighted.
We live in a corrupt, benighted time
When a PM can nominate his own brother
For a peerage without being considered nepotistic
Or cronyist – so populism hands
Legislative judgment to unsuitables and cronies.
Your poet shakes his head: decline, decline.

Like a nightjar uttering incomprehensible churs
Johnson's speaking on his post-Covid-recovery plan,
He justifies the economic chaos
With colourful language that exonerates him:

"If Covid was a lightning flash, we're about
To have the thunderclap of economic
Consequences" (suggesting the consequences
Will have nothing to do with him, like thunder).
His plan is for massive borrowing and spending
Which he calls investment, it's "build, build, build",
Borrowing a trillion pounds at low-interest rates
(For now) when the pound won't be devalued as
Other countries are affected similarly,
And spending on renewable energy
(Cleaner fuels) and a new Silicon city,
With fibre-optic cables throughout the UK
For a high-speed internet, roads, rail, housing,
Forty hospitals, and subsidies for
Industry with many apprenticeships
To create jobs for all – and leave repayment
To coming generations, and future PMs.
And perhaps, despite all this, to go into 'no deal'
Unopposed now the twenty-one have been expelled
For seeing 'no deal' as a gigantic risk.
Now another opponent of 'no deal' has gone:
Sedwill, Johnson's Cabinet Secretary
(Head of the Civil Service) who clashed with Cummings,
And National Security Adviser,
Replaced by Frost who will accept 'no deal'
And effect a Whitehall revolution for
Civil servants are impartial and independent.
It is said that Sedwill's Cabinet job should go
To a Brexiteer (someone who'll be happy
With 'no deal') and take on borrow-and-build.
Meanwhile crowds flock to Bournemouth in a heatwave,
And there's disorder in London and Liverpool,
And multitudes disregard distancing.

Like a peacock displaying a hundred eyes
As if each one's truth, not a hundred lies,
Now Johnson is making his "build" speech in

Dudley, calling for a New Deal (like Roosevelt's
Rebuilding after the Great Depression
In the thirties) and for "project speed" to build
All the projects Governments have shunned for thirty
Years, an infrastructure revolution
To stimulate the economy that's twenty per cent
Down this year so far. He calls for innovatory
Projects like a zero-emission long-haul plane,
So the UK'll be a "science" superpower.
There'll be spending on new schools, homes and trees,
Hospitals, rail and road; oh, and a bridge
From Scotland across to Northern Ireland.
There'll be a shake-up of planning regulations
To allow commercial properties to be
Converted into housing or "repurposed"
From shops to cafés or to offices.
There'll be massive Labour-like investments
On borrowed money, to use Covid-19
As a springboard, with the private sector
As the bedrock of the economy.
There should be doorstep clapping for wealth creators.
He'll rush forward five billion from an investment
Of six hundred and forty billion pounds
And there may have to be higher taxes
To cover some of the enormous costs.
He says he's not a Communist (like Corbyn),
But will keep all employed (on borrowed money).
Like a dog in a French window, he barks
And barks and barks to see off a danger,
But nothing's changed out in the large garden.
The barking's to no avail and solves nothing.
    The Bank of England says more than half the British
Population's unemployed or underemployed.
Johnson wants to get the diggers in and build now –
Hospitals, schools, rail, road – to "build, build, build"
The way back to health, meaning "spend, spend, spend".

What about "jobs, jobs, jobs"? A chill like a breeze.
How can the coming unemployed in retail
And hospitality learn building skills?
 The extra Covid spending now totals
A hundred and nineteen billion; furlough
Fifty-six billion; welfare twenty-three
Billion; grants to small business fifteen
Billion; NHS and extra spending
Fifteen billion or six per cent of GDP;
And Johnson is bringing forward five billion
Already promised. The capital investment
Is tiny beside the outgoings, add to this
A fall in receipts and existing deficit
And the total is fifteen per cent of GDP,
Higher than any year of the financial
Crisis or New Deal, more borrowing than
In any single year in the fastest
Economic decline in forty years.
So Brexiteers thought they'd left the EU for
A more deregulated, low-tax economy,
And this interventionist Rooseveltian
New Deal is State-regulating and high-tax
And Johnson's claiming he's in favour of both.
 Super Saturday – or super-spreader-day?
As people emerge from lockdown into pubs,
Restaurants and hairdressers, go to weddings
And civil ceremonies and theme parks
The infection rate is higher than when the UK
Went into lockdown. And it's now emerged
The Government was advised in early
April that staff should not move between care homes,
And it took them five weeks to act on this,
With twenty thousand deaths as the result.
The most vulnerable elderly were not shielded
Effectively. And now the Government
Has broken its pledge to give ten billion

To the NHS to clear the backlog on
The eve of its seventy-second birthday,
And after NHS staff have risked themselves
And have been clapped on doorsteps every week.
    Now there's news of the virus's consequences.
The Institute of Fiscal Studies has warned
It will take decades for the UK's finances
To recover from the last four months. Taxes
Will rise some forty billion pounds a year,
The equivalent of 1.5 per cent
Of GDP. The Chancellor has spent
A hundred and eighty-eight billion pounds
Of public money on the economy
During lockdown. Borrowing will be half a trillion
Pounds during the next two years, and increasing
Taxes will reduce economic activity
And employment – and also the tax take.
There are many costs. The reward to employers
Will be a thousand pounds for each staff retained,
At a cost of 9.4 billion pounds.
Thirteen years of progress in tackling
NHS waiting lists have been destroyed
In these four months. And the EU Commission
Has invited the UK to join the new
EU vaccine strategy to provide tens
Of millions of doses to its member states –
And the UK's been barred from the steering committee
That will decide which country gets the first doses,
And, fearing the EU'll limit doses to the UK,
Has declined to join as a delay in receiving
The vaccine could cost the UK economy
Tens of billions of pounds. The UK now
Understands that care-home workers should be
Isolated and not work in multiple homes
To avoid spreading the virus, which has led
To twenty-two thousand deaths in UK care homes.

Johnson wants all to go back to work now,
Wear masks into shops, and eat less to cut
Obesity, which the virus heads for,
And 'eat out to help out' on half-discounts
(A mixed message, 'Don't eat' and yet 'Eat more').
But many are preferring to stay at home,
Not sure if the pandemic's over or just starting,
Cautious about the virus and preferring
Working from home to the old way of working,
And the economy's missing the stay-at-homes' spending.
   Now masks are obligatory in shops
With fines of a hundred pounds for a breach.
The rules have been released just hours before
The change and there seems to be no logic in them.
You must wear a mask in a bank or post office
But not in a gym or a theatre, and why
Do you need to wear a mask if you're shopping
In a supermarket but not if you're working there?
You have to wear a mask in a take-away
But the person serving need not wear a mask.
You needn't wear a mask in a library
Or a place of worship but have to if buying clothes.
   Much gold was promised for the NHS.
Now it's announced, no pay increases for nurses
Or anyone in the NHS beneath
The rank of a consultant or GP.
It was vigorously denied the NHS
Would be for sale to US companies:
Before the election promises were made,
"We will never sacrifice the NHS
As part of a US trade deal. The NHS
Is not on the table" and "We will never allow
Food standards to be compromised as part of a trade deal".
Now an amendment to the Trade Bill's clause 17
Designed to protect the NHS from being
Subject to control from outside the UK

In any future post-Brexit trade deal
Has been voted down by every Tory MP.
Down, protecting the NHS from foreign control,
And from being compromised by any future trade deal.
Down, protecting its public funding so it's free
At the point of delivery, and so its staff
Don't have their wages or any of their rights slashed.
Down, controlling pricing of its medicines.
Down, preserving the quality and safety
Of its many health and care services.
Down, protecting patients' data from being sold off
Under a future trade deal with the US.
And down, Parliament approving trade agreements.
    Lockdown, and the worst death count and economic
Hit in Europe – with that failed policy
Johnson has fallen out with the scientists.
In a briefing he says as the death rate
Is falling, the R rate's low and the virus
Can be targeted locally with test-and-trace,
He wants all office workers back at their desk
If employers decide, and using public transport,
And a timetable for lifting social-distancing
(Hoping for the best but planning for the worst).
Vallance, the Chief Scientific Adviser,
Has said there's no reason to stop working at home,
Which is crippling town- and city-centres,
And that social distancing should remain
Until a vaccine against the virus is found –
And is not at the briefing to dissent.
It's the economy or public health,
Balancing the two may increase infections.
    Just as iguanas bask in the sun and recharge,
Now there's a false contentment as people
Are on lockdown holiday, their salary paid,
Sitting in sunny gardens with their children
Like summer birds wafted in on mild winds,

Like a blackbird warbling contentedly among lilacs
Or a grasshopper warbler in sweet-smelling honeysuckle
Near where goldfinches are drawn to thistle-seeds,
Admiring rhododendrons and wisteria,
Laburnum and pale-blue forget-me-nots,
Unaware their companies are in dire straits
And they'll soon be unemployed, basking
In the sunshine of a fools' paradise,
And a rude awakening is ahead
As it's announced that England has suffered
The worst coronavirus death toll in Europe,
More excess deaths than any European nation.
There'll be satellitehood or else 'no deal'.
The economy's shrunk twenty-three per cent
During the first half of 2020
(21.3 per cent between April and June).
Trade will be thirty per cent down under WTO rules,
As bad as in the Great Depression in
1932 with five million unemployed,
And 'no deal' will be worse than a satellite deal –
Or a fudge, a 'deal' that doesn't change things for
A long time, that comes in at a future date,
So Johnson will be able to say he's the victor
And the EU will be able to say that they have won.
    A rude awakening.... Now the PM
In a briefing has slammed the brakes on easing lockdown:
People in Blackburn can't be in the streets,
There's been no warning, and now throughout the UK
Openings have been suspended for beauty salons,
Bowling alleys, theatres, county-cricket crowds
And such gatherings, including the Muslim Eid,
And schools can only open if pubs close
As the virus is spreading and is taking hold.
There are fears Europe will follow the US
(Which suffered a 9.5-per-cent slump
Between April and June, its biggest collapse

In growth since the Great Depression) into
A double-dip downturn in a fog of lies.
The new slogan's: "hands, face, space" ("wash your hands,
Cover your face, observe two metres' distance").
It's government by slogans and no one's listening.
Half the English public don't understand the rules.
The virus is permanently all round us in the air,
There are no waves, it's not like the sea whose tides
Come in and then go out, drawn by the moon,
It's airborne, blown by wind, caught or not caught.
We wall it out with masks, distance and tests,
But our wall's cracking, crumbling, it's a leaky wall
As we go out and intermingle with all.
We were told the virus is in retreat – not now.
It's confusion, upset and total chaos
Caused by Johnson's imprecision and bluster.
(A young woman says on TV, "I stopped
Listening to that idiot weeks ago.")
There's a lot of Brexit legislation to do,
People need to know it's reasonably safe
To start functioning normally again,
But the Government's incapable of reassuring them.
The UK faces economic devastation
If it waits for the virus to be eliminated
Before leaving lockdown, yet there's silence,
Lack of judgment and lack of leadership.
An EU diplomat asks, "What has become
Of your country? We see only a ship of fools,
And a plague ship at that, heading for the rocks."
  The latest Bank of England report forecasts,
Like a dog barking at an unseen intruder,
That recovery will be slower than expected
But not as severe, the worst economic downturn
For a hundred years, since Spanish flu, not three
Hundred years, with the economy shrinking
9.5 per cent, not fourteen per cent,

And unemployment doubling to 2.5
Million, not four, and 9.5 per cent
Growth in 2021, and a V-shaped
Recovery in one or three years' time –
All dependent on whether there's a second spike
And more lockdown, and a permanent switch
From shops to online, offices to home.
But no one knows what's going to happen now.
    With hindsight, there should have been two weeks' lockdown
In March before the peak, and the economy
Should have been restarted with the vulnerable
Still shielded, but what was needed was foresight
And Johnson did not attend five Cobra meetings
In January and February, and so there was none.
Hancock's been blamed for not getting to grips
With Covid-19 at poorly-focused
Cobra meetings in Johnson's strange absence
Until the meeting of February the twenty-eighth.
    So where does the virus leave us today?
Ferguson's modelling report predicted
"A reasonable worst-case scenario"
Of some five hundred and ten thousand deaths
Which could be averted by indefinite
Lockdown until a vaccine is produced,
Otherwise a second spike would be even worse.
The Government's gone for lockdown long enough
To allow the NHS's intensive-care
Capacity to catch up – which took a month,
Not four months and a damaged economy.
Sweden did social distancing in March,
No lockdown and lower deaths per million
Of the population and half the UK's
Damage to its economy. So now
We all await a vaccine, and meanwhile
Our liberty has gone, to converse, work,
Play, eat out, drink, debate in the Commons,

Sing, watch sport, be in an audience, take part
In all collective activities – and now
Our humanity's gone with depersonalised
Masks and a fear of living together again.
Europe was largely untouched by MERS, SARS,
Hong-Kong flu, H1N1 and Ebola.
HIV reached Europe, and the UK's
National Risk Register published in 2008
Says a new strain of flu could cause between
Fifty thousand and seven hundred and fifty
Thousand additional deaths in the UK,
And new diseases originating in
Animals are a growing threat. For all
Under fifty, the risk of death from Covid
Is tiny, less than seasonal flu or
Tuberculosis, and while we can respect
Those who continue to socially distance
We now need to drop distancing and stop
Running away and get back to normal lives
And live alongside Covid as if it were flu
Rather than the Black Death spread by rat fleas
That killed within twelve hours of a flea-bite,
Turning necks, armpits and inner thighs black.
The Black Death took nearly half of the entire
Population of Europe and the known world
In just four years from 1347
And resurfaced forty times in three hundred years
Until 1665, when Milton shielded
And dictated *Paradise Lost* with the plague outside.
    Now it's said the economy will shrink
Fourteen per cent this year (19.1 per cent
Between March and May). The deficit
May top six hundred and sixty billion pounds
Over the next two years, and a second wave
Of the virus this winter would result
In a hundred and nineteen thousand more deaths

In hospitals in the UK, excluding care homes.
Amid all this the UK has to prepare
For the end of the Brexit transition period.
There will be four hundred million new customs
Declarations each year, and too few officials,
And borders can't cope with the searches.
The UK is woefully unprepared.
But a Government contract says Leave voters are
Less likely to prepare as they do not believe
There will be negative consequences for leaving the EU.
Fools believe their fools' gold is valuable.

All's not as described, the passengers are seething.
They've been misled by a captain they saw as sincere.
They've been taken in, and have been complicit
In being duped, and they're bitterly critical.
They lie like rags and bones strewn on the deck,
No energy, many gasping for breath.
Two more have died and still there's no docking
For the plague ship that's still in quarantine.
All rue the day they chose to join the voyage,
Convinced their prosperity was guaranteed.
They're victims of the plague and of the lies
That led them to follow this new captain
Who seemed to embody their hopes and dreams,
Now demonstrated to be fantasies.

Canto XVI
'No Deal' Looms

Sing, Muse, of talks from entrenched positions,
Of fears there will be no trade agreement,
Sing of the prospect of dreaded 'no deal',
Of less demand for British goods and fears
Of job losses amid a pandemic,
Sing of tariffs and eleven-mile lorry queues,
Of businesses unprepared for chaos.
And sing of borders, of how independence can be
Good if it's for England, bad for Scotland,
Sing of double standards and Unions
And of hopes that are dashed and mendacity
As 'no deal' becomes 'an Australian deal'.
    Like a squirrel that's been waiting for a refill
Of an empty nut feeder, and has given up,
Johnson's reconciled to Brexit talks ending –
Breaking up – without a trade agreement.
The UK would be under WTO rules
And would have the same trade terms as Australia,
Which has no trade agreement with the EU.
Some say a breakthrough is still possible,
That eighty per cent's already been agreed,
But others say the differences are still too wide
And a crash-out's now inevitable.
And Johnson believes the economic fall-out
From the coronavirus crisis will dwarf
Or mask a severe hit from a hard Brexit.
    A 'no-deal' Brexit would be a disaster
As unpublished Government forecasts confirm
And can't be reconciled to Johnson's "FDR"
Ambitions of a New Deal for all: "borrow,
Borrow, borrow", "print money, print money,
Print money", "spend, spend, spend", "build, build, build", no

Austerity. The UK's left the EU
And wants to dump key parts of the Withdrawal
Agreement, which keeps the European Court
Of Justice and will cripple stand-alone Britain.
Johnson will go down in history as having
Recklessly – madly – heaped colossal debts
Onto the younger generation and the next,
And for rashly not staying as close as possible
To the EU as the majority of Britons
In a time of dearth with no new trade deals want.
As when white geese are disturbed by their pond
There's a honking and cackling warning in the air
And your poet can just hear on the wind
"Quem deus vult perdere prius dementat"
("Those the gods wish to destroy they first make mad").
His foolish way's madness, and destruction's ahead –
By irate people who see their country crashed,
And a Union left and a Union being smashed.
The same week the EU's taken a huge step
Towards becoming a federal superstate
By agreeing to pool debt to fund its vast
Coronavirus recovery program
And putting up 1.6 trillion pounds,
Officials in Brussels becoming bankers
With borrowing and spending powers. Had the UK
Remained it would be the second-largest
Once-off bailer-out of countries now enmeshed
In the greatest jump in EU integration
Since 1999, when the euro was born.
It looks like the beginning of fiscal union
With political union not far behind.
Brexiteers say that the UK has left
In the nick of time, but the forward-looking
See the UK's missed out on being a part
Of a United States of Europe that can grow
Into a federal democratic World State.

Now it dawns on your poet this is what Rothschilds
Always wanted and the UK was obstructive,
So for the greater good the UK's been
Allowed to leave so the EU can integrate.
    Like two parakeets flying off to left and right,
Now formal talks between Frost and Barnier
Have ended and there's not a breakthrough
But they'll continue to meet and there may be
A deal in September, both British and EU
Negotiators have said, as the EU
Has quietly dropped its demands that the ECJ
Should have a role in enforcing the deal
And the UK'll now accept an overarching
Enforcement structure to settle disputes.
Barnier's thumb-upped as he leaves in his car.
But fishing rights and anti-competition
('Level-playing-field') guarantees, and state aid
Are still problems which have to be resolved
In September or at the latest October
So a deal can be ratified by the deadline.
But the clean and total break from the EU
The Brexiteers wanted cannot happen
As there are no trading agreements with other states
Following the virus, contrary to what all were told,
And so the UK will be an economic
Satellite to the EU but excluded
From the decision-making process. The UK
Will be free to depart the playing-field
'Voluntarily' 'as a sovereign nation',
No longer bound by Brussels rules when it chooses,
But it won't as forty-seven per cent
Of UK trade's with the EU – forty-three
Per cent of its exports, fifty-one per cent
Of its imports in 2019 – and there's nothing
To replace it. Johnson's father says the PM
Is living in "cloud-cuckoo-land" if he thinks

The EU will give the UK a trade deal
Without signing up to strict 'level-playing-fields' rules
And its farming standards. The UK could diverge,
But it won't. So that's the likely outcome.
Thanks to the Brexiteers (who are furious
Or else sheepishly silent) the UK, drawn
By the glittering world of many trade deals,
Has surrendered its place at the European table
So others decide, and with a basic deal.
Humiliated by Brexit ('Covid-20'),
The UK'll await a Labour Government
To renegotiate a place at the EU's table
Which will mean rejoining without the old terms,
The Thatcher rebate and Major opt-out,
And how foolish the Brexiteers will look then.
Like sheep herded from a field up a ramp,
Some running off in the wrong direction
But all driven away in a lorry
By the field's gate, the issues including
Fishing and competition are being rounded up
So the UK can become the EU's satellite,
And vote Leave all along meant vacating
The UK's seat at the decision-making table
In return for gold which has turned out to be fools' gold.
The alternative is worse: no deal at all –
What Disaster Capitalism's always wanted –
As the EU won't give ground as the twenty-seven
Want to punish the UK for leaving
Their integrating union – Barnier also
Waved goodbye from his car to talks and a deal
And to the UK as it leaves the EU.
If there is 'no deal' the UK will trade
With the EU on WTO terms,
The same terms the US trades with the EU,
But this will result in longish delays
In the passage of all goods entering

And leaving the UK, a backward step.
Brexit was billed as progress, but is now
Seen to be a retreat, into tariffdom
Or at its best into satellitehood.
    This was not what the British people were told
Before they voted Leave in the referendum.
But, no worries, more gold has been offered:
Johnson's promised the 1922
Committee of back-benchers the economy
Will be back on "an even keel" before
The next election in 2024,
Meaning the three-hundred-billion-pound cost
Of coping with the coronavirus pandemic
And the dozens of billions of pounds from leaving
The EU will be coped with in the next four years.
And although fifty-four per cent of Scottish
Voters want independence from the UK,
All will be well as the single market
Of the UK matters more to Scotland
Than the single market of the EU, we're told.
Gold, glittering gold for those who'll still believe.
O let all hope again as in the early
Nineteen-seventies that the EU will kindly
Let the UK back in so it can be part
Of the EU's decision-making process
For the ongoing trade terms of the single market.

The cost of the UK's divorce from the EU
Has been engulfed in the Covid catastrophe.
But it's still there, the IMF have costed
Brexit at a 3.6-per-cent loss
Of GDP after two years, or if
The UK leaves the single market and trades
On WTO terms, a six-per-cent
Loss of GDP, a hundred and twenty-five
Billion pounds (four years of economic growth).

But that's not all, for now it has come to light
The Withdrawal Agreement keeps the UK tied
To payments issued by EU agencies
Such as the European Investment Bank
And the European Financial Stability
Mechanism, and the UK's twelve-per-cent share
Could total a hundred and sixty billion pounds
Of unpaid loans, four times the thirty-nine-
Billion-pound divorce deal, a huge burden.
It's in the small print, unnoticed by many.
So there's another hundred and sixty billion
To repay on top of the Covid-and-Brexit
Half trillion. Duncan Smith voted against
Proper scrutiny of the Withdrawal Agreement,
And for the Bill, and is now complaining
That he did not understand what he voted for.
That's why European leaders beamed at
Johnson in Brussels after the deal was reached –
He too had not read the commitment to which he signed up.
Many Tories don't just want a clean-break Brexit
But to renege on the Withdrawal Agreement too
As it ceded too much liability
And sovereignty less than a year ago.
    And, like a farm with holes in its hedge, so crops
Can be eaten by intruding rabbits and deer,
The UK has a problem with its sovereign borders.
Migrants paddle inflatables from France.
The UN Convention on the Law of the Sea
States there are no international waters
Off Kent, only British and French waters,
And there's no right to deport migrants
Leaving the EU to the country they came from,
And an agreement to deport them back to the EU
Ends with transition. So the Government
That told all that borders would now be safe
Is now coping less well than when in the EU.

France wants thirty million to stop the dinghies.
    And there's Scotland, another border problem.
Having spent five years telling British voters
They've nothing to fear from independence,
Businesses will adapt, the economy thrive,
Johnson has gone to Scotland and tells voters
Independence is fraught with risk, businesses
Would be damaged, the economy will suffer.
He's still advocating a Portpatrick-to-Larne
Twenty-eight-mile bridge between Scotland and Northern
Ireland costed at twenty billion pounds
(Unlike his planned bridge across the Thames, costed
At two hundred million), and is pictured
In Stromness harbour, Orkney, holding two
Gigantic crabs upside down in his power,
Their enormous legs clawing the air in vain.
    But their pincers are soon going to hurt Johnson
For his legacy may be the break-up
Of the United Kingdom, it feels inevitable
That Scotland will break away from the Union.
He's coming back on holiday to Scotland
To demonstrate his support for the Union,
At a time when fifty-four per cent of Scots
Want independence from the Union,
And to have paternity time with his new son
And found a ten-year plan for government.
On his mind will be coping with the virus
(Opening schools and saving the red-wall seats),
Saving the economy (by soaking the rich
And going over to seaside wind power),
Saving the Union and a Brexit deal.
There's an economic and public-health crisis
And a deepening recession, and the end of the Union,
The cost of the divorce, border problems
And on top of it all satellitehood and reneging
On the Withdrawal Agreement, caused by Johnson's

Brexit and pursuit of sparkling global gold.
The news is out, a 20.4-per-cent
Fall in GDP in the second quarter to June,
Tipping the UK into its first recession
In eleven years and the biggest in its history,
The biggest quarterly fall in GDP
On record, making it the worst performing
In the G7. The economy stopped in April,
And the Government's second-quarter borrowing
Was 127.9 billion pounds.
May saw 2.2 per-cent growth and June
Eight-per-cent growth, a bit of a bounce-back,
But now the UK's national debt has reached
More than two trillion pounds, as Government
Borrowing's reached a hundred and fifty
Billion pounds since April, three times last year's
Forecast in just four months, and twice Corbyn's
Plan to borrow an extra seventy-nine
Billion pounds a year in his manifesto.
Racking up the national debt's not a Tory
Way of governing. The UK's debt's now more
Than a hundred per cent of GDP,
The first time the UK's owed more than it earns in a year
Since from the First World War to 1963.
The UK is now technically bankrupt.
And now Johnson and his Chancellor have split
Over Sunak's plan to slash tax relief on
Pensions as it breaks election promises
And Johnson's denouncing of austerity.
In racking up debt and refusing cuts
Johnson appears confused and incompetent.
There are hard times ahead, and the British
Will have to leave their Brexit fantasy
And face up to reality, and now
The public have lost faith in Johnson's promises
To deliver game-changing post-Brexit

Trade deals that will bring more jobs and prosperity.
The British Establishment got the virus wrong.
Lockdowns lengthen the spread of infection,
But don't reduce them, decisions have been made
Without considering the economic cost.
Sweden's GDP fell 8.6 per cent
In the first half of the year against the UK's
22.2 per cent, and its excess deaths
Rose twenty-four per cent against the UK's
Forty-five per cent, and it didn't have lockdown.
Half the UK's catastrophic collapse
In GDP was needless, caused by lockdown –
Two hundred and fifty billion pounds wasted,
A quarter of a trillion, and millions of children's
Education ruined, due to the British State's
Systemic incompetence and trust in modellers
Rather than proper scientists: British
World-beating exceptionalism found out again
As complacency and sickening delusion.
Just as a sacred flock of geese living
In Juno's temple on the Capitoline Hill
Honked when a Gallic tribe sneaked in to alert
Guards to save the Roman citadel, so
Geese honk a new alert that sounds like boos.
A boo for the public-policy blunders
Of the UK's arrogant quangocrats
And State experts who thought they all knew best.
And a boo for the UK's trade negotiators
As New Zealand's blamed them for their slow progress
Towards a trade deal, they are thirty years
Out of date and not fit for such negotiations.

Barnier says the Brexit trade talks are going
Backwards, and a German paper now doubts
That a deal will happen before the deadline
And says, "It's time to let Boris finally

Jump over the cliff." While a Brussels commentator
Says the lemmings will in all likelihood
Be "driven over the cliff and into the sea",
And the EU should drive them to plunge as the British
"Have cost us enough nerves". It's all a mess.
    Like a newly-arrived puffin trying to impress
Johnson's been on holiday in Scotland,
Sleeping in a bell-tent on a cliff's edge
The other side of a stone wall from his cottage
(Having climbed the wall via chairs on either side),
Blown by the wind that can power the economy,
Keeping in touch with the GCSE results,
U-turning an algorithm to mock grades.
The idea was to U-turn the Scottish polls
For independence from fifty-four per cent
By showing his love of the Scots with his fiancée
And child in a papoose in a Scottish field,
And lighting a camp-fire in the twilight,
But unfortunately he's been trespassing:
The field belonged to another landowner
Whose permission was not asked, and there's burnt turf.
Pictures of his tent have appeared in the press,
It's not safe now, he's back in Downing Street
And greeted with news that 'Rule Britannia'
And 'Land of Hope and Glory' will be performed
At The Last Night of the Proms without any words
As "Britons never will be slaves" now jars
With 'Black Lives Matter' descendants of slaves
Who want to erase all slave-owners and their past
And brand all British history as racist.
And not a peep of protest from Johnson.
But it won't happen, common sense will prevail.
    The pandemic's vastation has rendered
The economics of Johnson's Brexit irrelevant.
Now a leaked Cabinet report, the Transition
Task Force Dossier, shows emergency plans

Have been drawn up to protect the UK
From a winter second wave of Covid
Coinciding with a 'no-deal' Brexit:
'No-deal' restrictions on all trade (as no
Political EU intervention
From Merkel and Macron breaks the impasse) with new
Customs procedures, visa requirements,
Travel insurance, residency rights
And multiple certification regimes
Combined with winter floods, flu and Covid
Could overwhelm hospitals, cause power cuts
And petrol shortages as eight thousand
Five hundred trucks are stuck at Dover, causing
Shortages of medicines and animal disease
In the countryside, and the Channel Islands
Could need air drops of food to prevent starving
And the Navy will have to protect the UK's fishing fleet
From hundreds of illegal European
Fishing-boat incursions. One in twenty
Town Halls could go bust in a second wave
Of Covid, and the economic impact
Of the virus and Brexit could cause public
Disorder, shortages and price rises.
Troops may have to be sent on to the streets
As supplies of food and fuel are blocked at
Dover over Christmas. Gove is working
On contingency plans for an unruly exit
From the EU transition period at the end
Of December, with trade barriers going up
On the first of January. That day France will enforce
"Mandatory controls on UK goods"
And the flow between Dover and Calais will be down
Forty-five per cent for three months, there'll be queues
Of HGVs in Kent, and there'll be shortages
Of the thirty per cent of UK food imported
From the EU, and medicines, chemicals

To purify drinking-water, and fuel
And there may be water rationing and power cuts
And panic buying. And pandemic flu,
Severe flooding, a second Covid wave
And industrial action will affect mental health.
   Gove says the Cabinet Office is working
Flat out to make sure the UK is ready
For the changes and huge opportunities
As it regains its political and economic
Independence for the first time in almost
Fifty years, and there's "a great deal in January".
Those who said the UK will have a better future
Will now have to deliver their promises
In the face of coming winter disaster –
The winter Disaster Capitalism bet on.
Soon all will see if their promises were gold.
Vote Leave said there will be a brighter future
And now they'll have to cope with a blocked Dover.
The gods are just and place the promisers
In positions where their hollow rhetoric
Before the referendum will be exposed
If their promises turn out to be worthless,
And they will then be voted out to obloquy.
   Like a demanding great tit wanting more feed,
Tapping its beak on the window to say "Where is it?",
The EU's said there are just two weeks to save
Post-Brexit trade and security talks, the UK
Must reveal its state-aid and competition
Policy, it can't subsidise steel and cars
And adversely affect EU industries
And jobs – the twenty-seven are united
On state aid and will declare a 'no deal'.
There will be queues at ports and airports,
Tariffs on goods for the first time in nearly fifty years
And a collapse in security co-operation.
Brussels is serious, a 'level playing-field'

Must be preserved, competitor third countries
Can't have more attractive terms than EU members.
Satellite status is demonstrably inferior
To full membership, and Johnson must choose
Between a 'no-deal' clean break and a safety-first
Compromise, a 'deal' that betrays his hard-liners.
Johnson has concluded he should not soften
The UK's determination to go it alone
On state aid so it can have its own control
Of subsidies, and not be subject to the EU's.
But Gove's worried a failure to get a deal
Will fuel Scottish demands for independence
And tarnish Johnson's premiership with the abrupt
Break-up of the fragmenting Union.
There's an autumn of discontent ahead, and a plan
To claw back thirty billion in a tax raid.
The PM's subdued, lacks his normal ebullient
Optimistic confidence and self-belief,
Has lost his grip, with default-position U-turns –
Power without admitting responsibility –
Despite having an eighty-seat majority.
    Johnson denies responsibility
For incompetent Covid management,
Yet the UK has: the highest confirmed Covid
Death toll in Europe; the second-highest
Confirmed Covid deaths per capita in the world;
The highest excess per capita death count
In Europe; the third-highest in the world;
The worst case mortality rate globally;
And one of the worst *economic* losses anywhere.
And there's more chance of a young person dying now
From a tortoise dropped by an eagle from the sky,
As happened to Aeschylus, than from Covid.
Parliamentary private secretaries, the PM's
"Eyes and ears", are failing to be a conduit
To the Government, whose lead over Labour

Is down to two per cent while Johnson's own
Rating's minus fifteen, Starmer's plus eight.
Look, geese are flying in a perfect V
Formation (each slightly above the bird
In front to reduce wind) and are signalling
That a victory over the Government's on the way.
There's a Brexit crash ahead, and the PM
Has fallen out of favour with voters:
He's lost a twenty-six-point lead in five months,
Now the Tories are level with Labour at forty per cent.
The hollowness of the Brexiteers' rhetoric
Before the referendum has now been exposed.

The ship is lurching and rolling on the waves,
All lie listlessly in the wind and rain,
Dubious about their cargo of glittering gold
And in bitterness at the sacrifice they made.
Their illness has swept their ambitions aside,
No longer do they believe that they will have
A better life as a result of this voyage,
The prosperity and comfort of their dreams.
When a fool dies he is thrown overboard.
All now know there's no triumphant return
And a better standard of living than if they had
Never joined the voyage to Narragonia.

Canto XVII
A Bill to Change the Withdrawal Agreement

Sing, Muse, of treaties that cannot be changed,
Written into stone like the NATO treaty,
And sing of politicians who don't read them
And are shocked that they've signed to a border
That splits a Union down a communal sea,
Sing of attempts to bring a cancelling Bill
To Parliament to break a solemn promise
And of the shock and outrage round the world
That a nation-state whose word was always its bond
Should be duplicitous, not honour what's signed,
Sing of lack of trust and lost integrity,
Of an honoured realm now a pariah state,
Sing of unscrupulous lack of principle.
    Crisis talks on state aid in London, Barnier
Won't discuss a fishing deal until the UK
Has moved on state aid but the UK will walk
Away from a free trade deal unless it gets
The right to undercut the twenty-seven
And prop up failing British companies
With state aid so they can compete better.
Now the trade talks with the EU have stalled
Over fishing – and state aid, as usual,
As the UK wants to build its own technology
Sector like Silicon Valley with state aid
And not be dependent on the US or China.
Barnier's said the UK can have sovereignty
Over its waters but not over its fish,
And he's demanding a veto on all
The UK's post-Brexit laws and regulations.
    Like a swaggering muntjac that won't retreat
Now Frost has said that Britain will not blink,
Will not become "a client state" of Brussels

By accepting restrictions on fishing rights –
The EU "want to have their fish cake and eat it" –
And vetoes on its laws as this Government
Is more steely and determined than May's,
Which blinked and had its bluff called every time.
The UK won't accept level-playing-field
Provisions that lock it into the EU
Or yield control of its money as it's
An independent country, a sovereign state.
Frost had Covid in March and struggles for breath
When jogging but's grasped the key to negotiation:
To make demands that can actually be achieved
And let the other side know you mean business.
Johnson's appointed Abbott, the ex-PM
Of Australia, to make trade deals in the East,
And has said Britain will "prosper mightily"
Whatever the outcome of Brexit, deal or 'no deal',
Another way of promising more gold.
With hints and subtext promises of gold,
Johnson has moved decisively to break
The deadlock, setting the European
Council's meeting on the fifteenth of October
In thirty-eight days' time as the deadline
(Two weeks earlier than Barnier's end date)
For a deal and will walk away if there's no deal,
And failing to sign would be a "good outcome"
As the UK would trade on the same terms as Australia –
Whose ex-PM's now UK trade adviser –
And the UK will "prosper mightily". Gold, gold.
An Internal Market Bill will formalise
Rules so the UK can sign new trade deals
And iron out legal ambiguities
In the Withdrawal Agreement regarding
Northern Ireland, and there's now an outcry:
This will undermine the Northern-Ireland
Protocol to avoid a hard border on

The island of Ireland, and will undermine
The Withdrawal Agreement, which has to be implemented
In full, Barnier's said. And to renege on this treaty
Would be an "incomprehensible miscalculation"
That would be "the beginning of the end"
Of the UK-EU relationship.
    Like a con-man selling his failure as a success
Johnson says a 'no-deal' Brexit's a "good outcome".
Really? That wasn't what was said during
The referendum campaign. It all looks grim.
A 'no-deal' Brexit looks very likely now.
The odds are less than twenty per cent on a deal.
The UK's facing mass unemployment
As a result of coronavirus and the biggest
Recession for many years, and Brexit will do
Terrible damage to UK industries,
To farming, agriculture, manufacturing,
Financial services. The British State is strutting
And posturing and threatening 'no deal',
And a 'no deal' could happen by accident.
Cummings hopes the UK will have the new
Giants of tech and found the new Google,
Amazon and Facebook in Milton Keynes
Through creative disruption and build global Britain,
But huge tariffs will be slapped on beef and lamb,
And Dover will become a lorry park
And all this was always going to happen
As the UK is too near Europe to have
State-aid rules that compete with the EU,
The level of taxpayer support the UK
Will be able to provide for businesses.
There's a new plan to undermine the Withdrawal
Agreement, which has the force of a treaty,
And the UK is now becoming a rogue state
And is not honouring May's hard-fought-for deal.
The UK's planning not to do what it has promised.

Sturgeon says this means repudiation,
Ditching the "oven-ready deal": "What charlatans!"
    After a meeting with Gove, Sefcovic,
The Vice-President of the EU, is threatening
To sue the UK if it doesn't withdraw
The Internal Market Bill as it overrides
Key parts of the Withdrawal Agreement
Like a red fox adapting a badger's lair,
And breaks international law and has seriously
Damaged the EU's trust. The EU's demanded
The measures should be withdrawn by the end of the month.
The EU has said that the Withdrawal Agreement
Which contains the Northern Ireland Protocol –
Which replaced the backstop and signed Northern Ireland
Up to EU state-aid rules after transition –
Is a legal agreement signed by Johnson
And passed in Parliament. The EU's threatening
Legal action against the UK, to take
It to court for hundreds of millions of pounds
If the Bill's not withdrawn within twenty days
As it violates an international treaty,
And if there's 'no deal' the EU will cut off
All British imports to Northern Ireland.
The EU does not accept that the Bill
Is a legal safety net, the EU's position
Has now stiffened the Government's resolve.
    The Internal Market Bill will give ministers
The power to override commitments in
The Withdrawal Agreement treaty to ensure EU
Customs controls are carried out on all goods
Entering or exiting Northern Ireland.
Johnson's accused of sabotaging the trade
Negotiations and moving the UK
Towards 'no deal'. Gove's said the Government
Will not withdraw the Internal Market Bill.
    But, led astray by a confidence trickster,

The UK, which has always kept its word,
Is now planning to break its word, and rebels
Are gathering to oppose Johnson on principle.
In the Lords Howard accuses Johnson of showing
Scant regard for the UK's treaty obligations.
Barnier's spoken of the consequences of 'no deal'.
And the Speaker of the House of Representatives
In the US has said there will be no chance
Of a US-UK trade deal if Johnson
Overrides the Brexit Withdrawal Agreement
And imperils peace in Northern Ireland.
But as sovereign will's the ultimate authority
In the creation of international law,
International law is only valid if
It does not subordinate sovereign will.
Johnson is facing a pincer movement
From angry Remainers and right-wingers.
Will the Government face a double rebellion
From the two wings of the Conservative Party,
Get this legislation done in the Commons
And then head to a 'no-deal' Brexit? Or
Will it look at the numbers of the rebels
And compromise? But they won't voluntarily back down.
It's announced the UK economy's 11.7
Per cent smaller than before the Covid crisis,
And debt in Britain rose in August as much
As in the whole of the nineteen-seventies.
Johnson's spending a hundred billion pounds
(Of which half a billion's been committed so far)
On getting ten million tests a day, a "moonshot" –
Or should it be called "a long shot" or "moonshine",
Mass testing of the population twice a week –
That's widely thought to be unachievable.
The three *amigos* – Johnson, Whitty and Vallance
(The Chief Medical and Scientific Advisers) –
Have announced a 'rule of six', meet no more than five

Indoors or be arrested by marshals and fined
Even though thirty-eight million Brits live in places
Where infections are not rising at all
And hospitals are empty, with few deaths.
    The Cabinet's at war as the EU,
Like a bull stamping and snorting in its rage,
Has given the UK twenty days to retreat
On its Brexit Bill or face the collapse
Of the Brexit talks and legal action.
Britain's rejected the EU's ultimatum,
The Brexit talks are on the brink of collapse.
Johnson's defying the EU and will see
Them in court, it's the feel of proroguing again.
Disagreements between the EU and the UK
Can be resolved by a Joint Committee
And then arbitration, as set out in
The Withdrawal Agreement, but this collision between
The UK and EU will make agreements less likely.
And the Internal Market Bill won't pass through the Lords.
But if a deal is reached, the Internal
Market Bill won't be needed, so it might all be
Elaborate pressure on the EU to reach a deal –
Or it might be a sabotaging of the talks
So the EU can be blamed for 'no deal'.
    Now it's announced the EU Parliament
Will not ratify any free-trade agreement
Between the UK and EU unless
The Withdrawal Agreement's implemented intact.
It will block a trade deal with the UK
Unless the UK backs down on its plans
To override the Withdrawal Agreement.
Johnson's held an online meeting with his MPs
To quell unease at his willingness to go back
On the UK's international-treaty commitments.
He's said the EU's trying to blockade
The UK by not letting its goods into the EU.

The UK's created a trade war with the EU.
How often we see it, it's sadly true
That wherever there are nation-states there's war
Or trade war, it happened in imperial times
And in two world wars, man has not learned
That national 'I, I, I''s self-destructive.
    Now Barnier's set to deny the UK
"Third-country" status despite starting
From a place of alignment as its biosecurity
Rules would mean British farmers could not export
Meat and dairy produce to the EU
Worth five billion pounds, from January.
The UK would be below Afghanistan,
The Yemen, Angola and Azerbaijan.
    Like a liar blaming another for his past lies
Johnson, speaking on a video link to MPs,
Has accused Brussels of trying to break up
The UK – if the UK doesn't agree
With the EU's interpretation of the checks,
"There'd be nothing short of an economic barrier
Down the Irish Sea with tariffs." He repeats,
"What we can't have is the threat of a border
Down the Irish Sea and the threat of the break-up
Of the United Kingdom" – the very reason
For not voting Leave as it was clear before
The referendum the UK'd split up.
Johnson's "light-touch checks" are now a hard border
That threatens the integrity of the UK.
So Brussels is to blame for the "food blockade"
Down the Irish Sea, not Johnson's lack of detail.
It's Brussels' trying to "carve up our country",
Not Johnson's blindness, what he failed to see.
It's a misunderstanding of the Withdrawal Agreement,
Or did Johnson see it all along and lie
That there'd be no hard checks to win the election?
Did he promise goods could flow each way across

The Irish Sea, so he could amass votes?
Johnson says the EU threatens the integrity
Of the UK, a blockade down the Irish Sea –
Using the Withdrawal Agreement that he signed,
Over which he resigned, prorogued Parliament,
Fought a leadership, and general, election.
He campaigned for this very Withdrawal Agreement,
Got it through Parliament, got the Queen to sign it off,
Got the EU to sign it off, relied on it
For nine months of negotiations,
Then turned round and said, "Oh, I didn't know
It contained a border down the Irish Sea,"
And he's accusing the EU of using
His words against him, in a Continental way.
He was warned by the British civil service
Of the border earlier this year. If it's not
A negotiating ploy to force a concession
From the EU, it's a Brexiteer leader
Taking back control of British laws without
Reading them for a year, and plunging
The British people into a stinking bog.
The Government needs assurances from the EU
That it won't blockade the Irish Sea.
A deal's still possible, and if this is a gambit
To bring the EU to a deal, it has backfired
As the EU no longer trusts Johnson.
The border in the Irish Sea's not resolvable,
It was always going to be impossible,
Johnson promised he had a solution, and now
It's clear he hadn't, and his promise of gold
Has turned out to be a promise of fools' gold.
Back of the class, dunce, for not reading the small print
When you were promising gold, gold, gold, gold.

Like badgers appalled that a fox has found a home
In a lair they abandoned some years ago,

And is making changes to the mouth of their burrow,
Ex-PMs Blair and Major, the architects
Of the Irish Good-Friday Agreement,
Have written an article in *The Sunday Times*
Saying "shocking" Johnson shames the UK
As the Internal Market Bill will jeopardise peace
In Northern Ireland; destroy Britain's standing
In the world so it's unable to negotiate
Trade deals; and break international law.
Johnson signed the Withdrawal Agreement
And crowed it was a "negotiating triumph"
And won an election for an "oven-ready" deal
And is now saying he didn't read it.
His empty promises have been revealed.
It doesn't protect the Good-Friday Agreement
But imperils it, it's not a safety net.
    But as Blair and Major warned in 2016
The open border between the North and South
Of Ireland is vital to the peace process
And the Good-Friday Agreement and is threatened
If the UK leaves the European single market.
The Good-Friday Agreement guarantees
There'll be no border on the island of Ireland,
Even if that means having customs checks and tariffs
In the Irish Sea if there's no free-trade deal.
The UK needs to stay aligned with the single
Market and customs union. Either
The open border must be abandoned or
Northern Ireland stays in the single market.
If Britain leaves the single market and Northern
Ireland stays it would be separated
From the rest of the UK. The backstop had
Northern Ireland tied into the single
Market and the whole of the UK in
The customs union. Johnson resigned as
May's deal was "a betrayal". And when he

Succeeded her, he replaced the backstop
With a "front-stop" that keeps Northern Ireland
Tied to the EU's single-market rules
And keeps the border open. Johnson knew
This as he negotiated it. It's not "unforeseen".
 The EU may limit the UK's financial
Services' access to the single market
In retaliation, the integrity
Of the British nation-state is at stake.
If Parliament passes the Bill the UK will be hauled
Before the European Court of Justice,
Which under the Northern Ireland Protocol
Retains jurisdiction over EU rules.
If the UK loses, its international
Reputation for keeping its word will be lost.
For centuries the UK has furthered the rule of law
All round the world. The Government has shamed
And embarrassed the nation before a world
That's now aghast at such chicanery.
 Now Brussels' collapsing trust in Johnson,
Like a magpie's deep suspicion of a fox,
Is revealed in leaked EU documents:
The deal is on the brink, about to collapse.
Johnson will tell Barnier the Withdrawal Agreement
Is contradictory in relation to the UK's status
Of having a sovereign Parliament.
Barnier's cautioned Johnson that if he rewrites
The legally-binding Withdrawal Agreement,
The Brexit deal, talks will collapse altogether
On a matter of trust, and Von der Leyen will not
Do business with Britain in the future.
 Like a con-man blaming the contract he's breaking,
Johnson has said the Withdrawal Agreement
Is "contradictory" and ambiguous
And would leave Northern Ireland isolated
From the rest of the UK, which was "unforeseen"

When he agreed to it last year. Hold on,
It was clear to your poet there was a border
Down the Irish Sea, why wasn't it clear to him?
Did he not read the Withdrawal Agreement?
Like a fox prowling near a magpie's chicks
He now says it has "legal ambiguities"
After the removal of the backstop,
And that the peace process would be compromised
By "unintended consequences". What
A euphemism for "I did not realise"!
It's now clear Johnson didn't read the small print
Of the Withdrawal Agreement and did not realise
His "oven-ready deal" would place a border
In the Irish Sea between Britain and Ireland.
Hence the Internal Market Bill.
Back of the class, Johnson, wear a dunce's cap;
Front of the class, poet, you were right at the time.
    Now it emerges that Article 4
Of the Withdrawal Agreement makes it clear
That areas covered by the treaty take
Precedence over the UK's domestic law.
Now it also emerges that Clause 38,
The clause drafted by Cash, in the Withdrawal
Agreement Johnson signed, gave the UK
The right to put sovereignty above the EU:
"The Parliament of the United Kingdom
Is sovereign... notwithstanding the European Union
(Withdrawal Agreement) Act 2020."
What's more: "Nothing in this Act derogates
From the sovereignty of the Parliament
Of the United Kingdom." Without the deal
In a Remainer rebellion Brexit would be lost,
But with it Britain was tied, to its cost,
Into a Northern Ireland Protocol.
So there are contradictory clauses
In the Withdrawal Agreement, and Johnson's challenge

Is based on Brexiteer Cash's insertion.
    Like a con-man admitting he's breaking the law
To justify his denials in the past –
And like a fox heading for a magpie's nest –
Now Brandon Lewis, the Northern Ireland
Secretary, has admitted in the Commons
That the Government will break international law
In its proposed changes to the Withdrawal
Agreement, and Starmer has said that's wrong
And merely a negotiating tactic.
A senior minister's expressed astonishment
That the Government's saying it intends to break the law.
If the UK goes back on its word, it will
Not be trusted, how can the UK criticise
Iran, Russia and China for breaking the law
When the UK is breaking it too? May asks how
The UK will be trusted to abide by
The legal obligations of the agreements
It signs, and a senior Government lawyer's resigned
Over this breach of international law
And the illegal plan put forward by Downing Street.
Starmer says the public were promised a deal
And the Government need to get on and get a deal
That helps business thrive, brings job opportunities
And peace in Northern Ireland. Johnson won
The election by promising a deal,
Now he needs to deliver on his promise,
Not renege on what has already been agreed,
And 'no deal' will be his failure of statecraft.
    Now it emerges Brussels has threatened
To disrupt food exports – as leverage –
From mainland Britain to Northern Ireland.
All food exports leaving the UK's mainland
For Northern Ireland will be under EU oversight
And if there's no deal could be declared illegal.
Hence legislation for a safety net.

That's why the Northern Ireland Secretary
Has said the UK now wants to rip up
A signed treaty in a specific and limited way.
The Internal Market Bill overrides
Parts of the Brexit Withdrawal Agreement.
Major says that if the UK loses its
Reputation for honouring promises
It will have lost something that's beyond price,
That it may never regain. Johnson, asked,
Now says there is a risk that extreme views
On the Withdrawal Agreement treaty
May endanger the peace process in Northern Ireland
As it can put a barrier down the Irish Sea,
And checks on goods passing within the UK
Could inflame unionist sentiments;
And he is putting a safety net in place
To protect all the United Kingdom.
Von der Leyen has said, "*Pacta sunt servanda*",
"Agreements must be kept", the foundation
Of all states' prosperous future relations.
Sturgeon's piled in: "Break the treaty? What charlatans!"
There's an internal Government row over the extent
Of the subsidy needed for Johnson's economic
Reform plans, which encourage the development
Of high-tech companies. This has contributed
To the UK's insistence on rejecting EU
State-aid rules. As the UK repatriates
EU internal market powers, powers ranging
From air quality to building regulation
Are being taken back from Scotland to England,
Which the Scots see as a "wrecking ball" to devolution.
It's the holy three, Johnson, Cummings and Gove,
Who despise experts, who've thought this up.
Cummings and Johnson are delivering
What Disaster Capitalism wants.
Johnson's making the UK a pariah state,

A global Britain that disregards what it's signed,
That despoils the judiciary's independence,
The BBC's success, the civil service's
Impartiality and Parliament's authority,
And tainted the rule of law with proroguing
After giving the Queen illegal advice,
And is now tearing up the rule of law.
It's a treaty-breaking renegade, delinquent state
And's threatening a trade war, with tariffs on champagne.
Johnson's a political opportunist,
Cummings a political ideologue.
As the ex-PMs say, we have almost lost
Our capacity to be shocked in recent times
But it is nevertheless still shocking.
While the Attorney-General is taken to task
For damaging the UK's global reputation,
For saying, when supposed to uphold the law,
That internal UK law can be trumped
By Parliamentary sovereignty,
And for signing off on a Bill which breaks the law
By deliberately overlooking the ministerial
Code and the advice of senior Government lawyers
To secure the passage of this Brexit Bill.
There's anger in the back benches and rebellion.
It will soon be seen if this Bill is a bluff
To ease the negotiations towards a deal.

Now Johnson is opting out of the several key
EU human rights laws that have been sacrosanct,
To ease the deporting of immigrants who land
In flimsy dinghies from France and criminals
Back to their countries, and prevent soldiers
From being prosecuted for past service.
The European Convention of Human Rights,
Set up after the war to prevent a recurrence
Of fascism and places like Auschwitz,

Protects the right to life and to free speech,
The right to fair trials and to hold elections.
Of all the European nation-states
Only Belarus has also opted out.
    Johnson's asked the UK to obey Covid rules
But then announced that he's breaking the law
"To protect the unity of the UK".
'Do as I say, not as I do' seems to be
The unspoken message from Downing Street.
There's irrational advice on Covid –
You can exercise in groups and play sports and meet
In restaurants and pubs, but there's no good track-and-trace
And a family of five can't meet two grandparents –
And now there's irrational treatment of Europe.
    Only one side wants to break international law,
And the EU wants a deal. The UK's saying,
'Give us what we want, or we'll pass a law
To make it happen anyway.' The reputation
Of the UK is being damaged. The UK
Is doing this because Barnier's not giving
It third-country status, but he's been clear
A third country must respect international law.
How can the EU have a trading relationship
With the UK if it's breaking international law?
Now Labour say they can't support a Bill
That blatantly breaks international law.
The UK's always stood for the rule of law.
The EU will take legal action if the Bill's passed.
Johnson says the Bill's an insurance policy
But he said the Withdrawal Agreement was a "fantastic deal"
And went to the country on that, and now says it's a bad deal –
Was he lying or did he not understand it?
Is he posturing and blustering to get a deal?
    Now Barnier has tweeted that he denies
Refusing to list the UK as a third
Country for food imports. Frost has posted

Seven tweets saying he has, in a public spat
That's made the negotiations more difficult.
The issue of avoiding a hard border
And checks and controls for the rest of the UK
If there's no deal boils down to replacing
The Joint Committee of the Withdrawal Agreement
With a sole UK voice to review issues.
Cox, ex-Attorney-General, whose Brexit
Connections are unimpeachable, will vote against
The plan to break international law – which is
"Unconscionable", for the consequences
Of the Withdrawal Agreement were the unpalatable
Application of tariffs and customs procedures
To certain goods entering Northern Ireland
From Great Britain. The battle lines are drawn.
Johnson's circulated among ministers
A banned list: 'Brexit' (which suggests it's not done
And his election promise is not honoured)
And 'no deal' (which now has to be expressed
As 'a trade deal like Australia's'), and 'state aid'
(Which must now be 'subsidies'). So murking language
Can obfuscate the truth for the voters they take for fools,
Who need to believe all's good when it is not.
In the same spirit, perhaps the 'rule of six'
With Covid marshals and breaking up the UK
With a food blockade are ploys to camouflage
A no-deal Brexit amid anxiety
And chaos, so there's less coverage and challenge?
    The Internal Market Bill's second reading –
The Bill was introduced without any debate –
And Johnson takes the Business Secretary's place
Like a fox that's just emerged from its burrow,
A hole in the ground where it can skulk and plot,
And argues that the EU has threatened
To divide the United Kingdom by
Blockading goods bound for Northern Ireland,

Refusing to list food and agricultural products
For sale anywhere within the EU,
Prohibiting UK animal products
From passing from Great Britain to Northern Ireland,
And imposing huge tariffs on such imports
In clear breach of the UK's sovereignty.
He says the EU has not complied with its good faith,
And Brussels is refusing to "take its
Revolver off the negotiating table".
He speaks at length and says the Bill's necessary
(Bringing in the 'no deal' Disaster Capitalism want)
As an insurance policy. He says
He was unaware of how the Withdrawal Agreement
Could be misinterpreted by EU bad faith
At the time when he negotiated it.
He dresses it up as a business Bill
And says he'll use remedies before invoking the Bill.
Interventions condemn breaking the rule of law.
The last five Prime Ministers have condemned him,
Also the last five Conservative leaders.
He sits down to jeers and shakes his head.
Has it just been political theatre to get a deal?
    Now Miliband speaks, deputising for
Starmer, who is isolating. He says Johnson
Is whipping his Party to get Brexit undone,
To vote against the Withdrawal Agreement
Which won him the election. He launches
A full-scale onslaught on the PM, wagging
His finger oratorically, stressing
The rule of law which the UK founded,
And challenging Johnson on Northern Ireland.
He asks what clause in the Withdrawal Agreement
Mentions a blockade so we need to protect
Goods being sent from GB to NI,
And says he'll give way, and sits down.
Johnson just scowls and doesn't rise. Miliband says,

"He doesn't know, he hasn't read the Withdrawal Agreement."
He takes Johnson's five arguments apart,
And his "specific, limited" breaking of the law.
He says, "This is his mess and failure. For the first time
In his life it's time to take responsibility."
Madam Deputy Speaker Laing watches
Attentively as Johnson looks stricken.
It's been a barnstorming speech, he sits to cheers.
Cash speaks, shouting that the Bill is justified,
But still Miliband's speech echoes resoundingly.
Johnson scuttles and hides behind a wainscot.
Blackford speaks about Scotland, then O'Neill
Airs concern at breaking international law.
A hundred and one MPs want to speak.
Javid will abstain, there'll be more abstentions.
    Now MPs are voting on Labour's amendment
Which rejects the Bill because it "undermines
The EU Withdrawal Agreement" and "breaks
International law". The amendment is defeated.
There's another vote on the thrust of the Bill
To allow goods and services to flow freely
Across the four UK nations after the UK
Leaves the EU's single market at the end of December.
The Government has a majority of seventy-seven.
Now all eyes are on O'Neill's amendment next week
That powers should be given to MPs to vote
On whether to break international law. There may
Be a rebellion, and resistance in the Lords,
But can Johnson's aggression secure a trade deal,
Is this political theatre to that end?
    Or is the Government trying to blow up the talks
And implement an appalling 'no deal'?
A secret report claims seven thousand lorries
Will be stuck in post-Brexit chaos, and the EU
Is considering whether the City of London
Should continue to handle its hundred and fifty billion

Pounds a day trade in euros on its Stock Exchange
As Paris and Frankfurt seek to challenge London's
Dominance of the financial markets.
And the EU has started locking out British
Travellers with new quarantining thresholds.
    Thirty Conservative MPs withheld support.
Like a fox complaining at a magpie's screech
Johnson's said the EU are "abusive",
And now it's announced he will compromise
On the Internal Market Bill to stop a revolt.
He got his large majority by promising
That he will act on the rebels' concerns
And rewrite bits of the Internal Market Bill.
He is set to accept O'Neill's amendment:
The Commons must vote for ministers to use the powers
That break the deal reached with Brussels last year.
The amendment puts a Parliamentary lock
On the Internal Market Bill and breach of law.
However, Johnson's devolution 'power grab'
While Westminster gets powers back from Europe
Has left UK-Scottish relations broken down.
And your poet, born three months before the war
When the UK ruled a quarter of the world,
May live to see it shrink to Little England,
Having lost Scotland in an independence vote,
Northern Ireland to an Irish-Sea border
And Wales, still hankering to be in the EU.

The ship's still quarantining off the coast,
And the plight of the crew and passengers is dire.
All are unwell and are being left to toss
On the dipping sea and shiver at night.
All have a stake in the cargo in the hold,
But all have now lost interest in their haul,
Which has left them and their prospects less well off.
All are miserable and long for the old days

When all believed they were gaining lifelong wealth
And now they are weakened and have lost their health.

Canto XVIII
Covid's Second Wave

Sing, Muse, of a pandemic's second wave,
Of universal dread it will be virulent,
Sing of local lockdowns and Labour calls
For a circuit-breaking national lockdown.
Sing of the bankruptcy of a nation,
Of four hundred billion borrowed to keep
The elderly protected, the over-fifties well.
Sing of fear and ruin, and of the relief
That the new wave's killing fewer citizens.
Sing of cures that are worse than the disease.
    Covid cases have just doubled and yet
The testing system's completely collapsed.
There's a vacuum at the top, the Tories are losing
Their reputation for competence as no one
Can get a test, tests are being rationed
And those tested have to wait three days or more
For a result. There's a testing crisis,
The nearest test may be eighty miles away
And though half may have T-cell immunity,
There's a temporary solution in a new lockdown.
Ten million Brits are living under restrictions
And there's talk of a national lockdown over half term
When schoolchildren are home, a "circuit-breaker".
No one knows what will happen, there is drift,
The leader has no strategy and may cave in
To SAGE, it's all chaos and confusion
And a Cabinet of lightweights has no control.
    Covid's fatality rate's now 0.3
Per cent or lower, it's less dangerous now,
More infectious but less fatal. But it's taken its toll
On the PM, who's subdued and not lively,
Has misery on his face, it's all weighed heavily,

He's not enjoying being at the helm in rough seas.
He's short of money, has under half of his
Former salary with four children to support.
His flat in Downing Street's taxed as a benefit in kind,
His illness and his baby are exhausting,
He feels and looks unwell, and has bad days,
When he forgets his briefing and does not know
The answer to a question, he's without
The grounding his ex-wife Marina gave him.
The Spectator, which he edited, has asked,
"Where's Boris?" and accused him of presiding
Over "disorder, débâcle, rebellion,
U-turn and confusion". He's lurching from
Crisis to crisis, he's not fit to be PM.
He always knew there were contradictions
In the Withdrawal Agreement he signed.
Progress in the Brexit negotiations has run
Late because of lockdown, and their crunch point's
Coincided with the virus's second wave.
He didn't think through his Internal Market Bill,
He didn't expect protests at his breach of the law
And now Oliver Lewis is blamed for giving
Brandon Lewis the statement he'd be breaking the law.
There's no direction or leadership, the public
Has grown confused, divided and resentful
At his overpromising, moonshots when there are no tests.
The confusion's inseparable from his character.
He's handled the crisis poorly and's being found wanting.
And he's got the UK leaving with a thin deal.
A journalist asks if it wouldn't be wise
Not to leave the EU at the time of the virus –
A bird in the hand is worth two in the bush.
Trade with the EU's better than more trade out there
When there is a plaguey virus abroad
That may delay a deal with India.
The second wave is with us, it will be

A W-shaped, double-dip recession.
Excess deaths to the fourth of September
Are sixty-five thousand, and in the same period
Nearly fifty-seven thousand have the cause
On their death certificates as Covid-19.
The flu season's with us, preserving society
And our liberty must be balanced against
Preventing deaths. With his weak grasp of detail
The PM, like a pedestrian treading
In dog's muck, does not look where he's going,
Does not see ahead and overpromises,
And his character's the reason why he can't
Anticipate and address challenges.
And he's got the UK leaving without a deal,
His most calamitously wrong forecast of all.
    Now it's announced there's a briefing by Whitty
And Vallance as the virus is doubling
Every seven to ten days, it's a critical week
And there'll be more restrictions, the Government's
Hoping the public will listen to the scientists
More than to the politicians. The briefing happens,
The two men sit in gloom at a long desk
And in turn show doomsday graphs and data:
The rise in Spain and France the UK'll follow
Six weeks behind, how the infection rate's doubling
Every seven days and if there's no action
Will hit fifty thousand cases a day
In mid-October and two hundred deaths a day
In November and rising – a grim picture
As their unsmiling faces show, hard truths indeed.
They sit like two Horsemen of the Apocalypse,
Like Death and Hades sitting side by side,
Serious, quietly exulting in mortality.
It's a worst-case scenario, the actuality
May be only ten thousand cases a day.
But it's said the virus has mutated – evolved –

To transmit faster with one more ammonic
Acid, spread faster as 614G
Than as 614D – a mutation
More contagious that could be adapting
To bypass barriers: masks and hand washing.
And the R rate's now approaching 1.5.
They set out the facts clearly and concisely
As a possible trend, not a prediction.
It's spin, as a SAGE report, 188 pages long,
Also says seventy-five thousand could die
From non-Covid causes in a new lockdown.
Now the PM is speaking in the House
Like a sheepdog driving sheep into a pen,
Announcing restrictions to reduce infection.
All must sit at tables in pubs, bars and restaurants,
Which will close in England at 10pm, intimate time –
Daily curfew that may last for a Draconian
Six months, and all should work at home if they can,
And a two-week "circuit break" could be introduced soon.
The rules controlling how people should live
Have changed almost two hundred times since March.
Starmer's told his Party's virtual conference
Johnson's just not serious, he's just not up
To the job, and "the Government's incompetence
Holds us back and angers me". He sounds a PM.
Now in the Commons he says the Government
Has no strategy – workers were told to go back
To the office, and are now told to work at home.
Johnson says Labour's logic's irrational
As 'test and trace' does not transmit the virus.
Eh? It's now said that Johnson just misspoke.
Johnson speaks to the nation reading from
An autocue, punching the air – your poet
Thought he was going to be punched through the screen –
And hitting out at, speaking at, not to, the viewer,
Saying the new curfew may last six months,

Boasting – when no one can book a test – just how
Good moonshot testing will be, saying the Army
Will help the police keep everyone distancing.
He seems to be saying he'll bring in martial law
Without consulting Parliament's MPs,
Draconian measures for thirty deaths a day,
Compared with four hundred and fifty from cancer
And only three hundred and seven who had not got
An underlying condition have died
Of Covid-19 under sixty since March.
Restrictions have increased as furloughing stops.
So it's six months of curfew every year
Until a vaccine's found, tried and tested?
Ten million Londoners face local lockdowns.

Now like an inflamed bull showing its horns
Barnier's come to London for information talks
And says Brussels is now planning for the future
On the basis of a 'no deal' with Britain
As the Withdrawal Agreement's been called into question
And there can be no going forward without trust.
How can a state make a second agreement
With one that's undermined the first agreement?
It's a question of trust following the new Bill.
If this Bill isn't withdrawn by September
The thirtieth, Barnier says, the EU won't deal.
He leaves without a breakthrough. But the EU
Have backed down from blockading Ulster's food
And there's cautious optimism on a deal
If the gun (the Bill) is taken off the table.
Meanwhile the EU plans to build a capital
Market union so it's no longer dependent
On the City of London after December.
    UK businesses need to know what to prepare for,
Deal or 'no deal'? And Gove's in the Commons
Making a statement. He says only a quarter

Are ready, three-quarters are ill-prepared
For January the first, and lorries without the right
Paperwork will be forced to U-turn, and there will be
A queue of seven thousand lorries behind them.
The Government has promised several new measures
To cope with a 'no deal' but they haven't happened.
The Opposition spokesperson Reeves says it's like
Baking a cake and forgetting to turn on the oven.
Now lorries will need permits to enter Kent
To keep two-day-long queues down. Kent will be
A border, within it will be a no-man's land
Where seven thousand lorries can queue two days,
Sixty per cent without the right paperwork.
Opponents of Brexit ridicule this pass,
Gauke says it's clear who is responsible:
"Kent access permits would not be necessary
If Queen Mary had not lost Calais in
1558." Are they serious?
You'll need a passport to go to Tunbridge Wells?
That was never promised during the referendum.
Hauliers are reacting angrily to this news.
There are further questions on Johnson, who is now in thrall
To blinkered scientists who are running the Government,
In confusion, contradiction and mixed messages,
Governing by diktat, refusing to discuss his rulings.
He's saying 'Stay at home for six months' and spouting
Churchillian nonsense about 'We'll make it through' –
With devastating repercussions on jobs.
Now Sunak, who's facing the biggest UK
Deficit in peacetime, having borrowed
221.4 billion
Pounds in the first five months of the current year,
And another 35.9 billion
In August, is revealing new borrowing
To subsidise wages of part-time jobs
In place of furloughing, a job-support scheme

That won't help the three million who cannot work
In aviation and hospitality.
It won't be enough to stop business closures.
It will cover fewer people than furloughing.
It will cost nine billion more, but who cares?
In thrall to science, the Government's lost touch
With commercial reality as Sunak knows:
He says, "We must learn to live with this virus
And to live without fear," a new slogan
Which opposes Johnson's slogan "Stay at home".
There's a rift between Sunak and Johnson. Look,
Johnson's not in the chamber, he's visiting
Police in Northants as Sunak's charting
A new economy-improving course.
    There's a rebellion gathering under Brady
To put lockdown measures to an MPs' vote.
As sheep long to return to their pasture
And all look longingly out from their pen
And a "baaa" bleats out their deep frustration,
It's now announced MPs will decide
If Johnson's 'rule of six' is to go ahead.
Quibbling has turned into a mutiny.
It's clear Johnson simply doesn't understand
How business depends on orders and bookings,
The economic damage of more lockdown
And how temporary economic change
Can become permanent and destructive.
There's speculation he could soon step down
As the mess increases, the debt and chaos:
Lockdown was to be reviewed after three weeks,
Then it was flattening the curve, then "the second hump
Of the camel" and is now "suppressing the virus
Until we have a vaccine". Now quarantine
Has put hundreds of thousands of jobs at risk,
There's the 'rule of six', there are fines of ten thousand pounds,
Now students may be banned from their homes over Christmas,

And only sleep with someone if you're in
"An established relationship" – liberty's under threat.
He has to pay for guests' food at Chequers
And is short of cash, can't live on his salary
Of a hundred and fifty thousand pounds as he
Supports four of his six children, and his divorce
Cost him two million and cleaned him out – and Marina
Has taken out a charge in her maiden name
On his Oxfordshire farmhouse so he can't sell it.
She's boxed him into the consequences of his deeds,
Compelling him to try and rent it out.
He can't afford a nanny for his new son,
And if he resigns he can earn big money again.
It's come out that his son was baptised as
A Catholic in Westminster Cathedral
As Carrie's a Catholic – a pro-European gesture
As if King Henry the Eighth had turned Catholic
After breaking with Rome. Since his Covid
He's been having dark moods, and there are concerns
For his physical well-being and mental health.
As his ignorance of business translates into a failed
Economy and mass unemployment,
His only way out may be to resign.
And in the middle of all this is Brexit:
The London School of Economics' report
Forecasts the economic cost of a 'no deal'
Could be two or three times worse than Covid's impact
And will be hugely damaging for the UK.
And, having promised gold before the referendum,
Johnson will be principally to blame.
The pressure is mounting for him to step down.
And your poet, like a hen in a farmyard,
Pecks scraps from blowing newspapers and picks out
Salient details like juicy corn or grubs,
And wonders like everyone else what is ahead.

And now it's emerged, Whitty and Johnson
Agreed a two-week "circuit-break" lockdown
Immediately, and Sunak opposed this
And, fearful he would leave, Johnson backed down.
Hence the rebellion, and Brady's amendment,
Hence MPs want the politicians to snatch
Back control of policy from the scientists.
In all this Johnson's damaged, exhausted.
Labour are three points ahead in the polls.
Johnson seems no longer up to the job,
His diktats are deemed disastrous, he's worn out
From Covid and his domestic problems.
There are rumours in Westminster he's split from Carrie,
Who interferes in the running of the country:
She's struggled to be First Lady, and marches
Into ministerial meetings and thrusts his son
Into his arms, and is more interested in
Badgers than Brexit, and is disliked by MPs.
Hence she's holidayed with friends by Lake Como.
There are rumours that he's missing Marina.
And now he's engulfed in the UK's deficit.
 Johnson said austerity's over, but it's now
A necessity to pay for the borrowing.
And so is inflation, to whittle the huge debt down.
And Gove's terrified of a double whammy –
A 'no-deal' Brexit on top of Covid debts.
There's a new desperation for a deal
With the EU to ease the dire economy,
And China's hostile in view of Hong Kong,
And is accused of grabbing world control
Of many states by using loans and debts,
And wooing Barbados with its 'new silk road'
And overseeing its turning against the Queen
So it now wants a Barbadian Head of State.
 Like sheep that have been shepherded into a barn
And are locked in for a spell of bad weather

The country's exasperated by changing rules,
Tightening restrictions and whopping fines.
Snow, interviewing Hancock, jabs his finger
And heatedly says: "Parliament is for once
Deeply representative of the country,
It's completely asunder, nobody
In the country or Cabinet knows what's going on,
And you know nothing about what's going on.
The Cabinet and the country are at sea,
We're a laughing-stock." The world's laughing at the UK.
But a million have died from Covid throughout the world.
    Now Johnson's got extra Covid restrictions
In the North-East wrong. He's said to apprentice builders,
"It's six in a home, six in hospitality,
But as I understand it, not six outside."
He means that six people can meet in pubs,
But a new law bans households from mixing
Indoors within the region of the North-East.
He doesn't understand his own rules, he's befuddled.
The *Daily Mirror* shows Johnson standing,
Scratching his head, and its headline proclaims:
"The fool of six." Now there is confusion
Over the rules, and Johnson's apologised
And said that he "misspoke". And the unrest
On the back benches is now palpable.
Even the PM doesn't know the rules,
And the 10pm rule for pubs and restaurants
Doesn't apply to the House of Commons bars
As MPs (including Hancock) have been drinking
Much later than closing-time, 10pm.
There's widespread lack of trust in the Government
And Johnson lacks moral authority.
He appears clueless and paralysed by events,
Even May would have looked more competent than this.
The UK'll end up with the worst per capita death
Rate and worst-hit economy of all

The industrialised nations, and the rules won't have worked.
    Now it's announced the UK economy
Is 21.8 per cent smaller
Than this time last year, and while Patel
Is considering sending asylum seekers
To Ascension or St Helena islands
In the South Atlantic, four thousand miles away,
There's a call for European immigrants
To replace those who would not register
On an app and left feeling unwanted,
To fill positions in hospitals and care homes
And get the economy moving once again.
    It's revealed in a biography, Johnson's
Father broke his mother's nose when he was ten,
And because of his father's absences in his boyhood,
Troubled, Johnson took his mother's side and now
He says he could only have a woman as a soul mate.
It seems he was genuinely torn over Brexit
When he wrote two newspaper columns, for and against,
And then opted to head the Leave campaign
Because he opposed his father, who worked for the EU.
His Brexit stance may be anger with his father.
    It's now said the virus is not on surfaces
But is transmitted between people, so wiping down
For seven months may have been unnecessary,
And that R doesn't reproduce exponentially.
It's also revealed that Ferguson got it wrong.
He forecast 1.5 million British dead
From Covid, and panicked Whitty and Vallance
Into the lockdown that ruined the economy.
Johnson's been bamboozled by scientists' advice
And has not considered the damage and lives lost
By the restrictions, and has broken his promises.
He's crashed the economy, to trenchant criticism.
A poll shows fifty per cent think Brexit's a mistake,
And only thirty-nine per cent support it,

And all are braced for a new economic hit.
Now a shock. Trump's been helicoptered to hospital
Coughing and tired, with a fever, and has tested
Positive for Covid, and been given oxygen.
He's being treated with a cocktail of drugs
Made from antibodies of genetically-
Engineered mice and blood that's been taken from
Covid survivors, made by Regeneron,
And the antiviral drug remdesivir
That shortens all patient recovery times,
Which no one's been given before; and dexamethasone,
A steroid to help lung function. A video
Shows him working at a desk, what will he be like
On day ten of his Covid, and what effect
Will his illness have on the election campaign?
Will he win on a sympathy vote, or be replaced?
Now he's shown driving past his supporters,
Waving from a car amid security men,
And now he's out and back at the White House,
Campaigning with Covid, on nine cocktailed drugs.
The virtual Tory conference. Johnson,
Like a sheep baa-ing again and again and again,
Speaks of the UK as the greatest place on earth
In ten years' time, levelled up and soaring
Economically, exclusively powered by wind –
But what will happen on windless winter nights? –
And tax cuts and help for young home buyers,
And private enterprise that will create
A golden future, a new Jerusalem,
Much gold. But now there is a bleak present,
Ruinous lockdowns, rising Covid and deaths,
Bankrupt firms, job losses, locked-up students,
And boosterism won't balance the books.
Most seek to survive now, not dream ahead.
Most don't look beyond next week, and how can
The economy grow on wind if there is none?

Most look for gold *now*, not in ten years' time.
    The UK has the highest rise in Covid
Cases in Europe and the fourth-highest in the world
After the US, Brazil and India.
Liverpool has the highest R rate in Europe.
A new clamp-down on the North. Van-Tam, Deputy
Chief Medical Officer, gives a briefing,
Says cases have quadrupled over three weeks.
R's 1.2 to 1.5 instead of 2.7 to 3
As it would be if there were no restrictions.
He says we cannot let the virus rip
Or have another lockdown and close schools,
And so there must be a more balanced way
With more restrictions. Powis shows a graph:
Forty per cent of all Covid cases
Are in the North-West. The virus is transmitted
In enclosed, crowded and close-contact spaces
Such as pubs and packed places. Only by
Decreasing the R rate to below 1
Can hospitalisations and deaths be decreased.
A graph shows rising infections, hospitalisations
And deaths rise after a time-lag. It's fifteen
To thirty days from infection to death or discharge.
NHS staff will be regularly tested,
Nightingale hospitals must be ready in the North.
    In Parliament Johnson unveils a new
Three-tier system: 'medium', 'high' and 'very high'.
Starmer says September's measures did not work.
Now there's a conference: Johnson, Sunak, Whitty.
The measures are in consultation with Mayors,
Getting the local leaders on the Government's side.
Johnson says the measures will work if they
Are implemented properly, but if not
Then new action will have to be imposed.
The rhetoric's about the country, but so far
Only Liverpool's in the 'very high' tier.

Johnson has gone against the SAGE advice
To have a circuit-breaking two/three-week
Lockdown (excluding schools) across half-term,
And noticeably Vallance was not to be seen
At Johnson's briefing or press conference.
As a goldfish in a pond with large *koi* carp
Is always the last to rise for its fish food
And is well behind the greedy gobbling *koi*
At feeding time, so Johnson's slow to lock down
Among the sleek and gleaming EU carp.
　　And now Starmer's challenging Johnson, calling
Combatively for a 'circuit-breaker' that stops
The virus's current just like the flow
Of an electrical circuit's current, saying
Johnson's policies have failed and need resetting,
Calling for full-pay furloughing, not two-thirds.
Sunak replaced Vallance, and Whitty said
That tier 3 would require more restrictions.
Now Starmer's allied with SAGE against the PM.
There've been seventeen thousand new Covid cases
And a hundred and forty-three more deaths.
The London Mayor says London's at 'high' tier.
There've been more excess deaths in homes than in care homes.
　　Soon London and Essex are in tier two,
And Lancashire, and reluctantly Manchester –
Where Covid hospitalisations have doubled
To more than in the whole of the South-East and South-West –
Have been elevated into tier three,
Or as the Mayor put it, "levelled down, not up".
There's Northern ill-will, Johnson's lost the North.
There's loathing in the stand-off between Johnson
And city leaders, businesses and Brussels.
Twelve per cent of the economy is now in tier three.

The ship is riding at anchor and buffeted
By steepling waves as the frail clutch and cling.

The fools are sick and rueful they've been conned
And have some knowledge of their own folly,
The too-high hopes that brought them to the voyage,
Their too-easy belief in the gold they were shown,
And the waste of their time in hewing out gold
And loading it onboard to bring it home.
All see they will be worse off for the voyage
And vent their anger against the captain, who
Hides from them on the bridge and will not speak
When they try to complain and seek compensation
For their foolishly-bought ticket for this ship.
All see they were wrong and have been grossly misled.
The fools, understanding their folly, are becoming wise.

Canto XIX
Second Lockdown and Vaccine

Sing, Muse, of a second lockdown after a leak,
Of dubious data and reluctance to comply,
Sing of a spreading virus, and the joy
When a new vaccine's announced, bringing the prospect
Of a return to some normality
In half a year's time, for parts of the world.
And sing of hope amid the grim despair.
Now a study by Imperial College
(Which has always opposed Oxford's herd immunity),
Based on the results of finger-prick tests
Of three hundred and sixty-five thousand
People between June and September, shows
That antibodies which give immunity
Fall away over a few months, which means
There can be re-infection by Covid,
There's no herd immunity, and vaccines
Will only work for a short time, like flu jabs,
And must be boosted at least annually.
The Government's been trying to contain
The virus until a vaccine arrives,
The lockdowns just delay until that time,
But this antibody study's exposed
A fatal flaw in Number Ten's strategy
At a time when fifty Tory MPs want
A "clear road map out of lockdown" from Johnson
Amid mass complaints the North's been ignored,
Not levelled up, but slapped with unfair lockdowns.
Two hundred and twenty-six thousand Americans dead
From the virus, more than were killed in World War One,
The Korean War and the Vietnam War combined,
A fifth of all the world's deaths from Covid,
And a hundred thousand new cases a day.

The polls are with Biden and twice Trump's been
To the Supreme Court to block a grand jury
From seeing his accounts and tax records,
When he only paid seven hundred and fifty
Dollars a year in his presidency's first two years.
And now he's lost, he's lost immunity
From a probe into his criminal fraud and if
He's convicted could face fifteen years in prison,
Could go from the White House's West Wing to Sing Sing.
But he's just appointed a new Associate Justice
Of the Supreme Court, Judge Amy Barrett, who
In return for her appointment may be obliged
To refuse to look into his tax returns.
A leaked SAGE report forecasts eighty-five
Thousand dead in a second wave to the end
Of March – a million are now infected –
And a rising number of cases. There are
Now widespread calls for a second lockdown,
As is happening in France and Germany,
Like a new round-up of farmyard animals
And incarceration from a coming storm,
And the Government's pinned its hopes on a new vaccine,
Backed by Pfizer, to be ready for Christmas
And has bought twenty million Pfizer doses.
There are fears Spain will force a 'no-deal' Brexit
And Spanish farmers will lose their UK market
For fruit and vegetables to Morocco.
Three-tier Blackpool, now walk deserted streets
Past the first tramlines for electric trams built in
1885, and see the distant Tower
Built in 1894, five years after the Eiffel,
And look at the Pleasure Beach, whose rounding planes
Were soaring in 1903 (before
The Wright Brothers' first flight), a fantasy
Of flying like swans become a reality,
And think of the amazed Edwardian crowds

And of its enlargement and opening in
1923. Your poet wanders past
The 'high-tide' organ above where high tides
Foam at the sea wall and eerily blow the pipes
Of a monumental organ on the promenade.
Blackpool, which had one of the first tramlines,
Had pleasure planes and tangled scaffolding,
Now ravaged by Covid, so on the south pier
Shop- and stall-owners loll with no customers,
O Blackpool, your industrial greatness
Has been tier-threed to shut-down by the pandemic.
The second Covid wave's stronger each day,
It's a sudden increase, cases have jumped fifty
Per cent since last week, it's spreading faster
Than the Government's own worst-case scenario
Which says there will be eighty-five thousand dead
By March, every UK hospital full
By mid-December. The economy will shrink
10.4 per cent after disintegrating
Before the second wave, a different strain
Of the virus that spread throughout Europe from Spain
And has caused eighty per cent of new infections,
A genetic variant first seen in
Spanish farm-workers, 20A.EU1
With six mutations. Like the Spanish flu
Of 1918 that killed fifty million
Its second wave will be deadlier and kill
Young adults as well as the elderly.
After a week toes turn purple and swell
For two months. There'll be no normality
Till 2022, Dr Fauci has said,
Director of the US National
Institute of Allergy and Infectious Diseases.
Hallowe'en, trick or treats. Flanked by cadaverous
Harbingers who don't consider L-shaped
Economic damage or social cost,

Grim Whitty and Vallance with dubious charts
Presented to four men (Johnson, Sunak,
Hancock and Gove) for a snap decision
And hurried and calamitous U-turn,
Brought forward from Monday after a leak
And delayed nearly three hours by speech-writing,
Johnson observes as the scientists (in charge)
Exaggerate evidence: soon deaths will be
Worse than the worst-case scenario of two
Thousand a day – or perhaps four if
A Public Health England/Cambridge study
Compiled a month back, pre-tier, out of date,
Can be believed, up by between fifty
And a hundred and fifty per cent more than thought,
And rising until the end of December;
And hospitals are close to overflowing,
Though 232 of 482 NHS
Hospitals have no Covid patients, who now
Number nine thousand against seventeen
Thousand at the peak in the height of spring.

Like a vacillating deer in a dither,
Looking this way and then that, and frozen with fear,
Swayed by their manipulated data
And biased conclusions that terrify,
Johnson announces a four-week-long national
Lockdown from Thursday the fifth of November
So strict measures can be eased before Christmas
But it may continue into the new year:
A stay-at-home order, non-essential
Shops, retail and hospitality will shut.
(Furloughing has been extended by a month,
Costing seven billion, when Johnson could not find
Five million to settle with Manchester.)
Schools and universities will remain open.

Having told Downing-Street aides in September,
"I'd rather let coronavirus rip

Than impose a second lockdown," now at the end
Of October in a rage at the decision
To lock down Johnson's shouted in his study,
Overheard through open doors to his office,
"No more f—ing lockdowns," and when Cummings said,
"If you do that the bodies will pile up in their thousands,"
Irritated, Johnson replied, "So be it,"
Words later echoed in *The Daily Mail,*
Confirmed from their independent sources by
The BBC's Kuenssberg and ITV's Peston.
He'd prefer thousands of deaths to another lockdown.
Research at King's College, London has shown
That the rise in Covid cases is much lower
Than Imperial College's report:
Thirty-six thousand new infections each day
Against Imperial's ninety-six thousand.
The ex-chief scientist at Pfizer says
That SAGE has got its facts wrong: 22.5
Million people have been infected by Covid
In the UK, 33.5 per cent,
Not the seven per cent according to SAGE,
And 26.5 per cent of people are susceptible,
Not SAGE's ninety-three per cent. SAGE's
Forecasts are too high, lockdowns may not be the way.
Lockdown will cost 1.8 billion a day,
That's 50.4 billion over four weeks.
The IMF now expects the economy
To shrink by 10.4 per cent this year
In a double-dip recession, and be in debt
With a five-hundred-billion-pound deficit.
An adviser to Biden had said in Germany
Biden will support "European integration",
And Barnier's warning there's a lot more work to be done,
So there may be no UK-EU trade deal next week.
It's clear to most Johnson has lost his way.
A poll shows seventy-nine per cent of Scots

Don't want him to lead their country, hence
The rising support for separation.
It's said (by Toby Young) Covid damaged
His brain, and he's exhausted and forgetful –
The Times has reported he did not know the age
Of his new son, so big was Covid's impact.
He's ready for 'no deal' but long waits in
Lay-bys for thousands of lorry-drivers will spread
Covid, and going ahead with Brexit in
A time of plague is irresponsible.
He's passed the tipping point, he's lost control
Of the virus, the political narrative
And the Conservative Party, which is rebelling.
He has no clear sense of direction, and is now
A liability to his Party, five points
Behind Starmer, and may be visited
By men in grey suits (Brady and Walker)
Who may demand an end to his PMship.
SAGE called for a two-week circuit-breaker
And now there must be a shut-down for four weeks
And perhaps longer. It's more stop-start-stop,
And the economy must take a second hit,
Another U-turn by a weak PM
Who's under the thumb of the two Hallowe'en reapers.
Scotland's banned travel to and from England,
Wales will end the 'fire break' on Monday as planned.
In the countries that acted earlier – Greece, Germany,
South-East Asia and China – cases are less.
Lockdown is a blunt instrument but there is no other
And ahead is going from one lockdown
To the next without a strategy, hoping
That somehow a vaccine will save the day.
And just when the Brexit talks are concluding,
Belgium, Germany, France and the UK
Will all be stuck in a second lockdown,
And lockdown may stop play and consign the UK

Economy to a third hit that may bring
Three million unemployed and a Great Depression
As French fishermen block British goods at
Calais if Macron fails to strike a deal.
The UK-EU negotiations are all
Tangled up like the Blackpool Big Dippers
Loops of rails, the negotiators climb
And are then plunged down, screaming, with arms in the air,
Hurtle sideways, almost overturning, then rise,
Go under, then above, then inside out,
And go round in a circle back to the start
And don't get anywhere until their 'car'
Grinds to a halt: no deal. A lot of scares
And anguish have led nowhere, and all that's left
Is rail lines in the sky and tangled loops
Of negotiations that went nowhere.
    Your poet has watched from the Boulevard Hotel
And must now leave Blackpool and the North for
A month of staying at home, having taken
A tram to the Euston Railway's northern end,
New Euston, whose hotel Victoria
Visited in 1847 where
Your poet had morning coffee, and realised
The railway paved the way for the trams and Tower,
The industrial revolution turned to earn
From giving pleasure to working masses.
And as your poet takes one final ride
On an illuminated ship (a tram covered
With lights) for an hour's round trip to look at
Twinklingly-lit children's cartoon favourites,
Garish materialistic baubles that grew
Out of the Victorian end of the line
(Not a Ship of Fools, your poet hastens to add,
Even though a ship in lights was sailing on roads),
A last look at the glittering economy,
A look at the hotels and businesses

Already shut when tier 3 was announced,
To deplore the new closures on Wednesday
That will turn the North into an industrial wasteland,
Johnson's promises to level up the North
Are in ruins, all businesses need funding,
The gold was never there to deliver.
The North has been conned, a red wall of fifty
MPs in ex-Labour seats are up in arms,
And Starmer, having withdrawn the Labour whip
From Corbyn, has at last reoccupied
Blair's centre ground and will win back the Northern votes
That Corbyn lost, it'll be curtains for Johnson.
Your poet sits in his window as the wind gusts
And whistles and the calm sands stretch to the sea
And laments this latest loop in England's tangled decline.

Like farmers debating when their dairy cows
Should be locked away in sheds, and if battery hens
Should do nothing all day except lay eggs,
The Commons is debating the new lockdown.
May rises two rows behind Johnson to speak.
Johnson, who described her plan as "trying
To polish a turd" (unseemly, crude language
Before a vicar's daughter, who just stared),
Plonks his notes on his green bench and walks out
As May tears into the new lockdown rules:
Four thousand deaths a day "was wrong before
It was even used", the data was "dodgy".
It "looks as though the figures are being chosen
To support the policy, rather than the policy
Being based on the figures". Now she demands
The data on the costs of the decisions
Being made, the cost to the economy.
Fifty Tories vote against lockdown or abstain.
Whitty admits Liverpool cases are falling
Although he misleadingly said they are rising.

Like a naughty schoolboy told he must write
A letter of apology, Johnson's written
A letter of apology for his walk-out,
Telling May he had to attend a meeting.
    Another U-turn, just as a clover field's
Manna to all deer, Sunak extends furloughing
To March, adding umpteen billions to costs.
It's now transpired the death-toll graphs were wrong,
The projections for Covid fatalities
By the two Grim Reapers. It should have been
A thousand deaths a day, but the modelling
On which lockdown was based was incompetent.
Is the policy based on the data, or the data
Chosen to reflect the policy, as May asked?
Yet another U-turn, a hundred and seventy
Million given for more free lunches at schools
Footballer Rashford's campaigned for. So who is
Running the country, scientists or footballers?
    It now seemed that Covid was in decline
Before lockdown began, and the second wave's
Peak had already passed, and there would be no more
Lockdowns following Vallance's dodgy data
Forecasting one thousand five hundred dead a day
Or even four thousand, which bounced Johnson
Into lockdown on a lie, with loss of trust,
That the public wouldn't be locked up any more
Or go along with the contradictory rules.
The Great Plague of 1665 killed
Two hundred thousand over eighteen months.
Our ancestors used social distancing,
Lockdowns, disinfectants and track-and-trace,
And paid by dropping coins in vinegar.
The King's plague orders were: whitewash your walls,
Quarantine and don't trade clothes – which all worked.
    The US election's over, and after two days
Of Trump protesting the Democrats have gained

From illegal votes during the extended count
And starting legal actions in several states,
Which the Supreme Court will rule on in due course,
Biden seems to be the winner. He's of Irish-
Catholic descent and supports the Good-Friday
Agreement, sees Brexit as a major mistake
And won't give the UK a trade deal with the US
Unless it has a deal with the EU first.
    Now Biden is resetting the globalist world,
Reversing Trump's agenda, returning
America to the Paris climate-change
Agreement, confronting China and Russia,
Reinvigorating global institutions –
The WTO and WHO –
And defending the global rule of law
And human rights when the UK's in breach
Of international law and the global
Rules-based order by reneging on its treaty
Obligations through ill-judged clauses in
The Internal Market Bill, and has said
It does not wish to commit to applying
The European Convention on Human Rights.

But now, great news, as Biden's announcing
A task force to combat Covid-19
Pfizer confirm their vaccine (tested in
Six countries on forty-three thousand five hundred,
Coded BNT162b2)
Is ninety-five-per-cent effective and no
Safety concerns have been raised. Pioneered by
Two children of Turkish migrants to Germany,
Sahin and Tureci, husband and wife
Who founded BioNTech, it's a two-dose
Vaccine that has to be kept below minus
Seventy, and the UK has bought enough
To immunise twenty-five million people.

The American scientists have saved
The world from the coronavirus nightmare
A few days after the US election.
Did they delay the announcement so Trump could not claim credit?
Did they wait to announce it until after the election
So Trump would not benefit from a surge of hope?
Dolsten, Pfizer's Chief Scientific Officer,
Says jubilantly it's one of the biggest
Medical advances in a hundred years
And the scientists jumped up and down and cheered
With joy for humanity and medical progress.
It's an important scientific breakthrough.
The US Pfizer and its German developer
And manufacturer BioNTech, and Belgian
Distributor, can supply 1.3 billion
Doses in the coming year. The vaccine uses
A tiny part of the spike, the genetic
Sequence, of the virus rather than the actual
Virus itself. It works when mRNA,
Synthetic material, synthetically
Created genetic instructions, is injected
Into arm muscles and this stimulates
The creation of antibodies that identify
And destroy cells that have been infected,
Y-shaped proteins that bind onto coronavirus,
Prevent future infections and produce killer
T-cells that eliminate coronavirus.
　A news briefing. Johnson urges caution
As the vaccine hasn't passed the regulator.
Van-Tam says it's like a train two miles away.
It has to come into the station safely
And the guard must think it's safe to open the doors.
NHS workers will be first in the seats,
Then those in care homes and over eighty –
Your poet – and the two doses will take two months
For the body to work with the vaccine.

It must be stored at minus seventy-one degrees.
Johnson says the cavalry's bugles can be heard
Over the hill, but it's still strict lockdown.
    The markets are soaring at the optimistic news.
It's not peer-reviewed, volunteers have been followed
For weeks and need to be followed for months.
It's the first mRNA vaccine ever produced,
And won't make an impact until the spring.
More data needs to be pored over. Does it
Protect the elderly? We don't know yet.
How long does protection last, are boosters needed?
Does it protect against illness or infection?
If not against infection, we can get
The disease asymptomatically.
It can still spread, and the pandemic's not over.
But it's really good news, our old life will
Soon be back, we can be global again.
The cattle and sheep can roam the hillside
And crop the grass without being locked away.
The vaccine may prevent all future waves,
We may be waking from the Covid nightmare,
Back to the old normal of travel and crowds.
    Now Covid deaths in the UK have reached
Fifty thousand, the highest in Europe,
But at long last there's now hope in the air,
There's a vaccine, and two more are on the way,
Including a British vaccine by Christmas
That's one dose and can be stored at normal fridge
Temperature and costs just over two pounds
Against nearly thirty for Pfizer's double dose.
We'll soon be living normally again.
And soon the US will be leading the world
And the rules-based global order will be back.
Only the UK's at odds with the global
Rule of law because it's breaking a treaty.

The ship's tossing about in a rough sea
And disease is spreading among passengers
And the crew, who are back in their quarters.
The deck's deserted, there's no sign of life.
The passengers sit below, backs to curved sides
Between the bow and stern, and feel wretched.
All are in dismal mood, and feel unwell
And loathe the quarantine enforced on them.
All wish they had never embarked, and calls to hope
Are falling on deaf ears and a fixed gaze.

Canto XX
Brexiteers Sacked

Sing, Muse, of disloyalty and breach of trust,
Of briefings against the boss and mockery
Of his girlfriend, and of high-handedness,
Sing of an outsider's meddling in politics
At a time when 'no deal' seems most likely.
Sing of fifty thousand dead and squabbling,
Of turf wars that ignore a spreading plague.
And sing of dismissal and betrayal,
Of summary sackings of loyal friends,
And sing of a stunning eight-billion-pound bet
And of expectations and loyal gratitude
As a country's fortunes depend on a gamble.
Sing of shadowy things that cannot be spoken.
    Fifty thousand deaths, when Vallance had said
Twenty thousand would be a good outcome,
And questions as to whether Johnson was too slow
In locking down and mishandled the care homes.
Fifty thousand, and turmoil in Downing Street.
The Director of Communications at Number Ten
Has resigned in the middle of the pandemic
Because Carrie (our Catherine Parr, though still
Just a fiancée) felt strongly he should not become
Johnson's new Chief of Staff, and Cummings is now
Considering resigning. There's a crisis
In Downing Street, and Johnson must get a grip.
    The PM's fiancée was openly opposing
An appointment her husband-to-be was making.
What's going on, territorial disputes
When fifty thousand are dead? It's a disaster.
Number Ten is run atrociously, there's chaos.
Fifty thousand deaths, and in dysfunctional
Downing Street staff are fighting like rats in a sack,

And Johnson looks an incompetent, useless PM.
    Another briefing, by Sharma, who says
The economy grew by fifteen per cent
In the third quarter but has shrunk 8.2
Per cent since where it was in February.
Three hundred and fifty million vaccines have been
Secured from six suppliers, but when pressed
He won't answer if their procurement will be
Affected by the UK's exit from the EU.
And there's talk that the vaccine will arrive too late
As the second wave is spreading really fast:
Thirty-five thousand cases yesterday,
And three hundred and fifty dead today
Even though there's full lockdown – the cases
Could reflect infections just before lockdown.
    Everywhere the Tories are in uproar
Like flocks of flapping, pecking, screaming gulls
That flutter and drop on a shoal of pilchards.
Brexiteers in the Lords hammered the clauses,
A hundred Tory MPs oppose lockdown.
Johnson's gone to a loyal praetorian
As Chief of Staff, the man who ran the country
When he had Covid, Cain, his right-hand man,
And has been overruled by his girlfriend.
Why is she making decisions on who works for him?
Cummings is no longer in charge. And no one person
In Number Ten's implementing the PM's will,
Just factions fighting each other, and MPs
Are saying they want Johnson to get a grip
On the chaos surrounding the PM
As the Vote-Leave group around him break up.
Johnson is leading the country during the biggest
Crisis in decades, and he looks weak and wanting.
He's lost control and looks like an average bloke
Who's being told what to do by his girlfriend
Amid squabbling over who has what powers.

He doesn't know where he's going or what to do.
There have been many U-turns, there's no leadership.
He does not seem in control of his destiny.
And, like Penrose's black holes in space that can run
Out of fuel and collapse, the black hole in Number Ten
May implode, and the Government cave in.
    A power struggle between aides: the "mad mullahs"
And the new press secretary, who Carrie's backed.
Cain wanted more powers and was enraged by
The appointment of Stratton, who's supposed to conduct
Daily White-House-style TV press briefings,
And a compromise of making him the boss
Of all Number-Ten staff had a backlash
From Stratton and Johnson's unelected partner
Who, aghast, has become an assassin.
Stratton wouldn't work with Cain but wanted
To report directly to the PM.
In the middle of Covid and Brexit,
A turf war at the heart of Government.
As a minke whale surrounded by a pod
Of orca whales in the Southern Ocean
Turns and heads out before it is attacked
And the sea turns red beneath the swooping gulls,
Cummings announced he will leave by Christmas,
And again Carrie can be seen as behind the blood.
Senior Tories have asked him to leave now:
The main issue of Covid should be focused on,
And nothing has been achieved in the Brexit talks
With six days to go before the deadline,
Energy's been wasted on internal squabbling.
    Now like a pit pony that works underground
And surfaces, blinking, into daylight
Cummings has emerged from a dark passage by his house
And, blinking, has again braved reporters' shouts,
And has now been seen leaving Number Ten
Carrying a cardboard box of his belongings,

He's left for good and will work his notice at home.
He's later seen carrying in wine and champagne.
His few allies who remain in Downing Street
Claim they can hear boisterous sounds of a 'victory
Party' coming from Carrie's upstairs flat.
Six days of Brexit talks, and Vote Leave's gone.
Does this mean Johnson's going to compromise?
Does it mean he's breaking from Disaster Capitalism?
Have they lost their eight-billion bet in another betrayal?
 Now Vote Leave has fallen, there is a power
Vacuum in Number Ten, and the shape and tone
Of Government after Brexit will soon be known.
Now the Augean stables can be mucked out.
Johnson bounces between Vote Leave and Carrie,
Often changes his mind and puts off difficult decisions,
He agrees with one group to do one thing and then
Agrees with another to do another thing.
Carrie blames Vote-Leave aides who hold key posts
In Downing Street for isolating Johnson
From his own MPs, turning the media against
The Government and overseeing mistakes
On the pandemic that have squandered his majority.
She wants a different tone, less aggression.
It's a power struggle for who has access
To the PM, and influence over him.

Now it's emerged that Cain and Cummings spoke
To the PM at lunchtime, and said it was
Better that they should both go at Christmas.
It's puzzling and intriguing why they went.
Cummings was ordered to leave with immediate effect
After being accused of briefing against Johnson.
The move was warmly encouraged by Carrie.
Cummings left with a parting shot at Johnson:
He's been dithering and failing to act decisively
On Cummings' advice, which Johnson ignored.

Johnson is still searching for the aide who leaked
Lockdown, and Cummings, who used to work for Gove,
Who knew, may have meant that Johnson needed
Leaks to bring him out of his dithering.
Cummings came out of the front door of Number Ten
And he won't be going quietly. There are still feuds
Within the top team just days before Brexit.
Have Vote Leave been cleared out of Downing Street
In advance of a climbdown on Brexit,
A cave-in by the UK which Vote Leave
(Cummings and Cain) would have vigorously opposed?
"Get out," Johnson told the Brexit squatters
In Downing Street, according to one source.
    More details have emerged on the departures.
Cummings had drafted his Vote-Leave ally Cain
In as Johnson's Director of Communications
As he'd been Johnson's Special Adviser when
Johnson resigned as Foreign Secretary
Over Chequers, and took all his calls, and along
With Cummings was the closest to Johnson.
Now Cummings urged Johnson to make him his
Chief of Staff in Downing Street. Stratton
Said this would be a mistake, and her supporter,
Johnson's fiancée and mother of his child
And a former Director of Communications
For the Conservative Party (who resigned
When accused of abusing her expenses), who texts
Him up to twenty-five times every hour
With her opinions on his policies,
Agreed, and vetoed Cain's promotion, siding
With messages received by the Chief Whip
From MPs urging him to block this move.
Carrie felt he was abrasive and mishandled
The pandemic, and believed the PM
Was not getting good advice from Cummings,
And Cain should not be her husband-to-be's

Right-hand man. She resented she'd been kept
Out of the limelight. She'd applied to be
Johnson's Special Adviser when he was Foreign
Secretary before they became romantically attached,
And Cain had got the job, and she loathed him.
Stratton had not spoken to Cain for two weeks,
Having clashed with him over access to Johnson.
Cummings suggested Watson for Chief of Staff,
Another ally, but Johnson rejected this.
There were raised voices, Cummings was shouty.
It's puzzling that Carrie did not seem to know
Disaster Capitalism, who bet on Vote Leave
And funded Johnson's campaign to be PM,
Had bet eight billion there will be 'no deal'
And that Johnson would be on Cummings' side.
Did Carrie not understand that Johnson
Was obligated to Disaster Capitalism?
Will Cummings settle scores, criticise Johnson
And the Government, knowing where bodies are buried?
There's been strain in Downing Street for many weeks:
Lockdown rows, leaks and attacks on Carrie,
Boasts that Vote Leave were running the country now,
U-turns over 'A' levels and school meals,
Tensions over the Covid pandemic
That drove the factions into civil war.
Cummings and Cain were accused of the leak
That bounced Johnson into a second lockdown
And of trying to frame Hancock as the culprit.
Cummings' parting shot at Johnson, that he's
"A ditherer", may have applied to lockdown,
That he had to be pushed into decision by a leak,
It was Gove they went to for a decision,
Did they leak lockdown for Gove to get a decision?
The champagne and wine carried into his house
Were to celebrate getting Brexit done
And achieving the re-election of the PM

By him and Cain, and perhaps a looming 'no deal'.
    Like a hungry orca whale, with the help of its pod,
Savaging a minke whale and drawing blood
As it twists and turns and tries hard to escape,
After a week of turmoil Johnson's told
His most senior adviser – the second most powerful man
In the kingdom – to go with immediate effect, and not
Work out his time in Downing Street until Christmas
To end the toxic rows at Number Ten.
Others will leave, there'll be a huge clear-out.
Cummings had quit after the PM withdrew
His offer of promotion to Cain as Chief of Staff
Following objections by Carrie, and both
Were accused of briefing against Johnson
(That Covid had impaired his mental powers)
And also against Carrie in a tense
Forty-five-minute meeting with the PM
And were shown incriminating text messages
Forwarded to Carrie, referring to her
By their nickname "Princess Nut Nut", emojis
Of a Princess and four peanuts, saying she's 'nuts'.
Johnson raged they must leave immediately
As he would no longer tolerate their presence.
Cain's said the meeting was warm and full of laughs
As they reminisced, and he and the PM wore
Boxing gloves to camera saying 'Get Brexit Done',
Signed by Johnson (suggesting that politics
Are pugilistic), who said: "I hope we can get
The band back together before the next election."
Downing Street said the meeting was to "clear
The air", improve "morale" with a clean break.
Now they are on gardening leave, working out
Their employment at home until Christmas.
It's a rancorous, acrimonious end
To a relationship that began with Vote Leave.
And Team Cummings say they will now "set fire"

To Johnson's premiership with toxic briefings.
Someone's briefed the PM's not listening to back-benchers,
That the talk in the tearooms is of how soon
Johnson will be gone and who will replace him.
    There's been a purge of the Brexiteers in the wake
Of a maverick adviser and meddling fiancée:
Cummings' shouty confrontation with the PM
Over the ousting of Cain and briefings
Against his fiancée Carrie. Now Vote Leave
Are out, and perhaps Disaster Capitalism
With them, six days before the Brexit talks'
Deadline. Is a sell-out to the EU looming?

Now stories are coming out from Team Cummings.
Carrie wants to be a new Princess Diana,
She holds court as the most important person
In Number Ten, with her own spin doctor,
Soirées for invited friends and journalists,
And does not help Johnson, it's all about her.
It's said that Carrie can be heard prompting
Johnson when he's on the phone to ministers
And officials in confidential calls,
Chivvying on her favourite issues
Such as the environment, which is disconcerting.
And texts sent from his PM's official account
On the messaging service appear to be sent
By someone other than him as they lack his style,
They're short and sharp, don't sound or look like him,
He's courteous and colourful, with erratic spacing.
He's making top-secret policy decisions
On WhatsApp and has clashed with Case, Britain's
Most senior mandarin, who's said it's not secure.
'Government by WhatsApp' can be eavesdropped on.
    She's "running the Government by WhatsApp" from Number Ten,
She calls Johnson's private office from her flat
About twenty times a day and texts him

Up to twenty-five times an hour on policy
Issues, usually on the environment.
The PM goes upstairs and from 9pm
WhatsApp messages arrive and change his mind.
Carrie matchmade Stratton at a drinks party
At Chequers held for her in the summer
When Johnson asked her to be his spokesperson
And slowly she was reeled in. Cain wanted
Price to be her deputy but she saw
Downing Street could control her by getting Price
To take televised briefings in her place.
Carrie "went wild" when she heard Cain had been offered
Chief of Staff – he'd pipped her to be Special
Adviser to Johnson when he was Foreign Secretary
Four years back. Allies of Cummings and Cain
Say Johnson's "running the Government by girlfriend".
But then she's a professional communications operator.
Many have said that Cummings and Cain ran
Downing Street like the Mafia, with macho
Talk of knee-capping those who disobey orders.
Team Cummings say, "The story's as old as time,
Mad Queen destroys the court," meaning Carrie
Will bring Johnson down. Now it's said that he
Will not be in Downing Street in a year's time.
    It's said Johnson rebuked Cummings and Cain
In the final meeting for calling Carrie "Princess
Nut Nut", briefing against her on social media,
Referring to her through emojis that suggest
She thinks of herself as a Princess, and she's 'nuts'.
And as the sea turns red round two minke whales,
And orcas pile in and take bites of their flesh,
So the two sacked Brexiteers were savaged by
An orca team led by Johnson and Carrie.
It's said Stratton was in tears all Saturday
Morning after critical briefings by Cain.
Is she the right person to hold such a position

If she's in tears? And actually, her position
Is unconstitutional, for the UK
Is a Parliamentary democracy,
Not an executive presidency like the US.
    It's emerged Johnson's said he appointed Stratton
To prevent Carrie from going "f—ing crackers".
Her courtiers are hailing her for ending
The "macho culture" within Number Ten.
It's said she went to Cain and tried to stop
The PM hosting a Covid meeting
In March so he could complain to *The Times*
About a report (that she thought stemmed from Cain)
That she wanted to get rid of her dog.
It's said an official suggested top-secret
Information should be kept from Johnson's red box,
His Government briefcase, in case she looked.
She bombards him with texts, and all who work
In Downing Street know about their rows. He
Looks unhappy as if he's a hostage.
She used to work for Javid and wants him
Recalled to counter Sunak's rising star.
Is the gossip in the newspapers not the fault
Of the PM for allowing such chaos?
The PM offered Cain Chief of Staff on
A Sunday, when he cooked sausages in
The Downing-Street kitchen with him. Cain mashed
Potato and swede, and they ate together
In the garden and talked for two hours. Next evening
The story was leaked to *The Times* that only
Cummings, Cain, Case and Lister – not Stratton –
Should have access to Johnson. Two days on
The PM's told him to leave. Does he agree
With the last person he has spoken to?
So now will government be about wind farms,
Trans. rights and woke, which turn the public off?
    Like a dog that wags its tail when anyone

Bends and strokes it, wanting to be liked,
Johnson absorbs opinions and ideas
From those around him and will bend to please
Whoever he's spoken to last, so he's incoherent
And inconsistent. And now he's approaching
The sunlit uplands, those who sold sunshine
Are leaving, and the politicians will blame
Covid while the rich funders of Vote Leave
Get richer by betting against Britain.
    So did Johnson ask Cummings and Cain to leave
As Disaster Capitalism had funded
Vote Leave during the referendum campaign
And then Johnson's campaign to become PM,
And now expected them to deliver 'no deal',
And it was wise to 'break up the band' while
'No deal''s declared, and keep a low profile,
And regroup when it's safer in due course,
And did they let Carrie believe she had won
A power struggle against macho aides?
Or did he 'break up the band' because there's a deal
In the offing, and he's going to betray DC
And doesn't want any Vote-Leave in Downing Street
While this compromise with the EU happens?
Or was Gove using his old aide Cummings
To brief against Johnson and begin a *coup*?
Conspiracy theories on make-believe
Events are wrong, but those on actual events
Illuminate history and underline
The need for men of letters to hold to account
Politicians and their aides to protect
The cultural health of Europe and the state
Of the European civilisation to which they belong.
    So why did Cummings and Cain leave Johnson?
Because the Princess outmanoeuvred them
Or because they need to lie low from DC?
Or because Gove pulled them out to topple Johnson?

Or because Johnson's going to compromise for a deal?
Or a mixture of all four, a bit of each?
Did the Princess manipulate and they had to lie low
And Gove was intriguing to succeed Johnson,
Who was betraying DC for a compromise deal.
If it's 'no deal' for DC and lying low
While all the other things were happening,
The lurid stories of laddish events,
Then they can all remain friends and soon the band
Will be re-formed for the next election.
    Already the agenda has moved on.
Johnson's been rung by NHS Test and Trace
And told to isolate for fourteen days
As a contact has tested positive,
A Tory MP who came to Downing Street.
Immediate tests would prevent such waste of time.
Moderna's new vaccine's announced with joy.
It's 94.5 per cent effective
In stopping symptoms, and stores in an ordinary fridge.
The UK has bought five million doses
But declined to take part in the EU's bulk
Purchase of a hundred and sixty million
Doses as it's independent of Europe.
And without Cummings and Cain to guide him,
Johnson's fanned Scottish-independence flames
By saying from home devolution's been "a disaster
North of the border" as it's been used by
Separatists and nationalists to break up the UK,
And not foreseeing this was Blair's biggest mistake.
He's goading the Scots into a referendum.
Sturgeon says the Scottish Parliament's under threat
And must be protected by independence.
Johnson's announced a green revolution,
At Carrie's urging. Cummings disapproved,
Six hundred billion pounds over five years
To level up infrastructure in the North

Was his priority, Northerners don't want green.
Johnson's investing four billion. Will it lead
To a green industrial revolution?
And Johnson's said the international situation
Is more perilous and competitive
Than at any time since the Cold War, and the era
Of cutting the defence budget must end.
He's investing 16.5 billion
Having cut the Overseas Aid budget,
Making 24.1 billion with previous pledges.
He wants Britannia to remain the most formidable
Naval, and military, power in Europe,
Britannia unchained from her EU shackles.
It's a response to Biden and Brexit,
To reboot Western resolve and confront China
So a Western alliance stands up to the Dragon
And the UK stands alongside the US.
And once again nationalism's leading to war,
And billions that could be spent on humankind
Are going to be spent on warships and fighter planes.
And where is the UK's global leadership
As a moral force for good in a troubled world,
A force that shows respect to the rule of law?
Now Johnson's stuck at home and cannot meet
EU leaders face to face to head off
'No deal' during the last critical week
Of the most important talks since the Second World War.

Now there's a storm and there are mountainous seas
And there's squabbling as to who will take the wheel
And steady the ship at this tumultuous time.
One of the crew's gone overboard, and one more,
The arguments are about power on the bridge.
Long gone are thoughts of gold within the hold.
All are listless, and stare blankly ahead
And hold on, feeling sick, as they're tossed about,

And the captain pulls away from some of his crew.
Loud voices are raised in the engine-room.
All have one thought, not to be swept overboard.
Everyone's stuck in a querulous nightmare.

Canto XXI
'No Deal'

Sing, Muse, of negotiations and stalemate,
Of entrenched positions as one side seeks to maintain
The existing rules and avoid competition
And the other side stands on sovereignty
And independence, as if they increase trade.
Sing of stubbornness and of sticking to a course
That leads to a collision and a crash.
Sing of a country's ruin through recklessness
And of looming disaster no one can avert.
    The EU's been working on a 'legal text',
A joint draft version of a free-trade agreement
Amid whispers of a breakthrough behind the scenes,
Although Sefcovic is saying that the Bill
Is a serious violation of the divorce treaty
And that the EU will retaliate.
    Like a badger seeking to reclaim its sett
From a vicious fox that's broken all the rules,
The EU's started legal action against
The UK because of Johnson's breach of good faith
In breaking aspects of the Withdrawal Agreement
Signed by twenty-seven EU states and the UK
And will not sign any agreement reached
Until bits have been removed from the draft
Internal Market Bill. Von der Leyen says
A letter of formal notice is being sent
And the UK has a month in which to reply,
But both sides are still talking. Will there be a deal
By the end of October? This dispute could end
In the European Court of Justice.
Article 5 of the Withdrawal Agreement
Mentions the obligation of good faith,
Which the UK is now imperilling.

However, under international treaty
Practice sovereign states cannot be bound by
Rulings of courts of another treaty party –
Although May's Withdrawal Agreement allowed
The ECJ to have long-term jurisdiction
Over the UK – and clauses do not break
International law, they authorise action,
It's actions that break international law.
Now the two sides, the UK and the EU,
Like a fox and a badger face to face in a sett,
Are to go into the tunnel, *"le submarine"*,
For secret intensive talks to break deadlock
Which may last three weeks, and while they are haggling,
As if to encourage the mutual trust required,
Eustice is saying the UK is ready to fight
A new Cod War against EU trawlers
And has doubled the Royal Navy's patrol craft in
'The Cod Squad' from three to six. So nationalism
Shows yet again, for the ten-thousandth time
Since the beginning of history, that nation-states'
Competition ends in war. The lessons have not
Been learned from the two world wars that this is the case.
Your poet lived through the Second World War and recalls,
As these ministers – too young to remember – can't,
The ringing nationalism and deadly bombs.
October the fifteenth, Johnson's deadline,
And no sign of a deal as the EU summit
Reviews the position. Barnier has told
Member states at a meeting in Luxembourg
There's no sign of progress on fisheries,
The level playing-field or enforcement
And has fixed the end of October as the deadline
By which ratification of a deal must begin.
Merkel, who holds the EU presidency,
Has told European mayors that a deal's urgent
"From the Irish perspective", and has called for realism.

In Brussels, hidden by masks, the EU leaders
Agree to keep talks going to November
To reach a fair deal, but not at any price.
Macron won't "sacrifice" French fishermen for a deal.
A draft of the summit's conclusions proposed
That Barnier should "intensify" his talks with Frost
But now the European Council members
Have dropped the word 'intensify', stating
The two sides should continue negotiating
In the coming weeks – to UK disappointment.
The EU will not work "intensively"
For a future partnership as Von der Leyen agreed.
Von der Leyen's now isolating as an aide
Has tested positive for Covid, it seems
Covid has priority over Brexit.
Johnson's considering bringing the talks to an end.
Now Frost has told his counterpart Barnier
Not to come to London next week for more talks
As there is no basis for continuing them
Since the EU won't agree a Canada deal.
He's accused Brussels of abandoning an agreement,
And has said the EU should prepare for 'no deal'.
Johnson's said he has to make a judgment
On the likely outcome and get the UK "ready",
And, given that the EU has not negotiated seriously
And that its summit appears to have ruled out
A Canada-style deal, he has concluded
That the UK should get ready from January the first
For arrangements that are more like Australia's,
Based on the principles of global free trade.
The talks are deadlocked like two dogs straining
On leashes and growling, and seem to have come to an end.
The negotiations are finished – unless the EU
Fundamentally changes its position.
Barnier and Von der Leyen want to intensify
But the summit of twenty-seven have blocked them

And it's not for the twenty-seven to keep the British
PM happy, Macron's said, it's the UK
That wants to leave. The trade talks are over,
Is it theatre? Is it reckless brinkmanship?
Is it delivering what Disaster Capitalism want?
Time's running out, Johnson has paused the talks,
And the atmosphere is now tense and stressed.
Johnson's walked away, blaming the EU,
And the UK's Fisheries Bill will end the right
Of EU vessels to fish in British waters.
    Now there's a W-shaped recession,
A double dip from new Covid shuttings-down,
And Moody's have lowered the UK's sovereign debt
Rating by a notch to Aa3, citing
Weakening economic and fiscal strength
Stemming from Brexit woes and Covid shocks.
And the UK's shrunken Brexit ambitions
Mean that UK investment banking won't be
"Equivalent" from next year, and Britain needs
"Equivalence" to replace EU "passporting"
To maintain its three-hundred-billion-pound
Financial-services revenues – to lose them is not
What the referendum voters were promised.
And the Office for Budget Responsibility
Forecasts that the UK's national debt will rise
To 2.6 trillion pounds within five years
And four hundred per cent of GDP
In fifty years' – five decades' – time (when now
It's thought a hundred per cent's ruinous).
    It has all gone wrong for the Brexiteers.
'No deal' and a big economic hit
For leaving the EU, and now Trump out,
And Biden, whose great-grandfather emigrated
From Co. Louth in 1850, is hostile
To the Johnson Government as an Irish Catholic
Who won't see the Good-Friday Agreement undermined.

And Biden's said for some while there'll be no
Early US-UK trade agreement.
    Now the recriminations. The UK's
Negotiators say they can't face Eurocrats
For years after how they have been treated.
It will be several years before the UK
Can meaningfully return for new negotiations,
And Brussels could be frozen out for years.
There are calls to tear up the Withdrawal Agreement
And not pay the thirty-nine billion pounds,
Not pay a penny more than the UK owes.
Just words? Can't they just sit down and reach a deal?
The next deadline is the twelfth of November,
Just before a summit when a deal could be signed
Off by the twenty-seven EU leaders.
    But even a thin deal will damage the UK's trade.
And lorry-owners don't know what permits they'll need,
A queue of a thousand sixty-foot lorries
Will stretch eleven miles. 'No deal' and the three-
Hundred-and-thirteen-year-old Union
With Scotland is dying, fifty-eight per cent
Of Scots would now vote for independence,
And Sturgeon's written in *Die Welt* saying
Independent Scotland would rejoin the EU.
Scotland, Wales and Northern Ireland have gone
Their own way by announcing their national
'Circuit breaks', Wales for seventeen days, Northern
Ireland for six weeks, and England, home to eighty-five
Per cent of the UK's sixty-eight million,
Is divided in the face of a second wave
Between lockdowns and keeping businesses open.
The Union's run its course and's unravelling,
And how can Britain remain one of the five
Permanent members of the UN Security Council,
And keep its army and nuclear deterrent?
The Union's dying of neglect, and with it

Britain's place in the world, and it now seems
The Brexiteers have misjudged the EU's talks
And the future of the post-Brexit UK,
A colossal misjudgment that's leading to decline.
And where are the sunny uplands, the new Golden Age
The Brexiteers promised referendum voters?
Where's the promised prosperous, united society
Now there's a dithering Covid casualty
Trapped in Downing Street with a crying baby
And a girlfriend twenty-four years his junior,
A looming second wave and an imploding
Economy that's more ruinous each day?

Now Barnier is saying the EU will
Genuinely intensify talks, but Downing Street
Says talks cannot resume unless there is
A fundamental change in approach from
The EU, so talks are between sovereign equals.
Barnier says he's working on a legal text
And has agreed to increase the pace of the negotiations
But Johnson is miffed the deadline he set
For the fifteenth of October has been ignored,
And Downing Street has said the U-turn
Is not enough for talks to be resumed.
The EU's not ready to move from its demands
For access to fishing waters and state aid.
But will offer mini-deals for road and air links
But police will lose access to EU
Databases on criminals and terrorists.
Is it posturing to avoid being blamed for 'no deal'?
    Now it's being said Johnson will see Brexit through
To a 'no deal' that's independent of Europe
And will then resign on the grounds of ill health.
He's unwell, exhausted from Covid and hard up.
He envies May, who's making a million a year
From speeches when he's unable to live on

His hundred-and-fifty-thousand PM's salary.
He will walk away from his mess and make money.
Disaster Capitalism will be appreciative.
Sunak will have to end the financial chaos,
But the damage will take generations to sort out.
    Now, like a mole and a vole in one burrow,
The EU talks have restarted, intensive
Daily talks on all eleven subjects. Barnier's
Saying a deal could be struck within two weeks.
Frost's sure he's bringing a fundamental change
To the stalled negotiations after
Giving a conciliatory speech to the European
Parliament in Brussels, and he's speaking
Of the autonomy and sovereignty of both sides
And talking of a balanced compromise,
A zero-tariff, zero-quota deal
That can be signed off at November's summit.
What turned the stand-off round was the UK's
Deal with Japan, its level-playing-field
Guarantees on subsidy law were more
Substantial than the minimum for the EU.
The UK's resistance cracked when negotiators
Were confronted with what was conceded to Japan.
There's now a new baseline, and talk of France
Conceding over fishing – unlikely talk.
    Now there's a six-hundred-page legal text
And both UK and EU negotiators
Are haggling over red tape and fishing,
And the EU's deadline is the coming summit.
If it's breached, there will be legal chaos
As the UK and EU Parliaments
Must ratify a deal, which may take weeks,
So it can come into force on January the first.
    Brussels has taunted that the UK's been stalling
The Brexit talks to see if Trump loses
The US election, and it will face

A tougher trade deal with the US – and will
Make concessions in the talks with the EU
To secure an EU trade deal at all costs.
Barnier's refused to elevate the talks
To leaders' level so the final round
Of talks becomes a bargaining session,
And has said they are heading for 'no deal'.
The chances of a Brexit deal are slipping
Away as Barnier won't budge from his hard-line
Fishing demands, and the leaders are not stepping in
As fish have no passports, they swim between
Jurisdictions, mackerel spawn off Western
Ireland and are caught off Scotland, they move
Between countries' bordered fishing waters.
Talks on a deal could fizzle out, there's no
Sign of EU compromise now Biden's won.
The UK are ready to compromise, the EU aren't.
It's at last crunch week for the Brexit talks.
Is it breakthrough or collapse? Both sides must move,
Or compromise, to get a deal in the talks
In Brussels. The UK's red lines haven't changed,
And Frost will leave if he has to sign a deal
He does not agree with. Four years ago
Frost said the UK'll have to make concessions
To get a deal as it's smaller than the EU.
He had a sense of perspective and context then,
But now he's swaggering on sovereignty
And throwing his weight around, 'No concessions'.
Will there be a deal within the next few days?
It doesn't look like it. There are still disputes
On environmental, social and state-aid
Protections, and the Government is concerned
That a future Labour Government will sign
Up to these details the Tories oppose.
Now Frost says he can see a Brussels deal
Early next week, but the talks could still collapse

Over fishing and red tape. Sunak has urged
A compromise, Gove's warned 'no deal' will lead
To Scotland's breaking away. The quality
Of the deal is poor, 'no deal' is still likely.
    But Biden's win's made a difference, and a deal
Is now essential as Johnson can't be at war
With both America (breaking a treaty
And disrupting the Good-Friday Agreement)
And Europe, which is saying it will deny
The UK access to its energy
Unless it recognises fish swim in shoals
And cannot be fixed within bordered waters.
And if the UK breaks the existing law
By cancelling clauses in the Withdrawal Agreement
Which Johnson himself signed only a year ago,
Why would the EU sign up to a new deal
When the previous one's only lasted a year?
    The future King of the UK's reasserted
The bond between the UK and Europe.
He's been received by Germany's President
And laid a wreath at Berlin's Neue Wacht
War memorial, and's addressed the Bundestag,
Germany's Parliament, in German and English
As befits an eight-times-great-grandson of George I.
He's urged Europe to stand with the UK,
The Anglo-German relationship's "essence"
Is the connections between its people,
An interdependent bond, for the fortunes
Of all Europeans have been dependent
On one another for many centuries,
Connections that have been obscured by wars
And revealed in their rebuilding of the continent.
He's said the English poet John Donne wrote
"No man is an island entire of itself,
Every man is a piece of the continent, a part of the main",
And no country's an island, as histories

Bind together, destinies are interdependent.
The UK remains in the European civilisation.
    Seven days to reach a free-trade deal before
A video summit of EU leaders.
There won't be a deal this week, negotiations
Will run to the eve of the summit and are deadlocked
Over level-playing-field guarantees
For state aid, tax, labour rights and the environment.
There are two competing visions, and the talks
Could fall apart if they can't be reconciled.
'No deal' gapes like an abyss from next week.

Like the captain on Plato's ship of fools, Johnson
Has no knowledge of the sea – or of the costs
Of Brexit or Covid, or pandemics
Or extending furloughing until March,
Or lockdowns that drain the economy.
Like a Rottweiler outsmarting a sly fox,
The Lords are deleting clauses from the Internal
Market Bill that endangers the Good-Friday
Agreement, and Johnson, mindful of Biden,
Should accept the excisions, bearing in mind
He's walked away from forty-seven per cent
Of UK trade and now won't make it up
From the US, but being stubborn he won't.
But with a second lockdown taking billions
Avoiding 'no deal' must be his best chance
Of having a good relationship with Biden.
    The Lords voted for a motion to strip out
The bits of the Internal Market Bill
That break international law regarding
The Irish border – designed to prevent
A trade border down the Irish Sea as Johnson
Signed up to, in the event of 'no deal' –
By 433 to 165, massive.
The Government says it will reinstate these clauses

But the Lords can delay them for a year.
    In a speech Major's said the UK's no longer
A great power, and will be passed by larger
Countries' growth. Ahead's a barebones deal or
No deal at all; a betrayal of what electors
Were led to believe, and Brexit may be
More brutal than anyone expected,
With the risk the UK will break up as there's
Support for Scotland to leave the Union
And Northern Ireland to unite with the South.
    The ex-PM castigates the incumbent:
There are three great powers – the US, China and EU –
And liberal values have stalled in a new Cold War
And trade wars. Russia and Turkey meddle
And are subversive. The US and EU
Have been divided but both now deplore
China's authoritarian direction.
Free trade and globalisation are questioned.
Autocracy's outgrowing democracy.
The UN, WTO and WHO
Are paralysed, and now Covid's diverted
Trillions of dollars from growth, and nostalgia
And complacency are symptoms of decline.
No longer a great power, with under one
Per cent of the world's population, since
Brexit the UK has ceased to be a bridge
Between the US and the EU and is
No longer relevant to either now.
Covid has sunk the economy for decades,
Cost billions and increased the national debt,
And Brexit has been hidden behind it,
The worst foreign-policy decision
In our lifetime. All polls are against it.
The promises that the UK would stay
In the single market, take back control,
Save billions, cut back on bureaucracy,

Not encourage Scottish independence
Or a united Ireland or separate Wales
And have lucrative trade deals with America,
India and China have all turned out to be false
And the UK's trade will be less profitable.
Like a fox blocking a badger underground,
Ministers are giving themselves powers to break the law.
Freedom of movement has gone, food and holidays
Will be more expensive. It will all get worse.
    Then there's the debt our grandchildren will be repaying.
In the past six months the UK's national debt
Has risen by two hundred and sixty
Billion to 2.08 trillion pounds,
Up a trillion over the last ten years.
By 2024 it will be nearly
Three trillion, and the international
Current account deficit will be five per cent
Of national output during the same time.
The Treasury'll borrow five hundred billion this year,
And its Debt Management Office has already
Sold three hundred and eighty-eight billion
And the Chancellor will also have net borrowing
Of 394 billion by next April.
By the end of this Parliament the deficit
Will still be above a hundred billion.
And the only way out's growth in an expensive time
Of Covid and Brexit, when there have been
Four thousand mutations of coronavirus
And new strains may resist vaccines and treatment.
There's a black debt hole in the economy
Of forty billion a year, ahead's hard slog,
And the OBR will signal the slump in growth
Is similar to the Bank of England's
Forecast of an eleven-per-cent fall,
The worst since the Great Frost of 1709.
But there's an opportunity, eighty-five

Per cent of the world economy's outside
The EU, including the fastest-growing countries.
But the UK's standing alone as a small island,
Isolationist, without its vast wartime empire,
With nostalgia for war, seeing Brussels as Berlin,
Exceptionalist Little England unable
To sort its economy out in today's bleak world.
    Now Johnson has to unite both England
And the United Kingdom round a common cause.
But like a butting stag with prickly horns
He's fighting everyone – Mayors over tiers,
Schoolchildren by denying free lunches
At half-term, as well as the Europeans,
And crowing over EU compromise is divisive.
It's said he's wanting to hear if Trump wins
Before deciding whether to go for 'no deal'
And have an American trade deal with Trump,
So the two-trillion debt's at last sinking in.
Johnson's fractured the two post-war pillars
Of UK foreign policy: the close
Relationship with Europe and the US,
Driven by power-hunger and ineptitude.
    There can only be a deal, Frost says, if the UK's
Sovereignty is fully recognised and respected
And solutions take back control of the UK's laws,
Trade and waters, and do not tie the UK
Into the EU's *acquis communautaire,*
Its body of laws and objectives. It will be
A hard Brexit: leaving the single market
And customs union amid the worst hit
To public finances since the Second World War,
With the economy eleven per cent down.
    'No deal' comes at a cost to the Union
For the three-hundred-and-thirteen-year-old
Union between England and Scotland, the most
Successful economic and political

Partnership in history, would end, and there'd be
New paramilitary action in Northern
Ireland, the Troubles all over again.
In such a divided kingdom, the Commons
Would become the seat of an English Parliament
And the Union would decline into a federal state
Of four separate nations only loosely joined,
A Federation of the British Isles,
And Johnson would be the last PM of the UK,
His legacy: precipitating decline.

Negotiations to lift the quarantine
And allow passengers and crew back on dry land.
All feel sick from the stormy conditions,
And hold on, waiting for calm to return.
The ship's become a queasy prison, and all
Would gladly settle to leave their cargo on board
Just to get off and return to dry land
So they can terminate this disastrous voyage.
All think of the wonderful life they led before
They embarked on the ship in the hope of bettering themselves.
All realise how content they were with life
Before they undertook this awful ordeal.

Canto XXII
Deadlock

Sing, Muse, of the confusion and chaos
As the country lurches towards 'no deal',
The goal of the PM's funder, Disaster
Capitalism, who backed all his campaigns.
Sing of the end of the second lockdown,
And of the breakdown of deadlocked talks,
Of looming and disastrous 'no deal'
And of gloom on both sides of the Channel.
It's the final push for a trade agreement.
Both sides grapple like polar bears mauling.
If there's no deal by tomorrow there won't be time
For it to be translated into the bloc's
Twenty-eight languages, and the EU
Governments will demand that the Commission
Launches emergency 'no-deal' plans, which could
Poison the ongoing talks in Brussels.
But now the talks with the EU have been suspended
As one of Barnier's team's tested positive
For Covid, and Barnier has to isolate
For ten days. Frost has said, "The health of our teams
Comes first." There can be no face-to-face talks
In Brussels, perhaps they'll move to London
With little time left, and hundreds of pages
Of legal documents to be combed through
In European capitals and eventually
The European Parliament, and to be signed up
In time for ratification in December,
And that task looks extremely difficult.
Eurocrats are considering a last-resort plan
In which parts of the deal come into force
At the end of transition on January the first,
And an EU-only deal that does not need

To be ratified in national parliaments
Or by Members of the European Parliament
Even though Barnier's promised MEPs a vote.
Barnier and Frost could not chat outside the talks
And build a relationship and have a rapport,
And Johnson's refusal to agree to extend
The transition period now looks reckless
As the negotiators now can't even get
Into a room but must negotiate online.
    Now, meeting meekly like a herd of deer,
The EU Ambassadors have been told
That ninety-five per cent of a trade deal
Has been locked down, but it could still collapse
Because of "wide gaps" on fishing and state aid.
Johnson must make political choices
To seal a deal, and Barnier and Frost
Are talking again on a video link.
But nothing's agreed till everything's agreed.
Johnson's been warned he will lose the North
If he gives in to the EU's demands
For clarity on environmental
Standards and workplace contracts, and reciprocal
Access to fishing waters and markets
As the departure of the UK is not
Supposed to hurt workers in the EU.
    Now civil servants are drawing up legislation
For a deal to pass through the Commons and Lords
"At breakneck pace", but the draft legal text
Has square brackets round clauses on road haulage
And energy that are conditional
On a wider deal. There's a new starting-point:
A review of fishing quotas after ten years
That will be locked to the wider trade deal.
Macron's demanded a translation into French
Which will further delay a deal, and many
EU countries feel they've not been consulted

And are unhappy at an EU-only deal
That's not ratified in national parliaments.
    Barnier's leaving quarantine for final talks
On Brexit in London, and now a trade,
Security and fishing deal's in sight
With a review clause of fishing and trade
In three to five, or ten to fifteen years
After line-by-line talks on a draft legal
Treaty text. But the EU has made
A derisory offer of fifteen to eighteen
Per cent of the fish quota caught at present
In British waters. The UK's said No.
The gap's wide. Barnier's exasperated
At "British blockages" and has told MEPs
He fears the talks – stuck for weeks on fishing,
State aid, competition rules for businesses
And enforcing a future deal – are doomed.
As a cormorant sits on a breakwater waiting for fish
And then dives in and emerges with a sardine,
So Barnier bided his time on fishing rights.
    There's growing disquiet from EU member states
Barnier'll give too much away to the UK.
In an online briefing for EU Ambassadors
In Brussels, from London, he says he won't
Succumb to British demands, but will hold firm
On red lines. The Commission has received
A firm and serious warning from France
That concessions risk dividing member states.
Barnier's also told MEPs Johnson's
Agreed to keep Britain tied to European
Human rights rules so Britain can retain
Access to shared intelligence on criminals.
    It's leaked there will be a hundred and fifty
Billion pounds more of QE in November,
Bringing the amount of twenty-first-century
QE to a trillion pounds, ruination.

The Government's reaction to Covid
Has obliterated three years' growth and left
An economy scarred, since Brexit output's collapsed
And ahead's a Britain facing ruin
As, promising endless gold in give-aways,
Heedless that interest rates can suddenly rise,
The Tory Party's ruining the economy.
  Goldman Sachs economists have warned
The blow to the UK of 'no deal' would be
"Two or three times" more costly than dealing
With the worst pandemic in post-war history.
Now the Governor of the Bank of England
Has warned that 'no deal' would cause more long-term
Damage to the economy than the pandemic
As it would be more difficult to adjust
If the UK reverted to trading with the EU
On new World Trade Organization terms.
'No deal' would lower the national income by
7.7 per cent over fifteen years
And even a deal by almost five per cent.
  The OBR say a 'no-deal' Brexit
Would shrink the economy by two per cent,
Push unemployment above five per cent,
And put three hundred thousand out of work
So there would be three million unemployed,
And send house prices tumbling by ten per cent.
And annual borrowing could rise by twelve billion.
And even with a deal, GDP would be
Four per cent lower than if the UK'd remained
In the EU, and sterling would plunge five per cent
With a longer-term fall of three per cent.
  Like a fox sensing victory by hook or by crook
Johnson's said the UK will thrive with or without a deal.
It's more of the false Brexit prospectus.
In the 1930s Britain used its empire
As an extension of its home market.

Seeing the US, China and India
As alternatives is fantasy, the UK
Needs the EU single market and customs
Union and membership of the EU.
    Sunak presents his November spending review.
He says the health emergency's not over
And the economic emergency's only just begun.
The UK economy will be three per cent
Smaller than forecast in March. Britain will borrow
Three hundred and ninety-four billion this year,
Equivalent to nineteen per cent of GDP,
And is providing two hundred and eighty billion
To get through Covid. Underlying debt
Will be 91.9 per cent of GDP
This year. When the emergency's over the UK
Must return to sustainability.
GDP growth slowed to 2.7 per cent
In the first three months of this year, and then took
The biggest hit to the economy in three hundred years.
The economy will contract 11.3
Per cent this year, and the damage will be lasting.
And that excludes Brexit's two-per-cent shrinkage
Which Biden's Secretary of State's called "a mess".
Biden's said Brexit must not erect a hard border
Between Ireland and Northern Ireland, Kerry
Has said Brexit could be "walked back" – reversed.

The end of second lockdown, but it's still not safe.
There are three new tiers, and the virus is still
Virulent with more than six hundred deaths a day.
Thirty-four million Britons face tougher restrictions,
Now Labour leads the Tories in the polls,
Which put the economy ahead of public health.
As Britain emerges from Covid, the old Britain's gone.
It has been replaced by a jaded, indebted,
Risk-averse Britain with a collectivist

Economy. There's been an authoritarian
Banning of centuries of freedom and human rights
As the State decides who Britons can meet or hug,
And SAGE scientists, blind to economic health,
Force all apart. It's back to the Civil War,
The Puritan Johnson, like Cromwell, has threatened
To ban Christmas, having been a lifelong
Cavalier. The dream of a dynamic,
Post-Brexit buccaneering Britain is dead,
Britain's among the worst-performing European
Nations, doomed by Covid and Brexit self-harm,
A prosperous nation broken by ruinous
Predictions from a panicking coterie,
Borrowing for bail-outs, in defeatist decline.
    The economic carnage of lockdown
Is beginning to be revealed, thirteen thousand
Jobs lost from the collapse of Arcadia,
Thousands of lay-offs from Boots and John Lewis,
And twelve thousand jobs lost at Debenhams,
With three million hospitality workers at risk
And businesses in the North, Midlands and Kent
On the point of closing. MPs are demanding
A cost-benefit analysis, and have received
A rushed cut-and-paste document with no
Regional economic analysis while a leaked
Whitehall study shows lockdown-related job cuts.
There's no longer a health crisis, but instead
A total economic catastrophe,
And no sign of a boom after the pandemic
As in the Roaring Twenties in America.
    A news conference on the first vaccine, Pfizer's.
It's the start of mass vaccination in the UK.
It's ninety-five-per-cent effective across
All ages and will shield twenty million.
Relief and exultation, but a warning
From Van-Tam that we'll be living with Covid

For ever, it may become like seasonal flu.
Johnson's using war imagery again,
The "searchlights of science" have picked out "the enemy"
As if permanent Covid was a temporary Blitz.
There are now sixty thousand deaths from Covid
In the UK – seventy-five thousand
If deaths attributed to Covid on
Death certificates are counted. And the first
Doses of the Pfizer vaccine have just arrived.
    Hancock's welcomed the vaccine, which was researched
By two German children of Turkish immigrants
For a German company with a production
Plant in Belgium, an EU operation,
Under an American corporation.
He's said, "Because of Brexit the UK's been able
To make a decision based on the UK regulator...
And not go at the pace of the Europeans."
He's referring to UK's Regulation
174 which fast-tracks fighting pandemics.
A month's delay would cost economies billions.
Rees-Mogg's said, "We could only approve this vaccine
So quickly because we have left the EU."
But the chief executive of the MHRA,
The UK's Medicines and Healthcare Products
Regulatory Agency, has said they used
"Provisions under European law
Which exist until the first of January".
    Dr Fauci urges vaccine caution,
The vaccine's been approved quickly in the UK.
Spectacular advances in technology
Have discovered a vaccine within months, not decades,
It's not cutting corners but must be reviewed
For people to trust it. The US will take longer.
The feeling is the UK's gone too fast
And has approved the vaccine too hastily.
Williamson's said the UK's got the vaccine first

Because it's "a much better country than the rest",
Even though it was discovered by Turkish Germans
And produced in Belgium, under the EU –
Another instance of British exceptionalism.
It's an unseemly and pointless argument
With European health regulators about
The merits of Brexit, and was not very wise
As it's enraged Barnier at a crucial stage
In the talks on a deal, when the UK needs his goodwill.
Starmer says a deal's in the national
Interest, and is likely to vote against 'no deal'.
The CRG, the Covid Recovery Group,
Is resisting the virus restrictions
And wants a levelling-up agenda,
And will oust Johnson if he has no plan.
There's a febrile atmosphere, it's being asked
'What is Johnson for? What are his principles?'
After Brexit and Covid he has served
His purpose and may be ruthlessly replaced.
The Brexit talks are at a critical stage,
There's turbulence in the windowless, clockless
Business department's negotiating room
Known as "the cave", over late-night pizza.
Like polar bears fighting in a snow burrow
The UK and EU representatives
Huff and growl and rise onto their hind legs
And bite to disarm their adversaries.
The UK's dropped from eighty to sixty per cent
Of its share of fish caught in British waters,
And France, Belgium and Denmark are insisting
Barnier keeps to the red lines on fishing,
And the EU has rejected this offer
And introduced new demands that the UK
Should grant ten years' access to its waters
And stick to EU standards after Brexit.
Barnier's brought back a ratchet clause to make

The UK follow future EU laws.
    Shocked, Frost walks to Number Ten for a face-to-face
Talk with the PM, who says, "There's no way
We are going to do that," and later can be heard
Singing 'Waltzing Matilda', an Australian song,
Signalling it's Australian-style WTO
Rules ahead (what Disaster Capitalism want
As it wins their bet of eight billion pounds).
The next afternoon Frost returns and briefs
The PM again, who says "That's not acceptable",
And instead of pizza the Europeans are served
"Manky sandwiches in plastic". There's a huge gulf.
And the EU aren't pleased Hancock and Williamson
Are crowing about being first with a vaccine
When it's been approved too fast, they've soured the talks –
As has the return of the Internal Market Bill
From the Lords to the Commons, with the removed
Clauses put back, which could bring the talks to an end.
    A US-UK trade deal's receding,
Biden's said he'll concentrate on building up
US industries before agreeing
A US-UK trade deal in detail,
A set-back to Johnson if there's no deal.
    Frost and Barnier are pausing their talks while
They inform their Principals of "the state of play",
So their leaders can decide the next step.
They've agreed the conditions for an agreement
Have not been met due to significant
Divergences on a level playing-field,
Governance and fisheries. It is a path
To a deal and also to a 'no deal'.
Johnson is phoning Von der Leyen, who
Can change Barnier's mandate to making concessions,
But France and the Netherlands can veto the deal
If they don't like what's agreed on fishing,
And Johnson has to carry his hard-liners

And Northern voters without selling them out.
There will be a political decision
Outside the chamber, and Berlin and Paris
Will influence what Von der Leyen says.
It will go to the EU summit later this week.
Two days for a deal to be ratified
By the end of December, or there may be a freeze
Till ratification in January.
By then the UK will be just a "third country",
Global Britain's "new trade deals" will have faded.
'France derails Brexit talks' *Times* headlines scream.
Businesses have been left floundering,
Facing 'no deal' in four weeks and not knowing
What procedures they must begin to change.
There's a blockage and Johnson can clear it
And be hailed for a triumph as he sells the deal.
Both sides can find compromises to go back and say
They both won something to sell, and neither lost,
And Covid can hide Brexit's massive costs.
Four weeks and the Royal Navy may be turning
French fishing boats back from British waters
As French customs officers check papers
With a queue of lorries for the Channel tunnel
Stretching from Folkestone to the M25,
And a warring Continent targeting Britain.
Like a fox on best behaviour with a deer
Johnson and Von der Leyen have spoken,
Johnson from Chequers where Frost's been staying.
He's talked for an hour on the phone, and caustically
Told Von der Leyen that her team's demands
Are "unrealistic", and that the process was wrecked
By EU time-wasting on legal texts.
The call was supposed to rubber-stamp a deal
But's now a last-ditch attempt to save one.
A joint statement from the EU and UK
Governments says differences remain

On a level playing-field, on governance
And fisheries. Both sides underlined that no
Agreement is feasible if the issues aren't solved
And while recognising the seriousness of these differences
They agreed that a further effort should be
Undertaken by their negotiating teams
To assess whether these issues can be resolved.
　Negotiations will resume in Brussels
Tomorrow, Sunday, and the following day
There will be a second call, they'll speak again
On the very day the Internal Market Bill –
And two days before the Taxation Bill,
Both of which override last year's Brexit Treaty
And thereby break international law –
Will be brought back to the Commons with clauses restored,
And the EU's warned this could mean the end of talks.
There's a final EU summit of the year
Later in the week, when the EU leaders
Could approve a deal, giving the UK Parliament
A week to sign it off before Christmas.
No agreement by December the thirty-first
Means the "oven-ready deal" promised last year
In the election campaign has not materialised,
And there's a 'no-deal' Brexit after all.
As Davis has said, the final three weeks matter
More than the first three years in a deal or 'no deal'.
　Is it theatre, is it all a charade?
Are there real differences between the two sides?
Is it a mixture of both? Are both sides
Reassuring their backers they've got the best deal?
There have been rows and screamings in corridors,
If they're getting rattled with each other, it's real.
The Europeans have always believed the deal
Must reinforce a strong single market
And a strong European Union, and anything less
Is not worth having and must be rejected.

Johnson's staring at deadlock and no deal:
Operation Yellowhammer to keep the UK
Functioning when borders are clogged with customs checks.
Hauliers will be stopped from approaching Channel ports
Unless they have the correct paperwork,
And thousands of lorries will queue at sites in Kent.

Deadline Monday has come, and no sign of a deal,
And time is running out, and there'll be no deal.
Monday when international law's broken
As the Internal Market Bill has clauses restored
And there'll be upset in Europe at the breach of trust.
And Barnier's told the EU Ambassadors
In Brussels that there is no deal so far.
The UK's Paymaster-General has said
"The only deal that's possible is one
That's compatible with our sovereignty"
And "the UK's prepared to leave without a deal".
Like two bears claiming an animal carcass
Both sides are now protective of their kill
As they prepare to leave their dark burrow,
The UK Government's said it will remove
Three controversial clauses from the Internal
Market Bill following discussions in
The Withdrawal Agreement Joint Committee,
Deactivate clause 44 on export
Declarations, and 45 and 47
On state aid if there's now a deal, as an olive branch
Offered to EU negotiators.
It's a negotiating ploy, the EU's unmoved.
If you say you'll break international law and then
Say you won't, the law-abiding won't be impressed.
It's now emerged that when Barnier isolated
And was replaced by Von der Leyen's deputy
Chief of Staff Riso, who was making progress,
Johnson was preparing to agree a 'non-

Regression' clause that would see the UK
Maintain existing standards on state aid,
Workers' rights and also the environment,
But was stopped by the demand for the UK
To align with future EU regulations,
Barnier's response to pressure from Macron.
Pictures show Johnson holding a giant crab,
Brandishing it aggressively as if to say
'Watch out for my pincers, I grip and pinch',
Or that he's been clawed in a pincer movement,
Ambushed by Barnier and Macron, or, perhaps,
Merkel and Macron, and that he will burrow
Into the sand and escape the predatory sharks.
    Like a cunning fox wheedling an elegant deer
Johnson and Von der Leyen have spoken
For an hour and a half, and have taken a break
To talk with colleagues, they have paused the talks.
There's silence, suggesting there's still deadlock.
Johnson's asked to meet or speak to Merkel
And Macron, but President Michel's blocked him.
Johnson must only talk to Von der Leyen
To preserve the EU bloc's unity.
There won't be a Franco-German summit.
Von der Leyen's invited him to dinner instead.
    Now like a courteous fox and a suave deer
Johnson and Von der Leyen have released
A joint statement saying: "We took stock today
Of the ongoing negotiations. We agreed
That the conditions for finalising
An agreement are not there due to the remaining
Significant differences on three critical
Issues, level playing-field, governance
And fisheries." And their negotiators
Have been asked to prepare an overview
Of the remaining differences, which will be discussed
In a physical meeting in Brussels in the coming days,

Talks that will define Britain's place in the world,
And his administration's, for decades to come.
Telephone diplomacy hasn't worked,
It has to be face to face now, looking in eyes.
Johnson hopes he can see Merkel and Macron.
The EU leaders have agreed a new mandate.
He's dashing to Brussels for a private dinner
With Von der Leyen before Thursday's summit.
If he doesn't sell out there will be 'no deal'.
But the process is being extended with no
Real sign of actually reaching a conclusion,
And he may be showing he's tried everything
Before coming away empty-handed.
The ERG are saying he'll be ousted
If he compromises on sovereignty.
The Internal Market Bill's clauses have been
Voted through by overwhelming majorities.
Barnier's gloomy, there's a mood in Brussels
That a Brexit deal will never happen.
The pound has tumbled against the euro.
Johnson's statecraft is questionable, to say the least.
He risks sacrificing food, drink, clothing
And vehicle exporters so UK fishing can grow,
But it's just 0.01 per cent of the economy.
He's preparing to renege on an agreement
He signed a year ago, but does not understand
Why the EU wants effective enforcement
In a new agreement. It's poor statecraft.
Johnson's faced with leaving with no agreement
To preserve a political principle
That leaving the EU was about the UK
Getting back its sovereignty and control,
But all trade's interdependent, all agreements –
With the UN, NATO and WTO –
Reduce independence and limit sovereignty.
Last year Johnson said a 'no-deal' Brexit "would be

A failure of statecraft for which we would all
Be responsible" – so it's now looking as if
His premiership's been a colossal failure.
He promised a deal, he promised – gold, gold, gold.
    So what does sovereignty amount to?
A country controlling its borders, money and laws.
Total sovereignty means not being in the UN,
Not being in the Geneva Convention,
Not being subject to international laws
Regarding sea and air, or any trade deals.
Nationalism leads to war – and sovereign states
Fight trade wars and resist all who would infringe
Their territorial integrity
Including intruders into their waters –
And does not advance peace and prosperity.
Ted Heath, once your poet's boss, said when joining
The European Community, "Everyone
Gives up a little sovereignty to bring peace."
Where there was war in every European state
There's been peace for seventy-five glorious years.
    Brexiteers said the UK was reclaiming
Its sovereignty, but that was a massive lie
As it was never lost to be reclaimed:
Hobbes showed in *Leviathan* that sovereignty,
The ultimate authority in the state,
Is indivisible, so when Parliament
Voted to join the European Common Market
It did not surrender any sovereignty.
If it had, it could not have voted to leave
The EU without seeking the approval
Of the European Commission, and would have
Been chastised as a province in revolt
Against its lawful ruler. By enacting
Brexit, the UK's Parliament showed all
That its sovereignty had not been eclipsed.
    It's been said the UK's lost its way.

The old Britain was pragmatic, hard-headed
And full of common sense, knew what it wanted.
It's now indecisive and is pursuing
Incompatible objectives. Vote Leave's wish list
Is about to grate on reality like a ship
Crunching on rocks, and Johnson appears weak,
Pushed around by back-benchers, not leading
From the front. And so instead of standing for
Reliability and stability
It's attacked its respected institutions,
Parliament and the judiciary,
It's scrapped the Department for International
Development and the aid budget,
And it's threatening to break international law,
Which worries those who are considering
Whether to enter a trade deal with Britain.
Britain looks untrustworthy and confused,
And now inward-looking with misplaced belief
In British exceptionalism, and won't accept
That sovereignty and market access are balanced.
Its national superiority's bragging,
And braggarts are not liked out in the world.
Britain's not a part of global diplomacy.
    Like brawling polar bears with thick, curved claws
The UK and EU have now arrived
At an agreement on the Irish Protocol,
How to avoid a hard border in Ireland.
And Johnson will drop all clauses from the Internal
Market Bill that would breach international law
As his olive branch to the EU.
There's still a border down the Irish Sea
As Johnson and Varadkar agreed a year ago
As is in the Withdrawal Agreement Johnson signed.
Gove and Sefcovic have shaken hands, the UK's
Backed down on blocking the movement of chilled meat
Between Ireland and Northern Ireland, and's allowed

EU border inspectors to be based
In Northern Ireland and inspect goods crossing
The Irish Sea without warning or permission,
And in return Great Britain's mainland firms
With a presence in Northern Ireland can receive
British state aid. If there's no deal ninety
Per cent of goods crossing the Irish Sea
Will not be subject to EU tariffs.
Some goods will have tariffs if they are "at risk"
Of being sold in Ireland, part of the EU,
But the tariffs will be refunded if the goods
Remain in Northern Ireland, and do not move on.
    Northern Ireland will remain in the single market
And, to Brexiteer anger, will accept EU laws
And checks on food and medicine will increase.
There's definitely a border down the Irish Sea:
Gove says Northern Ireland is "different
From other members of the United Kingdom".
Northern Ireland and Ireland are in the EU,
Great Britain's not, how long before Ireland
And Northern Ireland unite within the EU
And leave Great Britain to fend for itself?
    At the dinner Johnson and Von der Leyen
Like a fox's finagling and a deer's courtesy
Will see if negotiations can be restarted
But at PMQs he's been under pressure
From back-benchers not to shift his red lines.
It looks a blame game. Johnson will say
He went and did all he could, the EU wouldn't budge.
Six Tory PMs have been brought down by Europe.
Will Johnson avoid becoming the seventh?
Having got the country into this quandary,
He has to consider the economics of Brexit
And deliver a Brexit with a deal
Or go down in history as a disaster.
    There's talk of the chaos if there is no deal,

Of factories shutting and food rotting on docks,
Of chaos at container ports, and at the Channel
Tunnel, where two thousand extra trucks are heading
Daily for the UK, and queues are already
Stretching for miles up the M20 as
Traffic management systems are put in place.

The ship is tossing, buffeted by wind.
There's vomit on the deck, the captain shouts
They'll soon be landing, but can't persuade
The authorities to let them disembark.
It's feared they will never land, each passenger sits
And stares at the choppy waves and their crests of salt,
At the briny swell that throws them from side to side
As they huddle with sore throats and dull headaches
And wonder if they have a new strain of the plague.
They are all too ill to think of their cargo,
The gold they've brought back from Narragonia
Doesn't enter their thoughts as they stare listlessly
And wait for news of another who has died.

Canto XXIII
A Perfect Storm

Sing, Muse, of a dinner that went horribly wrong,
Sing of sovereignty and the single market,
Sing of exceptionalism and punishment.
Sing of two sides that are still far apart.
Sing, Muse, of a closed border (with Zeus's blessing)
To panic a PM into a deal.
Sing of the passing of stark deadlines and of how
Covid and Brexit made a perfect storm.
    A dinner date with destiny, and decision
In the EU's Berlaymont HQ, where
The UK's Union flag's flying for the first time
Since the thirty-first of January – upside down.
Like a horse that's nervous before a thunderstorm
And is ready to run for cover when it rains
Johnson looks flustered posing with Von der Leyen,
Who witheringly warns him "Keep distance" as they stand.
Like a fox being polite alongside a deer
Johnson takes off his mask for the cameras.
Like a deer anxious to obey the rules
She tells him to put it back on again.
They attended the same school in Brussels.
She's had seven children, and is coaxing him like a child.
A three-hour dinner on the thirteenth floor
In the *Salon de la Convivialité*.
The British team have had to surrender their phones.
Scallops and steamed turbot – fish, in 2018
There was confrontation as the British can fish
For scallops all the year round, the French for only
Just over half the year – are on the menu
With Australian pavlova pudding.
But the trouble with British waters is that when
UK fishing boats were given licences

Many sold their track records on quotas
To Spanish and French fishermen
Who are therefore legally entitled to fish
In British waters as they hold licences.
Johnson again asks to meet Merkel and Macron.
As graceful as a flamingo, and poised,
Von der Leyen says he can ask but she knows what they'll say.
Johnson's made three requests and been snubbed each time.
Brexit's not on tomorrow's summit agenda.
    Frost and Johnson set out the British position.
Johnson tries to propose three ways forward.
As in a divorce the aggrieved party turns hard line
There's a muted reaction, the EU won't engage.
As a cow sits down on grass before a storm
And swishes its tail in annoyance at coming rain,
So Von der Leyen sits with her arms folded.
They sit and listen, there's a wall of silence.
    The talks hang in the balance, there are deep
Disagreements on fishing and level-playing-field
Regulatory alignment, and Johnson
Suggests a minimal deal on areas
Of existing agreement: "We could even
Show a willingness to co-operate
With a treaty on foreign policy and defence."
Von der Leyen and Barnier are stunned
Like a deer and stag receiving a dead rabbit
Dropped at their feet by a suddenly friendly fox,
Johnson doesn't seem to know his negotiating
Position. Barnier says, "But, Boris,
It was you who refused to put in a chapter on
Defence, co-operation and foreign
Policy in the negotiations."
Johnson looks at his officials and replies,
"What do you mean, me? Who gave this instruction?"
You did. Get a grip, you're supposed to be PM.
He's confused about Britain's position on

A key aspect of the negotiations,
And has forgotten he's already ruled it out.
At the end of the frosty dinner they will consider
Whether the gap is now unbridgeable.
    Now a statement from Downing Street: Johnson
And Von der Leyen have had a frank discussion
And they have both agreed significant
Obstacles remain in the negotiations
With the EU, and it is still unclear
Whether these can be bridged. Both Von der Leyen
And Johnson have agreed a firm decision
Should be taken about the future of Brexit talks
By Sunday, after the EU summit,
And after twenty-seven EU leaders
Have been able to approve Von der Leyen's stance.
    Like an elegant deer reporting truthfully
Von der Leyen has said they had a lively
And interesting discussion about the outstanding issues,
And have a clear understanding of each other's positions.
But they remain far apart. They agreed
The teams should immediately reconvene
To try to resolve these issues and will come
To a decision by the end of the weekend.
As all eyes are on a speckled great-crested newt
With tiny webbed feet in an aquarium,
So Von der Leyen's held the attention of all.
The Walloons say they'll veto any deal unless
The UK signs up to regulatory alignment.
The mood is gloomy, the two teams have failed.
'No deal' is nearer than it's ever been.
    Separate statements rather than a joint statement
Are not a good sign. The talks have gone badly.
Next day Von der Leyen's tweeted "There's no guarantee
That if or when an agreement is found it can
Enter into force on time" and: "We have
To be prepared for not having a deal

In place on the first of January." The UK's
Paymaster-General has told MPs, "It's clear
The UK and EU remain far apart." It's gloomy.
    Like a fox licking its lips at an ensuing kill
Johnson's told the Cabinet in a conference call
That outrageous EU demands have pushed
Negotiations to the brink and they should prepare
For a 'no deal'. He says on television
That there is a strong possibility
There will be an "Australian deal" rather
Than a "Canadian deal" – meaning 'no deal'
Rather than a deal. Johnson wanted
To speak to Merkel and Macron, Von der Leyen
Said no. He says an EU official said
Reciprocating laws on a level playing-field
In the EU's future relationship with the UK
Would be like the relationship of two twins:
If one has a haircut, so does the other,
Or else there is a punishment. If one buys
An expensive handbag, so does the other,
Or else it faces tariffs. The UK's baffled,
Not knowing Von der Leyen has twin girls.
The EU haven't understood it's about control.
Brexit was supposed to undercut the EU
By turning the UK into Singapore-on-Thames,
But that's never been possible as the EU will block.
Ireland's urging the UK not to walk away
As the deal is ninety-seven-per-cent done.
It's announced the EU has reached a budget deal,
Which is more important to the EU than Brexit.
The twenty-seven won't go against Barnier,
And don't want Johnson anywhere near the summit.
Global aspirations, with an "Australian deal"?
Sadly, the reality's a backwater.
    The EU Commission has set out contingency plans
In case Brexit trade talks fail and there is 'no deal',

To avoid air and road disruption for six months
And for the EU to retain access
To the UK's fishing waters for a year
After the end of the transition period.
Nothing has changed for months, it can only be
A flimsy deal or no deal that's being called
'Taking back control'. The UK has no control,
It's a supplicant, leaving the EU and saying
'Change your rules' because it has an illusion
About its place in the world, its sovereignty
Means 'no deal' with its biggest market.
    Your poet has lived through the trauma of war
And heard all past PMs seek a treaty
To influence peace, and now the UK's prestige
And influence are being given up and incalculable
Damage is being done to its economy
By severing connections with its biggest trading
Partner because a faction saw a route to power
By telling untruths to people who were fed up
After the banking crash and felt they'd missed out
In austerity, who were told their plight could be blamed
On foreigners, immigrants and civil servants –
In short, on the European Union.
But 'taking back control' allows cuts in standards
And does not create any jobs or investment.
It's the worst peacetime decision of modern times.
    In Brussels the summit dinner's in progress.
The budget's been approved, all are content.
Von der Leyen's giving a debriefing
On talks with Johnson, President Michel
Is keen Brexit should not be discussed
As there is no deal for them to look at. It is still
At the level of negotiations. Coverage
Will be short. The mood in Brussels is 'no deal'.
    Next day. Doleful, sincere, like a polite deer,
Von der Leyen says both sides are still far apart,

And it will be "new beginnings for old friends".
Johnson says WTO rules would be wonderful
As the UK could then do what it wants,
But three of the devolved nations are desperate
And are strongly urging a deal at all costs.
    Von der Leyen says fair competition's the condition
For entering the single market, but that's not to say
The UK has to follow every change.
Johnson says if a regulation changes
In the EU, it has to change in the UK,
But the EU's saying No, tariffs will be imposed.
So why does the UK not sign up for tariffs
And escape 'no deal' that will bring tariffs later?
Johnson seems lost in a fog on what's not agreed
And seems out of his depth, says 'You know' several times.
    Now there's planning for 'no deal'. Priority
In the lorry queues on the M20 goes to Scotland's
Live fish exports and chips transported by truck.
There will be taxes on all imports and exports,
And EU countries have been warned by the EU
Not to engage in side deals with the UK
If the talks fail, the EU must act as a bloc.
And four Navy patrol vessels will board
French boats to prevent incursions in British waters
Even if they own track-record licences –
One Dutch ship owns a third of the UK's quota.
It's said the UK may compensate French fishermen
In return for exclusive rights to their waters
Twelve miles off the French coast, so perhaps
The UK is now taking licences into account.
It's back again to gunboat diplomacy,
Aggressive threats, throwing the UK's weight around.
So once again, nationalism leads to war.
    Like a fox looking to justify its treachery
Now it's clear Johnson's seen that tens of millions
In Britain believe the British are much better

Than the rest of the world, and that since the war
Britain's been held back, shackled by the EU,
And should in one week become unbound,
The way of looking of British exceptionalism
Conveyed by a charlatan who does not believe
In a hard Brexit but's on the 'we're better' side.
And the only reason to leave the EU
Is to have a clean break, 'no deal' as exceptionalist
Disaster Capitalism want, for which they've bet.
The Cabinet don't believe in a clean break
And squirm to avoid the eyes of history
As they reinforce their leader's duplicity
With shameful support for damage they fear.
    Now it's emerged Tory donors have urged
Johnson to declare 'no deal', they include DC.
And it's also emerged Frost and Johnson proposed –
Like two self-interested foxes baring their teeth –
Over dinner there should be freedom from tariffs,
The UK would be released from EU rules
And would accept that duties would be slapped
On diverging British exports to the bloc.
But Von der Leyen wasn't interested
In accepting that Brexit means the UK
Would be free to set its own rules. Merkel,
The Puritan daughter of a Lutheran
Clergyman, has distaste for the libertine
Johnson, does not trust him and quashed the idea.
At the bottom of the EU's rejection
Of UK ideas is Merkel's dislike
And she joined forces with anti-Brit Macron.
Number-Ten officials were taken aback by
The inflexible EU position, and one said
Merkel wants Britain to crawl across broken glass.
    It's come out Johnson himself briefed journalists
That Merkel wants the UK to crawl across
Broken glass, the ensuing headlines echo

Johnson's words, not Merkel's, and *Kristallnacht*,
The Night of Broken Glass or November Pogrom
Against Jews by SA forces on the ninth
Of November 1938, while German
Authorities watched without intervening.
It was not Merkel who said this, but Johnson,
Fox-like making things up out of self-interest.
At a critical point in the negotiations
Johnson's suggesting Germany's treated
The UK like the Jews on *Kristallnacht*.
    An upsurge of Little Englandism has meant
Its nationalists need an enemy and a war
Just as Irish nationalists need Troubles,
And have picked on the European Union
As if it's Fascist and not a state that's brought peace
And respects equality under the rule of law,
And so the Navy's patrol boats are ready for war.
English nationalists now have their enemy,
And the German mood in the trade talks has soured.
    Saturday evening, and Tory grandees,
Senior Conservatives, have criticised a looming 'no deal'.
There's fury at the "undignified reports"
That the Navy has been deployed against the EU
When it's already overstretched. Confrontation
With the UK's closest partner in Europe.
The UK's saying the EU's offer
Is unacceptable, and talks have broken off.
The UK didn't start the two world wars, but started
Brexit, and it will cost three times the amount
Of Covid according to the Bank of England,
And the OBR says two per cent will be added
To GDP, and many livelihoods will be lost.
To inflict such damage unnecessarily
Is the act of a sociopath because jobs will be lost.
It's the end for sheep-farmers, your poet's ancestors
Were Cambridgeshire sheep-farmers from Brugge.

The EU have said they'll impose tariffs if
The UK diverges, so why not accept a fair deal
Rather than have tariffs on all goods through 'no deal'?
The damage is of Johnson's own making.
O Zeus, please can we vote to ostracise
A public menace to remotest Syria.

Sunday dawns drizzling, the day of decision.
But it's not decision, Johnson and Von der Leyen,
Both restless like cattle under thunderclouds,
Have spoken by phone, they're carrying on talking
Till New Year's Eve if need be, it's extra time.
They will see if disputes on divergence can go
To arbitration and at what stage either side
Can impose retaliatory tariffs.
Like peaceful deer perpetuating peace
The twenty-seven have told Von der Leyen
To reach a deal and avoid disruption.
But Johnson is not trusted, he's seen as the problem
As trade deals are not made to assert sovereignty
Or independence, but to manage interdependence.
    The UK's politicians have had a blind
Belief the EU would agree a deal that gives
Unfettered access to the single market
With none of the obligations and budget constraints,
And the EU will now punish the UK
To deter others from following suit.
    Like a congress of deer following rules
The EU is saying the UK must accept
The 'ratchet' clause and be locked into Europe's
Regulatory and governing structure
Permanently. It's an ultimatum
And the European Commission's instructed
Member states to engage in a systemic
Non-co-operation policy to force the UK
Back to the table as soon as possible,

Believing the trauma of port chaos,
Pauperisation and further fracturing
Of the Union will snuff out resistance
As happened to Greece when the ECB
(The European Central Bank) cut off funds
Until its financial system collapsed.
And this choice between surrender or 'no deal' –
This deterrence – is happening just as
A new variant of the Covid-19 virus,
A mutant strain that is fast-infecting,
Has been identified, which might be associated
With Covid's fast spread in South-East England,
Much of which, including London and Essex,
Will go into tier 3 in two days' time.
    Like a robin alighting on a garden fork
And offering companionship to a gardener
Bending and weeding, looking out for worms,
Johnson is now trying to get a deal.
He seems to have accepted that the UK
Is the weaker partner in this negotiation
And will have to concede on a level
Playing-field and perhaps also on fishing.
Barnier's said that the UK's accepted
A "rebalancing mechanism" which means it could be hit
By tariffs if it splits from EU rules
By trying to set up Singapore-on-Thames.
Johnson's red lines are evaporating
And some Tories have called for him to resign
If he does not reach a deal, which means
Walking away from his exceptionalist dream,
The illusion that he's mightier than the EU
And can call 'no deal' and terrify Europe.
    Monday. Von der Leyen has rung Johnson
And, coaxing like a gentle, bashful deer,
Said there's a now-or-never chance to clinch
A tariff- and quota-free pact or else

There will be a long 'no-deal' period
With sector-by-sector talks that will take years.
Like a graceful swan floating to a moat's bank
And bending its long neck to nod its head
Several times to the owner who keeps its feed
She's persuasive in the interests of her bloc.
Barnier's given the UK just hours to accept
A demand that the EU can impose trade tariffs on
Britain if its access to fishing is cut,
And Johnson has rejected his ultimatum
Like a fox with saliva dripping from its lips.
The deal is on offer now, but the UK
Will have to water down its fishing demands.
MPs and peers had been put on stand-by
To vote on a Brexit deal within days,
But Johnson has sent them home for Christmas,
Signalling to the EU the UK won't cave in
To its fishing demands, but they could be recalled
Even on New Year's Eve to approve a deal.
    Friday. Johnson's rung Von der Leyen and urged her
To help him clear two final hurdles to a deal.
Downing Street's said the talks are in a "serious situation"
As the EU's stance on unfair competition
Is "offensive" and fishing is still in stalemate.
The EU says it should be allowed to subsidise
Industries across Europe while denying the UK
The same rights, to which Johnson has countered
The EU's Covid recovery package
Of six hundred and eighty billion pounds
Cannot be exempt from state aid restrictions
In a Brexit agreement. The EU've
Cut their demand for access to British waters –
And the UK's control of all its stocks of fish –
From ten years to eight, when the British suggest three.
But it looks as if the EU won't budge,
And the UK isn't budging on state aid.

Meanwhile, the virus is raging, it's everywhere,
And more counties are going into tier 3.
It seems Britain's lost control of the virus.
A third lockdown is looming in January.
Your poet's received a call and is going
To a local clinic to be vaccinated
With two three-week-apart Pfizer vaccines.
He can still be infected but may not be at death's door
If he's put on a dreaded ventilator.
There are reports there are no ventilators left
And always new body bags in A&E.
A new transmissible strain of the virus
In the South-East and an announcement at 4:
Johnson, no longer buccaneering Cavalier,
Now Cromwellian Roundhead, introduces
A new tier 4 for London and the South-East.
Johnson says that the UK has the best
Genomic sequencing in the whole world.
(Exceptionalism? No, true.) Vallance describes
A new variant that has increased transmission.
It was first identified in September.
It moves fast and's the dominant variant,
But isn't more severe. Johnson was told
On Friday, it's a Saturday panic
And flip-flop, his eyes heavy with sadness.
He looks a man who was swollen with pride,
With hubris and then atë, above himself,
And has just been cut down by nemesis,
By microbes sent by Zeus to level him down.
It's one of the worst moments of the epidemic
Because of its infectivity, but there's
A prospect that vaccines will slow it down.
The nation's in shock, thousands mass in stations
To escape London and tier 4 before midnight.
It's like crowding on the last train out of Saigon.
Johnson's said vaccination will change things

And it will be a different country by Easter;
But he promised Christmas would not be cancelled
And tier 4 has dented the nation's morale,
Yet again he's overpromised and under-delivered.
    Downing Street says the talks have now entered
"The final hours" and it's "increasingly likely"
The UK will leave the bloc without a deal
As the EU's mounted a last-minute ambush
On fishing rights. Barnier wants to impose
"Lightning tariffs" if the UK restricts
EU access to UK fishing waters.
The UK's message is, there's no trade deal ahead
Without a substantial shift from Brussels
In the coming days, as the talks are stuck
On state aid and fishing access and rights.
Johnson now faces a Churchillian choice:
He can hold out and ensure the UK takes
Back control of its laws, or he can give ground
And leave the UK trapped in the EU's
Regulatory orbit indefinitely,
Which would be selling out the ERG –
And, of course, Disaster Capitalism.
    Disaster Capitalism, Johnson's backers,
Friends of the fox who've put him where he is,
Bet eight billion on a 'no-deal' crash-out.
If challenged Johnson could say the UK's never
Been European, but has fought Continental wars
While being an Asiatic power in India,
Singapore, the Far East, Australia and New Zealand –
And will be global again, turning its back
On the European Union to revive
Its old Empire: a fantasy, as it's passed
Into the Commonwealth and exists no more,
But he can tough out criticisms he's
Intrigued 'no deal' by blaming the EU's
Intransigence on state subsidies and fishing.

As 'no deal' looms, Operation Capstone,
Whitehall's war-game, lists eventualities:
Ferries laden with food and medicines
Blockaded by French fishing vessels, and stopped;
And lorries full of vaccines hijacked by
Criminal gangs demanding a ransom.
And the pound plummeting on foreign-exchange markets.
A variant strain, sixteen million in tier 4,
Including your poet, a new lockdown;
Another hit to the UK's economy
With businesses closed, travel restrictions in Europe;
And the prospect of Brexit trade talks' 'no deal' –
A perfect storm of devastating decline
For which no soft-power export of culture
And industrial innovation can compensate.
The Sunday deadline's gone, no deal's in sight.
The new strain of the virus in the UK
Has turned the Europeans against Britain.
The UK-France border has just been closed
And the Eurotunnel has been shut down.
The port of Dover's closed to all traffic.
Belgium, Italy, Austria, Holland, Germany,
Bulgaria and Turkey have suspended travel
From the UK because of the new virus strain.
The UK's been put into isolation
By Europe as the virus is out of control.
British travellers are being banned in the week
When the Brexit decision must be reached, and lockdown
May last for months. The UK is besieged,
An island cut off from the mainland now,
And there's anger at the chaotic U-turn
By Johnson, the new strain has been known about
Since September, and a day's notice to go
Into lockdown for months hasn't gone down well.
It's emerged that NERVTAG's behind tier 4,
New and Emerging Respiratory

Virus Threats Advisory Group, which includes
Neil Ferguson, whose wrong modelling brought in
The first lockdown. Hancock's been told the variant,
B.1.1.7, has been detected by
Britain's world-leading genome-sequencing
And unique genomic monitoring,
And is "seventy per cent" more infectious
And running riot, the NHS is at risk.
But Heneghan, professor of evidence-
Based medicine at Oxford, says that you can't
Establish a quantifiable number
In such a short time, some parts of the country
Are free from the variant. All viruses mutate,
And Covid has twenty thousand variants,
And exposure to them stimulates the immune
System to produce a response and protection.
The panicky idea of one mutant virus
Spreading out of control is wrong, lockdowns
Don't work, this respiratory virus
Will be with us for ever and kill few.

The Government's panic has panicked France.
Zeus is alarmed at the prospect of 'no deal'
And Hermes visits Macron and whispers in his ear:
"Is the rapid spread because of the virus
Or because of human behaviour? It's best to be safe."
Macron blockades Britain with travel bans.
Exports from Dover have been suspended
And Manston Airport will be a new lorry park.
The UK faces a double-dip recession.
Major was doomed when the UK crashed out
Of the exchange rate mechanism (ERM),
Blair after the dodgy dossier that led
To the Iraq War, which took time to percolate,
And Johnson after cancelling Christmas –
Again the fox has betrayed its promises –

After letting an extremist coterie
Of scientists force umpteen businesses to close,
For a panicky, wrong view of viruses.
Did he have any idea what he's doing
Or where he's going, is he not all at sea,
The captain of a rudderless ship, controlled
By currents rather than steering a steady course?
O Zeus, you see it all from Olympian heights,
How hubris swells to atë, and then nemesis.
Another deadline's been missed, the talks go on.
Ten days to the end of transition, and now no time
For MEPs to approve a deal, but EU
Law does not require the European Parliament
To approve a deal before it takes effect.
Now forty countries have banned travel from the UK,
Reacting to Hancock's "the new variant
Is out of control". France will lift its blockade
Of passengers and also of their freight
If lorry drivers are tested in England.
Is the new variant being deceptively
Used as a smokescreen so Johnson can hide
'No deal' disruption behind travel bans
And blame it on the variant, not Brexit?
There's a shiver down the national spine
That the Dover route for imports and exports
Has closed not just as retaliation
For patrol boats threatening fishermen,
But as a dress rehearsal for 'no deal',
As if Macron has said, 'Do you like this?
There's a lot more of this if you serve up "no deal."'
And lorry drivers will be banned for taking in
Ham and cheese sandwiches bought in England.
Now Macron's backed down, with lorry drivers
Saying, "This isn't about Covid, it's about Brexit,
He's blackmailing us into doing a deal,
Saying, 'This is what it will be like if you don't.'"

The European Commission has issued a rebuke,
Saying his reaction to the new Covid strain
Has been over the top. In the small hours
Of Wednesday morning the Army's begun testing
And all found negative within twenty minutes
Can drive on to ferries. There's a huge tailback
Of stranded lorries on the M20 in Kent
And two thousand parked on Manston Airfield,
Near Ramsgate, it will take several days to clear,
And truckers have been pushing a police cordon
Near the Dover port which is still open for freight
That is not accompanied by drivers,
As they demand immediate use of the port.
Scuffles have broken out, and a blaring of horns.
    There have been regular secret phone calls as Johnson
And Von der Leyen push on for a deal,
The cunning fox and transparent deer bartering,
And Merkel and Macron have been backchannels,
Even Barnier does not know what has been said.
Frost has tabled a new fishing offer.
Barnier's rejected it, but Von der Leyen
Is urging Macron to accept it, and has
Ordered him to open his borders to the UK.
Johnson's waiting for movement from the EU.
It's said a trade deal is imminent,
And Germany's sent a plane laden with food
To counter anger at French border closure.
    There's another new variant from South Africa
Which is even more transmissible than the UK's.
There are thirty-nine thousand new cases a day
And seven hundred and forty-four Covid deaths,
Nearly seventy thousand Covid deaths in all.
At a press conference, Hancock expands tier 4.
The Continent's full of Brexit-induced *Schadenfreude*.
Britain's a plague island, ten days from Brexit
And it's cut off from Europe and the world

With a PM making promises he can't keep,
Promising false dawns that never happen,
Trying to make the situation look better
Than it is and causing loss of confidence.
Britain, mired in inaction, is the sick man
Of Europe with a new out-of-control plague.
    Now it's out, the richest man in the City,
Cruddas, is to be made a peer like Botham,
One of fifty-two Johnson's stuffed into the Lords,
A former Tory Treasurer and funder
Of Vote Leave and Johnson's leader's campaign,
A spread-betting tycoon from wagering
On the outcome of events, such as 'no deal',
With links to Disaster Capitalism.
Johnson has overruled the House of Lords
Appointments Commission's reservations.
He's funded Johnson's campaigns and's linked with DC.
Like a fox rewarding a hen for betraying a cockerel
It seems Johnson's dumping DC for a deal
And is offering the peerage to make up for the lost bet.
    Now talks are in the "end phase" but no sign
Of a deal yet. Perhaps a 1am
Announcement is the speculation. Now
After one thousand six hundred and forty-four days
Signs of white smoke? It's back down to fishing,
Will the EU compromise? Johnson has a call
To the Cabinet, which he'd have to make before
He sells a deal to the country. The headlines
Of *The Telegraph* are 'Johnson poised to seal
Brexit trade deal'. Johnson and Von der Leyen
Have cleared the final hurdles in their talks,
The fox and the deer are near an agreement.
Johnson's betrayed DC and lost its bet,
He's put his own interests above his funders
And will escape close scrutiny of how
His promises of gold have not been fulfilled.

The deal won't match the lofty rhetoric
Before the referendum. Labour will back it,
It will go through but it's not what was promised.
It won't be a frictionless arrangement,
And money's been squandered preparing for 'no deal'.
That's been a fools' errand, and soon there will be
A third lockdown and a new recession.
    There's a deal on the table, the Cabinet
Is discussing it but talks are continuing
In Brussels, pizzas are being delivered.
The text runs to more than twelve hundred pages.
It will shape the UK's future for years to come.
The UK'll be out of the single market
And customs union. It's a harder Brexit
Than many thought they were voting for. Now
Johnson will claim a victory on fish
As he's had to give way on alignment
With Europe over a long period of time.
It's a Johnson-and-Von-der-Leyen deal,
The ex-European-School pupils in phone calls
Like an anxious horse and cow when thunder growls.
    A leaked Government report has warned Britain
Faces a perfect storm of disasters
After Brexit: an economic crisis
As it battles Covid and a third peak;
Worsening weather and severe flooding;
Pandemic flu; a novel infectious
Disease; industrial action; the end
Of the transition period and customs checks
On goods bound from Great Britain to Northern
Ireland and the European Union;
Disruption to food supplies and millions
Of vaccine doses being shipped from Belgium
Across the English Channel. And the poor
Will be hit hardest in this perfect storm
Of a series of once-in-a-generation

Crises all crashing in at the same time.
At the very time the UK has cut adrift
From its moorings to the EU and headed
For the high seas, it's been struck by a perfect storm:
A global pandemic's caused catastrophic
Economic devastation that has
Brought back a culture of dependency
On State hand-outs when taxes should be reduced;
A new US president is unaligned
Politically with the UK's Government,
And wants a new coalition of the West,
And a US trade deal looks more difficult;
In one year the UK has moved away
From seeing China as friend to as pariah;
The UK's departure from the EU will transform
Britain's place in the world for the worse for decades
Even if it revives its trade with the Commonwealth's
Fifty-three other global nation-states,
And, excluded from the deal, financial services –
Bankers, insurers and fund managers – will lose
Unfettered access to EU markets
And will not be able to trade freely
Across the bloc, and London will lose clout
To Frankfurt, Dublin and Paris, which will steal its trade.
It's a leaky Ship of Fools on the high seas
And all its 'victories' have proved to be Pyrrhic:
To pass the Withdrawal Agreement Johnson
Capitulated to EU demands
On the Irish border, and then tried to reverse his cave-in
With the Internal Market Bill; he imposed
Tier-3 restrictions on Manchester's and other
Northern leaders and said No to free lunches
For hungry children when school's out, and U-turned on both.
His Conservative and Unionist Party
Looks State-led and has lost the Union
Due to Covid and his lack of leadership

And his U-turns are fuelling the separatist cause.
There are rumours that having concluded the Brexit
Negotiations, leading the UK out
Of the second wave will be the PM's last
Political act before he quits his job.
All political careers end in failure,
And Johnson's will be a most destructive failure.
    It's a perfect storm: Covid and Brexit,
Slow roll-out of vaccines, slow recovery
And empty shelves in Northern-Irish stores,
A trade war between the EU and UK
That can add tariffs to half British exports
And take the City business to Amsterdam,
A consequence of the folly of sticking
To the Brexit deadline while there's a pandemic.
The EU's threatened to cut off top-up access
To European electricity and gas pipelines
If there's 'no deal', there may be power cuts.
Brexit's a bad idea for all livelihoods,
The UK's national wealth and its direction
As it turns its back on togetherness in a time
Of insecurity and division.
    Jupiter and Saturn are closely aligned in the sky
Above the south-west horizon, for the first time
Since 1226, for eight hundred years,
A bright star that was seen in 7BC,
Allegedly (on dubious foundation)
The star of Bethlehem the three wise men
Followed – which could also have been the conjunction
Of Jupiter and Venus in 2BC;
A Great Conjunction that together will form
One big light in the sky above Bethlehem.
O star of wonder, heralding a deal
And guiding wise men to the right terms, sent
By Zeus as a beacon of harmony,
May clouds not intervene between you and those

Who have been negotiating for four long years.
   An orange western sky, a clear sunset.
Your poet walks to look across a field
Where horses graze all summer, to the south-west.
No sign of parted planets in the orange,
No sign of unity or disunity.
Your poet stands and gazes in the dusk
And mourns the split in a Union that was good
But is consoled that old conflict won't be seen
In the sky-filling orange of a new World State.
Alas, clouds have now covered the twilit sky,
And hopes for a guiding deal have been concealed
As darkness now falls on benighted men.
   O Britannia, who ruled the waves and now
Waives the rules and is doddery with dementia,
A boo for Boudicca, for not supporting
The civilising Romans who built its roads.
When the Romans left in 408AD
And imperial troops withdrew, it seemed they took
Civilisation with them and left behind
A benighted Britain and Continent
Of subsistence farms and warring factions,
A Dark Age that ended a lavish life.
The UK faces a grim destiny.
A boo for Johnson, who's viewed with hatred
As an English nationalist, not a Conservative,
As an extremist exceptionalist,
Not a One-Nation Tory for all citizens,
For promising gold, gold, and delivering dross:
Hardship, austerity and national ruin.

The ship is battered by a lowering storm,
Jagged lightning hurtles round its flimsy sides,
Thunder crashes and growls, the passengers cower
From the pelting rain and are soaked and miserable,
All ill from a fast-spreading infection,

Some gasping to breathe, some staring listlessly.
A small boat draws alongside, the captain
Leans over a rail and shouts down to its pilot.
Suddenly the captain shouts, "We can berth,
We're going into shore, it's our pilot boat."
Some stir and raise themselves in driving rain,
Some sit apathetically, indifferent
To what they wanted so much not so long ago.
The captain shouts, "Get your things from below,"
And returns to the wheel to follow the pilot.
None move to recover the gold stored in the hold.

Canto XXIV
A Satellite Deal and Decline

Sing, Muse, of a deal at last, but a thin deal,
Of broken promises and discontent,
Of a hard Brexit and trade-breaking paperwork,
Sing of a deal that turned the sad UK
Into a satellite of the EU,
Dependent on its trade, not in it, without
A seat at the decision-making table
But in orbit round its centre of gravity.
Sing of an economic satellite
That's off the coast of Europe and has no say
In the decisions on the economy
Of the emerging United States of Europe,
Sing of winning back national sovereignty
And loss of trade and economic slump.
Sing of national decline and disunity
And of delusion of being a great power.
Sing of the grand illusion hubris feeds.
Sing of the pursuit of humankind's harmony
And the opted-out island that is waiting,
After learning its lesson, to reapply
To join the EU under a wise Government.
Sing of folly and then sing of wisdom.
Sing of foolish choices and wise amends.
And sing of the oneness of the planet earth.
    Christmas Eve. A news conference on the deal.
Like a fox on a snowy field that stands and stares
Defiantly as its owner opens the gate,
As if she's a trespasser on her own land,
Johnson, on his own, wearing a fish-patterned tie,
Between two pairs of Union Jacks, says it's
Four and a half years since the British people
Voted to take back control of their money,

Their borders, laws and waters, and to leave
The European Union, and the Government
Fulfilled that promise when they left on January
The thirty-first with the "oven-ready deal",
And has brought in the new immigration system
And done free-trade deals with fifty-eight countries
And prepared for a new relationship with the EU.
People said that the transition should have been extended
Because of Covid, and he rejected this
To bounce back strongly next year, so he's pleased
The UK's completed the world's biggest trade deal,
Worth six hundred and sixty billion pounds a year,
A Canada-style deal sending goods to be sold
Without tariffs or quotas in the EU market
While taking back control of its laws and destiny,
Outside the single market and customs union.
Laws will only be made by the British Parliament
And interpreted by UK judges and courts
And the ECJ's jurisdiction will end.
The UK can set new standards to innovate
In businesses and financial services,
Artificial intelligence, in which the UK
Leads the world. The deal means certainty
For aviation, hauliers and the police,
The security services and scientists,
And for businesses. He claims that jobs will be
Stimulated in new freeports and green zones.
The UK can back the farmers and agriculture
And be an independent coastal state
With control of its waters, with UK fish
From half to two-thirds in five years' time
When there will be no restriction on its fishing.
He claims it's a good deal for the UK and EU
And will assist the prosperity of both.
Johnson says the UK is culturally,
Emotionally, historically,

Strategically and geologically
Attached to Europe, and their goals remain the same.
  A picture's released of Johnson with arms raised
As if surrendering his seat at top table,
And thumbs up as he hears the deal is done.
He's not been triumphalist in his conference.
Fox-like and shallow, he's betrayed his friends.
The ERG are simmering to rebel
But Labour will vote for. Farage has said
The UK will be too near the EU.
The EU's saying the UK can't step out of line,
And an arbitration committee will determine this.
There's disappointment in fishing and Ulster.
It's a very hard Brexit, there's no mention
Of financial services, or recognising
Professional qualifications, including doctors'.
It's much worse than the deal the UK's got.
Johnson's emollient towards the EU,
His "partners", little sign of a clean break.
He claims it's a good deal, but the caustic
Language of four years ago has gone. It seems
The deal is not really done as there will be
Mini-negotiations, which will bring
Tariffs, revenues and divergences.
The new relationship's an ongoing negotiation.
Johnson says integration was not for the UK,
But many Remainers are tweeting it's not the deal
They wanted, they would rather have stayed in.
  The EU press conference was earlier
Than Johnson's, and is full of deep regret,
A sombre unhappiness the UK's leaving.
Like a mournful-looking but elegant deer
That's been deserted and is lugubrious,
Von der Leyen says it's been "a long and winding road"
And expresses satisfaction and relief
For a fair, balanced and responsible deal.

Competition will be fair, standards will be maintained,
Co-operation with the UK will continue
And fishing communities have five and a half
Years of predictability. Sovereignty
Is about pooling strength and being together
With great powers, and the twenty-seven pulling
Each other up, so the EU's one of the giants.
She laments, "Parting is such sweet sorrow".
She's alert to British culture, to McCartney
And to Shakespeare's *Romeo and Juliet,*
And now she quotes Eliot's 'Little Gidding':
"What we call the beginning is often the end.
And to make an end is to make a beginning."
She speaks in three languages with dignity.
  In contrast Johnson's said with faux-populism,
Like a fox salivating at its coming meal,
"That's it from Brussels, now for the sprouts," stressing
Britain's become uncultured and boorish,
Full of bad jokes, lacking humility.
Ratification cannot follow in the time,
The deal will be voted on in the new year.
The EU Ambassadors will meet Barnier
On Christmas Day. The level playing-field
Is in the agreement, and can be renegotiated
Every four years. Two-thirds of fish in fishing
Waters will be retained by British fishermen
In a five-and-half-year transition period.
Services, eighty per cent of the British economy,
Will not have the same access to the EU.
  The deal's a compromise that will affect trade
And security, sharing information
And working together in years to come,
A cunning fox and a deer in partnership.
Both sides have pushed hard to get the deal done,
Von der Leyen instructed by the twenty-seven,
And Johnson realising the calamity of 'no deal',

Not wanting more lorry queues round Dover.
The UK appears to have what it wants, a zero-
Quota and -tariff deal which gives access
To the huge trading bloc of the EU it has left,
And although tied to the EU's regulations
There's a freedom clause which allows divergence
So it won't be determined by the EU's rules
Without having a UK say, but there are bits
Of the trade deal that will be negotiated
Every four years, for ever. The European
Court of Justice won't have an explicit say
In what happens. The deal won't cover services.
It's been a gigantic compromise, a Christmas fudge
As the best was always going to be not as good
As the arrangement the UK walked away from
With a seat at the table to determine things,
But not as bad as a 'no deal' for supply chains.
After four years the whole deal can be terminated
If either the EU or UK believes
It's not working, and the first four-year review
Will take place just after the next election.
Both sides have moved, and scrutiny will show
How far it departs from the early promises.
Is it gold, gold, gold, this thin bare-bones deal?
No, no, no, no, no! It's all fools' gold.
    It's emerged in a call at 8pm on Monday
Von der Leyen said the EU should impose trade tariffs
On the UK if it did not let them fish in
British waters for ever. She called it "the hammer".
Johnson said it was a deal-breaker, "I can't sign
This treaty, Ursula. I can't do something
That's not in my country's interests. Unless
You change tack we'll trade on Australian terms."
He likened the hammer to a Monty Python sketch
In which a giant hammer hits a car
Every time it tries to drive out of gates.

He was prepared to forfeit a six-hundred-and-sixty-
Billion-pound deal for a billion's worth of fish:
"Viel hummer, kein hammer," "lots of lobster,
No hammer". Negotiations resumed.
    On Wednesday there were four calls on fishing
And car parts. Finally on Wednesday evening
Von der Leyen said of the time EU boats
Could carry on fishing UK waters, "Six years?"
Johnson said, "Five." A silence for three minutes,
The switchboard operator said, "We seem
To have lost the European Commission."
A German voice said, "No, no, I'm still here.
Five and a half years?" That unlocked the talks.
Around 1.30 Frost rang: "I think we've got there."
Johnson said, "Go and close it out." Twenty
Minutes later, a video call with Von der Leyen.
Johnson asked, "So do we have a deal, Ursula?"
She replied, "Yes, we do." The Number-Ten staff clapped
But three per cent of the UK's fish stock
Had disappeared, hence a delay until Christmas Eve.
After eating take-away burgers from Five Guys,
Johnson held a Cabinet call and gave the news.
    Next day Johnson sat in the Cabinet Room
With eight of his team. Frost rang: the deal could be signed.
Von der Leyen Zoomed Johnson saying the deal had been signed.
Johnson raised a thumb, his team applauded.
Johnson's pictured in his Downing-Street bunker,
Lolling back on a chair, shoed feet on his desk
Like a fox wiping its fur paws on a treaty,
As an aide covers his face with both his hands.
He has announced a new Turing programme
To fund thirty-five thousand students overseas
In place of the EU's Erasmus programme –
The wartime imagery of Bletchley Park's
Turing cracking German Enigma codes
Has replaced the cultural Renaissance

Imagery of Erasmus's knowledge.
  So like a fox betraying another friend
Johnson's dumped Disaster Capitalism,
Who bet eight billion pounds on a 'no deal'
And lost their money – after backing Johnson's
Vote-Leave campaign, and his leadership contest.
He'll say no US trade deal forced his hand.
Hence he's tried to make spread-betting Cruddas a peer.
But he's delivered what many said could not be done:
Win access to the single market without
Accepting EU laws. But many feel
It would have been far preferable to stay
In the EU and have world influence
And trade without new barriers or go backwards
Into past nationalism, not forwards to a World State.
And what will the UK do with its new 'freedom'
That gives it more world influence than it had
At its seat at the EU's decision-making table?
  Like a herd of orderly deer in a park
The Ambassadors from the twenty-seven EU
Member states have unanimously approved
The deal, and it has now been signed off by
Von der Leyen and the President of the EU
Council in Brussels and is being flown to London
By RAF plane for Johnson to sign.
  Now Parliament is meeting to debate
The EU (New Relationship) Bill. Johnson says
The Bill's purpose is to trade and co-operate
With European neighbours in friendship
While "retaining sovereign control of our laws
And our national destiny", which was deemed impossible;
And (seeking to unite Leave and Remain)
That the deal will make Britain both European
And sovereign and that the UK will be
The best friend and ally the EU could have.
He says the UK'll open a new chapter

In Britain's national story: making trade deals.
Starmer says a thin deal's better than 'no deal'
Which would mean immediate tariffs and quotas
That would put up prices and break businesses,
Leave huge gaps in security and reduce
Workers' rights and protections, and damage
The Northern Ireland Protocol. The moment
The PM exercises sovereignty to break
With the level playing-field, tariffs kick in.
He says that though the deal should be accepted
To escape 'no deal', it can be criticised.
    Other speakers are critical. Benn says,
Like a deer in a pack – a skulk – of wild foxes,
There will be no frictionless trade, there'll be checks,
Costs of red tape that will expose businesses,
And what's missing includes data transfer,
Financial services, conformity
Assessment, rules of origin, mutual
Recognition of qualifications
And now reduced SPF record checks,
And there's still no agreement on Gibraltar.
All say voting for the deal's better than 'no deal',
But voting for does not mean voting for Brexit,
It's making a bad agreement a bit better.
The Government's prioritised sovereignty
And interpreted it as isolation,
And it has been faced with having to choose
Between sovereignty and the economic
Interests of the country, and however hard
It tried to pretend it could have the best of both,
That was never possible, there would always be
A trade-off that can be seen in the agreement.
    Now's not a good time for a bad deal. Davey
Of the Lib Dems, like another deer among
Foxes, says there are two crises: Covid's
Left the UK's hospitals stretched, and the British

Economy's in the worst recession
For three hundred years. A responsible
Government, faced with crises in health and jobs,
Would not pass this rotten deal, which will make
The British people poorer and less safe,
It's not a 'trade deal' but a 'loss-of-trade deal',
The first deal to put up barriers to trade.
We were told Brexit would cut red tape, this deal
Represents the biggest increase in red tape
In British history, twenty-three new committees
To oversee this trade bureaucracy,
Fifty thousand new customs officials,
Four hundred million new forms, which will cost
British business twenty billion pounds a year.
It's not the frictionless trade the PM promised.
The reels of red tape will put more jobs at risk
At a time when jobs are being lost to Covid,
And all these new barriers will raise prices
In shops at a time when families are already
Struggling because of Covid to make ends meet.
From the failure to agree a good deal for
The services sector, eighty per cent
Of the British economy, to the failure
To agree a stable deal investors will trust,
This was a lousy deal. For this deal the Tories
Can no longer claim to be the party of business
And law and order, for the police won't have access
To European crime-fighting databases
Like the EU's Schengen Information System
Which British police use six hundred million
Times a year – and criminals will escape.
There are many things wrong with the agreement,
From environment failures to breaking promises
To the young by pulling out of Erasmus.
The deal that 'restores' Parliamentary sovereignty
Has hours of scrutiny, Europe has many days;

And businesses have little time to adjust,
But the Government no longer cares about business.
Is this deal that costs jobs, increases red tape,
Hits Britain's services, undermines the police
And damages young people's future a good deal
For the British people? No, it's a bad deal.
Churchill said after Dunkirk, "Wars are not won
By evacuations." Brexit's an evacuation.
    The Bill is passed five hundred and twenty-one
To seventy-three, goes through the committee stage
And its third reading by the same margin,
And has passed through the Lords and received Royal Assent,
An evacuation rushed through in a day.
The most important decision since the war
Pushed through with very little scrutiny
Of the Bill's twelve hundred and forty-six pages.
Johnson's father, who's eighty, younger than
Your poet, has applied for French citizenship,
Saying his mother was French and that he
Has always regarded himself as European.
    But despite the Brexit decision being confirmed
It's rampant Covid that dominates the news:
Seventy-two thousand five hundred deaths now passed,
Nine hundred and eighty-one deaths in twenty-four hours
And more than fifty thousand new cases
For the second day running, and hospitals swamped –
Essex has appealed for help, and the military
Will be running community hospitals there.
New tiers, all England's now in tiers 3 or 4,
Three-quarters of the population are in tier 4.
No celebrations of the new year are allowed.
The Oxford/AstraZeneca vaccine's been approved
And will be given in two doses, separated
By twelve weeks. Three billion doses will be produced
In the coming year with a rapid roll-out.
The public's more worried about the pandemic

Than the loss of decision-making in Europe.
    One thousand two hundred and forty-six pages to read,
And the deal's shortcomings are becoming apparent.
It makes the UK less safe from the point of view
Of security, and police access to data,
It's a bad deal for trade, business and services.
And in the small print it says there must be a review
Every four years to see if the deal's working –
Renewed negotiations every four years
During our entire lifetimes. It is now clear
Europe will be a central issue in
British politics for the next fifty years
And at some stage the UK will go back in
And rejoin the union of its own civilisation.
This may be sooner than many believe, if Brexit
Turns out badly, in four or eight years' time,
When the EU has a single currency.
Brexit may come to be seen as a nationalist blot.
    Like a confident fox, lord of all he sees
Although he's ready to run into a thicket,
Johnson claims to have delivered on every one
Of his manifesto commitments, to take back
Control of money, laws, borders and fish,
And hopes his tottering premiership's bolstered.
But it's not what the Brexiteers promised
During the referendum campaign for
Trade won't be frictionless, there will be tariffs
And new customs and regulatory checks.
The fishing settlement's less than forecast.
The EU's only returning twenty-five
Per cent of the value of fish caught in
UK waters to UK fishermen,
Not thirty-five per cent as he demanded.
As grasshoppers once sawed all summer long
But now cannot be found, so fishermen
May no longer sell their fish to the EU.

There's nothing for financial services
And there's a goods border down the Irish Sea
That's between Great Britain and Northern Ireland
And separates Ireland from the mainland.
And the UK's trading future has to be reviewed
Every four years, and is at the mercy
Of the EU's whims and possible resentment.
Was it worth the upheaval to have reached
Where the UK is now? The UK's economic
Position is now weak, and its influence in Europe,
Which the US has valued, has been forfeited.
New decisions on trade, environmental
And health standards by the EU will affect the UK,
But the UK, being a satellite, without
A seat at the decision-making table,
Has no power to influence EU decisions.
Brexit is a declaration of British
Exceptionalism, "We're too good to be in the EU",
But Johnson does not know what to do next,
He seems to be unravelling before our eyes.
Will the UK's economic and political
Performance live up to its claims of specialness
In a time when leaving will be brutal to businesses?
The think-tank IPPR has warned the deal
Is remarkably weak, it "isn't far off a 'no deal'",
And will introduce major trade barriers
Between the UK and the EU. Starmer has called
It a "thin deal", not the deal the Government promised.
The UK will have to toe the Brussels line
Or face penalties on businesses and exporters.
The UK's committed to a level playing-field,
Maintaining high levels of protection,
And a Joint Partnership Council will make sure
The Trade and Cooperation Agreement
Is properly interpreted by both sides.
There'll be no joint foreign-policy action

And on the coming first of January
The EU and UK will form two separate
Markets, there will be barriers to trade in goods
And services, and cross-border mobility:
The free movement of persons, goods, services
And capital between the UK and EU will end.
    Like a fox that's frightened all the deer away
Johnson's inflicted a hard Brexit on the UK
During the Covid pandemic because
He's always wanted British sovereignty
Disentangled from the EU's enmeshing,
And a sovereignty clause to allow Parliament
To overrule decisions from Brussels.
Now Britain, outside the EU, will be
Diminished, isolated and irrelevant.
The public were told a free-trade agreement
With the EU would be "one of the easiest
In human history", and it would be "a great deal"
With "the exact same benefits" of EU membership
Without any of the obligations or financial costs.
But the deal Johnson's agreed will inflict all the costs
He denied it would, it will erect barriers
To trade, and subject goods to new customs
And regulatory checks, and financial services
Which make up eighty per cent of the British
Economy are not covered, and the OBR
Has forecast this kind of deal will reduce
Britain's long-term GDP by four per cent,
Dwarfing the long-term costs of the pandemic.
    The deal will make the UK much poorer
And will reduce its global influence.
We live in a globalised world, most countries use
Regulatory alignment to facilitate trade
And reject isolationist and old-fashioned
Notions of sovereignty, pooling sovereignty instead.
And countries in superblocs will prosper more

Than those that are isolated and diminished.
There could have been a soft Brexit that kept
The UK in the single market and customs union.
(The Brexiteer Cabinet ministers had to have
The single market explained by Ivan Rogers,
Former Ambassador to the EU, when they met
After the referendum result – they didn't know
The difference between the customs union
With zero tariffs for intra-EU trade,
And the single market which gradually
Eliminated non-tariff barriers.)
The Vote-Leave campaign misled the public
With easy populist solutions to discontents:
Reduce immigration, give the EU's entry fee
To the NHS, as the EU's 'taken your money',
Leave Europe and level up inequalities –
Even though that needs sustained investment.
Britons will live with the consequences for decades.
Vote Leave promised Britain will not have to think
About the EU or Europe after Brexit,
But the UK's been part of Europe for two thousand years,
Under the Roman superstate and again
Under the Danes and the Normans, and, after the divorce,
Henry the Eighth's Reformation, again
Under the Dutch, and after Waterloo
And two world wars, now under the EU,
And will be part of Europe for decades to come.
The hard Brexit will deepen rifts within
The Union, Scotland and Northern Ireland will leave.
An unscrupulous gaggle of politicians has wreaked
Great damage on the UK through tawdry politics,
And our grandchildren will look back in astonishment
That such a failure of vision could have triumphed.
Johnson's said a new Golden Age has begun,
And the deal is a new beginning for Britain,
Which will become an economic powerhouse.

But a lot of businesses have been damaged
By the Government's bad handling of Brexit
And a lot of economic problems have been caused
By Covid, and now there has to be restructuring,
And the debts are massive, there's unemployment
And what looks like a double-dip recession.
Johnson calls, "Gold! A Golden Age ahoy!"
No, his promises are folly, it's fools' gold!

Your poet's seen the crisis in the West.
It's not "a moment of national renewal" (Frost)
But a teetering on the edge of a steep decline
When, as in the nineteen-sixties, the UK
Could not balance the books, was in deficit
And came to be known as the Sick Man of Europe.
Once again the UK's the Sick Man of Europe.
British exceptionalism has been dealt a blow,
The belief, that helped drive the departure, that the UK
Is not one European country among many,
But's a special, chosen country that's better.
It will now find out how small is the part it will play
On the world stage following the populist sentiment
That carried an out-of-touch Britain, obsessed
By past glories, into the folly of thinking
It could exert global influence again
From a position of wartime isolation.
Like a swaggering fox that will soon bolt to hide
Johnson has said there's a Golden Age ahead
In the coming decade, but it's an illusion
That, debt-ridden, despite trade barriers, it can bring in
A prosperous time when all will possess gold
(Now worth over two thousand dollars per troy ounce)
When the reality is: his promises are fools' gold.
   It was always going to be a satellite deal,
Leaving the UK an economic satellite,
Or 'no deal' if Johnson supported his funders.

He seems to have dumped his funder, DC –
Who were behind his Vote-Leave and leadership campaigns,
And tried to make up for it by making Cruddas a peer –
But not dumped his ex-schoolmate Von der Leyen,
Who loiters elegantly near at hand,
A gentle deer too nice to be savaged,
A deal's safer for his survival than 'no deal'.
The deal's worth six hundred and sixty billion pounds,
Twelve billion less than the two-way UK-EU
Total trade last year, so it's in the region
Of the UK's previous trade with the EU
(Forty-three per cent of its total exports),
But, as the OBR have forecast, GDP
Will be four per cent lower under the deal
Than if the UK had remained – six per cent lower
With 'no deal' – and its reduced access to the EU
Will affect GDP. As the US and other
Nations won't come up with whopping trade deals –
So far the UK has found nine hundred billion
From sixty-two countries whereas last year's
Trade deals totalled one thousand four hundred
And twenty-three billion pounds, it still has to find
Five hundred and twenty-three billion pounds
To break even, not improve the status quo –
The UK will still be dependent on the EU
For the bulk of its exports and supply chains, and will be
An economic satellite of the EU,
Not in it, without a seat at the decision-
Making table but in orbit round the EU,
Its centre of gravity for forty-three
Per cent of British exports, while the UK dreams
Of the Commonwealth volunteering to return
With new trade deals worth more than five hundred billion
Pounds, and of becoming a new financial Empire.
    Now reality shines on the darkened scene
Like the sun breaking through clouds in a dark sky:

The Queen's Christmas message is about the Light,
The European civilisation's Central Idea
Your poet stands for, the Light of the World
That fills with Truth and exposes illusions,
The Light of hope and her own inner Light,
And the star of Bethlehem, the Light that led
The wise men to Bethlehem; and about inner peace
And not about matching last year's trade deals.
    Reality's about to end Brexit delusions.
The deal's damaging for the British economy
Compared with remaining under the EU,
But it's better than 'no deal', and giving businesses
Days to adjust to new paperwork in a pandemic
Makes it seem foolish and unnecessary.
Brexiteers have had the delusion that a deal
Would be easy but the UK's had to make concessions:
Money owed to the EU, the Irish border
And EU demands for a level playing-field.
It's been said the negotiation's between sovereign equals,
But the UK economy's a sixth of the EU's,
It's not as powerful, and rebalancing will impact
More on the UK than the EU. Another delusion's
Taking back control, the UK already has control
Of defence, education, housing, health and regional
Development, public investment and welfare.
And as the British will lose opportunities
To do business or live, study and work
In the EU, the UK will lose control.
Immigration from the rest of the world
Increased by a hundred and fifty thousand
Last year. The UK fought harder for fishing
Than for services, which generate eighty per cent
Of its GDP as opposed to fishing's
0.04 per cent. Johnson has said
The UK'll "prosper mightily" even without
A deal, but most economists agree,

The UK will be poorer in the long run
Under this sort of a deal than if it had
Remained in the EU. Scotland may leave
The Union to join the EU, Northern Ireland to join
Ireland and so the EU. England's borders
May then be the Tweed and the Irish Sea.
Brexit's almost certain to damage the UK's
Prosperity and influence permanently.
A boo for Johnson for not realising this.
But at last the UK's beginning to find out
That reality's dispelling the delusions.
    Your poet finds consolation in a wall clock.
Aged under one, he was evacuated from
The bombing in London in 1940
To his grandmother's home in East Grinstead,
And his early wartime childhood memories
Are filled with the safe, mellifluent Westminster chimes
Of an American Ansonia clock
That's now on his wall and has been silent for years
And, after a clockman's visit, is again
Filling the house with safe melodic chimes
Every quarter of an hour during this plaguey time.
His infancy and advanced years will have been filled
With the same reassuring languid chimes
Of a stable time in the Edwardian era
Despite the medieval dangers now.
    Your poet lay awake as a five-year-old
Listening in the dark for the drone of doodle-bugs
And when one cut out counted up to ten
And was relieved it did not land on his house
And blow his young life into smithereens,
And he has been grateful for the noble Union
Of then-warring nations which has protected
His children and grandchildren from rockets and bombs.
    Standing by Loughton war memorial where
Your poet recalls hearing Churchill speak

As tribal leader of victorious Britain
On the sixteenth of June 1945
At the start of the election campaign he'd lose,
Just fifteen months before he called for "a kind
Of United States of Europe" Britain would assist
And presumably be part of. Your poet stands
Where he stood before the United States of Europe
Was first announced, at the start of a movement
That has brought peace to Europe in our time,
And regrets the return to the stand-alone Britain
Of his boyhood in bleak war-torn Europe.
    So what is the global Britain Johnson wants?
The dream's that global Britain, free from the EU,
Will stride the world as a great trading nation
With its own large technology sector
Independent of the US and China,
A bridge between East and West, with English
As the international language, a location
Within a direct flight of ninety-six per cent
Of the global GDP, with a legal system
And an ingenious, entrepreneurial people,
A small island that's the fifth largest economy
In the world, supporting thirty-three million
Jobs as it's good at international trade.
Forty per cent of its exports go through Heathrow,
Planes head for far-flung countries, filled with goods,
Engineers, accountants, lawyers who make things work,
And a plan to unite the world into a World State –
All stifled by quarantine that stops planes flying,
Flights to US cities and China,
And assumes all have Covid, not one per cent,
So France and Germany take its passengers.
A plague island in the cold Atlantic.
    The dream is that Britain's as it used to be,
It's a neo-imperial, pre-Suez country
Trading with the world, sending an aircraft-carrier

To the South China Sea, having a global
Presence and activating the Commonwealth,
Hunting the world as a fox hunts a field.
Johnson's merged the Department for International
Development with the Foreign and Commonwealth
Office to stop aid to dictatorships
Whose policies are anti-British and see
UK aid as a giant cashpoint in the sky,
So Britain can influence the policies
Of all the world's nation-states and 'rule the waves'.
    But your poet sees delusions of grandeur,
Brexiteers haven't accepted the UK's diminished role:
Can it go back to the days of the Empire
And Britannia, when it has so few gunboats?
It claims to be one of the world's top five powers,
Has the best legal and financial services,
The most professional Armed Forces and is one
Of nine nuclear states and one of five
Permanent UN Security Council members,
And is home to the global language and the world's
Capital city, and no comparable nation
Laments its decline or is lacking self-belief.
Milton said, "Remember what nation it is
Whereof ye are," and the UK exported
The idea that laws and taxes must be
Passed by elected representatives,
That the world should follow the rule of law,
And it ended slavery and stamped it out globally
And defeated the Nazi and Soviet tyrannies
And liberated hundreds of millions of people.
The UK has stood for an enduring peace,
And though bankrupt and exhausted after the war
And letting the US assume its global role
So the UK was Greece to the US's Rome,
It is now engaging in global commerce
And, now Western Europe is no longer threatened

By Soviet expansionism, can revert
To an island nation trading with the US,
Australia and New Zealand, Canada and Singapore.

But your poet thinks of the fall of Singapore
Which ended the British Empire in the Far East
In a 1942 catastrophe,
And of the incompetence and self-delusion
Of the Britons in their military stronghold,
Their self-righteous, unjustified self-belief
That underestimated the Japanese threat –
The exceptionalism and superiority
Of the Brexiteers that all would go excellently,
The 'excellentism' and wrong assumptions
That stranded the UK without trade agreements
In a world in which a Chinese virus accelerated
The liberal West's fall from world dominance
And elevated tyrannical China
(Which does not compensate or do furloughing)
To the position of number-one superpower.
And your poet shakes his head in profound sorrow
That sees deep into the malaise of decline.

Your poet has charted – on a seven-foot-long chart –
Twenty-five civilisations, eleven dead,
Fourteen living, all of which go through sixty-one
Parallel stages, and each of the hundred
And ninety-three nation-states in the UN
Belongs to one of these civilisations.
No nation-state can leave its civilisation.
European civilisation's in its union stage
(Stage 43, in a conglomerate),
And if a member state secedes it may be
To a stage of cultural purity (a yearning
For a lost past, stage 45, to return
To its civilisation's religious grounding
And mystic art, its core) that co-exists
With syncretistic Universalism

(Stage 44) and is its civilisation's
Next stage, further towards its long decline
To a new federalism (stage 46).
The Soviet Union passed from Communism
(Stage 43) to the Russian Federation
(Stage 46), with a Russian Orthodox
Revival, and if the UK has left
The European Union for English
Cultural purity there will be a revival
Of national Protestantism that will co-exist
With Universalism, on its way towards
Becoming a federation like Russia.
    But Brexit is a xenophobic nationalism
And may be very short-lived. It's not yet
A revival of the cultural purity
Of Christendom, as happened in Russia,
Of the medieval Light, the mystic trance
And a new Baroque vision of spirit and sense;
And so may not be a shift from one stage to another
Within the European civilisation.
If the UK stays out of the EU
And Covid brings a Protestant revival,
Then Brexit's beginning stage 45;
But if the UK returns to the EU,
Brexit's a temporary lurch towards decline,
Towards federalism and stage 46
And the civilisation's final stage 61,
But the lurch will have been unlurched, and the federalism
Of stage 46, and decline, will be delayed.
    For Brexit was an English withdrawal.
The Scottish, Welsh, Northern Irish – and London –
Wanted to remain. And the revival of England
Has turned iconoclastic as statues
Of slave-traders and colonialists are attacked,
A purity rid of colonial slavery.
England's behaviour's breaking up the UK.

The United Kingdom may soon become
A British Federation without Northern Ireland,
With English, Scottish and Welsh Parliaments.
Lockdown has intensified a cultural war
Between the ex-oppressors and oppressed,
A pre-revolutionary state of affairs,
A left-wing fight for an English purity
That resists the pro-imperial hard-line rule.

Your poet, who was born before the war
When the UK ruled a quarter of the world
And the greatest Empire the world has ever known,
Which the Brexiteers are hoping to revive,
Can see it shrink to just Little England,
An eighty-year decline of staggering melt,
And shakes his head at the sheer ignorance
Of leaders who believe they are in progress
When their folly's brought in massive decline.
Why didn't they read some of your poet's books?
Why didn't they study the seven-foot-long chart?
The West is in decline, and few have smelt
The decay and putrefaction, and the rot,
The corruption, the deceit and rigged rules,
But Russia and China have not been fooled
And are challenging its weakness with their hacks,
Their brazen 'rule-for-life' dictatorships,
Their undermining of liberal democracy.
If Covid leaked from a Chinese laboratory
Either by accident or by design
(To promote China as sole superpower)
And if China has covered this up, we are in
The middle of Cold War Two, and China's military
Expansion within the South China Sea
And dominance will have seismic consequences.

Your poet, an admirer of the West's
History, tradition and institutions,
Held his mirror up to Nature to reflect Truth

And detected decline fifty-five years ago
And put it in his works, which challenge folly,
The swagger of populists who've fallen short,
And request a return to the high standards of the past,
A message those in power won't want to hear.
His mirror shows a country trapped between
Two superpowers that hold 'global Britain' down.
His analysis in 'Old Man in a Circle'
And 'Archangel' (on Russia and China)
Fifty-five years ago remains unchanged.
So what has happened in this long decline
Of the UK from great imperial power
Ruling a quarter of the world to (soon)
A federal group of four nation-states, no
Longer a United Kingdom? The European
Civilisation declined, its Light grew weak,
Two world wars broke down all its certainties.
Its religion weakened, it turned secular,
All was scientific materialism,
Philosophical rationalism and scepticism,
There was imperial decline and colonial conflict
Until it passed into a conglomerate
With loss of national sovereignty over its laws,
There was syncretism and a Universalist
Vision of the oneness of the world and sects
Drawn together with the Light as their common source.
There was a reaction to the unBritishness
Of the secularising conglomerate
(The EU) and a rejection of the present
And a yearning for a lost past and greatness,
A revival of an imperial phase
In the UK's history – Brexit – and the lost past
And Universalism co-existed
As is reflected in your poet's *oeuvre*,
For your poet has observed the process
In his long lifetime from stages thirty-five

To forty-six in the scheme he worked out
More than thirty years ago. And the next stage
Is the UK's splitting into four separate
Federal entities with four Parliaments.
    Your poet has been a poet of decline,
Holding up a mirror to national events
And reflecting his civilisation's decay,
And he sees foreign occupation ahead
Which may turn out to be a new World State.
Johnson believes individuals chart history
But Universalist historians know
There is a pattern behind world events
And leaders are swept along by their currents.
It's the underlying pattern your poet
Is revealing through these surface events.
    The West is declining and now the East
Is taking over as China heads a new
Gold rush and corners the world's lithium
From Chile for batteries, tantalum
From the Democratic Republic of the Congo
For precision-guided missiles including
Tank missiles, and samarium from Chinese
Mines for wind turbines and solar farms in
A new industrial revolution.
Thanks to its conveniently worldwide virus
China now heads the world's marketing power
Despite economic sanctions by the US,
Under a nationalist leader who's bullying
His way towards global domination,
Who rules for life and crushes all dissent
And is buying access to the world's copper,
Iron, cobalt and all strategic metals
Needed to produce goods that will dominate
World trade and establish its pre-eminence.
    And it is now clear that Covid-19
Has hastened the shift in power from West to East,

Exposed flaws in Western governments and shone
On the strengths and resilience of Eastern states:
High death rates in the West – more in London
In April than in the worst four weeks of the Blitz,
Twenty-three thousand in New York against, in total,
Seven in Taiwan, twenty-seven in Singapore,
Thirty-four in Vietnam, twenty-three in Seoul –
And a looming economic crisis when China
Is supplying medical equipment to the West
And building two hundred and fifteen new airports
By 2035, and Singapore's schools are top.
The West has been liberal and democratic
And supported freedom and human rights, and yet
The UK's Government attacks the civil
Service, judiciary and Electoral Commission
Illiberally to shuffle off all blame,
And 'woke' cultural warriors intimidate
Diners into clenching fists and howl down 'Rule
Britannia' while the resolute strong-man East
Copes with the virus and grows its economies.
We are not yet at the coming of the end
When nation shall rise against nation, and kingdom
Against kingdom, and there shall be famines,
Pestilences and earthquakes in diverse places,
And all are afflicted in a great tribulation,
But the beginning of the end of something's in the wind.
There's a complacent end-of-empire feel in
The West as a plague undermines its institutions,
And exceptionalist pride is convinced it's invincible,
And I think of democratic Athens' plague-stricken plight
As it gave way to militaristic Sparta,
And I think of the two great plagues that contributed
To the fall of the mighty Roman Empire,
And I see a plague tilt the balance of power to the East
And sense we're witnessing the fall of the West
And call to the West, "Wake up – decline, decline!"

Midnight in Brussels on the thirty-first
Of December, and 11pm in London,
And Big Ben strikes the end of transition,
And the end of nearly half a century
Of being enmeshed in the European Union:
Bong. Free movement gone, points-based immigration
In place, Europeans replaced by Africans
In hospitals, schools and universities,
The European Investment Bank has gone,
Euratom, Europol and Eurojust,
And the Emissions Trading Scheme all gone.
Bong. Access to security and police
Records and terrorist tip-offs weakened
And students' Erasmus gone, architects',
Lawyers' and doctors' qualifications
No longer recognised, holiday disruption,
Queuing in "non-EU" lines at airports, checks
On insurance, passports, money and leaving dates.
Bong. Half the exports are still free of tariffs
But paperwork and border checks will slow.
Food's more expensive and there are shortages.
Bong. A lasting economic hit of four per cent
Of GDP for the new trading ways.
Bong. Reduced international influence,
Insufficient trade deals, not being listened to.
Bong. Scotland, Wales and Northern Ireland going,
A Federation replacing the Union.
Bong. No EU subsidies and set-aside
And farmers worried about their businesses.
Bong. Businesses' orders down, workers laid off,
Unemployment climbing, massive State hand-outs.
Bong. Debt of two trillion climbing out of control,
Huge borrowing to make up the deficit.
Bong. Sovereignty isolated from Union's help,
A satellite dependent on exporting to the EU,
An off-shore island with no seat at the table

And therefore reduced influence in the US.
Bong. You're on your own, no European
Workers' rights, food standards, air and health checks,
No check on your laws or on your Parliament,
Or on your politicians, are they good enough?
A chilly start to the new year: shivers of dread,
Excluded from ever-closer union
And the back-up to get through a new crisis.
The new year begins with a chilly frost.
In crisis, without fanfare, the UK's
Ended the era of its EU membership
Like a fox slinking off into the undergrowth,
Leaving a herd of deer peacefully grazing.
After nearly fifty years there is a new
Relationship, and both sides are weaker.
Johnson hails the UK's "amazing future",
Right-wingers see the start of a new era
With a global outlook no longer constrained
By EU membership, but fail to see
Britain's lost influence and reputation
Among the twenty-seven member states
Of the EU during the last four years,
That its dithering has diminished its stature.
The UK's prioritising sovereignty
And independence over its economic trade
With the EU, and by the same extremist logic
It should sever links with the UN and NATO,
The Geneva Convention and all trade treaties
Which detract from its sovereignty's purity,
To give it the pure isolation it seeks
As an "outward-looking, internationalist
And global power" that doesn't do 'joint' any more.
The UK's global outlook's forgotten
To include Gibraltar in the hasty deal.
Gibraltar's abandoned to the clutches of Spain,
It's 'no deal' and is joining the Schengen zone,

Only Spain, not the UK or Gibraltar,
Has access to the Schengen zone
And so Gibraltar's border's controlled by Spain
And its border fence with Spain's being demolished.
Scotland, Northern Ireland, Wales, now Gibraltar, going....
Macron criticises "the lies and broken promises"
That have led to this rupture in Europe.
The EU feel *au revoir*, not *adieu*,
But now the UK is out of the EU
And the divorce is at last finalised,
Where's the money coming from that will do
All the things you've promised, Johnson. Where's the gold?
    An hour after leaving the EU behind,
The UK's leaving the old year for the new.
Midnight in London as Big Ben strikes in
The new year of Britain's standing alone
And the non-delivery of promises
Made during the referendum campaign:
Bong. More money for the NHS, but this
Has not come from Brexit, it's from borrowing.
Bong. More money for farmers, there will be a new
Subsidy system tied to delivering objectives,
And this can't come from Brexit, and will drain.
Bong. More money in your pocket as there will be
Fewer immigrants, but immigration's risen
And all Brexit forecasts see real wages falling.
Bong. Trade will be frictionless, and there will be
No short-term economic disruption,
But GDP growth has slowed in the last four years,
Productivity's stagnant and the pound has plummeted,
And there'll be more paperwork and lorry parks,
Customs officers and installed IT systems.
Bong. There'll be new buccaneering free-trade deals,
But the promises have not materialised,
The quick deal with the US won't happen
And deals with sixty-two countries have only brought in

Nine-fourteenths of last year's trade, there's a shortfall.
Bong. The fishing industry will control all UK
Waters, but feels betrayed that promises weren't kept.
Bong. Immigration will be cut to tens
Of thousands, but though EU immigrants
Have greatly reduced, there's been an increase
Of a hundred and fifty thousand from round the world.
Bong. There'll be no controls on the Northern-Irish
Land border with the EU, but this has meant
A goods border down the Irish Sea, which has turned
Northern Ireland into an EU colony
From being an integral part of the UK.
Bong. The union with Scotland will be stronger,
But voters in Scotland and Northern Ireland
Think Brexit's made their departure more likely.
Bong. The UK's co-operation with the EU
Will be deeper, but the Political Declaration
Attached to the Withdrawal Agreement
Makes clear that it will be much shallower.
Bong. There's no reason for the UK to leave
The single market as a result of Brexit,
But after the referendum result was announced
That idea was immediately thrown away.
Bong. There'll be a Golden Age after Brexit,
But the economy will struggle and that promise,
Like all the rest, calls for gold – and it's fools' gold.
    It seems the European dream is over,
But amid the tears and stifled sobs there's hope.
The UK's cultural relationship with Europe
Is far from over. Just as Von der Leyen,
Poised like a graceful, elegant white-tailed deer,
Quoted from Shakespeare, Eliot and McCartney,
So a future courteous and cultured PM,
Shorn of false *faux*-philistine populism,
Will surely quote from Racine, Balzac and Piaf
And connect to our common cultural tradition,

The Europe of the Renaissance and Enlightenment,
Of Beethoven, Marie Curie and Van Gogh,
Our emotional, aesthetic roots in our common
European civilisation that began
Two thousand years ago with the Romans,
And continued with the Anglo-Saxons and Jutes,
The Vikings, Danes, Normans, Flemish and Dutch –
Your poet's descended from Flemish stock
In Flanders, from sheep-rearers in Brugge –
And our battles at Waterloo, Flemish Passchendaele
And Dunkirk, and bloomed in our free movement
Which allowed your poet to move between countries
And write his three hundred and seventeen
Classical odes on Europe's cultural tradition
Whose roots we hear each day in our language,
Greek, Latin, French, German and Nordic words –
'Democracy', 'sovereignty', 'tariff', 'parliament',
'Mutton', 'beef', 'fishery' – a patchwork quilt
Like our literature and our history
Of trade and wars, of genes and family names.
And just as Chaucer worked in Italy
And Basque Navarre and mirrored Boccaccio
And Dante, and Shakespeare set plays in Venice,
Verona, Illyria, Denmark and Greece,
So future writers will follow your poet's lead
And set works on the European continent
And see the cultural richness of Europe
As far more wonderful and significant
Than those who reduce it to trade, sun and snow.
O marvellous Europe, your poet bows in homage
To the wonders of the cultural past
Of our European civilisation,
Which we joined thanks to Julius Caesar
And to which we will always belong and return
As these islands will always look to the main
Whose history and culture we have in common:

Homer, Virgil, Horace, Dante, Goethe.
A boo for the philistines who can't see this.
    The UK will soon be a "foreign country"
To the EU with GDP 7.9 per cent
Of its pre-pandemic level, claiming
It's sovereign and free from European laws
But hugely in debt, shunned and despised by the world,
A satellite dependent on the EU
For its exports that's, with no say in decisions,
Worse off than if it had stayed in the EU.
Brexit was a wrong decision, a huge mistake.
The split has been a setback to the West,
Liberal democracies in the EU and UK
Can be seen as trailing authoritarian regimes
That have followed Russia and China and are stable.
One more boo for Johnson, who took a wrong path
And persuaded people to follow him into a bog.
A boo for the will-o'-the-wisp with dishevelled hair.
A boo for a new Dark Age, self-inflicted,
And a boo-hoo for the UK's exile from
The European civilisation
To which since Roman times it has belonged.
Europe's still central to British politics,
And there'll come a time when the EU superpower
Will have a prosperity and world influence
That will draw the UK to consider
Holding a second rejoining referendum –
With the support of the European Movement
Founded by Churchill after the Second World War –
And, using the break clause in a four-yearly review,
Reapply to re-enter the EU
Before Scotland, Wales and NI break away
And have far-flung world influence again.
A cheer for your poet who saw it all coming,
Who saw satellitehood on the first page
Of this work on fools' gold in heroic lines,

And unlike the wally called the outcome right:
"We will prosper mightily, mightily.
Gold ahoy! Gold, I say, gold!" No, fools' gold!
    So the European dream is far from over.
The UK's goods exporters have seen Europe
As a home market, but now holding pens
For lorries and border checks have hit hard.
Services – banks, insurance companies
And investment houses – have been welcomed,
But now have to ask permission to trade. London
Has suffered an immediate Brexit blow
As six billion euros of EU share trading
Have shifted to European capitals.
The City's lost its European share business.
Britain's out of the European Investment Bank,
Euratom, Europol and Eurojust,
And the EU Emissions Trading Scheme.
And now a third lockdown has been announced
While vaccination of millions takes place,
A new catastrophe for the UK's finances,
It will cost another hundred billion.
While in the US, urged on by Johnson's
Ally Trump, a mob storms the Capitol,
Seeking to destroy American democracy,
Incited to riot with false claims of fraud,
And, puffed up with egoistic hubris, Trump's
Destroyed his legacy and split his party
By casting doubt on the election result.
There are calls to remove him from office,
He's being impeached for inciting insurrection,
There's talk of the rural states seceding
And splitting the US into north and south,
And Zeus has ended his atë with a downfall,
A nemesis that's awesome and awful.
And power further slides from the West to the East.
    The UK's economy will be stagnant,

The Labour Government of 2029
(Or 2028 if Johnson has gone
To the country early in 2023),
The nemesis for Johnson's boastfulness,
His long hubris and overweening pride
That put an outdated sovereignty above
Europe's historic cultural tradition,
Will hold its promised referendum on
EU membership and a new generation will vote
To rejoin and end the troubled relationship
Between the UK and the expanding Europe
That is approaching fifty member states –
What Thatcher argued against in her Bruges speech –
And is with visionary global foresight
Working to herald in the long-awaited
Democratic World State of all humankind.
There's a storm looming like a thundercloud.
Covid has left the UK four hundred
Billion pounds down, Brexit three times as much,
More than a trillion pounds down, and the EU's
Unco-operative as it has been snubbed,
And the smell of a trade war is in the wind,
And China's offended as Huawei's been blocked,
And Russia's offended as it's been accused
Of meddling in the British referendum,
And the US is putting America first,
And ahead looms the end of the United Kingdom,
As a hunt and pack of dogs hunts down the fox,
And ahead's a third wave of the virus
Which may be more virulent in the late winter,
As nation-states attempt to vaccinate
Their populations as soon as possible
And until that's happened economies stagnate.
Everything has gone wrong at the same time,
A perfect storm like a purple thundercloud,
And the promises of paradise and gold

Are now seen to be illusory, delusions of grandeur.
And where is British pragmatic common sense,
The realistic eye that detects fools' gold?

Now disembarking's nigh. Shouting on the deck,
The captain is claiming success and praising their gold.
There's confusion, all now know it's worthless.
There's talk that the captain's deluded, the voyage has failed.
All that the fools were promised has not happened.
The fools are all in debt and cannot sell
Their worthless gold to fund their journey's costs.
All regret having embarked on this dreadful voyage.
Several are still ill, a few have died, there's
Misery in every quarter of the ship.
The enterprise has failed but is hailed a success.
Some are leaving behind their worthless bundles.
All hate the captain, who is in hiding
So he doesn't have to listen to their complaints.
O unhappy Ship of Fools, o Ship of State,
O plague ship, all face lives of colossal debt.

Epilogue

Paradise Postponed

Sing, Muse, of the gods and their struggle to understand
What is happening to the harmony in the world.
Sing of how Zeus still dreamt of unity,
And of how God of the One, his other form,
Longed to bring Paradise back to the earth,
Prosperity and peace among all nations,
Words stolen and put on Brexiteers' coins.
Sing, Muse, of the world Olympian Zeus dreams of,
A Golden Age to which all can aspire,
And the mess that's been made by self-interested men.
    Another gasp from the heights of Olympus,
Again of consternation, "*Hwaet*?" Zeus, stunned,
Had learned that Johnson had, through dissemblance,
While seeming to be working for 'no deal',
Delivered a thinnish satellite deal,
Thwarting Zeus's plans for a unified
United States of Europe that would prevent
A nuclear Third World War, and champion
A coming World State for tranquil humankind.
    Now Zeus, in dudgeon on Mount Olympus,
Like a bull (one of his forms in mythology)
Snorting and kicking back sand in a bullring,
A form of God of the One who loves harmony,
Sent a new variant to peak the second wave
Of the virus and confound Johnson's plans,
To punish his self-assertive hubris
With nemesis that will lead to his downfall,
And sent Hermes down to speak to your poet
At Connaught House. Hermes landed and lurked –
In three-hundred-acred Fairmead ('fair meadow')
Within view of Henry the Eighth's hunting

Lodge, completed in 1543 –
Beside the eighteenth-century statue of a boy
Holding a bowl and slowly wandered past
The fountain with Three Graces on its side
To the bust of Apollo by the winding stair.
    Your poet should have been having his second dose
Of the Pfizer vaccine but had been postponed
As the Government's extended the gap between
Pfizer's first and second doses to twelve weeks.
Hermes climbed the spiral stair to the balcony,
Tapped on the window like a gardener reporting
A leaning tree, and, as the door opened, said,
"Hello again, Zeus – God of the One – sent me
To speak to you, you can guess what about.
May I come in?" It was a sunny day,
And your poet was alone, isolating
From the virus at the vulnerable age
Of eighty-one. He said, "Yes, if we can stay
Two metres apart," and sat him on the sofa and said:
"We'll have to live with Covid as we live with flu,
It will always be with us but we'll be vaccinated.
It'll be like living with typhoid or cholera,
Some will still die but life will go on again.
The risk'll be managed, there'll be a new normal."
    Hermes, curly-haired and bearded like a pilgrim,
Said, "The UK's out at last, but Covid-19
Has messed up Johnson's future. Will there be
A Golden Age as Johnson has forecast?"
    Your poet smiled and said, "I am flattered
You've come to the Oracle for an update.
The Golden Age was the first in Hesiod,
When the golden race of humanity lived
In peace, harmonious, stable and prosperous,
When the earth provided abundant food,
The age of the natural man that Ovid sang
With echoes of life in Arcadia.

We still await the age when humankind
Will live at peace in a prosperous World State,
The true Golden Age the ancients yearned for,
And no backward nationalism can thwart this
Or claim it's enacting a Golden Age."
Nodding, Hermes interjected, "As Zeus knows,
Even though he is demoralised at the way
Humans wrongly assert their nation-states.
It's sunny, let's go down into the garden.
Zeus asks again, what will happen? Can you see
A way forward to the real Golden Age?"
Like a forest stag leading a verderer
Who has assumed the form of a fallow deer
Your poet led him down the spiral steps
Past the bust of Apollo and they strolled along the terrace,
Past the rose garden with paths like a Union Jack
Whose beds are based on the Union of four countries,
Past the spouting fountain washing the Three Graces,
Past the four bare oak trees on the sloping lawn
And the five horse chestnuts without white candles
And descended steps to the far lawn and walked
To the path between apple trees past an old sundial,
And, no bees humming in the lavender,
Studied the endless box-hedge knot of two
Eights, down and across, infinity signs
Based on the knot eleven-year-old Elizabeth
The First designed and embroidered on the cover
Of her manuscript book, *The Miroir or Glasse
Of the Synneful Soul,* she gave to her stepmother,
Henry the Eighth's sixth wife, Catherine Parr,
In 1544 – standing in the knot-garden
Whose twenty-five herb-beds represent civilisations.
Your poet said, "I have to unravel the knot
So you can see clearly what will happen.
Just as a plague plunged the Greek Empire into decline
From 430BC (typhoid fever

Or viral haemorrhagic fever) and killed
Up to a hundred thousand Athenians
Including Pericles and devastated
The Athenian army and ended its supremacy;
And a plague plunged the Roman Empire into decline
From 165AD (smallpox) and killed
Five million Romans including Marcus
Aurelius and devastated the Roman
Army and ended the *Pax Romana;*
So Covid's plunged Western civilisation
Into decline and destroyed the old order
Of liberal globalisation and replaced
It with nationalistic orders and travel bans –
Like the Great War, it's ended a sunny
Edwardian way of life, buying and investing
Worldwide. But conversely Covid's advanced
A World State that can control all viruses
And prevent new pandemics spreading like wildfire.
And like Thucydides or Galen, I
Describe the plague's symptoms and rampaging
In my current work, but also the future
That will come out of this most troubled time.
There have always been plagues, but this one's shut down
Western economies and societies
And is more cataclysmic than the ones of the past,
And the "plaguey London" of Donne and Milton.
The West's been levelled down by many wars,
Revolutions and independence movements
Against its empires, by division – Brexit
And 'America First', which has dwindled the West,
And a mob invading the US Capitol –
And by its economies being crashed by lockdowns.
We have been living through the fall of the West,
Its final falling apart from within.
"Covid marks the transition of one Age
To another, so what will the future be like?

There are those who see the pandemic having
Negative effects, from an era of stability
And advancement to conflict and turmoil,
Of disruption as a new Cold War begins
Between the US and China and bitter
Recriminations and a world economy
Less open and more protectionist, and less
Co-operative over climate change and racked
By destabilising debt with wealth taxes
To pay for public services and make
The UK's nation-states poorer; with a bigger State,
More surveillance, less privacy, and supply
Problems as businesses collapse, with high
Unemployment lasting for years, closed shops,
And a cashless society of contact cards,
And foreign holidays only for the wealthy,
A risk-averse age that shuns innovation,
Productivity and wealth creation.
Others see Covid-19 bringing blessings:
Forcing slowdown, grounding aircraft, bringing
Cleaner air, and a new sense of wonder
At Nature, helping us all to see that we
Are all connected, the unity of humankind,
And an opportunity to build the world anew.
Ahead's a collective opportunity
To unite the world against a common foe,
To re-evaluate our lives and bring in
An Age of world peace, love and happiness.
And the transition will be a tough tussle
Between the now destabilised old world
Of populist nationalism and its debts,
And the new harmony of a World State."
He added humorously with twinkling eyes,
"The virus seems to have been sent by Zeus
As a leveller, to reorganise the world,
To change the bad old nationalistic ways

And bring in a new way of living more
In keeping with a transformed environment.
"Let's start where we are, with sovereignty and what
The UK does with it. The PM must satisfy
New Northern voters and the old Southern guard,
He will prioritise border control,
The NHS and investment in the North
And import Northerners into the Cabinet
To improve Northern roads and railways
So regional trade in the North catches
Up with what is delivered in the South.
The exodus of skilled EU workers
Will be filled by skilled Commonwealth migrants.
Whether they'll be as skilful remains to be seen.
There will be an attempt to create new jobs
From reducing emissions and climate change.
Economic growth will suffer in the short term
And borrowing will replace austerity
And increase the UK's debt as if Labour
Were back in power with new borrow-and-spend.
And Scotland, Northern Ireland and then Wales –
In a karmic boomerang, what Johnson did
To the EU they'll do to him, the biter bit –
Will seek their own independence, and the UK
Will collapse from Union into a federation,
The Federation of the British Isles –
An offshore island with global memories,
Four nation-states functioning on their own,
A satellite dependent on EU trade,
Free from four years of pandemonium
When the EU felt Britain lost itself –
But with no decision-making in the EU
As it turns itself into the United States
Of Europe Churchill foresaw and helped to shape."
Your poet said, looking at the endless knot,
"To understand the future you have to understand

The past, and that means disentangling a knot
Of causes, grievances and misplaced hopes.
The problem was that the UK's sovereignty
And national independence was threatened by
'Ever-closer union', a confederation
Of nation-states in a federal union.
In the 1960s the UK fell behind
Mainland Europe economically,
But rejected an invitation to join
The merging union. Attlee opposed
British membership as ceding control.
Heath saw joining as gaining influence
And Thatcher supported this and helped create
The single market. Now, rejecting again
'Ever closer union' for sovereignty –
As being half in and half out from not joining
The eurozone had lost it some influence –
The UK is recapturing past glories.
"By seeking an independent global role,
The post-EU UK is seeking through
A hard Brexit a post-imperial role
That may oppose, not befriend, the EU.
Johnson's nostalgic optimism chimes
With the nostalgic pessimism of English
Nationalism, but putting Brexit first
Has alienated the Scots and comes across
As causing widening cracks in the Union.
The English felt hard-done-by when Scottish,
Irish and Welsh cries for independence
Were fed devolved power, which England rejected,
And railed against the 'totalitarian' regime
In Brussels, and longed to be once again
The buccaneering England of days gone,
An Anglosphere with ties to the US,
Former White Dominions and India –
Though trading with New Zealand and Australia

Is marginal beside trading with the vast
Four-hundred-and-fifty-million-strong single market
So near the UK, and the UK's trade
With Ireland wins it more than all its trade
With the BRICS countries. Please note, if the UK
Breaks up through Scottish independence or
Irish reunification as a result
Of Brussels' demanding that Ulster's treated
Similarly to the Irish Republic
Now there's a goods border down the Irish Sea,
Yes, Johnson – who's full of blithe confidence
Like Lord Cardigan who (on the basis
Of a misinterpreted order from Lord Raglan)
Led the charge of the Light Brigade to disaster
At the battle of Balaclava in the Crimea
In 1854, exceptionalism
That's a by-product of imperialism –
Will surely be the Prime Minister who
Delivered Brexit and, partly as a result,
Presided over the break-up of the UK.
But the UK may blame the EU for this
And angry England may be a permanent thorn
In the flesh of the Club it flounced out of.
    "Friendly Hermes, you managed to intrigue
A Labour leadership win for Starmer.
You may have a problem in making him PM.
Now the UK has left the twenty-seven
It's able to order vaccines swiftly
Without waiting for twenty-seven nations
To be consulted and reach a consensus.
Some say if there are vaccine-supply delays
Because the EU was slow in ordering,
Having to consult twenty-seven member states,
And if vaccine nationalism is blamed,
It will seem to UK voters that the EU
Impedes the ordering process, which is slow,

And though the EU's bulk ordering is cheap,
If the EU starts a trade war with the UK,
Slowing half the UK's exports to Europe,
The UK voters may be reluctant
To return to the EU, in which case the UK
Will be a precarious satellite of the EU
And discover it's ceased to be a global power
And has opted for mediocre and quiet decline.
"Yet a different outcome is still possible.
For a while Brexit will be hidden behind vaccines
And the success of the UK's vaccinations,
And many may say, "We wouldn't have been vaccinated
If we'd stayed in the EU." But the truth will out.
And sooner or later the UK's new plight will be seen.
When England's voters see the barriers
To free movement and trade and flow of goods –
Hear hauliers' lorries in London honking horns,
See fishermen's exports rotting on the quay
And supply chains cancelled because of poor paperwork,
Fishing clobbered, exporting and importing
Abandoned because of new form-filling,
Financial services outside the deal,
No new trade deals as were over-promised,
Businesses spending 7.5 billion pounds
A year handling customs declarations,
As much as they'll have spent under 'no deal' –
They'll see Brexit is not as it was described.
"There'll be talk of a trade deal with Australia
With Australian agricultural products
Competing with what our farmers produce.
They'll see British farmers will go under,
Their no-tariffs market's been twenty miles
Away, and would now be ten thousand miles distant
With increased costs and carbon pollution
When the UK's going for zero emissions.
They'll see it doesn't make sense, as Rachel Johnson's said.

They'll hear a Public Inquiry into the handling
Of Covid show how much has been badly done
In such a short time to the detriment
Of the people of the United Kingdom,
And they'll realise they have made a huge mistake,
And opinion polls will cry out for a return
To the high standards they enjoyed in the EU.
"Then Starmer'll apply to rejoin the twenty-seven
Other members of the European
Civilisation – and by then more who have joined
Since the UK left, who share their common
Origin with the UK – so European
Civilisation may again be politically
United and not divided by the shock
Defection of its co-foremost nation-state.
The real Golden Age is one of unity,
When Europe and all humankind are in one state."

Like a fallow deer, masking his own godhood
To put your poet's inner stag at ease,
Hermes said, "Zeus has been poring over
Your study of civilisations, and has been pondering
On stage 45 in your *Rise and Fall* tables.
It's about yearning for a lost past, a short-lived
Revival of cultural purity after
Rejecting the rule of a foreign conglomerate.
Zeus wants to know, is that what Brexit is,
The EU's stage 45, or is Brexit just
A group of nationalist ideologues wanting
To return to a lost past of the British Empire?"
Your poet, aware again that Olympian Zeus
Had little idea of how humankind would pursue
Its free will and, far from running the world,
Had to ask what was about to happen,
Replied, "I'm honoured that Olympian Zeus
Should be seeking to understand events

From my past books. I understand his difficulty.
As you know, in my study of civilisations
I see twenty-five civilisations
Going through sixty-one parallel stages,
And the European Union's in stage 43
Of the European civilisation,
A conglomerate, and after Universalism
There's a movement of cultural purity.
"Thirty years ago I wrote that in the European
Civilisation cultural purity
Would include a revival of national religion
And would co-exist with Universalism,
That it might be a renewal of the medieval Light,
A mystic revival that would be led from Britain
And create a new soulful Baroque Age
'After the dismemberment of the United Kingdom
When Ireland is reunited within the European
Conglomerate'. Brexit's a yearning for a lost past
But it's not a glorification of the Light-
Based medieval vision or a new
Classical Baroque spiritual movement.
It's just nationalism, and so may be short-lived.
Stage 45 is, yes, a short-lived return
To a lost past, and a rejection of foreign rule,
Of the union stage of the European civilisation,
The rule of its conglomerate, the EU.
"We have a revival of the sovereignty
And independence the UK enjoyed
During the reign of Queen Victoria
And during the rise of the British Empire.
It's a right-wing view that's strongly contested
By the left-wing anti-slavery and -Empire,
It may be normal right-left politics
That have boiled over into Brexit and rupture.
It's too early to say it's stage 45,
Sovereignty's only a part of that stage.

It's more complex than sovereignty for the civilisations
That have been through stage 45 all show
A revival of their old religion and culture,
A revival of stage 28, a renewal
Of the Fire or Light that's behind the universe,
The One life-giving principle behind
All civilisations that helps crops to grow,
Fields to be watered and plentiful harvests,
A return to the purity of Christian religion,
Like the Muslim revival of fundamentalist
Islamic values at the end of the European
Colonial presence, as Islamic State
Exemplifies, or Hezekiah and Josiah's
Making the Torah the law of the land
In a revival of the Torah-based
Judaism, and Brexit's missing that
Religious devotion, some would say fanaticism.
"I saw the European civilisation's
Stage 45's religious dimension as
A revival of the medieval vision
Of the Fire or Light and a new Baroque movement
Rooted in Baroque art and renewed interest
In the Metaphysical poets, combining
Sense and spirit, a blend of the visible
And invisible, the finite and infinite.
If Brexit opens the way to such insight,
Which can be found in my *A Baroque Vision*
And *The New Philosophy of Universalism* –
If the Brexiteers take up works like these
And add them to their return of sovereignty
To make a new mystical-historical
Movement that will have an enduring impact,
A revival of the religion of the past –
Then its rejection of the EU conglomerate
May be the beginning of the European
Civilisation's stage 45. But if not,

Then it's just a short-lived nationalist movement
Based on lies and broken promises by one-term
Right-wingers in the right-left ebb-and-flow
Of normal politics, and that is how
I see it now. Brexit's independence
Of foreign rule could be the beginning
Of stage 45, but in the absence
Of a metaphysical vision as exists
In other civilisations' stage 45,
It's not a full stage 45, and will fail.
If the UK stays outside the EU
And there's a revival of Protestantism,
The national religion, caused by Covid deaths
And people wanting to return to the Church
For comfort during the plague's ravages,
Then stage 45 will have begun. But if
It returns to the EU, there's no stage 45.
The UK needs to stay in the EU
As long as possible to head off decline."
    Hermes nodded: "That's more or less what Zeus thinks.
He will be in full agreement with your words.
He thinks Johnson's a charlatan and scoundrel
Who's fallen in with a group of nationalists
Despite having a Europhile father
And having had a Europhile education,
And has seen a route to power, which is not the full
Next stage and so will quickly peter out,
And to speed the process Zeus will block his boasts.
Watch out for problems as he under-delivers.
I know your writings, I have read your work
Over your shoulder as you've described
How Johnson's overpromised and under-delivered,
Has promised voters gold and given fools' gold.
Zeus wants a World State and as you are now
The only living writer who's called for one
He pays especial attention to how you see things.

I'll go and tell him now: no Golden Age,
No stage 45, and Brexit may be short-lived."
    Your poet said, "No, wait, there's more to say.
So how short-lived is the split from Europe?
The Tory Party's been transformed over forty years
From a pro-European to an anti-European party,
And Johnson's hard-Brexit policy will
Be his undoing during the next decade.
He's not been triumphalist and has called
For a national revival and has pursued
Popular levelling-up, rail franchises
And broadband, but he has had a Faustian pact
With his Mephistophelean right wing
To deliver a hard Brexit, and growth
Will slide to below one per cent per annum
(The forecast for the next two years – excluding
The impact of Covid), or below zero.
The Royal Haulage Association will say
Exports to the EU are two-thirds down
In relation to what they were last January,
And there's worse to come as the UK's imposing
Import controls on EU businesses
Which may be as ill-prepared as the UK's have been.
There's already a trade deficit in goods
And that will widen as UK services are denied
By EU markets, and competitors
Will take advantage of zero tariffs.
The UK'll join a new trading alliance,
The Trans-Pacific Partnership that includes
Japan, Canada, Australia and New Zealand,
But this will only replace a tiny amount
Of its exports to the EU that will be lost
Due to customs documents and ill will,
It won't bring in more than exports to Germany,
And an agreement with New Zealand will lose money,
It will just be about future possibilities.

And there'll be an unstoppable run on the pound,
Renewed austerity and recession.
"Brexit can be short-lived, as we both hope.
Johnson's Brexit deal will be disastrous.
There'll be a huge fall in trade to the EU,
UK exporters will stop exports and move
Inside the single market, losing jobs,
Investment and tax revenues in the UK.
The deal has gaps in services and fishing.
The Government's seeking conflict with the EU
On the agreed border in the Irish Sea
And departing from a level playing-field.
The Tories have wrapped businesses in red tape.
No country's 'an island, entire of itself',
It's 'a piece of the continent, a part of the main'.
There'll be weekly dips of disappointment
And Johnson can't convert to a soft Brexit
As he's imprisoned by his know-nothing right.
There'll soon be a hundred thousand Covid deaths,
The highest tally in Europe by far,
And the highest death rate per thousand in the world,
Twice the number the UK lost in the *Blitz*,
With the prospect of two hundred thousand ahead.
There'll be an Inquiry, Johnson will be found
To have been slow in lockdowns and stopping
Mingling, closing borders and providing masks,
And it will be found that tens of thousands died
Who needn't have died if decisions had been faster.
And the economy will then be dire.
"Johnson's legacy will be the huge number of
Covid deaths and the dissolution
Of the most successful political union
In modern times, rather than the triumph
Of Brexit and the recovery from Covid.
After presiding over one of the worst
Death tolls in the world, Johnson wants the narrative

To be how he steered his country through the worst
Modern crisis with statesmanlike prudence
And his hugely successful vaccine programme,
But the deaths can't be forgotten, they won't go away.
Johnson will hide the cost of Brexit behind
The Covid crisis and perpetuate
The myth that Britain liberated Europe
From Hitler on its own, without the help
Of the US and Russian pincer movement.
Global Britain's been lost among vaccines –
Condemning the fate of Navalny and the Uighurs –
But he can't pull the wool over the voters' eyes
And fool the public for ever, the UK's
Low standing in the world will at last be seen.
"The Tories will soon be riding high in the polls
Because of the vaccines and because Johnson
Has occupied Labour's territory
Of State borrowing and hand-outs, but their lead
Will not last long, the budget cannot hide
That two hundred and eighty billion pounds
Spent on Covid will force the Government
Into unpopular fiscal policies:
The UK has to save forty-three billion
To stabilise debt at a hundred per cent
Of national income, an interest-rate rise
Of one per cent would add twenty-five billion
To the annual cost of UK borrowing.
Figures will show the Government's borrowing
At its highest level since the Second World War,
And cutting carbon emissions will cost seventy
Billion pounds a year for the next three decades.
"The thieves will fall out, Cummings is smouldering,
And ready to incriminate Johnson
For lavishly refurbishing his flat
And getting a donor to pay the bill,
To get back at Carrie for his sacking.

And Cummings may blame him for late lockdowns
That killed tens of thousands of citizens,
May say Johnson saw Covid as a 'scare
Story' like swine flu and called it 'kung flu',
May say Johnson said that he should have kept
The beaches open like the Mayor in *Jaws*,
And say Johnson's unfit to be PM,
And may try to topple the scallywag.
There'll be mysterious leaks of Johnson's
Insecure emails promising tax breaks
In return for ventilators, there'll be cries of "Sleaze".
Johnson will bury all this with a wedding.
Baptised as a Catholic by his French mother
And confirmed as an Anglican at Eton,
He'll be rebaptised into the Catholic Church
And secretly marry Catholic Carrie
In a wedding planned when Cummings was sacked –
So she can host the G7 spouses –
In the Catholic Westminster Cathedral
With his Catholic son present, and will bury
Cummings' criticisms his dithering killed
Tens of thousands in late lockdowns, and care homes.
It will be Carrie's triumph over her critics,
And Johnson, who broke with the Treaty of Rome,
Will be back under Rome and Papal sway.
It will be as if Henry the Eighth married his sixth
Wife Catherine Parr in a Catholic Cathedral.
"When Cummings and Johnson, the two Brexit thieves,
Fall out and fight like rats within a sack,
Johnson's hubris will be swollen to atë
And nemesis is waiting to bring him down.
How apt if the Brexiteers fight to the death
And leave the stage in a cloud of scandal.
The opinion polls will swing towards Labour
And the Scottish polls towards independence
Amid the beginning of Johnson's end.

"I can see ahead, half a dozen investigations
Into Arcuri, Mustique and especially
The garish wallpaper that Carrie chose,
Which won't be to the taste of his successor.
I can see in my mind's eye an official
Investigation by the Electoral Commission,
Which regulates political parties
And their funding under the Political
Parties, Elections and Referendums Act,
To see if loans for the refurbishing work
Were properly declared by the Party.
I see the Conservative Party found guilty
Of not declaring it funded the refurb
Of the flat by getting Lord Brownlow to pay
For a fifty-eight-thousand shortfall on
A two-hundred-thousand-pound home décor
When the HMG allowance was thirty thousand –
To pay for Carrie's choice of gold wallpaper
At eight hundred and forty pounds a roll,
That's embossed, and her garish furniture.
If it finds the Party did not declare
A donation or loan for the work from Lord Brownlow
(Who's worth two hundred and seventy-one million
And whose company, Huntswood CTC,
May have received public contracts that are worth
Up to a hundred and twenty million pounds)
It can fine the Party twenty thousand pounds.
"I can see it playing out, his puffed-up hubris,
His lying denial that a donor paid
For the hubristic, fools'-gold wallpaper
Which he went along with so foolishly;
And his swollen atë, his expletive-filled
Rage that he'd rather see bodies piled high
In thousands than order a new lockdown;
And the nemesis of the Electoral
Commission – and of the UK's Parliament,

For if a recording of his bodies-piled-high
Remark, which he'll have denied in Parliament,
Surfaces, it will prove Parliament was misled,
And that is a resignation matter.
Meanwhile his betrayal of the DUP,
His lying denial of an Irish-Sea border,
Will trigger a *coup* against its leader
And a new leader will fiercely oppose
The Northern Ireland Protocol and the deal,
And threaten the Union with more Troubles;
And Johnson may invoke the Protocol's
Article 16, the unilateral
Safeguard clause, and suspend all checks on goods
Crossing the Irish Sea if the EU
Persists in its 'hard-line approach' which he signed up to,
And may block all EU exports to Ulster,
And the EU may start a trade war with the UK
For not honouring the post-Brexit Protocol.
"I can see what's coming like a thunderstorm.
The 1800 Acts of Union, parallel
Acts of the Parliaments of Great Britain
And Ireland to unite and so create
The United Kingdom of Great Britain and Ireland,
Will be repealed in the Republic of Ireland.
In a private hearing in the Belfast High Court
During a judicial review of the Protocol
A UK-Government counsel will claim
Article 6 of the 1801 Act
Of Union – that the Irish will be on the same
Footing as the people of Great Britain –
Was lawfully repealed when Parliament
Voted for the Withdrawal Agreement,
So the border down the Irish Sea's legal.
But no, the Brexiteers will be tinkering
With the law to abolish the Act of Union.
The Withdrawal Agreement and Protocol

Are illegal, and if this is not recognised
The Union will be broken illegally.
"I can see Johnson lose control of the narrative,
For these things will matter to Westminster
If not to voters, and will be raised each week,
The weekly narrative will be of deepening chaos.
All the ingredients are there: Cummings' proroguing,
Carrie's getting him the sack, the lavish refurb,
Johnson's mistake in hubristically
Accusing Cummings of leaking the second lockdown
To bounce him into it when he would rather
See thousands of bodies piled as in the plague,
Taxpayers' funding of Arcuri when he was Mayor,
Who paid for the holiday in Mustique
When a pandemic was blowing in the wind,
Johnson's amorality and blatant lying,
Expletive-ridden meetings and downright lies
In Parliament to the country, the Brexit lies,
His demeaning of European culture,
His cutting us off from our continental roots,
His inserting division into unity,
And his treacherous broken promise there'd be no border
Down the Irish Sea – they can all come together
In a nemesis in which Carrie's lavish greed
And his own lying cause him to resign.
"It's a nemesis with a perfect symmetry.
Like the tiger on Carrie's wallpaper he's been
Casual, chaotic and contemptuous of rules
Like the majority of the English nation
Who despise the rules of the regulating EU.
He's been careless, acted impulsively,
He and Carrie will have brought it on themselves.
If it happens it will be a consequence
Of his chaotic management of his own life.
I can see it, and if it happens, how apt and just!
"O Zeus, you lodge within us the follies

And vices that bring about our destruction
Unless we also quest for Reality,
The One that brings harmony to the soul
And fills us with honesty and integrity
So we live by sincerity and truthfulness.
"But back from what I have seen to the immediate future.
In due course Johnson will be struggling
And Starmer will then start making headway.
Labour will focus on the pro-EU
Voters in the UK's metropolitan
Cities and university towns, and will hold
Johnson to account for every Brexit-induced
Bit of bad news on Covid, and will insist
That all stagnation and fiscal austerity,
Division and decline are the result of being
Too far from Europe, and that the solution
Is to get closer, and eventually rejoin.
Europe, which has broken all his predecessors
Since Thatcher, will some time break Johnson too.
By then the UK may no longer exist
As I've said, but be four federal nation-states.
"Johnson could fall at any time because –
Regardless of probings into his refurb –
He's shown to have said something that's factually wrong
Like his speech on kippers at the last hustings,
Or a claim or promise based on make-believe;
Or his mistress Arcuri got taxpayers' money;
Or he stayed for free in a Mustique-Company
Villa without declaring it, in breach
Of the Parliamentary Code of Conduct,
And's suspended from attending the Commons.
He'll be praying for an unexpected war
In Europe to save him, for war leaders
Rally support and are seldom deposed.
"If he survives there are three outcomes ahead.
There is a long scenario lasting

Till the next election but one. The Tory MPs
Went for Leave to beat Labour, their victory
Contained a lot of marginal seats. Johnson
Is good at getting people to vote for him,
He's stolen the red-wall seats and their language,
The levelling-up, and he's scattered IOUs,
But there's been a huge rise in child poverty.
And he's got to deliver when councils' spending's been cut
Eight per cent and there's further austerity. Voters
In the Midlands and the North will want money
To be poured into their regions, and there's
Not enough money to pay for the promises.
Voters will be incensed at non-delivery.
They'll come to see their towns can't be transformed,
That there aren't the funds to bring prosperity
To the North, that levelling up's a populist lie,
It can't be afforded, unless funds are moved
From the South, which will vote against, and the promises
Of prosperous Northern towns are just fools' gold.
Voters have been lured by big promises
Transactionally, not by ideology.
They'll see his promises can't be delivered,
That his Party's policies are a wasteland.
Voters will be disillusioned with fools' gold.
Then voters will turn back to Labour again,
Starmer or his successor will get in
At the next election or the one after
And will reapply to rejoin the EU at some stage
If Labour can exploit the new political scene,
But the UK will have to join the eurozone
And lose its Thatcher rebate and Major opt-out,
And will have been self-harmed, will be set back.
"And there's a second outcome, a shorter
Scenario lasting only two years.
The Disaster Capitalism Club
Of hedge funds and private investors that backed

Johnson's Vote-Leave and leadership campaigns
And made a killing out of Leave, has now
Bet eight billion pounds on a 'no-deal' crash-out
And wanted Johnson and Cummings, who they funded,
To deliver 'no deal' in December
For a new killing. They will work for 'no deal'.
In four years' time, under the terms of the deal
There has to be a review and both sides can
Cancel the deal if it's not working for them.
Johnson could cancel the deal then, and go to 'no deal'
So DC don't lost their premium and win their bet
If the bet's time limit on 'no deal' is still in force.
Or the EU can say that they now want 'no deal'.
Even earlier than that, Johnson could precipitate 'no deal'
By calling an election in 2023
And unilaterally seceding from the deal.
Watch out for Frost to take over from Gove
As a Lord in the Cabinet, who will lead
Talks on trade and relations with the EU,
And a UK move away from state-aid rules
Resulting in tariffs and a forced 'no deal'
While Gove's to keep Scotland in the Union.
Under 'no deal' voters will see lorry parks,
Shortages of drugs and food, and will rebel
And riot. The Government will fall, Starmer
Will be PM and can restore order.
Such a circuitous route can restore
The UK's membership of the EU.
"And there's a middling scenario.
An emergency rallies voters to the PM,
A collective threat makes them more conservative.
As Britain emerges from the restrictions Starmer
Will take his mask off and show he should be PM.
Johnson will call an election in May
2023 when the economy
Has rebounded from Covid and has not yet

Flatlined and the Brexit dip has not begun.
By then he'll have celebrated marrying Carrie
And got a feel-good electoral wedding bounce.
Starmer will campaign to rejoin the EU
As sixty per cent of his members think he should.
He'll be more critical of the Government
And he'll be clearer on what he stands for.
Britain's had one of the highest death tolls
In the world, and the worst economic recovery
Of the G7, and millions desperately need
A strong Opposition that will speak for them.
He'll take his mask off then and do just that.
"You look shocked, let me explain a little more.
Brexit is a Conservative project,
Returning to national sovereignty –
Immune to all intellectual arguments,
Insulting and mocking intellectuals,
Show a fool the moon and he looks at your finger –
And Labour must oppose it and, when the time
Is right and the polls reflect disillusion
With the UK's trade and Brexit, then rejoin,
And Starmer's the man to do that. He'll be helped
By the way things will develop in the UK.
The UK'll be too militarily weak
And economically exposed to have
A credible foreign policy independent
Of the EU. Brexit has already
Cost the UK some two hundred and three
Billion pounds of lost output, according
To Bloomberg Economics, five per cent
Of its GDP according to the Treasury
And the IMF, the NIESR
Puts it at ten per cent of lost output.
And to that add the hole of the four hundred billion
(Some say three hundred and seventy-two billion)
Left by lockdowns, that was caused by the virus.

The economy shrank ten per cent last year
(9.9 per cent to be more exact),
The biggest decline since the 1709 Great Frost,
And debt's risen to 2.1 trillion,
The highest figure since 1962.
"If the UK refuses to accept
That it can only protect its European
Supply networks by continuing to implement
EU regulations, the deal allows
New EU tariffs, there will be frozen
Investment and escalating closures in
Auto, aerospace, drugs, chemical, food and drink
Industries. Japanese car makers and Airbus
Will be the first to pull out. New trade deals
With the US, China and India
Can't compensate for lost EU markets
And those countries won't open their service
Sectors to British exporters. There will be
The risk of a run on sterling, and all talk
Of reviving failing towns in the Midlands
And the North will be incontinent babbling.
Northern Ireland and Scotland will campaign
To split from Tory England, and the EU
Will become popular again as a way out
Of mounting internal chaos. If the UK
Wants to retain its manufacturing
Industry it will have to follow EU
Level-playing-field rules to allow market access.
"The UK'll be unstable and there'll be calls
To end the half-out half-in relationship,
And then calls to rejoin fully, to keep
The UK together. Johnson's promises
Will be seen to have no foundation at all,
They'll be like the seven hundred million the Cornish
Were promised to replace the subsidy
They received from the EU, and now won't get.

His policies that glittered will seem fools' gold.
His Golden Age will be a time of moans.
Chastened by its unsuccessful exile,
And more European, now an older generation
Has died out and been replaced by a new
Younger generation, the UK will find EU
Membership the second time round much easier.
All this will happen. The only question is,
Will it take place four or nine years from now?
Or three or eight years from now if Johnson goes
To the country in 2023?
Or will it take longer, four Parliaments?
Brexit can be short-lived, and may not outlast
The decade we're in if the right things are done.
"It all depends on what Starmer can do.
He must fight the next election with a coalition
Of parties committed to a second referendum.
He's been Shadow Secretary of State for
Exiting the European Union,
He was Director of Public Prosecutions
And Head of the Crown Prosecution Service.
He has the intellectual ability
As a QC to do all this, but needs
To be moderate and forget his 'Trotskyite past'
As serving on the editorial board
Of *Socialist Alternatives*, a Trotskyist-front
Magazine. He'll look Prime Ministerial.
He's forensic, he'll say he'll rebuild Britain
After the pandemic, like Attlee after the war.
He will become the next Prime Minister
When it's seen Johnson's promises were fools' gold,
And the UK is poorer outside than in
The EU, he will then take the UK back in
And the departure from Europe, the 'voyage',
Will turn out to have been circuitous.
But the UK will have to go in on EU terms,

Which include joining the euro and the Schengen
Area it's stayed out of until now,
With no Thatcher rebate or Major opt-out,
There'll be no half-in, half-out any more,
And if no future UK Government agrees
To join on these terms, the UK stays out.
It will take a little time, the public
Have to see all the promises of gold
Are nothing but illusory fools' gold."

Your poet spoke as if in a deep trance,
Peering into a future like an abyss:
"Starmer's saying now, 'We've left the EU,
The Leave/Remain argument is over,
And the only argument now is what sort of a deal
We have with the EU and what sort of deals
We have with the rest of the world. I don't think
There's a case for rejoining the EU,'
And, 'We'll improve bits of the deal, that's all.'
But that's positioning, he'll see what Johnson does
And criticise and oppose it, and when the polls
Show the British people want to rejoin the EU,
That is when he'll take the UK back in.
That British change of heart may not be soon,
The polls may not reflect it for some while.
The UK's speed in getting vaccines out
Is impressive, but there's more to consider.
The virus will make the people realise
That they need European protection
And most of all the protection of a World State.
Starmer has to become PM within the framework
Of Brexit set up by Johnson, and once he's PM,
Having been elected by people who voted Leave
He can then respond to the polls that begin to see
Leaving's been a disaster and the British should return
To the European fold of the civilisation

Which they never left, for the UK is European,
As Johnson's father's recognised by applying
For French citizenship so he can live in France.
"Then England will be firmly within the EU
But Scotland, Ireland and perhaps Wales will
All be separate states. And if Scotland,
Northern Ireland and Wales all leave the UK
And join the EU as separate states,
Then England will be applying on its own,
Greatly weakened. It's not impossible.
The EU wants to make an example
Of the UK for leaving its Union,
And its break-up would be a dramatic way
Of warning the twenty-seven not to go down the road
Of populism and xenophobic nationalism.
And the Brexiteers would be blamed for the break-up.
Johnson would go down in history as the man
Who broke up the UK. The EU'd benefit
From dealing with four small states, not one large one
That has always been difficult and demanding.
"It would be good if the UK could rejoin
The EU, but it won't happen until
The English are disappointed in their trade
Under Brexit, paperwork and costly delays –
Exports to the EU will be two-thirds down –
And if that's a long time in approaching
There'll be a quiet decline while the people
Still believe in Johnson's promises of gold
Without receiving it as the economy
Dwindles under new viral outbreaks
Of variants that vaccines may not contain
(Some of Covid's four thousand mutations).
SAGE has forecast a fourth wave with a hundred
And thirty thousand deaths, even though a boom
Is forecast, and herd immunity as soon
As sixty per cent of the population

Have been vaccinated, a speculation.
Johnson lied to the Northern Irish, he said
There would be no border down the Irish Sea,
And there is one, and the supermarket shelves
Are empty, what Johnson said he wouldn't do
He did, and inevitably there'll be rioting
And a return of the Irish Troubles,
And the beginning of the break-up of the UK.
Brussels will exclude London from its markets,
Brexit won't boost the UK's economy,
And bankers with EU clients will move
Out of London and onto the Continent.
The rest of the century'll be plagued by fools' gold.
It may be that Starmer does not rejoin
The EU, and the UK, broken up,
Sinks into a declining offshore island
Slowly realising the gold is not happening.
So which is it – rejoin or quiet decline?
Unless Starmer rejoins, the UK will decline
And a divided people will come to grasp
That the prosperity they were promised was always fools' gold.
    "And I, the poet who's mirrored the decline
Of the UK since Suez would live to see
The UK shrink from ruling one quarter
Of the world's population in the year of my birth
To a tiny part of an archipelago
Off the Continent, Little England indeed.
If in this way or through becoming a Federation
The UK broke into four separate states
It would be the end of global Britain
Living off the crock of glittering gold at the foot
Of the rainbow in English Narragonia."
    Your poet added as an afterthought
"A lump of fools' gold resembles the Light
Which breaks through inner dark into the soul
And purifies and fills the flesh and blood

With healing peace and may protect from harm,
Including (who knows?) deadly viruses.
What a good world society there would be
If the glitter of fools' gold could be converted
Into a mass awareness of the Light
As happened from the Dark Ages until
The seventeenth century and its reflection
In the enduring work of the Metaphysical poets –
A real religious cultural purity
Of the mystic Light and the Baroque vision.
"I was right in what I said last time we met,
We are heading for a World State if the EU
Can get the UK back within its fold.
Now Trump's gone, once again the US will work
For global unity and togetherness
And once again there'll be moves towards a World State.
In my study of civilisations
America's in stage 15, the stage
Of the Roman Empire, and will preside
Over the fall of the West into a World State
Under Biden and his successors, and backed
By England when Charles the Third becomes King.
The West will fall so a World State can thrive.
I sent *The Secret American Destiny*
To Trump, and received no reply, and I will send
The Fall of the West to Biden as the way forward.
There will be moves to integrate Europe
And set up a democratic World State.
I won't be there, but I'll have kept the idea alive
For my grandchildren's generation to bring it in.
There will then be a real Golden Age."
Your poet received these words in poetic trance
From his spring which bubbles up into his soul,
From his Muse on high, his link to Olympus.
Your poet channels what the Muses say.
They have always inspired him by sending

Words he has not thought into his soul in trance,
Informed by them, the words put in his head,
Which your poet receives as an oracular vision.
Standing by the endless knot in his knot-garden,
He spoke them like the sibyl at Cumae
Or the priestess in the Delphic Oracle,
And later recorded them like an amanuensis
Receiving dictation from a higher plane,
And lamented the low-level slogan politics
That had brought Chancer Johnson so much praise
(As when twelve months back he began his Christmas message,
"Hi, folks," trying to be a popular Northerner).
    Hermes said, "Thanks for sharing your vision,
That is exactly what Zeus wanted to hear,
I will tell Zeus straightaway your way forward.
I listen and report, I don't comment.
It's hard enough for the God of the One to see
The future, without me speculating."
    He made to leave but your poet stopped him
And, like a stag with seven-branched antlers,
Pulled himself up to his full height, towering
Above Hermes, a petite fallow deer,
And said, "Please give mighty Zeus this message:
'God of the One, your poet feels for you
In your exasperation at the follies
Of men. Please save us from taking the wrong course
Set for this offshore island, this corner
Of humankind, by a leader who cares about
His advancement, not the human race's,
Who thinks national and is blind to a World State,
Who sees partial and cannot see the whole,
Who's competitive and not co-operative,
Whose actions have set back the culture of Europe,
Who does not seem to know the higher plane
Where the gods of Olympus, having reconciled
All opposites, contradictions and conflicts,

Look serenely down with the wisdom of unity
And, yearning for humankind to be united,
Entreat the Muses to pour words into the souls
Of Universalists, urging a World State,
And long for one humankind to govern itself.'"
    Hermes nodded, and said, "Thank you for that,
I'll pass it on," and, patting your poet's arm,
He slipped away like a graceful fallow deer.

From his Cornish window your poet saw
A tall-masted ship tossing on the waves,
Waiting to enter the harbour below
With emaciated crew and passengers.
It looked like a plague ship, and then it seemed
The Ship of Fools back from Narragonia.
    Zeus, God of the One, looked down and, realising
That Johnson had not risen to divine vision,
Had not elevated his soul to higher things,
To a united humankind, all souls
Improving their lot under Universalism,
Shook his head in dismay at the UK's
Voters who had so selfishly chosen
The path of a nation-state based on a past
Imperial greatness and former riches,
And disregarded supporting the higher good
Of a unified and harmonious humankind
To which all leaders of vision have worked
From ancient, through Roman and medieval, times
Which is now well within humankind's grasp
In an age of international internet,
Mobile phones, air and space travel, and a new
Single market that can be expanded worldwide.
    Zeus, God of the One, disappointed so many times
During the last five thousand years, now wept
At twenty-first-century man's inability
To turn away from selfish nation-states,

From wars and violence and deceptive promises
Of Golden-Age prosperity that's fools' gold,
And bring a vision down from Olympus
Of a 'Heavenised' world the Muses know
And channel into your poet's trance-like soul,
Of a World State in which every soul has a place;
And create Paradise in every street.

Timeline

Main events of the UK's departure from the EU, in relation to the 24 cantos of *Fools' Gold*

24 Jul 2019	Boris Johnson becomes Prime Minister.
28 Aug 2019	Parliament prorogued.
24 Sep 2019	Supreme Court decides to cancel prorogation.
31 Oct 2019	The UK scheduled to leave the EU. This does not happen, new date 31 January 2020.
12 Dec 2019	General election, Johnson's Conservatives win 80-seat majority.
23 Jan 2020	The UK's EU (Withdrawal Agreement) Bill becomes law as the EU (Withdrawal Agreement) Act.
29 Jan 2020	The European Parliament approves the Brexit divorce deal.
30 Jan 2020	The EU (Withdrawal Agreement) Act is ratified by the EU.
31 Jan 2020	The UK officially leaves the EU at midnight CET (11pm UK time).
1 Feb 2020	An 11-month transition phase begins.
18 Mar 2020	The European Commission publishes a draft legal agreement covering the future EU-UK partnership.
23 Mar 2020	First national lockdown from Covid-19 announced in the UK.
26 Mar 2020	First national lockdown comes into force.
27–28 Mar 2020	Dominic Cummings drives to Durham.
5–12 Apr 2020	Johnson in hospital with Covid.
12 Apr 2020	Cummings seen in Barnard Castle.
26 Apr 2020	Johnson returns to Downing Street.
20 May 2020	UK Government publishes its approach to implementing the Northern Ireland Protocol.
25 May 2020	Cummings' press conference in the Downing-Street garden.
1 Jun 2020	Phased reopening of schools in England.

2–5 Jun 2020	Fourth round of UK-EU future relationship negotiations takes place.
15 Jun 2020	Non-essential shops re-open.
29 Jun–3 Jul 2020	Fifth round of UK-EU future relationship negotiations takes place.
30 Jun 2020	The deadline to request an extension to the transition period passes without an extension being requested.
4 Jul 2020	End of first national lockdown, beginning of first local lockdown in Leicestershire.
20–23 Jul 2020	Sixth round of UK-EU future relationship negotiations takes place.
31 Jul 2020	UK does not ask for an extension to the transition.
18–21 Aug 2020	Seventh round of UK-EU future relationship negotiations takes place.
8–10 Sep 2020	Eighth round of UK-EU future relationship negotiations takes place.
9 Sep 2020	The UK Internal Market Bill is introduced.
10 Sep 2020	The Withdrawal Agreement Joint Committee meets to discuss the UK Internal Market Bill and the Northern Ireland Protocol.
	The UK Government publishes its legal position on the UK Internal Market Bill and Northern Ireland Protocol.
	European Commission Vice-President Maros Sefcovic meets Michael Gove in London for an extraordinary meeting of the EU-UK Joint Committee.
11 Sep 2020	Leaders at the European Parliament say they will refuse to give consent to a future deal between the EU and the UK if London attempts to override the Withdrawal Agreement.
14 Sep 2020	'Rule of six' – social gatherings above six banned.
16 Sep 2020	The incoming European Commission President Ursula von der Leyen warns the UK Government

	against backtracking on the Withdrawal Agreement.
29 Sep 2020	The UK Internal Market Bill passes its Third Reading by 340 votes to 256.
29 Sep–2 Oct 2020	Ninth round of UK-EU future relationship negotiations takes place.
1 Oct 2020	The European Commission President announces the EU will initiate legal proceedings to prevent the UK attempting to override the Withdrawal Agreement.
3 Oct 2020	The UK Government sends a new Brexit plan to Brussels, including the removal of the backstop. It is rejected by the European Commission three days later.
8 Oct 2020	UK-EU talks all but collapse amid acrimony.
10 Oct 2020	UK and Irish prime ministers Boris Johnson and Leo Varadkar announce a "pathway to a possible deal" as they meet in England. EU and UK negotiators agree to intensify talks.
14 Oct 2020	New three-tier system of Covid-19 restrictions starts in England.
15–16 Oct 2020	European Council summit.
17 Oct 2020	The UK and EU announce that they have reached a new Brexit deal, ahead of a Brussels summit. It replaces the Irish backstop.
19 Oct 2020	In a special Saturday sitting British MPs withhold their approval for the deal until laws implementing Brexit are in place. Johnson is obliged to seek another Brexit delay from the EU.
22 Oct 2020	Johnson puts Brexit legislation on "pause".
28 Oct 2020	The EU agrees to offer the UK a Brexit "flextension" until 31 January. The offer is formally approved the next day.
29 Oct 2020	The House of Commons approves a general election on 12 December.

5 Nov 2020	Second national lockdown from Covid-19 begins in the UK.
13 Nov 2020	Cummings sacked.
1 Dec 2020	Ursula von der Leyen takes office as European Commission President, replacing Juncker. The new European Council President Charles Michel takes over from Donald Tusk.
2 Dec 2020	Second lockdown ends.
8 Dec 2020	First Pfizer vaccination in the UK.
9 Dec 2020	Johnson and Von der Leyen meet over dinner at the Berlaymont.
14–17 Dec 2020	Final European Parliament plenary session of the year.
24 Dec 2020	UK-EU trade deal agreed between Johnson and Von der Leyen.
31 Dec 2020	End of transition period, UK is a "foreign country" outside the EU. The UK's full economic and political independence from the EU commences, moving the UK from transitional to full third-country status outside the EU single market and customs union.
1 Jan 2021	New agreement on UK-EU relations enters into force.
5 Jan 2021	Third national lockdown from Covid-19 begins in the UK.
12 Jan 2021	Hermes' visit to the poet at Connaught House.
26 May 2021	Cummings gives evidence to a joint inquiry of the Commons Health and Social Care and Science and Technology committees for more than seven hours.
29 May 2021	Johnson secretly marries Carrie Symonds in the Catholic Westminster Cathedral.

O-BOOKS

O is a symbol of the world, of oneness and unity; this eye represents knowledge and insight.